The Corporeal Imagination

Divinations: Rereading Late Ancient Religion

Series Editors: Daniel Boyarin, Virginia Burrus, Derek Krueger

A complete list of books in the series is available from the publisher.

The Corporeal Imagination

Signifying the Holy
in Late Ancient Christianity

PATRICIA COX MILLER

PENN

University of Pennsylvania Press

Philadelphia

Published by
University of Pennsylvania Press
Philadelphia, Pennsylvania 19104-4112

Printed in the United States of America on acid-free paper
10 9 8 7 6 5 4 3 2 1

Library of Congress Cataloging-in-Publication Data

Miller, Patricia Cox.
    The corporeal imagination : signifying the holy in late ancient Christianity / Patricia Cox Miller.
        p.   cm. — (Divinations)
    Includes bibliographical references (p.   ) and index.
    ISBN 978-0-8122-4142-6 (alk. paper)
    1. Body, Human—Religious aspects—Christianity. I. Title.
    BT741.3.M56   2009
    235'.2—dc22

                                                                    2008040923

Epigraph: From Wallace Stevens, *Opus Posthumous*, ed. Samuel French Morse (New York: Alfred A. Knopf, 1977), 168.

The body is the great poem.
 —Wallace Stevens

Contents

Introduction

The relatively recent field of material culture studies has fostered scholarly analysis of the ways in which "things" claim a society's attention as well as analysis of how perception of things varies from one society to another. In one society, for example, things will be perceived as inhabited and animated, while in another, things will be perceived as insensate utilitarian objects.[1] But whether they are viewed as animate or inanimate, things have increasingly commanded the attention of cultural analysts: whole books have been written on the pencil, the chair, potatoes, and bananas.[2]

The field in which the present study is situated, the study of late ancient and early Byzantine Christianity, has participated in this "renaissance of the thing" by producing a number of studies on such objects as amulets and *ampullae*, relics, statues, shrines, and mosaics, as well as practices such as pilgrimage that celebrate the tangible expressions of religious devotion.[3] To this list of things I add the human body, which, as a "thing among things" in the phrase of philosopher Maurice Merleau-Ponty, has been much studied as a locus of religious meaning in late antiquity.[4]

Thing Theory

The focus of this book is on saintly human bodies in their various "thingly" permutations in ancient Christianity—as relics, as animated icons, as literary performers of the holy in hagiography. To understand these variations on the body as "things" rather than as mere objects, I am relying on cultural critic Bill Brown's differentiation between the two. In his elaboration of what he calls "thing theory," Brown writes: "We begin to confront the thingness of objects when they stop working for us: when the drill breaks, when the car stalls, when the windows get filthy, when their flow within the circuits of production and distribution, consumption and exhibition, has been arrested, however momentarily."[5] In other words, an object becomes a "thing" when it can no longer be taken for granted as part of the everyday world of the naturalized environment in which objects such as clean windows are so familiar as not to be noticed. When the window is dirty, one can no longer "natu-rally" see through it; suddenly, it takes on the character of a presence. Brown continues: "the story of objects asserting themselves as things, then, is the story of a changed relation to the human subject and thus the story of how the thing really names less an object than a particular subject-object relation."[6] For example, take the case of relics in late antiquity. From the perspective of the natural attitude, a relic is simply an object, part of a dead person's inanimate body. However, when a mar-tyr's dust, bone, or body becomes the center of cultic activity and rever-ence, it loses its character as a natural body and begins to function as a site of religious contact. No longer a mere object, it becomes a thing that does indeed signal a new subject-object relation, a relation of the human subject to the sanctifying potential of human physicality as locus and mediator of spiritual presence and power.

According to Brown's thing theory, things, as compared with objects, stand out against their environment and, like magnets of attraction (or repulsion), announce a change in habitual perception. They also indi-cate a locus of surplus value. Brown explains the second part of his the-ory as follows: "You could imagine things, second, as what is excessive in objects, as what exceeds their mere materialization as objects or their mere utilization as objects—their force as a sensuous presence or as a metaphysical presence, the magic by which objects become values, fetishes, idols, and totems."[7] Excess is "what remains physically or meta-physically irreducible to objects."[8] As Brown argues, it is also important to bear in mind "the all-at-onceness, the simultaneity, of the object/thing dialectic and the fact that, all at once, *the thing seems to name the object just as it is even as it names some thing else.*"[9] When it asserts itself as a thing, a relic is an overdetermined object, overdetermined because it is a finite object situated in an infinite field of meaning. To continue with the example of the relic: a bone becomes a relic when its surplus value is elicited aesthetically, in both art and rhetoric, and theologically, in terms of belief in saintly intercession. The term "relic" never ceases to name a body part of a dead person but, as Brown's thing theory indi-cates, it simultaneously names something else, a thing that both instanti-ates and signifies a belief system.

A good example of both the promotion of and engagement with the excess that signals a bone-become-relic, a moment when materiality and meaning are configured positively, is in the following encomium, which Gregory of Nyssa delivered in the late fourth century on the martyr Saint Theodore in the building that served as a martyrium for the saint's rel-ics. Early on in his address, Gregory directed the gaze of his audience to the art on the building's inner walls—images of animals, marble slabs so highly polished that they shimmered like silver, and colorful paintings of the martyr's deeds and torture that Gregory describes (rather incongruously) as a flowery meadow.[10] As Gregory presents it, the art functions as a lens through which to see and thus understand the significance of the martyr's relics. Indeed, Gregory insists, by its sensuous appeal, the art is a lure: it delights the bodily senses, especially sight, and in so doing draws the venerator near to the martyr's tomb.[11] Once at the tomb, several senses—"eyes, mouth, ears"—are engaged as venerators tearfully ask for the saint's intercession and blessing "as though he were whole and present."[12] And the artistic seduction that results in one's proximity to the tomb might also yield a material payoff: "If anyone," writes Gregory, "should take dust from the martyr's resting place, that dust is understood as a gift, and the [bit of] earth stored up as a treasure."[13] Even more fortunate are those granted permission to touch the martyr's relics, a boon of the highest value. The relic elicits a lavish sensory response, especially of sight and touch, that testifies to its magnetic religious power.

One might add that yet a further gift, for the modern reader, is Gregory's alluring rhetoric, which, like the martyrium's art, also functions as a lens through which to "see" the body parts of a corpse as spiritual objects. It is especially significant that Gregory seemingly felt compelled to enhance the artistic surround of the martyrium with his own rhetorical embellishments of it. Embellishing what was already embellished, he thus invokes the shimmer of the marble and the intrigue of the animal figures. Further, he presents the martyrium's paintings as a clear representation of the martyr's trials and death *and also* as a colorful, flowering meadow that functions "as if it were a book speaking" from the wall.[14] The excess of his rhetoric both creates and reflects the surplus value of the bones that, as relics, his audience of fellow Christians longed to beseech and touch.[15]

The Material Turn

Gregory's use of rhetoric as well as his appeal to the senses in order to convey the surplus value of a human body was part of a broader—and complicated—phenomenon in late ancient Christianity. In the first place, Gregory's loving attention to the significance of a piece of "matter" is representative of what I call "the material turn" in the fourth century, in which the religious significance of the material world was revalued. The phrase "material turn" indicates a shift in the late ancient Christian sensibility regarding the signifying potential of the material world (including especially the human body), a shift that reconfigured the relation between materiality and meaning in a positive direction. As Susan Ashbrook Harvey has argued persuasively, the major reason for what she calls the "shift in physical sensibility that marked late antique as distinct from earlier Christianity" was the legalization of Christianity by co-emperors Constantine and Licinius in C.E. 313.[16] Prior to legalization, Christians, while holding to the doctrine of God as creator of the world, "yet understood themselves to be living in a non-Christian world," in fact a sometimes hostile world in which persecution was a recurring threat.[17] As Harvey notes, "In the early Christian view, the model Christ had offered was to use the body as the instrument through which to seek eternal life; its purpose was not to focus on this temporary, ephemeral world."[18]

Once the actual violence and social marginalization ended with legalization, the world began to seem less ephemeral and more welcoming. "As Christians gained political and social power in the world around them, the world gained positive valuation among Christians as their context for encountering, knowing, and living in relationship with the divine."[19] There was a movement from "sensory austerity" to "a tangible, palpable piety" as the sensible world came to be viewed as a medium for the disclosure of the divine.[20] Indeed, it was only after legalization that the concept of a "holy land" with its attendant ritual practice of pilgrimage developed; only after legalization could Pope Damasus "invent" a Christian Rome by creating a cityscape based on the tombs of the saints; and only after legalization did Christian liturgical pageantry, as well as art and architecture, begin to flourish.[21] In this context, it was not only human sense-perception that became more important religiously; as Harvey points out, the human body itself "gained worth for Christians as a means for knowing God."[22] "Let no one tell you that this body of ours is a stranger to God," as Cyril of Jerusalem exhorted his catechetical flock. More stunningly, Ephrem the Syrian characterized the Eucharist as "the Bread of Life that came down and was mingled with the senses," a genuine sanctification of perceptual experience.[23]

While it is certainly true that the human body and its sensorium became a locus for religious epistemology, this does not mean that, beginning in the fourth century, Christians embraced the body and its senses without reserve. Christological thinking in this period saw that "the incarnation of the divine in materiality and corporeality confers extraordinary significance on the body."[24] But the rhetoric of the body that arose from the conjunction of the divine and the material had a double edge. On the one hand, and in a positive sense, the body could serve as a sign of the self in the process of being transfigured into its true status as image of God. One thinks of the profusion of hagiographical images, both literary and artistic, that present the bodies of the holy as suffused with light, whether in the angelic radiance flashing from the

faces of desert ascetics or in mosaic portraits of saints whose visages glimmer against a background of gold tesserae.[25] On the other hand, negatively, human beings could not be fully transfigured in the present, since
their very embodiment subjected them to the ravages of time, decay, spatial limitation, and ethical imperfection that were typically associated
with corporeality.[26]

The situation of human beings in the present was thus both a problem
and an opportunity. Gregory of Nazianzus formulated the situation of
human beings in cosmological terms: human nature was poised on a
boundary line between visible and invisible worlds, the "intelligible"
(νοητός) and the sensible (αἰσθητός).[27] Although occupying such a
position could be very positive in terms of access to intelligible reality, it
could also result in the problem of a divided consciousness. This
dilemma of the perch between two worlds could also be posed in terms
of sensual perception, for just as on the cosmological plane, human
nature straddled the earthly and heavenly worlds—"a new angel on the
earth," as Gregory of Nazianzus put it—so in anthropological terms
each individual was just such a composite of the spiritual and the material, with the powers of perception (αἴσθησις) forming the mediating
ground between the two, as Gregory of Nyssa argued.[28] The senses could
serve to unite, rather than to divide, the two components of human
beings.

However, there was also a double-edged dilemma concerning sensual
perception. This was a dilemma that was expressed with remarkable con-
sistency in late ancient Christian authors. In the mid-fifth century, for
example, Theodoret of Cyrrhus wrote a compendium of mini-hagiographies of monks in Syria, the *Historia religiosa*. In this work, Theodoret
declared that the exemplary holy men and women about whom he wrote
had "barred up the senses with God's laws as with bolts and bars and
entrusted their keys to the mind."[29] Once entrusted to "the mind," that
is, to spiritual guidance, however, those same senses became like strings
in a musical instrument, producing "sound that was perfectly harmoni-
ous."[30] Three-quarters of a century earlier, Gregory of Nyssa expressed
the negative dimension of the dilemma in his commentary on Jeremiah
9:21 ("Death has climbed in through our windows"). "What Scripture
calls 'windows,'" Gregory wrote, "are the senses," each of which could,
"as the passage says, make an entrance for death."[31] Yet this is the same
Gregory who thought that the senses could foster a spiritual experience
of the highest degree, exclaiming, as we saw above, that worshippers at
the shrine of Saint Theodore "embrace [the relics] as though they were
alive, approaching them with eyes, mouths, ears—all the senses."[32]

The "material turn," then, was complicated by the double valence of
both matter and the senses. The task for those who participated in this

turn was to redirect and re-educate the senses for, when the mediating senses were functioning properly, as at the shrine of Saint Theodore, they enabled a kind of apprehension that dissipated the *merely* material or corporeal without negating its function as sign of spiritual presence. As the chapters in this book demonstrate, the appeal to flesh and matter for meaning was not without its problematic aspects. Flirtation with idolatry, understood as reifying the holy in the human, was a constant problem. How was it possible to present human corporeality as a vehicle of transcendence without losing the mediating sense of "vehicle" and simply collapsing the material and the transcendent into each other?

The new enthusiasm for sensuous apprehension and instantiation of the divine in the everyday world required the development of interpretive finesse so that the excess, the surplus value, of things could be engaged and celebrated in non-idolatrous fashion. One of the interpretive gestures of this book is precisely to position the new embrace of the holy body as relic, saint, and icon vis-à-vis idolatry and, more particularly, vis-à-vis the iconoclastic controversy that erupted in the eighth century and roiled on into the ninth. Seen in hindsight—that is, reading backwards from the iconoclastic debates in which positions regarding idolatry and the role of images in Christian theology and ritual were argued openly—the theological poetics of material substance explored in this book can be understood as a strategy that in effect sidesteps an idolatrous impulse just as it anticipates the later celebration of material expressions of religion in the form of icons. I have used phrases such as dissonant sensibility, imaginative referentiality, ambiguous corporeality, ephemeral tangibility, and the uncanny doubling of saint and icon to characterize late ancient Christians' constructions of holy bodies. I intend these phrases to indicate the complexities that were sustained in the discourse of the late ancient Christian material turn, and I argue that the ambiguities and ambivalences of that discourse betray a hesitation in view of the material turn, a hesitation or even a nervousness regarding the potential for confusing the material and the spiritual.

Long before the material turn, Christians had brought to conscious articulation the problem of idolatry as a theological mistake. In their attacks on the pagan religious practice of idol worship, authors such as Athenagoras pinpointed the error underlying that ritual practice. In his apology addressed to the emperor Marcus Aurelius around C.E. 176, Athenagoras wrote as follows: "We distinguish God from matter, and show that matter is one thing and God another, and that there is a vast difference between them. For the divine is uncreated and eternal, grasped only by pure mind and intelligence, while matter is created and perishable."[33] As he says later in this treatise, the problem with idol worship is that "the populace cannot distinguish between matter and God or appreciate the chasm that that separates them."[34] According to this kind of argument, the material world and the spiritual world are so different ontologically that they are categorically distinct by their very nature. Athenagoras's referent for "idol" was, of course, a pagan statue of a god, which is not the same as a relic. Yet to the extent that a wooden statue and a human body part are both part of the material world, the formal ontological argument separating matter from divine holiness holds for the relic as well.

This marked degree of ontological separation between matter and spirit was precisely what the material turn diminished as, in David Frankfurter's happy phrase, late ancient authors imaginatively transformed "a pious human being into sacred stuff."[35] But the investment of human bodies with the holy was a new cultural practice, and it aroused anxiety, some of it vociferous, regarding how a material phenomenon like a human body can be a locus of spirituality without compromising the divine. In the fourth and early fifth centuries, there were both outright and implied charges of idolatry in regard to relics (as noted in the chapters that follow in reference to Vigilantius, Augustine, and Optatus of Milevis). And as for icons of the saints, Epiphanius roundly denounced them as false images, while Augustine, who preferred aniconic religion, lamented that the church had embraced such visual art in the first place and noted that pagans in Hippo had charged Christians with the very kind of idolatrous adoration of images of which Christians had accused them![36]

These detractors did not, of course, prevail against the heady conviction that objects such as relics and icons could give access to divine presence. As Robin Jensen has pointed out, Augustine's argument that "it would be wiser to pray directly to the saint rather than to the image of that saint" would only seem sensible "to a congregation that was unattached to such visual and material aids to prayer."[37] The polarizing positions that were later to be expressed in the iconoclastic controversies were not in place in late antiquity, but the fact that there were anxious rumblings suggests that negotiating the paradoxical relation between the infinite and the finite required a deft touch—hence the ambiguous corporeality of late ancient representations of holy bodies.

Corporeal Imagination

The phrase "corporeal imagination" can serve as an overall characterization of the techniques used by Christian authors to achieve the conjunction of discourse, materiality, and meaning that marked their turn toward the material. "Corporeal imagination" designates a kind of writing that blurs the distinction between reader and text by appealing to the reader's sensory imagination. In such texts, things such as relics, the invisible bodies of the saints in hagiography, and the saints' presence in icons take on visual and tactile presence. Achieving such a presence, they elicit either a corporeal response or else a synaesthetic response, requiring the reader to sense something that cannot strictly or literally be seen, namely, divine energy in action in the world. "Corporeal imagination" also designates textual images whose ocular and affective immediacy contributes to, or even creates, the religious significance of the thing that is their focus. As we have just seen, the body part of a dead human being only becomes a relic, a spiritual object, when aesthetically enhanced by this kind of writing. In short, this study analyzes pictorial strategies that draw on the power of discourse to materialize its effects in the world of the reader by attributing corporeal qualities to inscrutable objects (like the bodies of the saints) or by attributing spiritual qualities to corporeal objects (like relics, icons, or the dust at a stylite's column).

This ancient Christian turn toward the thing, together with the elaboration of a theological poetics of material substance to embody that turn was, in my view, part of a broad phenomenon in Western history that literary and cultural theorist Daniel Tiffany has termed the intrinsic role of word-pictures in shaping Western knowledge of material substance.[38] Western thinking about the material realm has been "inherently figurative."[39] Tiffany argues that "corporeality, and material substance itself," are "mediums that are inescapably informed by the pictures that we compose of them."[40] Focusing in part on the rise of atomic physics (natural philosophy) and microbiology in the seventeenth century, Tiffany rejects our modern habit of equating materialism with realism. The realism of modern physics, he says, relies on "a framework of vivid analogies and tropes"; thus "the foundation of material substance is intelligible to us, and therefore appears to be real, only if we credit the imaginary pictures we have composed of it."[41] That is, the only intuitive knowledge that we can possess of the inscrutable reality of material existence comes in the form of insubstantial pictures, or what Ian Hacking has called "the persistence of the image" in philosophical materialism.[42] Following Hacking, Tiffany argues that realism is founded on the act of representation: "First there is representation, and then there is 'real.'" What is considered to be "real" is a function of the pictorial imagination: "Without pictures, there can be no claim to reality."[43]

Such pictures constitute a "*poetics* of material substance . . . which calls for materialization of the invisible world."[44] Further, "when materiality is equated with invisibility, the invisible world becomes the province not only of atoms and [microscopic] animals but also, conceivably, of beings possessing the radiant body of an angel."[45] This last comment suggests the particular relevance of Tiffany's argument to what I have called the corporeal imagination of late ancient Christians, whose turn toward the material discovered precisely "radiant bodies"—holy men, relics, icons—that disclosed the reality of an invisible spiritual world. Ancient Christians were not, of course, philosophical materialists of the kind discussed by Tiffany. But, as I hope to show in this book, they elaborated a view of material substance, understood as the sainted human body, that relied heavily on a poetics of matter in order to redirect, indeed to form, sensuous apprehension of the presence of the spirit in the material world. Apart from such a poetics, flesh cannot be "real," because it has not entered the order of representation.

According to one interpreter, the pictorial turn in ancient Christian writers can be explained by pointing to their propensity to look out at the material world—at ascetic bodies, bones, dust—and "see more than was there."[46] Perhaps it might be more accurate to characterize such looking as "seeing the more that they believed was there," since their techniques for picturing the conjunction of matter and spirit were premised on a conviction not only that the material world was suffused with divine presence, but also that matter could provide an intercessory conduit for human access to spiritual power. In order to illustrate the point of "seeing more than was there" as an essential part of the theological poetics of material substance that is my topic, I turn to a discussion of techniques for achieving the transfigured eye needed to "see" the coinherence of the visible and the invisible in late ancient Christianity.

Ekphrasis

One of the major techniques used by Christian authors for articulating the relation between matter and meaning was ekphrasis. We have in fact just experienced an ekphrastic moment in Gregory of Nyssa's evocation of the artistic surround in Saint Theodore's shrine. Ekphrasis was one of the exercises in composition for students of rhetoric; in the *progymnasmata*, the rhetorical handbooks used in the late ancient period, ekphrasis was defined as "a descriptive speech bringing the thing shown vividly before the eyes," turning listeners into spectators.[47] The topics for ekphrases were varied—places, people, events, art, architecture—and their subjects could be purely imaginary. Thus when, as in the example to follow, a building, or a part thereof, is described in an ekphrasis, the reader should not expect a technical appraisal but rather a subjective, sometimes emotional, response to the topic at hand.[48]

A good example of the penchant to see more than was there comes from the Gallic writer and bishop of Clermont, Sidonius Apollinaris. In a letter to a friend, Sidonius recorded an inscription that he had written around C.E. 470 for the dedication of a new cathedral in Lyons.[49] Inscribed on the far wall of the cathedral, Sidonius's poem contained these verses: "Marble diversified with a varied gleam covers the floor, the vault and the windows; in a multi-colored design a verdant grassy encrustation leads a curving line of sapphire-colored stones across the leek-green grass . . . and the field in the middle is clothed with a stony forest of widely spaced columns."[50] Sidonius could look at marble and see grass. As Onians observed, Sidonius "could look at something which was in twentieth-century [i.e., contemporary] terms purely abstract and find it representational."[51] The question is, representational of what?

Sidonius was not simply ornamenting a marble wall with a poetic figure. This becomes clear when one remembers that the wall was in a cathedral, and that the image of verdant, grassy expanses had a long history in ancient Christianity's envisioning of paradise as a *locus amoenus,* an idyllic spot of delight and charm.[52] Sidonius was petitioning the surplus value of the marble wall as "thing," indicating in his ekphrasis that the inside of the cathedral was a paradisal spot. In this case, the excess of the object was theological; that is, the conjunction of matter and meaning produced a spiritualization of ecclesiastical space. A hundred years later, Paul the Silentiary could refer to the ambo in Hagia Sophia as adorned with "meadows of marble," and the anonymous author of the *Narratio de S. Sophia* made the religious surplus value of marble unquestionable when, quoting the emperor Justinian, he referred to the marble strips on the church's floor as "the four rivers that flow out of paradise."[53]

These ekphrastic images that present marble as organically alive and animated are not innocent poetic figures. Far from being "objective" descriptions of a building, they are in fact subjective judgments that establish and control perception of a church's interior space, conditioning the human subject's relation with that space in terms of its theological meaning. Further, such images defeat the binary opposition between the natural, the organic, and the representational, on the one hand, and the spiritual, abstract, and symbolic or nonmimetic on the other. In Sidonius's case, for example, the ekphrastic poem was affixed to the very thing, the slab of marble, that it purports to bring before the eye, thus making the vividness of the optical truth that it petitions all the more arresting, in that the viewer/reader is being asked to suspend the difference between word, thing, and image, all the while being aware of their separation. Late ancient arts such as this actually worked to subdue potential dichotomies between body and spirit, earth and heaven, material and immaterial by setting in motion an aesthetic play between planes of reality, a play, that is, with boundaries that are only apparently discrete, such that the ambiguity of referentiality is highlighted. This will 'il haven't met you yet' - Michael Bublé

Kameron Laylor (sp?)

-JV/9th Sball?

ELON UNIVERSITY

be as true of ekphrastic appropriations of the human body as of churchly marble, as the explorations of ekphrases of Asterius of Amaseia and Prudentius of Calahorra in subsequent chapters show.

Visceral Seeing

Ekphrasis was only one of the techniques of visualization that contributed to the theological poetics of material substance that is the focus of this book. Another is what I have termed "visceral seeing," in which the older Christian tradition of the spiritual senses was revised such that the "eye of faith" had a tangible as well as a metaphorical dimension. The older tradition of the spiritual senses, developed most notably by Origen of Alexandria in the third century, divided human consciousness into an "outer man" whose perception was carnal and an "inner man" whose perception was spiritual, spiritual understanding being, of course, privileged.[54] Even though, as David Dawson has argued, the doctrine of the spiritual senses rests on "an intrinsic connection between the visible and the invisible," it is difficult to argue that the man who famously (or infamously) stated that "in order to know God we need no body at all" truly appreciated the role of affect and materiality in discerning the presence of the divine in the ordinary world.[55]

In the course of the fourth century, the senses were accorded cognitive status and the intellect was materially engaged. Spiritual seeing became more visceral due in part to the dignity accorded to the senses by a new understanding of the Incarnation. P. W. L. Walker's observations on this development deserve to be quoted at length:

The fourth century was a time when the Church, now more settled "in the world," began to reaffirm the proper value of the temporal. Not surprisingly this would lead to a greater appreciation of the Incarnation in the Church's life and thought. If the Cross and the exaltation of Christ were always open to the danger of being interpreted in such a way as to cast a negative light upon the world, the Incarnation of Christ was the biblical principle par excellence that could effectively reverse that trend. . . . The Incarnation could allow a new attitude to physical matter, the very stuff of the world. It could be used to affirm not just the goodness of this world-order, of creation and humanity at a general level; it might also be used to inculcate a new approach to material objects and places, a new expectation that physical reality might in some way be important to the meeting between God and man. . . . The Incarnation was a true legitimation of the physical realm.[56]

Following Walker, Georgia Frank has concluded that "the Incarnation, in theory, legitimated all forms of sense perception as a means for knowing God."[57] In theory, and also in practice: Frank quotes Cyril, bishop of Jerusalem in the mid-fourth century, "boasting to catechumens that 'others merely hear, but we see and touch,' " and she goes on to demonstrate ancient Christian appropriation of vision as touch, indeed of "eyes as hands."[58]

"Visceral seeing" is a way of naming one of the results of the (re)physicalizing of the senses in light of the view that the Incarnation had legitimized the material realm. In particular, it designates the affective appeal of figurative language about saintly bodies, especially in late ancient and early Byzantine hagiography. Hagiographical images of saintly bodies taught the reader how to bring together the "real" and the transcendent, the material and the spiritual, in a single image. As ephemeral and tangible at once, saints were presented in hagiography as visual paradoxes, and these paradoxical bodies were signs of transfiguration at work in the world. The ambiguous corporeality of the saints, and the way in which pictured bodies, by appealing to the sensory imagination, provoke thoughts of spiritual transformation, is discussed in several of the following chapters. Here I would like to address the phenomenon of the affective image in one of its most visceral (and theological) modes, in which partakers of the Eucharist see the elements of bread and wine turn to "real" flesh and blood before their very eyes.

These images of a bloody Eucharist, contained in texts from the fifth and sixth centuries, had as background the effect of the new emphasis on Incarnation on ideas about the Eucharist in the fourth century. Especially, though not only, in the eastern part of the empire, theologians began to emphasize not the sacrificial, memorial, or symbolic character of the Eucharist, but rather the conversion or materialist theory that regarded the bread and wine as really transformed into the body and blood of Christ. John Chrysostom, for example, exploited "the materialist implications of the conversion theory to the full," speaking of "eating Christ, even of burying one's teeth in his flesh," though he admitted that the transformation could be apprehended not by the senses but only by the mind.[59] Ambrose expressed the perceptual conundrum straightforwardly: "Perhaps you may say: 'I see something else; how do you tell me that I receive the Body of Christ?' "[60] Not only did the bread look ordinary, so did the wine: "Perhaps you say: 'I do not see the appearance of blood.' "[61] Clearly, visceral imbibing of the Eucharist of the sort advocated by Chrysostom was difficult; as Georgia Frank has remarked, "receiving the Eucharist required a stretch of the imagination."[62]

A central player in this stretching of the imagination was Cyril of Alexandria, for whom the Incarnation was central to an understanding of the Eucharist. As Charles Barber has noted, in his Eucharistic doctrine Cyril "shifted emphasis from the death of Christ to the Incarnation, seeing in the transformation of the elements a sign of the power of the

Incarnation to transform man."[63] By taking on flesh, the Word had made possible the transfiguration of human nature, guaranteeing the resurrection of the body.[64] Hence it was essential that the Eucharistic elements be truly the body and blood of Christ because, just as Christ represented a transformed humanity, so also the sacramental elements were the vehicle through which the process of deification occurred.[65] "He offers us as food the flesh that he assumed," as Cyril argued.[66] The Eucharistic elements were material and divine at once; only thus could they effect metamorphosis.

Cyril's view of the Eucharist was central to his opposition to Nestorius, whom he perceived to have separated the human and the divine in Christ, thus rendering the Eucharistic "body" a merely human one and so incapable of producing the spiritual and physical transformation of humankind. One legacy of Cyril's theory of the Eucharist lay with the Monophysite monks of Gaza, who opposed the Council of Chalcedon's Christological formula that distinguished—too sharply, they thought—the two natures of Christ and so in their view represented a revival of Nestorius's thought.[67] One of those anti-Chalcedonian ascetics of Gaza, John Rufus (bishop of Maiouma, port city of Gaza, in the late fifth century), wrote a hagiographical account of his fellow Monophysite Peter the Iberian, in which he recorded the following scene: "And he [Peter] celebrated the entire [liturgy of the] Eucharist: when he came to the breaking of the almighty bread, with continuous weeping and disturbance of his heart and many fears, as it was custom to him, so much blood burst forth when he broke [the bread] that the entire holy altar was sprinkled [with blood]. [When he turned around he saw Christ next to him who told him:] "Bishop, break [it]! Don't fear."[68] In his treatise *Plerophoria*, a series of visions and prophecies that attempt to vindicate especially the Christology of the anti-Chalcedonian party, John Rufus recorded a similarly bloody event that occurred during Lent to a man in the church of St. Menas:

When the holy offering of the eucharist had taken place and everyone had received the terrifying mysteries, he, too, came forward, with tears, to partake. And when he opened his hand he saw, instead of bread, flesh soaked in blood, and his entire hand became blood-red. And trembling from the incredible wonder that had taken place, he said, "Woe is me, how is it possible that I have been found receiving meat when everyone else has received bread? How is it possible that I am partaking in flesh when this is a time of fasting?"[69]

As Lorenzo Perrone noted, such anecdotes are "the projection in image of the monophysite Christological dogma."[70] But what a projection! These images constitute visceral seeing at its starkest.

Like many of the hagiographical images treated in this book, these

Eucharistic images are constituted by a carnal rhetoric that has an ocular and affective immediacy. In keeping with the technique of visceral seeing, they appeal to the sensory imagination, and they certainly demonstrate the role of word-pictures in shaping knowledge of material substance—in these cases, the sacramental elements. But, as with images of relics and their connection with the notion of intercession, the Eucharistic images appeal not just to the senses but also to the intellect, to the extent that they invite the reader to "see" a belief system. Visceral seeing, then, denotes a pictorial idiom in which the senses have cognitive status and the mind is materially engaged. Above all, this idiom teaches readers to "see" what is visually intractable—here, the fleshly presence of Christ in the Eucharist; in chapters that follow, the presence of divine power in a human body or the animate quality of a seemingly inanimate work of art.

Pictorial Theatricality

In these techniques of visualization, the secret of the image's vitality is its spirited surplus as well as its pictorial theatricality. It is to this latter point that I will now turn in conclusion. The success of the material turn insofar as it was devoted to the paradox of spiritual bodies was due in large part to its cultivation of an inner visual imagination that was emotional and sensuously intense. Especially in the literature about martyrs that arose in connection with the cult of relics, the reader/hearer was situated as an active participant in the martyrial drama by the force of emotionally charged rhetoric. Augustine, for example, preached about the trials of Saint Cyprian by creating a form of spiritual theater of the mind: "Look, here am I, watching Cyprian; I'm crazy about Cyprian. . . . I'm watching him, I'm delighted by him, as far as I can I embrace him with the arms of my mind."[71] Who could remain unmoved by this dramatic inner spectacle that summons a past event excitedly into the present as though it were playing itself out before one's very eyes?

This sensibility, based on the visionary power of images—seen in the chapters that follow in such authors as Prudentius, Victricius, Asterius, and Paulinus, in addition to Augustine—might be illuminated by comparison with what art historian Norman Bryson, discussing a text of Philostratus the Elder, has called "the Philostratean 'Look!'"[72] Philostratus's *Imagines*, a series of ekphrases that summon forth a series of paintings in a (probably imaginary) gallery, is punctuated with moments when the author, in the midst of one of his descriptions, exclaims, "For look!"[73] With this exclamation, as Bryson observes, "the description at last reaches the moment of lift-off," as "one of the principal desires of the descriptions in the *Imagines*" is fulfilled: "to cease being words on the page, to come alive in the form of an image, to pass from the opacity of words to the luminous scenes behind the words." This is "a textual moment at which the description at last feels its own language to dissolve into the light of the scene it opens upon."[74] Late ancient Christian authors too were eager to summon the luminous scenes behind the words, and many of them animated "the dead," as it were, by using powerful imagery to make the invisible visible.

Enthusiasm for pictorial theatricality as a means for materializing the holy in the everyday world continued into the sixth and seventh centuries, particularly in hagiography. In the final chapters of this book, the focus is on hagiographies written in Greek in the eastern part of the former Roman empire. Although historians typically denote this geography and time period as "early Byzantine," I am considering it an extension of late antiquity insofar as the concerns of the "material turn" were intensified as well as problematized. As I read them, these hagiographies are testaments to the success of the process of materializing the holy, and also to its dangers, especially the danger of idolatry. Two aspects of these hagiographies are highlighted: first, their emphasis on tangible saintly presence, mainly connected with miracle-working, and second, their presentation of icons as animated with saintly presence. Whether an incorporeal saint is shown hugging one of her devotees, as in the case of Saint Thekla, or whether saints are portrayed as zooming in and out of their icon, as in the case of Saints Cosmas and Damian, these hagiographical images temper the pictorial realism with hints that these bodies are not so corporeal as they might seem. As "things," they are certainly excessive, but they are also ontologically unstable— "ephemerally solid," as I argue, and so safe from the charge of investing the human body with too much divine power.

The Body in Theory

The overall focus of this book, then, is on the human body and its refraction through various images and rhetorics, and I am aware that anyone who now approaches the topic of the body must do so with some trepidation, given how problematic and complex it has become in a wide variety of disciplines. In an article in the collection entitled *Fragments for a History of the Human Body*, classicist Jean-Pierre Vernant summarized the situation succinctly: in contemporary theory "the body is no longer posited as a fact of nature, a constant and universal reality, but as an entirely problematic notion, a historical category, steeped in imagination, and one that must be deciphered within a particular culture by defining the functions it assumes and the forms it takes on within that culture."[75] As a problematic phenomenon, the body has left the natural realm and entered the discursive domain. In light of—and indebted to—the work of Michel Foucault, contemporary social and philosophical theory has viewed the body in three basic ways, articulated as follows by Bryan Turner: (1) "as an effect of deep structural arrangements of power and knowledge"; (2) as "a symbolic system that produces a set of metaphors by which power is conceptualized"; and (3) as "a consequence of long-term historical changes in human society."[76]

As Turner observes, all three of these views "challenge any assumption about the ontological coherence of the body as a universal historical phenomenon"; one "cannot take 'the body' for granted as a natural, fixed, and historically universal datum of human societies," despite the fact that cultural conceptualizations of the body condition perception of the body in such a way that the body may *seem* natural.[77] And yet, despite their concern to historicize and particularize the body, sometimes such theories risk losing the body in a haze of abstractions. After some two decades of cultural obsession with the body, theorists are still "far from assured about its referent," as Sarah Coakley has remarked.[78] Already more than ten years ago, feminist philosopher Judith Butler, attempting to write on the materiality of the body, wrote about her own frustration in this regard: "I tried to discipline myself to stay on the subject, but found that I could not fix bodies as simple objects of thought. . . . I kept losing track of the subject . . . and I began to consider that perhaps this resistance to fixing the subject was essential to the matter at hand."[79]

As Butler goes on to say, her resistance was aimed at philosophical approaches, "always at some distance from corporeal matters," that "try in that disembodied way to demarcate bodily terrains: they invariably miss the body or, worse, write against it."[80] In recent years a host of interpreters has joined Butler in her quest for a more satisfying account of the materiality of the body, as the following litany of book titles suggests: *Transgressive Corporeality, The Body in the Mind, The Absent Body, Cutting the Body, Stately Bodies, Pictures of the Body, Volatile Bodies,* and of course Butler's own punning title, *Bodies That Matter.*[81] All of these, and many more, can be read as attempts to address Butler's question, "What about the materiality of the body?"[82]

Historians of ancient Christianity have also made significant contributions toward answering this question, especially regarding ascetic behaviors, gender construction, and sexual practices and theories. In various ways recent scholarly studies of the desert fathers and mothers, of resurrection, of such theologians as Jerome, John Chrysostom, Gregory of Nyssa, Athanasius, and Augustine, have all brought forward the body "as a tangible frame of selfhood in individual and collective experience, providing a constellation of physical signs that signify relations of persons to their contexts."[83] The perspectives that have provided the frame-work for these historical reconstructions have been drawn, in the main, from social history and anthropology, as well as from rhetorical and fem-inist theories. What my study adds to these is a broadly aesthetic perspec-tive, one that emphasizes the role of the senses and imaginative sensibility in any approach to the question of the body in late ancient Christianity. By focusing on the material turn in this time period, I hope to show how the life of affect, while fully instantiated in corporeality, was endowed with a creative, cognitive function.

My own approach to the question of the materiality of the body has focused in large part on analyzing the intrinsic role of word-pictures in shaping knowledge of material substance. In this I have been indebted to Michael Roberts's conception of what he calls "the jeweled style" in late ancient literature and art.[84] This was a style that privileged brilliance and dazzle, in art as well as in writing. It was a style that conveyed mean-ing by juxtaposing images, as in a frieze sarcophagus or collective hagi-ography, rather than by mounting a linear argument. The appeal of this style, that is, was to the fragment, like a colorful mosaic tile; the visual immediacy of the part was crucial to the role that this aesthetics played in the development of a corporeal imagination in late ancient Chris-tianity.

As I have put together this book, I have emulated something akin to the "jeweled style" of late ancient Christianity. In particular: most of the ideas in this book began as engagements with "fragments"—with a text's scintillating metaphor or oddly provocative anecdote. Textual images can themselves be considered "things" (to recall Brown's thing theory) whose excess or surplus value make them magnets of interpre-tive attention. I have thus been engaged with the dazzle of late ancient rhetoric from the beginning. In general: I have assembled the material in this book in chapters that circle around a common set of themes rather than following a linear, chronological argument. This means that some ancient texts appear in more than one chapter. As with the jeweled style, repetition is valued for the difference it can disclose. Thus each time texts appear they take on additional shades of meaning because each chapter presents a slightly different language and framework for the phenomenon under discussion. Finally, I have imagined that each chapter is a single "image" juxtaposed with the others, and I hope that this introduction has helped articulate the meanings that emerge from such juxtapositions, though it has certainly not exhausted them. For evocative disclosure, as contrasted with descriptive closure, lies at the heart of the jeweled style.

Chapter One
Bodies and Selves

The shift in sensibility that I have called "the material turn" was not limited to late ancient Christianity. The reconfiguration of the relationship between materiality and meaning was part of a wider cultural phenomenon, as several studies have shown. Beginning in the fourth century, there was an increase in appreciation for color, glitter, and spectacle, from public ceremonies to personal clothing.[1] This heightened appeal to the eye, variously characterized as a new theatricality and "a peculiarly expressionistic manner," can also be seen in poetry and sculpture—a "jeweled style" based on preference for visual immediacy, which was achieved by emphasis on the part at the expense of elaborations of organic wholes.[2] Petitioning the visual imagination of the spectator also marked the biographical literature of this period, as authors invited readers to "see" holiness in the bodies of their heroes.[3] As noted in the Introduction, an increase in the ability to "see more than was [literally] there" seems characteristic of the cultural scene that also witnessed a new appreciation for the role of both "things" and of the material imagination in understandings of self-identity.[4]

Central to the material turn was the use of the body as a tangible frame of selfhood, a phenomenon that was most strikingly manifested in Christianity and Neoplatonism. An example from Neoplatonism of this new function of the body as signifier of the self, particularly in terms of spiritual transformation, can serve to illustrate the import of this aspect of the material turn. In the late fifth century, Marinus of Neapolis wrote a biography of Proclus, his teacher and predecessor as head of the Neoplatonic academy in Athens. Midway through the biography, Marinus described Proclus as follows: "It was apparent that he spoke [under the inspiration of] divine thoughts, and from his wise mouth the words poured out like snowflakes. It seemed that his eyes were filled with a certain flashing, and further his face was suffused with a divine radiance."[5] According to Marinus, it was not only Proclus's radiant face and snowflake-words that reflected his hero's exalted self. Early on in his work he elaborated on characteristics of Proclus's body. In this regard it is significant that Marinus, who organized the biography around the virtues, expanded the traditional Neoplatonic canon of four virtues (political, purifying, contemplative, and exemplary) by adding physical, ethical, and theurgical categories.[6] In the context of the revalued material world in which Marinus was writing, it seems particularly significant that he could imagine a set of virtues that was specifically physical and revelatory of the relation of body and self. Proclus is accordingly described physically as having "a certain symmetry of organic members" and "the beauty of just proportions"; he possessed "an extreme delicacy of the senses that may be called 'corporeal wisdom,'" and "from his soul exuded a certain living light that shone over his whole body."[7] This, says Marinus, was the man "who was to achieve the presence of true being."[8] Proclus's body was a walking advertisement of his philosophical prowess.

The phrase "corporeal wisdom" is a good example of the new emphasis on the body as a positive locus for the construal of the self in this period. This chapter sets the stage for the book's focus on the material turn in late ancient Christianity by undertaking a comparative analysis of Christianity and Neoplatonism. In the following pages, thinkers who were participants in the material turn will be compared with thinkers from an earlier period in order to bring the new emphasis on materiality into sharper focus. Drawing on word-pictures of the self from the writings of each of these authors, I analyze a shift in ancient views of the embodied self, a shift from viewing corporeality as a mark of a self in disarray to viewing it as a site of religious and philosophical transformation. However, before addressing the issue of the body as signifier—that is, as a "thing" both negative and positive—it will help to explore briefly how the concept of "self" is being used here.

What Is a Self?

"Pleasures and sadnesses, fears and assurances, desires and aversions and pain—whose are they?"[9] Although Plotinus had struggled with this poignant question for many years and indeed had found an answer to it, he was still, at the end of his life, trying to articulate a vision of an authentic self free from the emotional entanglements of the embodied human being, entanglements that distracted the self from its genuine powers of self-discernment.[10] This worry about self-identity—"But we . . . who are 'we'?"[11]—arose in part from Plotinus's recognition of the soul's tendency toward fragmentation—its false tendency, that is, to define itself in terms of its attachment to cares and concerns of the moment. In his words, "all souls are all things, but each [is differentiated] according to that which is active in it; . . . different souls look at different things and are and become what they look at."[12]

This concern about fixating distractions that alienate and diminish the self was not limited to the Platonic tradition to which Plotinus adhered. Almost a century earlier, the Stoic Marcus Aurelius had asked himself, "To what use am I now putting the powers of my soul? Examine yourself on this point at every step, and ask, 'How does it stand with that part of me called the master-part? Whose soul inhabits me at this moment? Is it a little child's, a youngster's, a woman's, a tyrant's, that of a beast of burden, or a wild animal?'"[13] Characterizing Marcus as "criticizing himself relentlessly, like a bug under glass," Carlin Barton has argued that the "result of such a severe internalized critic" was "self-splitting," and "the shared, blurred social identity that ideally molded and formed the personality was experienced as a loss of identity, an unsightly chaos of the self."[14]

Worry about such a chaos of the self could also be found in Christianity. For Origen of Alexandria, an older contemporary of Plotinus, the "inner man" was unfortunately rent by demonic presences. Frequently interpreting images of beasts from Scriptural passages as figures for emotions, Origen interpreted them as fixating prisons—"serpent-man" and "horse-man"—and as grotesque masks.[15] When caught in the grip of negative emotions and false attachments, "we wear the mask (*persona*) of the lion, the dragon, the fox . . . and the pig."[16] An unsightly chaos indeed.

Although Plotinus, Marcus Aurelius, and Origen did not share the same thought-systems regarding the composition and destiny of the soul, all three did reflect in similar ways about the phenomenon of the self in disarray. Yet this is only part of the story, since they also expressed a certain optimism about the self that was both personal and cosmic. This is a topic to which I shall return. For the moment, however, I want to observe that these ancient portraits of a self divided against itself, bewildered as to its identity, seem strikingly "modern," I think seductively so, perhaps in part because the psychoanalytical traditions of the twentieth century appropriated ancient terminology such as "psyche," "persona," and words formed with *autos* (e.g., autism, autoeroticism) for their own understandings of the self. Although I have used the terms "soul" and "self" interchangeably in the instances of ancient thinking given above, there is in fact an interpretive problem in trying to reconcile an ancient terminology of "soul" with modern concepts of "self."

One example of such a modern concept will help clarify the problem. In a cogent analysis of ways in which Freudian psychoanalysis altered conceptions of the self, Gregory Jay offers the following succinct description of the self in the wake of Freud: "The argument of psychoanalysis, of course, becomes that we are not what we are—that our empirical selves are actors in a script whose authorship is essentially unconscious, both on a personal and a cultural level. Human identity turns out to be a speculation *par excellence*, an image formed as a reflective compromise between wishes and defenses that engage in a ceaseless struggle for ascendancy."[17] This staging of the self in terms of ambivalence, that is, in terms of a constant conflict between desire and repression, makes any attempt to formulate a stable *auto*biography impossible. "In autobiography psychoanalytically read," Jay continues, "the undecidable question, as Jacques Lacan pronounces it, is 'Who speaks?'"[18]

In light of such a definition, it is somewhat problematic to use the word "self" for ancient understandings of human identity expressed as "soul." Plotinus, for example, did not think that the question "Who speaks?" was finally undecidable. At the end of the very treatise that he opens by asking to whom the emotions belong, he again asks a series of self-definitional questions: "What is it that has carried out this investigation? Is it "we" or the soul? It is "we," but by the soul. And what do we mean by "by the soul"? Did "we" investigate by having soul? No, but in so far as we *are* soul."[19] Despite his worries about the soul's proclivity for errancy, Plotinus believed that the soul was a principle of self-cohesion anchored in a stabilizing transcendent reality.[20] Origen, too, despite his bestial scripting of the soul's debased desires, did not understand human identity to be a compromise formation premised upon ceaseless struggle; instead, he located the true self in an inner *logos,* incorporeal and changeless, through which a sustaining relation to the divine mind is established.[21]

Nonetheless, given the marked tendency of classical and late ancient authors to view soul as the locus of human identity,[22] I think that the term "self" can be used to characterize what ancient thinkers meant by "soul" as long as it is used to describe not actors in an unconscious script, but an orientation to context. When conceptualized as an orientation to context, the self-as-soul is not an entity that one "has." As Frederic Schroeder has observed, "the noun 'self' is *prima facie* embarrassing to the philosopher, since it seems to be little more than a hypostatized version of a reflexive and intensive pronoun. We may well ask, What is the difference between myself and my Self? How is either of these to be distinguished from me? The ancients were perhaps wiser in not rendering the equivalent Greek pronoun *autos,* or the Latin *ipse,* a substantive."[23] Given the virtual equivalence of *autos* and *psyche,* especially (but not only) in Platonic traditions,[24] soul is likewise not a substantive. In other words, as a term that describes the self, "soul" is a placing function that serves to orient the self in a network of relationships that are both material and spiritual.

The Self and Images of Place

The broad topic that this chapter addresses is a shift in the ways in which the self was represented in Neoplatonism and Christianity, moving from Plotinus and Origen in the third century to theurgists and theorists of relic-worship in the late fourth and fifth centuries. I intend this comparison of ways of thinking about the self, somewhat distant in time from each other, to serve as what Simon Goldhill, in another context, calls "paradigmatic moments"; as he explains, "these moments are not chosen because of any commitment to Foucauldian 'rupture' but in order to maximize difference for the sake of rhetorical clarity."[25] My argument focuses on the orienting function of soul insofar as it comes to expression in word-pictures of the self in relation to place, and the shift that occurs in such images of self-placement will be plotted along a continuum whose two poles I designate as "a touch of the transcendent" and "a touch of the real."[26] What I mean to specify by these phrases appropriated from the New Historicism is an aesthetics of self-identity that "places" the self by using cosmic imagery—"a touch of the transcendent"—that gives way to an aesthetics of self-identity that "places" the self by using material imagery—"a touch of the real." Furthermore, the word "touch" is important to this distinction because the distinction is not an absolute one but rather a matter of shifting emphasis concerning the relation between, and reconciliation of, idea and materiality, or the abstract and the concrete.

A picture of this argument regarding the shift in self-understanding as conveyed by images of place can be quickly drawn by considering how two Christians, Origen in the third century and Epiphanius in the late fourth, interpreted that notable feature of biblical geography, the heavenly waters that became the rivers of Paradise.[27] Commenting on God's creation and dividing of the waters in the first chapter of Genesis, Origen distinguishes between two kinds of water and immediately sees in them an anthropological image: "Let each of you, therefore, be zealous to become a divider of that water which is above and that which is below. The purpose, of course, is that, attaining an understanding and participation in that spiritual water which is above the firmament one may draw forth 'from within himself rivers of living water springing up into life eternal.'"[28] Origen is so eager that his reader "relate [the passage] to ourselves" that he opens out the self to encompass not just the "rivers of living water" but all of the features of the place that God creates: the seeds, the stars ("the heaven of our heart"), even the birds are all features of the human soul.[29] The force of Origen's interpretation is centrifugal, as the human heart is enlarged to encompass a spiritual geography.

This was, of course, the kind of allegorizing interpretation that irked Epiphanius, a major instigator of the Origenist controversy and famously critical of Origen's spiritual flights of fancy.[30] Wanting to have none of Origen's metaphorizing of Paradise in terms of the human, Epiphanius denied the validity of what he considered to be Origen's too-spiritual understanding: "In the beginning God made heaven and earth, which are not to be understood allegorically, but can actually be seen. And scripture says [that he made] the firmament, and the sea, plants, trees, pasture, grass, animals, fish, birds, and everything else which, as we can see, actually came into being."[31] This emphasis on seeing was also part of his attack on Origen in the *Panarion*, where he complained that Origen had deprived both the spiritual and the anthropological orders of seeing (the Son could not see the Father, the Holy Spirit could not see the Son, the angels could not see the Spirit, and human beings could not see angels).[32] The real clincher to his argument, however, was his personal experience of two of the rivers of Paradise: "I saw the waters of Gehon, waters that I looked at with these bodily eyes. . . . And I simply drank the waters from the great river Euphrates, which you can touch with your hand and sip with your lips; these are not spiritual waters."[33] Taking in the waters of Paradise with eyes and mouth, the "I" of Epiphanius is located in terms of a much more visceral, "this-worldly" geography than Origen's spiritually expansive geographical self.

Although it is clear that Epiphanius was not overtly theorizing human possibility as Origen was, it is also clear that there is more to this clash than a disagreement about scriptural interpretation. As Jonathan Smith has observed, a total worldview is implied in an individual's or a culture's imagination of place: "it is through an understanding and symbolization of place that a society or individual creates itself."[34] Epiphanius's tangible imagination of place signaled a shift in the role that "the real" might play in formulating human possibility. Peter Brown has remarked about the Palestinian monks who heard and approved of Epiphanius's rejection of Origen's view of Paradise that, for them, "paradise was not some supra-celestial, spiritual state, from which their souls had fallen on to the dull earth. Paradise was close to hand. It had always been on earth. . . . Paradise was within their grasp."[35] Hence Epiphanius's materialist appropriation of scriptural images of place was also a form of spirituality, but one that was more "centripetal" than Origen's in its this-worldly orientation. It is this shift from a transcendent to an earthy aesthetic that I will explore as a shift in ancient senses of the self, drawing upon an approach advocated by the New Historicism.

New Historicists Gallagher and Greenblatt describe their interpretive procedure as routing "theoretical and methodological generalizations through dense networks of particulars," and they defend their use of anecdotes in historical explanation in terms of their reluctance "to see the long chains of close analysis go up in a puff of abstraction."[36] In addition to the appeal to anecdotes, they borrow from the poet Ezra Pound "'the method of the Luminous Detail' whereby we attempt to isolate significant or 'interpreting detail' from the mass of traces that have survived in the archive."[37] In this I will follow in their footsteps, although I will extend Pound's notion of the luminous detail by adding to it his definition of an image as "that which presents an intellectual and emotional complex in an instant of time," "a cluster of fused ideas endowed with energy."[38] In what follows, then, "luminous details" will anchor my presentation of the imagination of "place" as a useful way to tap into ancient senses of "self."

Plotinus and the Touch of the Transcendent: The Transparent Sphere

Graeco-Roman authors were alert to the dangers involved in sight.[39] The eye could wither, devour, de-soul, or bewitch another, but it could also bewitch or consume the self.[40] Nowhere is the self-consuming function of the eye more striking than in the myth of Narcissus, to which Plotinus alludes in the course of a discussion about how the soul can "see" intelligible beauty and, ultimately, the Good:

> How can one see the "inconceivable beauty" [*Symp.* 218E2] which stays within in the holy sanctuary and does not come out where the profane may see it? Let him who can, follow and come within, and leave outside the sight of his eyes and not turn back to the bodily splendors which he saw before. When he sees the beauty in bodies he must not run after them; we must know that they are images, traces, shadows, and hurry away to that which they image. For if a man runs to the image (like a beautiful reflection playing on the water, which some story somewhere, I think, said riddlingly a man wanted to catch and sank down into the stream and disappeared) then this man who clings to beautiful bodies and will not let them go, will, like the man in the story, but in soul, not in body, sink down into the dark depths where intellect has no delight, and stay blind in Hades, consorting with shadows there and here.[41]

The tragedy of Narcissus, variously described by modern interpreters as an arresting self-fascination or as a conflictual splitting of the subject,[42] was for Plotinus a cautionary tale about the fate of the soul that mistakes sensory for spiritual (i.e., noetic) realities. When the self is placed with respect only to the material world, it gropes blindly after shadows. Thus Plotinus too, like modern interpreters of Narcissus, used this story to picture the problem of misdirected sight, that is, a form of attention that fixates and fragments the soul into a congeries of its own grasping desires.

Plotinus often, of course, linked this kind of woeful particularity to human physicality. Forgetfulness, for example, is due to the "moving and flowing" nature of the body[43]; the soul's "fellowship" (κοινωνία) with the body is "displeasing" because the body hinders thought and fills the soul with negative emotions.[44] This only happens, however, to the soul that "has sunk into the interior of the body" and has forgotten that the body belongs to it, and not the reverse.[45] There is a question about the extent to which sheer physicality was really the issue in Plotinus's presentation of the difficulties faced by the soul, since he admitted that "it is not evil in every way for soul to give body the ability to flourish and to exist, because not every kind of provident care for the inferior deprives the being exercising it of its ability to remain in the highest."[46]

Nonetheless, to the extent that the soul becomes "mixed up" with bodily stuff—"for every human being is double, one of him is the sort of compound being and one of him is himself"—it loses its proper focus and becomes "isolated and weak and fusses and looks towards a part and in its separation from the whole it embarks on one single thing and flies from everything else."[47] Even though Plotinus was genuinely concerned about the negative impact of "body," such passages can bear a more nuanced reading. As Stephen Clark has argued, for Plotinus the soul is not a "ghost in a machine."[48] The most devastating split is not between body and soul but rather between two kinds of consciousness: the "compound being" that "fusses" is identified by Clark, quoting Plotinus, as the "restlessly active nature which wanted to control itself and be on its own"; "it did not want the whole to be present to it altogether."[49]

Despite this positive reading of the Plotinian view of the embodied self, which emphasizes problems in the soul's orienting function rather than in the sheer fact of its physicality, there is a tension in Plotinus's thought regarding the self in its earthly context. His frequent use of the place-markers "there" and "here" to designate a metaphysical world of intelligible reality ("there") and its shadowy reflection in the material cosmos ("here"), when read anthropologically as the "there" of the soul's true home and the "here" of its cramping particularity, seems undeniably dualistic. Taking seriously Plotinus's language of "ascent," Stephen Halliwell sees "an ambivalence in his system of thought as a whole, an ambivalence that keeps Plotinian philosophy caught between ultimately irreconcilable ideals of 'flight' from the merely physical and, on the other hand, a commitment to finding the echo of higher realities in what it continues to regard as the rich and multiform 'tapestry' of life itself."[50]

Other interpreters, however, suggest that Plotinus's "here" and "there" should not be distinguished so sharply as a spiritual flight from the merely physical: as A. H. Armstrong has observed, "in the end we are left with the very strong impression that for Plotinus there are not two worlds but one real world apprehended in different ways on different levels."[51] Even when Plotinus occasionally imagined a time before time, as it were, when disembodied souls were "united with the whole of reality," he was quick to redirect attention to human life as it is lived now: "we were parts of the intelligible, not marked off or cut off but belonging to the whole; and we are not cut off even now."[52] But because "another man, wishing to exist, approached that man, and when he found us . . . he wound himself round us and attached himself to that man who was then each one of us," the task of the soul is to learn how to direct its attention to the whole—to detach itself, as Sara Rappe has argued, from "the narrow confines of a historical selfhood."[53] What the Plotinian self needs, in other words, is a touch of transcendence that, as Rappe continues, "does not consist in a denial of the empirical self [but] allows the larger selfhood of soul to emerge from behind the veil of the objective domain."[54]

In order to perform its proper placing function with regard to spiritual reality, the soul must direct its vision inward: "Shut your eyes, and change to and wake another way of seeing, which everyone has but few use."[55] Thus centered, the self expands. Plotinus developed techniques for achieving this kind of awareness, the so-called "spiritual exercises." Perhaps the most famous of these is his image of the transparent sphere, which I will read as an anthropological image, a way of picturing selfhood in terms of place:

Let there, then, be in the soul a shining imagination of a sphere, having everything [in the visible universe] within it, either moving or standing still, or some things moving and others standing still. Keep this, and apprehend in your mind another, taking away the mass: take away also the places, and the mental picture of matter in yourself, and do not try to apprehend another sphere smaller in mass than the original one, but calling on the god who made that of which you have the mental picture, pray him to come. And may he come, bringing his own universe with him, with all the gods within him, he who is one and all, and each god is all the gods coming together into one.[56]

In this image, according to Frederic Schroeder, "Plotinus is presenting us with a noetic universe in which there is no fixed point of observation: all is transparent to all."[57] It is a picture of intense inward concentration that opens the soul outward as it is filled with the "real beings" of the noetic world.[58] Both the image and the self disappear into their own luminosity; this process, whereby the knower and the known become one, is described by Schroeder as an "iconoclastic moment," a moment described further by Robert Berchman as a use of imagery and imagination "to the point of strain and shatter; at the moment of shatter, intelligible insight occurs."[59]

By engaging the image of the transparent sphere, the soul achieves self-knowledge, a knowledge that is distinct from the kind of objectivizing self- and world-awareness that Plotinus linked with discursive thought.[60] The sensible world is not so much abandoned as it is turned into light—a process of substraction that adds insofar as the soul is oriented in a nexus of relationships rather than in an "opaque" world of discrete objects. In order to be free from the attractive tug of particularity, especially in its material forms, the soul "must see that light by which it is enlightened: for we do not see the sun by another light than his own. How then can this happen? Take away everything!"[61]

What kind of self emerges in the light of the transparent sphere? When Plotinus directs the eyes of the soul inward, the vision that emerges is starkly different from the internalized self-watcher of Marcus Aurelius. A certain cosmic optimism pervades his thought, as "the levels of reality become levels of inner life, the levels of the self."[62] As "our head strikes the heavens" and becomes the transparent sphere, the illusions of personality and individuality vanish, revealing a "self" that is essentially divine.[63] Thus centered in the divine, the Plotinian self is, in Rappe's words, "infinitely expansive"; "no longer circumscribed by its historical, temporal, and emotional limitations, the Plotinian self embraces a vast domain whose boundaries extend to the fullness of what is encountered in every knowing moment."[64] Skittish to the end concerning the dangers posed by materiality, and especially by the human body (considered as a "hindrance": we must "cut away all the other things in which we are encased"), Plotinus offered a self touched by transcendence, a "self glorified, full of intelligible light—but rather itself pure light—weightless, floating free, having become—but rather being—a god."[65]

Origen and the Touch of the Transcendent: The Divine Library

As for Plotinus, so also for Origen, human corporeality could be troubling, a mark of a self in disarray. Commenting, for example, on Matt. 7:6 ("Do not give what is holy to dogs; and do not throw your pearls before swine"), Origen remarked, "For I would say that whoever is constantly muddied with bodily things and rolls around in the filthy things of life and has no desire for the pure and holy life, such a person is nothing but a swine."[66] Origen sometimes thought of human embodiment as the result of spiritual defect; the body in itself is not only "dead and completely lifeless" but is also "opposed and hostile to the spirit."[67]

Yet despite his sometime disparagement of the body, Origen seemed more concerned with how the soul orients itself with regard to the Pauline concept of "the flesh," understood as a willful attachment to false values that drag the soul in different directions.[68] The soul takes on the qualities of that which it contemplates: hence Origen's sense of the human dilemma as one of divided consciousness, which he frequently pictured as a kind of doubleness, an "outer man who looks at things in a corporeal way," and an "inner man" who sees spiritually.[69] In several of his writings, Origen developed this concept of doubleness at length, arguing that the empirical perceptions of human beings have as analogue the spiritual senses—having a nose for righteousness, an eye of the heart, the touch of faith, and so on through the five senses.[70] As David Dawson has argued, the doctrine of the spiritual senses rests on "an intrinsic connection between the visible and the invisible" and, "although the bodily realm always informs one's love for God, it should not become the object of that love."[71]

However, choosing an object for that love is just the problem. As Origen explained in his *Commentary on the Song of Songs*, "it is impossible for human nature not to be always feeling the passion of love for something." And he continued: "Some people pervert this faculty of passionate love, which is implanted in the human soul by the creator's kindness. Either it becomes with them a passion for money and the pursuit of avaricious ends; or they go after glory . . . or they chase after harlots and are found the prisoners of wantonness and lewdness; or they squander the strength of this great good on other things like these [including their jobs, athletic skills, and even higher education]."[72] This picture of a perverted self is very much like the restless and "fussy" self envisaged by Plotinus, a self that is placed only in relation to the material world and its enticements. Human love must be directed to the good, "and by that which is good," Origen concluded, "we understand not anything corporeal, but only that which is found first in God and in the powers of the soul."[73]

Unfortunately, the powers of the soul are not easy to harness. Frequently relying on scriptural animal imagery in order to picture the soul as a kind of menagerie, Origen argued that consciousness is multiple; it has "secret recesses" (*arcanae conscientiae*) and can "admit different energies, that is, controlling influences of spirits either good or bad."[74] The key to redirecting these inner powers is self-inspection, a probing of the false *personae* that make the soul "dingy and dirty."[75] Thus Origen called for a kind of reflexive self-seeing that is transformative: "If we are willing to understand that in us there is the power to be transformed from being serpents, swine, and dogs, let us learn from the apostle that the transformation depends on us. For he says this: 'We all, when with unveiled face we reflect the glory of the Lord, are transformed into the same image.'"[76]

That the self is capable of such metamorphosis is due in part to its ability to read Scripture properly so as to discern the spiritual metanarrative encrypted within it. Proper reading was, for Origen, allegorical reading, which spiritualizes the material realities of the text, its "sensible aspect," and at the same time spiritualizes the reader, who learns how to distinguish between "the inner and the outer man."[77] Learning how to make this distinction is crucial, because an allegorical reading of the biblical text "reveals a surprising and total isomorphism with the very structure of spiritual reality,"[78] a reality that is not only cosmic but also central to authentic self-identity as Origen understood it. In a passage in his *Commentary on John* devoted precisely to what he there calls "elevated interpretation," Origen wrote that "the mind that has been purified and has surpassed all material things, so as to be certain of the contemplation of God, is divinized by those things that it contemplates."[79] As Robert Berchman has argued, the purpose of this form of textual contemplation is "to foster the potential of intellectual self-awareness and so orient the self upon a path of self-knowledge that eventually leads to consciousness of the *Logos*."[80]

As the book becomes spirit, so the person becomes book: one of Origen's most powerful images of the self in relation to Scripture is presented as one of the figural meanings of Noah's ark in the *Homilies on Genesis*: "If there is anyone who, while evils are increasing and vices are overflowing, can turn from the things which are in flux and passing away and fallen, and can hear the word of God and the heavenly precepts, this man is building an ark of salvation within his own heart and is dedicating a library, so to speak, of the divine word within himself. . . . From this library learn the historical narratives; from it recognize 'the great mystery' which is fulfilled in Christ and in the Church."[81] This "library of divine books" is the "faithful soul" who, by internalizing the word, begins to realize a touch of transcendence in the self. As Dawson has observed, "the allegorical reader's necessary departure from Scripture's literal sense parallels her resistance to the fall of her soul away from contemplation of the *logos* into body, history, and culture. But the equally necessary reliance of the allegorical story on the literal sense parallels the reader's salvific use of her soul's embodiment (by virtue of the prior, enabling self-embodiment of the divine *logos*)."[82] Although by directing the attention of the soul away from temporal reality ("the things in flux") and toward the divinity within Origen envisioned the self's proper place as a cosmic one ("the heavenly precepts"), this does not mean that embodied life has no value. When the soul is "placed" in the context of a divine library, it is also placed with regard to the incarnation, as Dawson indicates briefly in the quotation above.

The full import of the image of the divine library can be seen in a remarkable passage from the *Philocalia*, in which Origen argues that "the word is made flesh eternally in the Scriptures in order to dwell among us."[83] That dwelling is not only the literal presence of the book *among* us but also the transfigured presence of Christ *in* us. Scripture embeds the incarnation in the world, but it also transfigures that world, as Origen went on to say: "those who are capable of following the traces of Jesus when he goes up and is transfigured in losing his terrestrial form will see the transfiguration in every part of Scripture" and will be transfigured themselves, since they have the key to the wisdom hidden in the text.[84] No longer divided, then, the Origenian self is as expansive and as embracing of a transcendent structure of reality as the Plotinian self whose "head strikes the heavens."

Origen's connection of the Incarnation with Scripture and, by extension, with the reader whose self encompasses a divine library, would seem to dignify the body; indeed, Dawson argues vigorously that "his celebration of allegorical transformation of identity is a spiritualization, not a rejection, of the body."[85] Such a spiritualized view of human materiality, however, is hard to reconcile with a valorization of the embodied human being, the historical self: as Peter Brown remarks, for Origen "the present human body reflected the needs of a single, somewhat cramped moment in the spirit's progress back to a former, limitless identity."[86] And, even though "body" would remain for Origen a marker of identity, it did so only as it was transformed into a spiritual body "gradually and by degrees, over the course of infinite and immeasurable ages."[87] Origen may have had a "heady sense of the potency and dynamism of body," as Caroline Walker Bynum argues; but as she goes on to observe, his theory of the body "seemed to sacrifice integrity of bodily structure for the sake of transformation; it seemed to surrender material continuity for the sake of identity."[88] Thus although Origen shared with Plotinus a sense of a self touched by transcendence,[89] he went one step further in spiritualizing the self by allowing even the body an eventual touch of transcendence.

From the Touch of Transcendence to the Touch of the Real

As I noted earlier, the ways of conceiving of the self that are the focus of this discussion can be located along a continuum, with the views of Plotinus and Origen representing a paradigmatic moment when the self is oriented toward the spiritual, sometimes at the expense of the material world. The later Neoplatonists and Christians to whom attention will

now shift also privileged spiritual knowing as a central and defining feature of the self, but they did so with greater emphasis on, and valuation
of, the this-worldly or material realm. Whereas Plotinus and Origen
directed the gaze inward in order to orient the self "outward" to a transcendent spiritual structure, later thinkers did the reverse, directing the
gaze outward in order to achieve inner vision.

The focus will continue to be on images in texts that can be read as
pictures of how a particular author orients the self. As with Plotinus and
Origen, the soul is placed by such textual imagery, but that imagery also
recommends a form of practice—spiritual exercises in Plotinus's case,
and introspective reading and interpretation in Origen's. However,
unlike the rather intellectual and even ethereal images and practices
seen so far, those to which I now turn—the animation of statues and the
devotion to relics—involve a kind of material engagement not characteristic of the earlier forms of self-construal. In fact, from the standpoint of
the earlier perspective, the later use of the material to enhance the spiritual will seem paradoxical.

Proclus and the Touch of the Real: Animated Statues

Although, in the wake of Plotinus, achievement of a "self glorified, full
of light"[90] continued to be the goal of later Neoplatonists, the means for
achieving that goal, as well as the cosmology and psychology upon which
those means were premised, had changed. The earlier tendency to suppress materiality as fundamental to self-identity was revised when the orienting function of the soul shifted with regard to the spiritual value of
the sensible world. This shift toward a sacramental view of the world—a
view, that is, that invests the sensible world with divine presence rather
than seeing the sensible as a shadowy reflection of the divine—was
already evident in the psychology of Iamblichus, whose views of the soul
Proclus largely followed.

Unlike Plotinus, who argued that part of the embodied soul never
descended but remained always in the intelligible realm, thus linking
human identity permanently to a kind of transcendent consciousness,
Iamblichus thought that the soul descended entirely.[91] No part of the
Iamblichean "I" is untouched by embodiment.[92] This has been viewed
as a kind of demotion and even self-alienation of the soul, and indeed
Iamblichus argued that the soul could not recover its own divinity by
itself but needed help from the gods.[93] Embodiment, however, was part
of a larger cosmogonic process: reading the *Timaeus*'s description of the
creation of Forms and matter as simultaneous rather than as sequential,
Iamblichus argued that "the separation of corporeality from its principles was an impossibility that could occur only in abstraction, not in

actuality."[94] Thus even though the embodied soul suffered dividedness—in Iamblichus's words, "the sameness within itself becomes
faint"—the material world provided it with resources for the recovery of
its divine nature, since traces of the divine were infused throughout the
world.[95]

Theurgy, a ritual process whose goal was self-unification and illumina-
tion by the gods, was based on this view of the material world as theophany.[96] As Iamblichus wrote, "the abundance of power of the highest
beings has the nature always to transcend everything in this world, and
yet this power is immanent in everything equally without impediment."[97] This power was present in the form of divine "tokens" (συνθή-
ματα and σύμβολα), those "godlike stones, herbs, animals, and spices"
that the theurgist combined and consecrated in order to "establish from
them a complete and pure receptacle [for the gods]."[98] By this ritual
use of matter, an altered sense of self-identity was performed and actualized, as the divine in the self was united with the god by the god's own
action: theurgical "ascent" was not an escape from the material world
but rather a deification of the soul through a unifying process that eventuated in what Iamblichus called "putting on the form of the gods."[99]
Shaw has put the matter succinctly: "theurgic rites transformed the soul
from being its own idol, in an inverted attitude of self-interest, into an
icon of the divine, with its very corporeality changed into a vehicle of
transcendence."[100]

This theurgical view of the self was inherited and developed further
by Proclus, whose view of the religious import of materiality was, if anything, even more emphatic than that of Iamblichus. Because, as Proclus
argued, "all things are bound up in the gods and deeply rooted in
them," everything in the sensible world is linked by lines of sympathy
with the god appropriate to it.[101] Indeed, according to the principle
expressed in Proposition 57 in his *Elements of Theology*, whereby the earlier members of a causal series have greater power and so extend
throughout all the levels of being that they illuminate, the divine is
directly present in matter. John Dillon has observed that "the theory
speculates that, in a powerful sense, the lower down the scale of nature
an entity is situated, the more closely it is linked with higher principles.
This provides excellent philosophical justification for making use of
stones, plants, and animals in the performance of magical [i.e., theurgi-
cal] rituals; they are actually nearer to one god or another than we are,
being direct products of the divine realm."[102] "Some things," remarked
Proclus, "are linked with the gods immediately [ἄμεσος], others
through a varying number of intermediate terms, but 'all things are full
of gods,' and from the gods each derives its natural attribute."[103]

Despite this rather ecstatic affirmation of "the touch of the real," Proclus, like Iamblichus, had a diminished view of the human capacity to realize its connection with the divine world by using its own powers. No part of the soul remains above, and it does not have the intelligible realm within.[104] Indeed, its knowledge "is different from the divine sort" due to our intermediate position in the cosmos.[105] Hence, Proclus continued, "it is while remaining at our own rank, and possessing images of the essences of all Beings, that we turn to them by means of these images, and cognize the realm of Being from the tokens of it that we possess, not coordinately, but on a secondary level and in a manner corresponding to our own worth."[106] Contact with higher levels of reality can only be made through their effects, and even those effects—the tokens or traces of the divine sown in the material world—are irradiations from the divine and not the gods themselves.[107]

In one sense, then, the Proclean self had no choice but to remain "someone," having lost Plotinus's heady view of the possibility of coming to identity with the divine.[108] In another sense, however, that same self was oriented in a world dense with divine power, and in a religious tradition that provided the techniques for making contact with that power. The network of relationships in which Proclus's theurgical self was placed continued, as in earlier Neoplatonism, to be both spiritual and material, but it now presupposed a realignment of perception and the senses with regard to the divine. Seeing more than was (visibly) there, the theurgist looked out at the physical world in order to fill the self with divine images.

In terms of orienting the self in the world theurgically, Proclus is probably best known for the practice of the animation of statues, a practice that Iamblichus eschewed.[109] Proclus thought that statues were, in effect, aesthetic elaborations of the gods: "through their shapes, signs, postures, and expressions," as Shaw notes, "theurgic statues revealed the properties of the gods."[110] Furthermore, when the material *symbola* proper to a specific god were inserted into hollow cavities in the statue, the statue was "animated" or activated with the divine power channeled through the levels of being by those *symbola*, revealing divine wisdom in the form of oracles and enabling human participation in that wisdom.[111] In his treatise *On the Hieratic Art of the Greeks*, Proclus listed examples of these material tokens: the bel stone, the lotus, the heliotrope, the lion, and the cock each make present a particular aspect of the sun god and ultimately of Apollo.[112] The religio-aesthetic basis for this practice was stated straightforwardly by Proclus: "for a theurgist who sets up a statue as a likeness of a certain divine order fabricates the tokens of its identity with reference to that order, acting as does the craftsman when he makes a likeness by looking to its proper model."[113]

This way of conceiving of animated statues, which shifts the relation of the spiritual and the material in a positive direction by affirming the likeness between them, brought a touch of the real into the area of human identity as well. There are passages in Proclus's writings that suggest that the animated statue functions as an image of the self in both implicit and explicit ways. The implicit connection between statue and human being is in Proclus's discussion about the three ways in which the cosmos, considered as the entire visible order, is related to the Forms. Defining these three modes as participation, impression, and reflection, Proclus then offered the following example of "the three kinds of participation interwoven with each other":

The body of a good and wise man, for example, appears itself handsome and attractive because it participates directly in the beauty of nature and has its bodily shape molded by it, and by receiving reflections from the beauty of soul it carries a trace of ideal beauty, the soul serving as a connecting term between his own lowest beauty and Beauty itself. So that the reflection reveals this species of soul as being wise, or courageous, or noble or a likeness of some other virtue. And the animated statue, for example, participates by way of impression in the art which turns it on a lathe and polishes and shapes it in such and such a fashion; while from the universe it has received reflections of vitality which even cause us to say that it is alive; and as a whole it has been made like the god whose image it is.[114]

In this passage, the human being, body and soul, is placed in apposition with the animate statue; at the very least, they are analogous as icons of a sacralized world.

Elsewhere, however, Proclus brought statue and human being together more explicitly: "the theurgist, by attaching certain symbols to statues, makes them better able to participate in the higher powers; in the same way, since universal Nature has, by creative corporeal principles, made [human] bodies like statues of souls, she inseminates in each a particular aptitude to receive a particular kind of soul, better or less good."[115] Here human body and statue relate in the same way that the human soul and *symbola* do. In another passage, this time from his fragmentary *Commentary on the Chaldean Oracles*, Proclus united divine tokens, human souls, and bodies in a single image: "the soul is composed of the intellectual words (νοεροὶ λογοί) and from the divine *symbola* (θεῖα σύμβολα), some of which are from the intellectual ideas, while others are from the divine henads. And we are in fact icons of the intellectual realities, and we are statues of the unknowable *synthēmata*."[116]

The Proclean "we" is as full of divine energy as an animated statue; indeed, it is itself a "statue" capable, when guarded by ritual, of being illuminated by the divine.[117] The qualifier regarding ritual is important. Since for Proclus the self was always in a world marked by division, it could not activate its own channels of connection to the divine apart from the material world and the ritual procedures whereby elements of the world provided pathways of spiritual communication. This was, of course, a "spiritualized world," as Rappe notes; but it was a *world* nonetheless.[118] Proclus's image of the self as an animated statue is a view of the self touched by the real, oriented to the divine world in such a way that materiality took on new meaning. A bit theatrical, perhaps, and even "peculiarly expressionistic," to recall Matthews' phrase, this expression of self-identity addressed the human being's lowered cosmic status with a kinetic sense of the tangible presence of the transcendent.

Victricius of Rouen and the Touch of the Real: Spiritual Jewels

In *Contra Celsum*, Origen had written, "In order to know God we need no body at all. The knowledge of God is not derived from the eye of the body, but from the mind which sees that which is in the image of the Creator and by divine providence has received the power to know God."[119] A century later, many Christians disagreed. Indeed, the fourth-century literature that describes desert ascetics provides ample testimony to a (literally) visual organization of meaning whereby observers of ascetic practitioners claimed to see with their own eyes men living a heavenly life, men whose bodies were illuminated with flashes of angelic light.[120] In this period, Christianity was, with Neoplatonism, "equally prepared to look for transformed persons," as Peter Brown has observed.[121] As he succinctly puts it, underlying the conviction that holiness could be seen was "the notion that body and soul formed a single field of force, in which what happened in the one had subtle and lasting effects on the other. . . . Somehow, the body itself was the companion of the soul in its effort to recover the 'image of God.'"[122]

This alignment of the body with spiritual attainment, together with an increased emphasis on seeing the touch of transcendence in human physicality, also signaled that a shift had occurred away from Origen's perceived tendency to privilege mind as the most essential aspect of human identity. In late fourth-century views of both the creation of Adam and the resurrection, body was an integral, if troubling, part of the human being.[123] Viewed as embodied from the beginning, the self was now in greater need of mediating channels to establish connection with the divine, since a gulf had opened between the uncreated God and the embodied created order.[124] Origen's view of the soul's contemplative ability to bring itself into accord with an inner *logos* gave way, especially in ascetic thought, to concentration on the salvific role of the incarnate Christ in making possible a restoration of humanity's relationship with the divine.[125] Curiously, as the body became more central to human identity, it became more dangerous, needing a fully divine Christ to assume it so as to make possible its divinization. Commenting on the Christology of the Nicene Christians of this era, Virginia Burrus has argued that "the assertion of the Son's absolute divinity and the divinization of humanity anticipated in his incarnation register their historical effect in the rigid discipline of fourth-century bodies resisting their own carnality."[126]

The thought of Athanasius is a case in point. In his view, Adam and Eve, having at first lived a life of ascetic self-control in Eden, became distracted by the body and turned their attention toward it and away from God.[127] Now corrupted, "the body took center stage," as David Brakke remarks, and he summarizes the function of the incarnation as follows: "According to Athanasius, the incarnation of the word made a successful ascetic life possible once again. . . . When the Word of God assumed a human body, and perfectly guided it, he divinized this body and made it incorruptible; through their 'kinship of the flesh' to the Word's body, individual human beings can restore a proper relationship between their own body and soul and thus live a virtuous life."[128] Those who came closest to this divinization of the flesh were those who, like the exemplary Saint Antony of the *Life of St. Antony*, practiced ascetic self-discipline.

In the wake of Athanasius's hagiographical master-text, such holy persons—whether alive or dead—not only gave "human density" to the need to connect heaven and earth, they also came to be seen as conduits of spiritual power.[129] If the fourth century witnessed the rise of the holy man and the boom in hagiographical literature devoted to this figure, it also witnessed the burgeoning of another form of visible holiness, the cult of the saints and their relics. Like the body of the theurgist, the living body of the ascetic holy man and the dead body of the saintly martyr were seen as vehicles of transcendence, their "matter" charged with religious meaning.

The body parts that were venerated in the cult of relics were mostly from bodies of martyrs, who had not necessarily been practitioners of asceticism.[130] Yet the view of ascetic practice as the highest form of Christian spirituality and the veneration of relics were connected, since it was precisely ascetics (Ambrose, Jerome, Gregory of Nyssa, and Victricius, for example) who promoted the cult of relics.[131] As forms of spirituality aimed at overcoming human instability, asceticism and the cult of relics were united by the need for a tangible locus of sanctity.[132] Furthermore, they shared similar views of the nature of divine presence in the world insofar as both demanded sensory expression, whether in a living or a dead body, for their abstract belief in conduits of divine power. Treading a fine line between the touch of the real and the touch of the transcendent, they espoused a spirituality that embraced earthy contact while avoiding idolatrous materialism.[133]

As one who developed a "radically incarnational theology" of relics, Victricius of Rouen, bishop from 385 to 410 C.E., is the only known theoretician of the cult of relics.[134] As his treatise *De laude sanctorum* shows, the performative as well as the religio-aesthetic dimension of "matter" was a feature of the Christian cult of relics as it was of the Neoplatonic animation of statues.[135] As part of his argument that "the truth of the whole corporeal passion [of the martyr] is present in fragments of the righteous," Victricius wrote that a proper understanding of relics called for an imaginative use of sight as well as language: "Why, then, do we call them 'relics'? Because words are images and signs of things. Before our eyes are blood and clay. We impress on them the name of 'relics,' because we cannot do otherwise, with (so to speak) the seal of living language. But now, by uttering the whole in the part, we open the eyes of the heart, not the barriers of our bodily sight."[136] One can only understand how "blood, after martyrdom, is on fire with the reward of divinity" when one interprets with the "eyes of the heart," not allowing "bodily sight" to be a barrier. This would seem to be a reversion to Origen's doctrine of the spiritual senses were it not for the fact that Victricius and his congregation were in fact literally looking at fragments of human bodies. What Victricius hoped to accomplish was a retraining of physical sight, such that one could apprehend how "an animate body" (*animatum corpus*) had been converted by God "into the substance of his light" (*ad sui luminis transferre substantiam*).[137] Victricius shared with Proclus an ability to see more than was there as he developed this strategy for retrieving what was visually intractable, the presence of divine power in an earthy object.

It is difficult not to notice the similarity between the theurgist's ἄγαλμα ἔμψυχον, the animated statue, and the relic venerator's *animatum corpus*, the animated body. Writing about Augustine's worry that agency might be attributed to the martyrs themselves rather than to God, Clark notes that "invocation of martyrs could too easily be assimilated to theurgy (which used 'sympathetic' physical objects to invoke divine powers) or, worse, to sorcery."[138] Assimilation of the two is understandable, since both were material objects that centered divine power, giving it a place from which it could be communicated to human beings, thus drawing them into the network of relationships that they activated. Unlike animated statues, however, whose function was to impart divine wisdom, the major performative function of relics was healing: because martyrs, who "heal and wash clean," are "bound to the relics by the bond of all eternity," they bring "heavenly brilliance" into human life in the very concrete form of physical restoration.[139]

Although Victricius mentioned healing at several points, recitation of miraculous cures was not part of his sermon. His main interest lay elsewhere, in explaining how such tiny bodily fragments can be so powerful. His argument hinged on his view of the consubstantiality of all bodies. Since the saints are entirely united to Christ and thus to God, and since God cannot be divided, therefore the whole is present in every part: "nothing in relics is not complete" and "unity is widely diffused without loss to itself."[140] Bringing out the full incarnational thrust of his argument, Victricius stated that not only the souls but also the bodies of the martyrs are united with Christ: "They are entirely with the Savior in his entirety . . . and have everything in common in the truth of the godhead. . . . By righteousness they are made companions of the Savior, by wisdom his rivals, by the use of limbs concorporeal, by blood consanguineous, by the sacrifice of the victim sharers in the eternity of the cross."[141] Much like the theurgical view of the diffusion of the transcendent in special material objects, Victricius's position was premised on the belief that "God is diffused far and wide, and lends out his light without loss to himself."[142]

Having established that "the martyr is wholly present—flesh, blood, and spirit united to God—in the relic," as Clark observes, "Victricius preempts a shocked reaction: is he really saying that these relics are just what God is, the 'absolute and ineffable substance of godhead' (8.19–21)? His answer, apparently, is 'yes.'"[143] Yes, but with an important qualifier: the martyr "is the same by gift not by property, by adoption not by nature."[144] Relics, that is, retained enough of the human so that they could function as condensations of the ideal self that ascetics such as Victricius hoped to achieve. Not only are the martyr-saints advocates, judges, and associates of their venerators, but they are also teachers of virtue who "remove the stains of vice" in the human, body and soul.[145] Perhaps the most astonishing aspect of Victricius's view of relics is their ability to remake human identity in their own image. When Victricius says, "I touch fragments," he is touching the fiery rays of his own transformation.[146]

In the presence of relics, one of the things that their venerators "see" is that the martyrs are "dwellers in our hearts" (*habitatores pectoris nostri*).[147] What relics put one in touch with, that is, are models of human identity toward which the soul strives. Victricius was fairly straightforward about this. In the following passage, in which he imagined the ceremonial entry of the relics into Rouen as a Christian *adventus*, he wrote:

There is no lack of things for us to admire: in place of the royal cloak, here is the garment of eternal light. The togas of the saints have absorbed this purple. Here are diadems adorned with the varied lights of the jewels of wisdom, intellect, knowledge, truth, good counsel, courage, endurance, self-control, justice, good sense, patience, chastity. These virtues are expressed and inscribed each in its own stone. Here the Savior-craftsman has adorned the crowns of the martyrs with spiritual jewels. Let us set the sails of our souls towards these gems.[148]

One feature of this passage that deserves mention first is its description of the ritualistic character of the entry of relics into the city. Underlying Victricius's imaginative portrayal is an important feature of the cult of relics: human body parts did not become the animate bodies that were relics apart from ritual practice, and in highly elaborate and aesthetically enhanced places that evoked the visionary atmosphere in which relics took their proper place.[149] Spectacle was as much a part of the cult of relics as it was of theurgical animation of statues.

Participants in such spectacles were confronted with spiritual objects to which they were not only related (as Victricius insisted, there is only "one mass of corporeality")[150] but in which they could see the "spiritual jewels," as it were, of their own selves, body and soul, touched by transcendence. When Victricius urged his congregation, whom he had extolled from the outset for its ascetic valor, to "set their souls towards these gems," he offered those spiritual jewels as an image for how soul "places" the self in regard to its own ethical ideals, since the gems represent virtues whose realization was the goal of the ascetic life. As an image of self-identity in the context of relic-veneration, "spiritual jewels" flirts with erasing the boundary between the material and the spiritual; however, the inescapable "touch of the real" in this form of devotion ensured that "body" would remain as a locus of religious meaning.

Toward an Embodied "I"

Two paradigmatic moments in the history of self-understanding in late antiquity have been presented in this chapter, each represented by striking word-pictures drawn from texts by the Neoplatonic and Christian thinkers upon whom the discussion has focused. My wager has been that these images—Plotinus's transparent sphere, Origen's divine library, Proclus's animated statues, and Victricius's spiritual jewels—can function as expressions, in condensed form, of their authors' views of self-identity and its relation (or not) to human corporeality. Following Jonathan Smith's argument that a worldview, as well as a view of the self, can be discerned through a culture's or an individual's imagination of place, I chose these particular images not only because of their vividness as figures or metaphors of place, but also because they reveal how each author thought that the self could best orient itself with respect to the spiritual and material aspects of human life. These "luminous details"—to recall the phrase borrowed by New Historicists from Ezra

Pound—are active in that they recommend a way of being-in-the-world religiously.

Each of these images not only envisions a place but also recommends a practice whereby proper placement can be achieved. Both Plotinus and Origen drew on images of actual places—a globe teeming with life and a library of sacred books—that are metaphors of interior dispositions from beginning to end. They turned these figures of place into images of a self transformed by the knowledge that the empirical, historically conditioned world is not the locus of true identity and can even hinder connection with the divine realm. Further, both are spiritual exercises that teach the reader how to turn vision inward; they both model a form of intense inner concentration that opens the self out to structures of spiritual reality that are the soul's true home.

By contrast, the images in the texts of Proclus and Victricius both begin and end in actual places—temples with animated statues, cathedrals and martyria with relics.[151] In a sense they provide snapshots of the self engaged in forms of practice that orient the soul to sources of divine power. But they are also figurations of self-identity and not simply descriptions of ritual behavior, since animated statue and relic are used to describe not only the object of practice but also the identity of the practitioner. In these images as well as the earlier ones, an imagination of place implies a view of the self.

When compared, these two sets of images, and the cultural preferences that they imply, demonstrate a shift in conceptions of the self with respect to materiality, broadly construed to include both the physical world as well as the human body. By plotting this shift as a movement from a religious orientation of the self that emphasized "the touch of transcendence" to one that emphasized "the touch of the real," I have not wanted to suggest that views of the self in the earlier era of the third century were somehow more spiritual than they were in the later era. Orienting the self in relation to the divine remained a constant. Rather, the shift involved a change in views of the soul's ability to make contact with the god or gods.

One way to describe the change is to consider how these two groups of authors thought about loss. For Plotinus and Origen, so confident that intense inner contemplation could bring about realization of the self's divine core, distraction was a major problem; loss of attention diminished the soul's consciousness of its expansive identity, and this loss was often attributed by them to the particularity of the material world and the body's involvement with it. For Proclus and Victricius, living in an age when the high gods had become more remote, loss was expressed as a loss of immediacy and as a diminished view of the human capacity to make contact with the divine by using the self's inner powers.

This loss of cosmic optimism concerning the makeup of the self, together with the felt need for figures who could mediate divine presence, eventuated in a new appreciation precisely for particularity. Now the sensible world, including human sense-perception, the body, and objects in the material realm, could be viewed not as distractions but as theophanic vehicles. This was the basic shift, and it entailed a re-formation of the viewing subject, who was newly dependent on rituals of transformation in order to see spiritual animation in the world and the self. Perhaps not surprisingly, when the tendency to suppress materiality as a locus of meaning was revised, the fully embodied "I" could see both more, and less, than in an earlier age.

Chapter Two
Bodies in Fragments

One aspect of the material turn in late antiquity was the development of an aesthetics that emphasized the visual and tactile immediacy of the part—a piece of bone, a single mosaic tile, a word in a poem—at the expense of the whole. In literature and art, compositional techniques such as juxtaposition and repetition were used precisely to highlight fragments rather than wholes. By virtue of these techniques, such fragments became "things" in the sense conveyed by Bill Brown's "thing theory," in which objects took on surplus value and stood out against their contexts as magnets of attraction.[1] When aesthetically wrought, these fragments took on force as presences both sensuous and metaphysical, and they both induced changes in the human subject's habitual perception and effected a virtual re-education of the senses. In this chapter, a wide spectrum of ancient arts—sculpture, poetry, ekphrasis, collective hagiography—will be surveyed in order to characterize the aesthetics of the fragment, which will be explored in more detail with regard to relics in the chapter that follows.

In his "thing theory," Brown does not discuss linguistic "things," but I think his argument concerning the metamorphosis of mere object into meaningful thing can illuminate the visionary power of verbal images as well as of actual physical objects. Images, too, can assert themselves as "things." Indeed, the affective appeal of figurative language was one of the forces that helped shape the tangible piety of the material turn. Hence the "things" in this chapter have a double referent, indicating not only concrete things like relics and holy men but also their linguistic images and the kind of narratives in which they were embedded. In terms of the aesthetics of the fragment, such image-things are both fragments of the whole and emblematic of the whole, where the whole is both a literary structure as well as what I call a narrative line.

An amusing example of the idea of a narrative line comes from Italo Calvino's *Six Memos for the Next Millennium*. Calvino wrote in a chapter in this work entitled "Quickness" that he "would like to edit a collection of tales consisting of one sentence only, or even a single line." He narrates a story by the Guatemalan writer Augusto Monterroso as one that he would include in this collection of narrative lines. Here is that story in its entirety: "When I woke up, the dinosaur was still there."[2] Like Calvino, I too am interested in narrative structures of a particular type, like his collection of one-liners, in which the genre of the collection is just as important as what it contains. Part of my interest in this chapter is in narrative "lines"—strategies of narration—that operate on the basis of two functional criteria: one, they leave out unnecessary details, and two, they emphasize repetition.[3] By omitting unnecessary details, such narratives foreground the objects—the fragments of the whole—around which they are structured. These objects are "charged with a special force" and become "like the pole of a magnetic field, a knot in the network of invisible relationships."[4] However, by emphasizing repetition, they enable a recognition of, and a certain pleasure in, the structure of the form itself, as when a child finds pleasure in fairy tales precisely because of the expectation that certain situations and formulas will be repeated in new-but-familiar ways. Narrative lines like this are effective, writes Calvino, because they are "series of events that echo each other as rhymes do in a poem."[5]

Dissonant Echoing

"Dissonant echoing" is the phrase that I am going to use to characterize a certain aesthetic of the narrative line which is found not only in literature but also in the art and ritual practice of the fourth and early fifth centuries of the late ancient era. Originally I was going to name this dissonant character of narrative lines as an "aesthetics of discontinuity" until I discovered that I had been anticipated in this by Michael Roberts's study of poetics in late antiquity, *The Jeweled Style: Poetry and Poetics in Late Antiquity*. Briefly, Roberts characterizes the aesthetics of discontinuity as a for the densely textured play of repetition and variation.[6] There is a preference for effects of visual immediacy, achieved by an emphasis on the part at the expense of elaborations of organic wholes.[7] Furthermore, the relationships among such parts operate at an abstract level and must be reconstituted or imagined by the reader or the observer.[8] Thus parataxis, juxtaposition, and patterning are among the formal principles that both govern and reveal the disjunctive composition of these "narrative lines." As Roberts remarks with an appropriately linear metaphor, "the seams not only show, they are positively advertised."[9]

The tendency of this aesthetics toward fragmentation can be seen linguistically in poetry, where words are handled as though they possessed "a physical presence of their own, distinct from any considerations of sense or syntax."[10] In fact, Roberts argues, "in late antiquity . . . the refer-

Figure 1. Arch of Constantine, detail. Rome, Italy. Photo Credit: Alinari/Art Resource, NY.

ential function of language [and] art lost some of its preeminence; signifier asserts itself at the expense of signified."[11] This "liberated" signifier then takes on the brilliance, dazzle, and value suggested by the "jeweled style" of Roberts's title.[12]

A brief look at certain stylistic features of the art of this period will add an important visual component to the aesthetic disposition that is my focus. While it may be an exaggeration to follow Ernst Kitzinger in characterizing developments in the art of the late Roman era as "a great stylistic upheaval," nonetheless there were striking changes in artistic representation in this era that have enabled historians of art to discern the emergence of a coherent stylistic tendency.[13] Although my focus will be on the sculpting of human figures, particularly on sarcophagi, similar stylistic trends have been discerned in the mosaic and painterly arts of the period.[14]

One of the basic changes is graphically represented in the contrast between the second-century roundels (literally "liberated" from monuments to Trajan, Hadrian, and Marcus Aurelius) and the early fourth-century frieze of the Arch of Constantine (fig. 1). As Kitzinger observes,

Figure 2. Marble sarcophagus with the Triumph of Dionysus and the Seasons, ca. A.D. 260–270. Phrygian marble. Overall: 34 x 85 x 36 ¹/₄ in. (86.4 x 215.9 x 92.1 cm). Purchase, Joseph Pulitzer Bequest, 1955 (55.11.5). Metropolitan Museum of Art, New York. Image copyright © The Metropolitan Museum of Art/Art Resource, NY.

the actions and gestures of the figures in the roundels are "restrained but organically generated by the body as a whole," and the group is held together by a "rhythmic interplay of stances and movements freely adopted by the individual figures," whereas the figures in the frieze are "so tightly packed within the frame as to lack all freedom of movement" and they cohere as a group by virtue of "an abstract geometric pattern imposed from outside and based on repetition of nearly identical units on either side of a central axis."[15]

A similar change can be seen in sculptures on sarcophagi from the fourth century in comparison to those from the third century; an "insistence on formal properties" replaces "representational integrity," and "patterns of repetition and variation run counter to scenic coherence."[16] Sarcophagi characterized by presentation of scenes that "form a single sequence with obvious narrative unity"[17]—as in an early third-century depiction of a Dionysiac procession (fig. 2), and a Christian sarcophagus from the late third century that depicts the story of Jonah (fig. 3)—give way to "frieze sarcophagi" such as the so-called "Dogmatic"

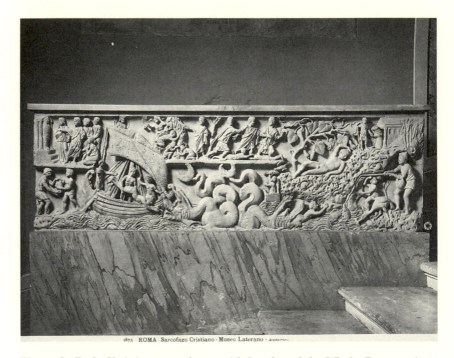

1875 ROMA Sarcofago Cristiano - Museo Laterano - Anderson

Figure 3. Early Christian sarcophagus with Jonah and the Whale; Resurrection of Lazarus, and other scenes. Museo Lateranense, Vatican Museums, Vatican State. Photo: Alinari/Art Resource, NY.

sarcophagus (C.E. 320–330) (fig. 4), in which scenic coherence is replaced by juxtaposed groups of two to three figures which depict scenes from the Old and New Testaments as well as from the life of Saint Peter. These groups of figures are not tied together organically; rather they are unified by the theological message to which all of them point: in Kitzinger's striking formulation, such a frieze is "like a line of writing which required the viewer's active participation" to discern the unifying narrative that the discrete sculptural groups exemplify again and again.[18] At this point I would introduce a modification to Roberts' argument concerning the disappearance of scenic coherence and representational integrity in this form of art by observing that frieze sarcophagi evince an *alternative* form of representational integrity that is not linear or narrative in the conventional sense. Such a view preserves precisely the aesthetic integrity of discontinuity insofar as it is rooted in the production of meaning by fragmentation.

"The predilection of late antique art for row formation" is certainly pronounced in double-frieze sarcophagi like the one shown in Fig. 4.

Figure 4. Large sarcophagus, including Creation of Adam and Eve, Adoration of the Magi. Early Christian. Museo Pio Cristiano, Vatican Museums, Vatican State. Photo: Scala/Art Resource, NY.

Packed with "shorthand pictographs,"[19] its "effect can be bewildering for the observer attempting to sort out the profusion of figures, and as the fourth century progressed further differentiation [was] introduced" by the use of "framing devices—columns or trees—used to separate the individual episodes, thereby creating self-contained compositional units and drawing attention to the episodic quality of the work as a whole."[20]

Column sarcophagi such as that of Junius Bassus, dated to C.E. 359 (fig. 5), not only display the taste for fragmentation and for ornamentation of the part characteristic of this form of late ancient aesthetics; they also suggest that a remarkably paratactic imagination was at work, requiring the viewer to construct narratives of theological meaning that arise from the juxtaposition of images rather than from straightforward linear development. In artworks such as these fourth-century sarcophagi, each individual image is a sensuous presense, a sculpted human body, but taken together they constitute a metaphysical presence, a set of spiritual narratives relating to salvation history. Because of the excess of meanings that the juxtapositions of images on the sarcophagi generate, the sarcophagi can be termed "things" that "exceed their mere materialization as objects" by becoming religious values.[21] Perhaps it might also be said that the "dazzle of the part" functioned simultaneously both to defer meaning precisely due to excess and to foreground, through difference, what Calvino called networks of invisible relation-

Figure 5. Sarcophagus of Junius Bassus, Roman prefect. Museum of the
Treasury, St. Peter's Basilica, Vatican State. Photo: Scala/Art Resource, NY.

ships. In any case, an ability to "move easily across the divide between
representation and abstraction" seems characteristic of the aesthetic
under consideration.[22]

Just as the stylistic features of the aesthetics of discontinuity cut across
differences of human expression, whether artistic or literary, so also they
were not unique to any particular religious affiliation.[23] In conversation
with Roberts and other theorists, my contribution to the exploration of
these stylistic affinities will be to suggest ways in which certain features
of late ancient Christianity cohere with or enact this cultural aesthetics.
Specifically, my focus will be on two phenomena of the fourth and early
fifth centuries that I think are related, aesthetically as well as theologically: these phenomena are, on the one hand, the ritual, literary and
artistic practices associated with the veneration of relics, and, on the
other, a genre of literature that I call "collective hagiography"—for
example, the *Historia monachorum* and related collections like Theodoret's *Historia religiosa* and Palladius's *Lausiac History*—a literary genre
that burgeoned with the establishment of desert asceticism. My aim is to
provide ways of addressing the following question: how can these two
phenomena of late ancient Christianity be seen as "narrative lines"
marked by the effects of an aesthetics of dissonant echoing?

Exemplifying the Aesthetics of Discontinuity

Before delving more deeply into the formal properties of this aesthetic
disposition, however, some concrete examples will be useful. These

examples center on the practices of three people, two of whom were near-contemporaries at the beginning of this time period, and one who lived toward its end. First, a Spanish noblewoman who lived in Carthage, dubbed "the famous Lucilla" by Hippolyte Delehaye: she possessed a bone from the body of a martyr and had adopted the ritual practice of kissing the bone prior to engaging in another ritual practice, taking the Eucharist.[24] Meanwhile, Optatian Porfyry, a poet and Lucilla's near-contemporary, sat down and wrote poems that can be read forwards or backwards either as wholes or line by line, such that "each poem contains a number of inherent permutations of itself."[25] He called his poems "chains" and "difficult bits."[26] Finally, toward the end of the fourth century, there was Ausonius, rhetorician and poet: he was a lover of catalogues and enumeration and at least twice he wrote six versions of the same joke.[27] He was also a master of the ekphrasis, a narrative description of a material artifact. However, his ekphrastic practice led him to see more than was there; as his friend Symmachus playfully remarked about one such ekphrastic passage, the famous catalogue of fish in his poem "Mosella," he had never seen these textual fish on any literal table![28]

What do these three have in common? I will address them one by one, attempting to weave them together toward a more formal statement of the aesthetic that is my topic.

Recall that Lucilla, a venerator of relics, kissed a martyr's bone before taking the Eucharist. Here are two ritual actions that echo each other, but dissonantly: ritual ingestion of elements considered to represent a whole body is preceded by ritual veneration of an element of a body that was once whole. Further, in each case the fragmentary elements are considered to be suffused with wholeness despite the literal absence to which they attest.[29] This structure of not-quite-congruent repetition, together with the focus on the part or the fragment, which is itself an uncanny repetition, are two of the components of the aesthetic that I wish to explore.

Despite the rebuke of her deacon,[30] Lucilla with her bone stood poised on the threshold of the dramatic expansion of the so-called "cult" of relics in the course of the fourth century, a "cult" better described as an aesthetic in which division—the parceling out of the bones, ashes, and other remains of martyrs' bodies—was paradoxically also multiplication, as in the analogous case of the holy cross in Jerusalem, which remained miraculously whole despite being constantly broken up into fragments, themselves considered to be "whole."[31] This was an aesthetic in which the tension between the demands of expansion and limit was made explicit; and also one in which the relationship between objects occupying space and abstract form was explored, particularly in forcing human body parts beyond the limits of the physical to new forms of aesthetic expression. I shall return to the topic of the aestheticizing of relics.

The knotty linear relationship between objects occupying space and abstract form was explored in a textual way by Optatian Porfyry, a sometime-poet in the court of Constantine the Great, exiled around c.e. 315 and recalled to imperial favor early in 325.[32] His poetic practice provides an intriguing literary parallel to Lucilla's ritual practice regarding relics. Described by one interpreter as representative of a tendency in fourth-century poetry toward "a kind of abstract literary extremism," Optatian's creations are pattern poems that "occupy space in two different dimensions."[33] Few would disagree with the estimation that Optatian's poems *as poems* are virtually unreadable; even a sympathetic reader has declared that "Optatian is not a good poet; he is not even a bad poet. His poems are prodigies, monsters in the literal sense."[34] A brief sampling of these poetic monsters will suffice to indicate the aesthetic at work in them.

Two types of poems are prominent in Optatian's poetic output, most of which honors Constantine.[35] First, there are the figurative poems in which red ink was used to highlight certain letters in particular words so as to form a picture or a geometrical pattern, and the highlighted letters themselves make syntactical and semantic sense when read as a sequence, forming a poem-within-the poem. Perhaps the most astounding of these is his Poem 19, in which the highlighted letters form the shape of an oared ship whose mast is the XP, the symbolic Christogram used here to recognize Constantine as victor. Further, the highlighted Latin letters of the Christogram "change their linguistic orientation and must be considered Greek, the Roman H becoming Greek *eta*, Roman C *sigma*, and so on," as indeed they do in other poems as well.[36] In Poem 19, the letters forming the Christogram begin an elegiac couplet in Greek that moves down the mast to encompass part of the ship, at which point a series of Latin hexameters takes over.[37]

Of course the poem as a whole, if read as a sequence of innocent linear lines, also makes sense in terms of a conventional semantic flow. However, "the impulse to verbal mimesis is conspicuously weak," consisting in the main of "stale praises of the emperor" like most of the other poems.[38] Further, the alphabetic line of narrative is interrupted by the pictographic line, and "the reader is pushed over the threshold of one order of experience—reading a text—into another—seeing a picture."[39] In terms of the aesthetic under consideration, what is striking is the poem's refusal to be continuous in the face of being continuous or whole nonetheless. Such pattern poems are fitting, if exaggerated, examples of the ocular dimension of the material turn and its aesthetic style. They enact a visual poetics as well as a poetics of materiality: as Susan Stewart has observed, pattern poets create "a poetry that is object-like or artifactual," due to the assertion of the part over against the whole.[40]

This interest in wholes whose "parts [make] their appeal constantly and all at the same time"[41] is also characteristic of the phenomenon of relics which, like Optatian's poetic artifacts, not only occupied space in two registers (heaven and earth, in the case of relics) but were also the subject of intense speculation about the relation between disjunction and continuity: as Victricius of Rouen explained, "Nothing in relics is not full [*in reliquiis nihil esse non plenum*] . . . Division must not be inserted into fullness, but in the division that lies before our eyes the truth of fullness should be adored."[42] As with poetry, so with relics: the impulse toward mimesis was weak, the relics referring not so much backwards to a literal body once alive as forward to the postmortem effectiveness that constitutes its real life.[43] If this were not the case, that is, if the impulse toward mimesis in the cult of relics had not been weak, it would have been idolatrous, and someone such as Jerome could not have viewed "loose ashes tied up in silk or a golden vessel" as though they contained the living presence of a prophet.[44]

This late ancient habit of relieving material and linguistic artifacts of conventional referential or mimetic impulses—that is, the habit of manipulating a little to get a lot—is characteristic of the other type of poem that Optatian wrote, the *technopaegnia*, poems with reversible verses and other linguistic tricks that advertise the linguisticality of the poetic works and function on an abstract level as explorations of the possibilities of language itself. Some of these poems are very complex in their demand for "re-combinatory" reading; they "progress," so to speak, but only by a series of disjunctions or dislocations.

As one interpreter has shown in great detail, "there are more verses in Optatian's poetry than a mere line-count will reveal: each poem also contains a number of inherent permutations of itself, a number of potential dispositions."[45] This is getting a lot from a little with a vengeance! Further, "writing no longer functions primarily as the record of speech but as the medium of a linguistic artifact whose interest lies in an aspect of language extrinsic to its reference, usually a sensory aspect."[46] When words take on this kind of physicality, poetry becomes "sensory" or tactile. As with pattern poems, so also here one finds the "thingly" aspects of language as poetic images assume a material presence.

This aspect of the aesthetics of late Latin poetry has an exact analogy in the cult of relics, where a dead body (like language) no longer functioned primarily as a record of human living (like speech) but rather as a material artifact whose referent lay outside itself in a spirituality that demanded sensory expression for its abstract belief in conduits of divine presence. Although I agree with Robert Wilken that "tactile piety, worship with the lips and the fingertips" was an important dimension of the cult of relics,[47] I would note that a relic is a curiously abstract piece of matter that signifies the many potential dispositions of the body of a martyr or saint: like a poem by Optatian, the martyr's body contained a number of inherent permutations of itself, as bones and ashes were "translated" to various points around the Mediterranean world. As Victricius of Rouen explained, each relic was a link in a "chain of eternity" (*vinculo aeternitatis*) that bound the martyrs together.[48] The fragments, that is, become properly intelligible when they are viewed as knots in an abstract "narrative line," the eternal chain of Victricius's theological imagination.

Relics as well as Optatian's poems were successful in one sense because of the visual immediacy they achieved by emphasizing the part at the expense of elaborations of organic wholes, as I pointed out earlier. In late ancient poetry, such visual immediacy could be evoked by using the techniques of the *technopaegnion*, but another technique was the use of ekphrases, which turned readers into active pictorial imaginers. Similarly, the literature that developed around relics aestheticized those objects by its insistent appeal to art and sensuous metaphors to describe them, often using ekphrastic techniques.

The technique of ekphrasis is the final component of the aesthetics of discontinuity that I will introduce by way of an exemplary figure, the late fourth-century poet Ausonius, probably best known in the context of late ancient Christianity as the teacher of Paulinus of Nola. In his literary output one finds an attitude toward poetic narrative and composition similar to that of Optatian in terms of experiments with words that depend for their aesthetic value on an abstract level of appreciation for the play of language itself. Thus among Ausonius's poems are the "Griphus Ternarii Numeri," a "Riddle on the Number Three" (an attempt to list all of the things that come in threes), and the "Technopaegnion," a poem that he describes as consisting of "verses begun with monosyllables and ended with monosyllables" that are "linked up so that the monosyllable which was the ending of one verse might also become the beginning of the line following."[49] His overall description of this little work is revealing of his aesthetic mindset: "It is small," he says, "yet it brings a sense of surfeit; it is disjointed yet tangled [*inconexa est et implicatur*]"—a succinct statement of the late ancient aesthetic embrace of narrative forms that convey intimate relatedness precisely by advertising disjunction.[50]

This much, however, has already been reviewed, but in his preface to this poem Ausonius adds one other significant ingredient. Referring to the monosyllabic words as *puncta*, "punctures" or "stopping points," he writes that "they merely hold together like the individual links in a chain." He says to the recipient of his poem: "*You* will endow them with a certain value, for without you they will be just monosyllables."[51] In other words, without the active participation of the reader, his poem will not be complete, its meaning left unconstrued. It is noteworthy that Ausonius's *puncta*—words that have become "things," magnets of attraction in Brown's sense—constitute the nodal points on which the meaning of the poem turns. In his book of meditations on photography, Roland Barthes used the term *punctum* to characterize the detail in a photograph that has the power of expansion: "While remaining a detail, it fills the whole picture."[52] For Ausonius as well as for his latter-day counterpart, the *punctum* is the fragment that draws the reader or viewer into an imaginative construal of a whole.

This petitioning of active imaginative engagement by readers or spectators was part of the aesthetics of discontinuity, and one of the literary techniques for eliciting this kind of active reading was the ekphrasis. In an ekphrasis, effects of visual and sensory immediacy come together as the writer attempts to bring a painting or other material object (whether real or imagined) alive in words.[53] As literary theorist W. J .T. Mitchell describes it, "the basic project of ekphrastic hope" is "the transformation of the dead, passive image into a living creature."[54] Ekphrastic writing was not invented in late antiquity,[55] but its handling by authors such as Ausonius was less linear, more dependent on dissonant parallels, and when embedded in longer narratives, late ancient ekphrases were "less open to [their] contexts" than earlier ekphrases were and tended to function as "self-contained and self-defining units."[56] Here once again is the aesthetic preference for "juxtaposition and contrast [over] logical relationship; contiguity no longer required continuity."[57]

The catalogue of fish in Ausonius's poem *Mosella* is actually an ekphrasis within an ekphrasis, since the poem as a whole purports to be a description of a river. There are two features of this catalogue that I want to highlight. One is the hyper-realism or pictorial theatricality of his descriptions, which creates a "reality-effect"—an illusion of reality— and suggests that such forms of representation are poetic effects rather than straightforward description.[58] As Georgia Nugent has explained, writing like this draws upon a kind of "synaesthetic response" in the reader, who must sense something that cannot strictly or literally be seen.[59]

The second feature of the catalogue that adds to an understanding of Ausonian ekphrasis is its context, a poem about a river that constantly alludes to the optical illusions created by the reflective qualities of water.

Frequently employing metaphors of mirroring to describe the unrelia-
bility of these watery visions, the poem is preoccupied with the deceptive
nature of images both verbal and visual.[60] With its use of terms like
absens, derisus, decepta, figura, and *simulacrum,* the poem issues a caveat to
its reader that "the ekphrastic encounter in language is purely figurative," as Mitchell has observed.[61] The catalogue of fish is only one of the
ways in which the poet underscores what he writes in line 239 of "The
Moselle": "pleasure is taken in sights which are ambiguously true and
false." As Nugent remarks, "Ausonius is a poet very much aware of the
ambiguities, deceptions, and substitutions inherent in representation,"
and by his ekphrastic technique he "invites the reader to enter into the
game of imaginative visualization based on what is fundamentally a verbal artefact."[62]

While there is no doubt that the writer of ekphrases was attempting
to transform the reader into a spectator and that sight was a privileged
sense in ekphrastic representation, it is also true that "ekphrastic rhetorical exercises often strove precisely to exceed the visual by evoking tactile, kinetic, aural and olfactory sensations as well."[63] For example,
Ausonius's poem "Cupido Cruciatus" purports to describe a painting of
the descent of the god Amor into the underworld, there to be tortured
by a series of lovelorn goddesses. It is an ekphrasis filled with images that
are difficult to visualize, and its "reality-effect" succeeds only by petitioning senses other than sight. In one passage of this poem, the underworld
is depicted as a place "where [Cupid's] wings move sluggishly in the
close darkness." As Nugent describes it, "the impression is that Cupid is
experiencing difficulty in plying his wings, because of the thickness of
the night. But what sense, precisely, does this make? While we intuitively
grasp its meaning, the image is not actually visual; rather, it seems to
draw upon a kind of synaesthetic response—the weight of night and
darkness is something that we may *sense,* but cannot (strictly speaking)
see."[64]

This kind of ekphrastic engagement of the reader's imaginative senses
is a defining characteristic of the literature, poetic as well as narrative,
that grew up around the phenomenon of relics in the course of the
fourth century and can in some ways be credited with the creation of
the meaning of relics. If it is true, as Victor Saxer has argued, that the
holy dead were truly materialized only when they were fragmented and
dispersed,[65] it is also true that those material bits came alive in the literary and artistic appeals that were made to the sensuous imaginations of
participants in this form of Christian ritual. These appeals aimed at a
virtual re-education of the human senses, teaching viewers to see that a
material object might have spiritual life.

Relics and Figuration

The phenomenon of relics was characterized by an insistent impulse toward figuration, both verbal and artistic. Damasus, bishop of Rome from c.e. 366–384, for example, appears to have had a hearty appreciation for the function of the trace as a condition of meaning: as he went around Rome establishing shrines at tombs of martyrs, he made the city into a network of traces that was at once geographically tangible and verbally material, since at each shrine he left lines of poetry, the epigrams for which he is famous.[66] In one of these poems, addressed to the martyr Felix, Damasus made puns on the martyr's name, engaging in the sort of etymological wordplay that became a standard feature of encomia to martyrs—Augustine, for example, punned on the names of Vincent and Agnes, and Prudentius on the names of Agnes, Hippolytus, and Cyprian.[67] Again the impulse to bring out the full aesthetic virtuosity of the fragment on two levels is evident. The linguistic filiations spun out of a martyr's name match the filiations of spiritual power that inhere in a fragment of his or her body. Relics became verbal as well as material artifacts.

The creative mimesis involved in the sort of dissonant echoing effected when poetry and relic were juxtaposed was also characteristic of late ancient ekphrases that described the art decorating the martyria. Gregory of Nyssa's encomium on Saint Theodore contains an ekphrasis on the paintings in Theodore's *memoria*. Gregory begins by privileging the metaphor of sight, describing the visual splendor of the building and its contents:

When one comes into a place like this one in which we are assembled today, where the memorial and holy relic of the righteous one are, one is first struck by the magnificence of what there is to see: a building as befits God's temple, splendidly wrought in terms of its great size and beautiful decoration and in which the woodworker has carved the wood into the shapes of animals and the stonemason has polished the marble slabs to the smoothness of silver. The painter has also colored the walls with the flowers of his art in images representing the martyr's brave actions, his resistance, his suffering, the brutal appearance of the rulers, the insults, that fiery furnace, the athlete's most blessed death, and the sketch of Christ, the judge of contests, in human form.[68]

In the passage that follows, however, sensibilities other than sight are brought into play: "All of this he fashioned by means of colors as though it were a book speaking. He depicted the martyr's struggles clearly and ornamented the church like a magnificent meadow, for painting, while silent, can speak from the wall and offer the greatest benefit."[69]

This ekphrastic passage contains a densely textured play of repetition and variation, as the reader is carried through a series of contiguously related parallels: from the relic that is the occasion of this spectacle, to the painted images, to the linguistic metaphor of the "speech of colors from the wall" that inversely echoes the passage of writing that gives expression to all this—an echoing, that is, of art and words that was also recognized by Asterius of Amaseia when, in a description of a painting of the martyrdom of Saint Euphemia, he says that "we writers [lit. "servants of the Muses"] possess 'colors' no worse than those of painters."[70]

Although Gregory and Asterius seem to be defending the congruity of art and words, the fact is that the art they describe exists as figurations in their texts, and both of them force the reader's imaginative participation to shift between two experiences, reading a text and seeing a picture. And there is more: how is one to imagine the visually difficult suggestion that a painting of scenes from a gruesome martyrdom blooms like a meadow? This is an ekphrastic "reality-effect" that borders on the surreal, akin to Ausonius's Cupid with sluggish wings or—to cite another ekphrasis connected with relics—akin to Paulinus of Nola's description of a mosaic in the apse of one of the basilicas dedicated to Saint Felix, a scene that according to Paulinus showed "the Father's voice thundering forth from heaven."[71] How might one picture a voice in the moment of its thundering? This image of Paulinus's certainly depends as much on auditory as on visual imagination for its aesthetic effect; it is an image that, in terms of the late ancient Christian corporeal imagination, helped the viewer achieve a transfigured eye.

Hyper-real images such as that of Paulinus were common in the ekphrastic literature that embedded relics in an aesthetics of discontinuity. The *praesentia*[72] or fullness of spiritual power thought to be present in a relic was an abstraction that could only be evoked by effects of visual and sensuous immediacy, as conveyed by Gregory of Nyssa in his well-known description of venerators of Theodore's relics: "Those who behold them embrace them as though the very body were living and flowering, and they bring all the senses—eyes, mouth, ears—into play; then they shed tears for his piety and suffering and bring forward their prayers of intercession to the martyr as though he were present and whole."[73] Passages such as this signal the late ancient mindset that valued the fragment for the narrative lines it was capable of eliciting. Like words in late ancient poetry, relics were "liberated signifiers" that took on a certain aesthetic dazzle far exceeding the referential function of a dead body part; as Victricius of Rouen noted, relics are "spiritual jewels" that "flower more and more in beauty."[74]

The mutual inherence of art, poetry, and relics in a tangled signifying network is nowhere better illustrated than in the *Peristephanon* of Prudentius. Since the techniques of Prudentius's visionary storytelling in his hagiographic poems are featured in a later chapter in this book ("Bodies and Spectacles"), I would only note here the pictorial theatricality of his notorious fascination with the bloody gore of martyr-stories, as well as his participation in an aesthetics of writing where "images, intertextual allusions, and etymological wordplay convey more meaning than plot and narrative."[75] "As impressive as the poems are as finished products, they are irresistibly more impressive as activities"—an estimation of the poetry of Optatian that is just as true of Prudentius's work.[76] The individual units of his collection are marked by the effects of uncanny repetition, in which the metonymic relations among words, wounds, art, and relics are constantly advertised; for example, looking at a painting of the martyr Cassian in his shrine, Prudentius describes him as "a page wet with red ink."[77] This is a stark example of the image as "thing" whose blunt affective appeal provokes a change in habitual perception, both of the martyr and of the written page that contains his story.

Jill Ross has argued persuasively that Prudentius's poems are "mimetic reenactments and representations of martyred bodies" and that they are "an attempt to gain the salvation he so desires."[78] I would add to this the observation that their shared poetic structure makes each of these poems into mimetic reenactments of the others in a narrative chain of *puncta* analogous to the structure of a column sarcophagus.[79] In order to "read" the *Peristephanon* properly *as a whole*, the reader must grasp the abstract theme that unifies the collection, Prudentius's theological belief in the "redemptive power of the written word" that functions as a conduit of spiritual presence and healing.[80]

Prudentius's collection exemplifies a particular aesthetic attitude toward the organization of narrative. Viewed as a collection, it has a "narrative line" formally structured on a principle of repetition that produces a series of things—in this case, martyrs—that are eye-catching when viewed as discrete units, but somewhat monotonous when viewed from the perspective of the collection as a whole. In this way his collection is less like a column sarcophagus, whose discrete parts contain different images, and more like a form of sarcophagus-art represented here by a sarcophagus from the end of the fourth century in which the framing devices have disappeared (fig. 6). In such "processional" sarcophagi, difference is still present in details of dress, posture, and gesture in such a way that the mimetic relationships continue to be dissonant, but difference is subordinated to the overall presentation of the individuals as members of a group.

Collective Biography and Dissonance

Certain features of the collective biographies of desert ascetics composed at the end of the fourth and early in the fifth centuries cohere

Figure 6. Sarcophagus with Christ and the Twelve Apostles. Early Christian, 2nd half of fourth century c.e. Museo Pio Cristiano, Vatican Museums, Vatican State. Photo: Scala/Art Resource, NY.

with the aesthetic style of the processional sarcophagi as well as Prudentius's collection. The aesthetics of discontinuity is at work in such collections in their organization by enumerative sequence, which draws attention to a certain abstract commonality that the reader, once past the prologues of these works, must infer, since there are no narrative connections supplied to link the parts in an organic or conventionally emplotted way. Further, each individual ascetic is differentiated by "a handful of individualizing features"—what they eat, how they pray, their ritual activities and performances of miracles—"that qualify the generic similarity of the figures and provide a subdued tension between synonymy and antithesis."[81] The individualizing details invite the reader to linger—but not for long, since the real interest in such collections is in the network of relationships that represent the theological vision of the collection as a whole. Here the positive relation of materiality and meaning that characterized the material turn is advertised: the parade of ascetic bodies shows how the sensible world can be a medium for the disclosure of the divine in human life.

Just as Ausonius characteristically wrote prologues to his poems, giving the reader hints about how to participate in constructing their meaning, so also the authors of collective biographies of desert ascetics wrote prefatory pages that encouraged readers to read in specific kinds of ways. For example, the author of the *Historia monachorum* describes his preference for narrative disjunction, that is, the preference for juxtaposition over continuity, by informing the reader of the virtual impossibility of writing an exhaustive narrative account of the lives of his holy ascetics: since their number is so large as to be virtually uncountable, as he explains, he has adopted enumerative selectivity as his principle of representation, a few standing in for the many.[82] Theodoret says the same, and even indicates how the reader should negotiate the divide between abstraction and particularity: "We shall not write a single eulogy for all together, for different graces were given them from

God—to one through the Spirit a word of wisdom, to another gifts of healing, to yet another workings of powers—but all these are worked by one and the same Spirit."[83] Each ascetic "fragment" is crucial because together they make tangible the spiritual theme of the collection itself. Thus there is difference, but the activities of each individual are all variations on an abstract theological line, an understanding of how human life can be suffused with spiritual presence. A particular form of religious anthropology, then, is the "narrative line" that is brought to the fore by the repetitive format that makes collective biographies read like processions of verbal icons.

The discrete parts of these collections are not full biographies but ekphrastic sketches that picture a "way of life" (πολιτεία) that the authors hope will be paradigmatic, as the reader is invited to participate in imagining those activities that embody the so-called "angelic life."[84] Imagination is paramount here, since each compositional unit is itself only a series of disjointed fragments; often only two or three anecdotes suffice to convey the paradox of fragmentary fullness that was also characteristic of relics. Representational integrity, in other words, is carried by the fragment.

Similarly, the visual immediacy of these literary "jewels" is emphasized: the authors of these collections constantly privilege metaphors of looking by calling attention to the fact that they had gazed at these ascetics, and this, together with their use of metaphors of light to describe the shining faces of many of these near-angels, calls attention to the permeability of the texts' boundaries as readers are drawn into the visual experience that the texts evoke.[85] As we have seen when considering the ekphrastic art of other texts, they often achieve their "reality-effect" by petitioning senses that exceed the visual. This is true of these collections as well. What reader of the *Historia monachorum*, for example, could resist the sensuous allure of an anecdote such as the one that pictures Macarius entering an eerie garden in the middle of the desert, conversing with and embracing the two holy men who lived there, and eating the marvelously large and colorful paradisal fruit that they provide?[86]

Like relics, the subjects of these collections have been aestheticized and function as verbal artifacts. Theodoret, in fact, was overt about his compositional goal of constructing word-pictures.[87] In his prologue, he explains that he is "honoring in writing" ascetics who are "living images and statues" (τινας εἰκόνας ἐμψύχους καὶ στήλας), but his descriptions, he is quick to note, are not sculptures in bas-relief (τὰ τούτων ἐκτυπώματα); that is, his ekphrases are not mimetic to mere appearances. Rather, what he has done is "to sketch the forms of invisible souls" (τῶν ἀοράτων ψυχῶν τάς ἰδέας σκιογραφοῦμεν),[88] a statement whose verb connotes the artist's practice of "painting with shadows" in order to achieve an effect of solidity. Theodoret, like Gregory of Nyssa and others, draws attention to the figural status of his verbal representations by suggesting their mutual inherence with painting; thus his collection occupies two registers at once, just as his subjects do, being simultaneously angel and human. As "things," Theodoret's subjects are these word-pictures, images that are both sensuous (human) and metaphysical (angelic). They signify both as fragments of the whole and emblems of the theology of the whole.

Finally, Theodoret's claim that his sketches do not reproduce mere appearance is a succinct characterization of what I see as one of the most significant aspects of the aesthetics of discontinuity, its creative understanding of mimesis. When Gregory of Nazianzus wrote the funeral oration for his friend Basil of Caesarea, he noted that many of Basil's contemporaries, acting on a kind of misplaced admiration for the man, had imitated his habits and person (his gait, the shape of his beard, his way of eating) and even his physical defects (his paleness and hesitant manner of speaking), so that "you might see many Basils as far as what appears to the eye, [but these are] just statues in the shadows," like an "echoing of a sound." In contrast to what he calls "ill-conceived imitation," Gregory commends the kind of mimesis engaged in by Basil: *he* imitated, not "Peter," but the "*zeal* of Peter"; not "Paul," but "the *energy* of Paul."[89] Gregory's comment is in the spirit of the material turn, in which the human model remains crucial but its "substance," as it were, is appropriated not literally but rather for its use-value in a meaningful life.

This understanding of imaginative referentiality gives the late ancient aesthetic explored in this chapter an immense appeal because of its refusal of fetishism and of what some construed to be an idolatrous identification of matter and spirit. Vigilantius, for example, was chided by Jerome for his too-literal conception of the kind of mimesis operative in the cult of relics.[90] As Jerome reported it, Vigilantius had accused venerators of relics of being "idolaters who pay homage to dead men's bones," mistaking the substance itself for the holy. Jerome in turn accused Vigilantius of "following the letter that kills and not the spirit that gives life" for misunderstanding relic-veneration as idolatry.[91]

To side with Vigilantius for a moment, it is true that the material turn harbored the possibility of an exuberant attachment to matter. A stunning example of this exuberance is captured in the following anecdote from the early fifth century regarding Megetia, a Carthaginian noblewoman who visited the shrine of Saint Stephen hoping for a cure of her dislocated jaw: "While she prayed at the place of the holy relic shrine, she beat against it, not only with the longings of her heart, but with her whole body so that the little grille in front of the relic opened at the impact; and she, taking the Kingdom of Heaven by storm, pushed her head inside and laid it on the holy relics resting there, drenching them with her tears."[92] From the perspective of a critic like Vigilantius, Megetia's association of materiality and meaning was too complete, leading to an idolatrous embrace of matter, in this case the relic. Even Evodius, who reported Megetia's act, put a somewhat negative spin on it with his reference to her "taking the Kingdom of Heaven by storm." From the perspective of relic-enthusiasts like Jerome, however, Megetia's act was witness to the wonder of a spirit-filled world, aptly characterized by Virginia Burrus as a "material cosmos exploding with its own self-exceeding transcendence."[93]

While Megetia, in the extremes of her despair, certainly seems to have lacked the dissonant sensibility explored in this chapter, a sensibility that was crucial to the material turn in terms of avoiding "taking the Kingdom of Heaven by storm," other Christians developed this sensibility in rich detail. In the following chapter, the role of the jeweled style's dissonant echoing in the fashioning of body parts as relics will be explored further, with particular emphasis on the aesthetic sensibility of those relic-minded Christians whose sensuous rhetoric made possible a non-idolatrous, because paradoxical, apprehension of spiritual substance.

Chapter Three
Dazzling Bodies

There is no better exemplar of Bill Brown's "thing theory" in late ancient Christianity than a relic. As a specifically *spiritual* object, a relic is a mere object, a body part of a dead human being, that has become a "thing" because it can no longer be taken for granted as part of the everyday world of the naturalized environment of the death and decay of the human body. In antiquity, the relic as thing was a locus of surplus value: because it was a vehicle for the mediation of divine presence in human life—that is to say, a crucial nodal point linking the transcendent and earthly realms—a relic was both the facilitator as well as a signifier of a belief system in which the concept of intercession placed spiritual power squarely in the midst of the material world. In short, as thing, the relic represents the seemingly paradoxical use of the material to enhance the spiritual, as noted in Chapter 1.

As both the sign and the carrier of a relation between materiality and theology, the phenomenon of relics aptly illustrates a major feature of the material turn in late ancient Christianity, namely, the revaluation of the religious significance of the material world in a positive direction. This revaluation was, however, problematic: in the view of some, relics signaled a corporeal imagination run amok by investing the material world, in the form of parts of the human body, with too much extra-human meaning. Given this troublesome aspect of the revaluation, the task of those who created positive interpretive frameworks for relics was basically twofold: first, to answer the question how a material object can have a spiritual life, that is, to explain how the necessary excess that marked relics as spiritual objects was not idolatrous, and second, to reeducate the senses of fellow Christians so as to enable them to perceive the material-spiritual relationship in relics. Their overall task was to articulate a religio-aesthetic environment within which the remains of special human beings could be apprehended as relics, that is, as spiritual objects worthy of ritual devotion.

This chapter focuses on how such relic-minded Christians as Prudentius of Calahorra, Asterius of Amaseia, and Paulinus of Nola created a context for apprehending body parts as relics by exercising what I have called a corporeal imagination, one that uses textual images whose ocular and affective immediacy contributes to, or even creates, the religious significance of the thing that is their focus. Their powerful verbal representations, often in the form of ekphrases, were a major component of the aesthetic style that vested in bones a signifying capacity that marked their emergence as relics. Further, their reliance on "dazzle"—that is, on the aesthetic sensibility associated with the late ancient cultural taste for color and brilliance—will be presented as an important contributor to the sensuously intense atmosphere within which the cult of relics achieved expression. Here, the "dissonant echoing" discussed in the previous chapter, which denotes a sensibility that avoided complete identification between matter and meaning, will be presented in terms of a poetics of the body that deformed ordinary perception in order to produce the figural gaze so crucial to the cult of relics.

How, then, does one evoke the "spirit" of the flesh? I begin with a modern example. In the early 1940s, an American photographer who went by the odd pseudonym "Disfarmer" ran a portrait studio in Heber Springs, Arkansas. The artfulness of his portraits, which created what might be called a hyperreal effect in the still life of the photograph, has recently been described as follows: "Disfarmer's technique was simple. His subjects—the ordinary people of Heber Springs—were placed before a plain, dark backdrop. Any props they chose were their own—a newborn child, an enormous catfish, a spouse, a friend, a cigarette. Disfarmer merely waited for a moment of clarity, that instant when everyday flesh caught fire, when he could see the weight of blood and bones the spirit carried and how beautifully, if wearily, they were carried after all."[1] My interest is in that "moment of clarity when everyday flesh catches fire," a moment when blood, bones, and spirit are so thoroughly fused that they convey a certain incandescent clarity—the "dazzle" of this chapter's title. In what follows, I will explore how certain late ancient Christian writers and artists achieved this kind of incandescent clarity in their artful engagement with the phenomenon of relics. Whether their medium was words or paints or mosaic tesserae, these Christians, like the photographer Disfarmer, managed to elicit the spirit of everyday flesh without separating the two from each other.

From Bones to Relics

As the cult of relics gathered momentum from the second half of the fourth century onward, Christians created richly articulated visual and verbal milieus for the bones and ashes of martyrs, those "very special dead" to whom the cult was largely devoted.[2] A "visual rhetoric of sanctity" in the form of the ornamented interior spaces of many martyria was complemented by a verbal rhetoric that was also highly figurative.[3] When viewed from the perspective of the artistic and rhetorical "surround" in which they were embedded, relics can be said to have derived their power in part as effects of an aesthetic style that "dissipates the material opacity without betraying the substance."[4] Neither wholly material nor wholly spiritual—"living dust," as Paulinus of Nola called them—relics occupied a signifying field that mediated between matter and spirit and so subdued the potential dichotomy between them.[5] Relics can thus be understood as "things" whose force was sensuous and metaphysical at once.

This "paradox of the linking of Heaven and Earth" in relics, as Peter Brown has observed, was the product of an "imaginative dialectic," one of whose effects was "to raise the physical remains of the saints above the normal associations of place and time," bringing "the first touch of the Resurrection . . . into the present."[6] Thus against the "plain, dark backdrop" of death—to recall the technique of the photographer from Arkansas—many late ancient Christian authors and artists introduced body parts of martyrs, opaque forms of everyday flesh that became relics when their meaning was elaborated by a certain intensity of the imagination—indeed, a form of imaginative clarity described by the American poet Wallace Stevens as a moment when "intensity becomes something incandescent."[7] Before returning to this fire, I will begin by exploring how the aesthetic milieus created by art and rhetoric not only aroused the viewers' affective responses but also engaged their cognitive skills by teaching them how to apprehend fragments of dead bodies as spiritual objects.

While the martyrs were considered to be human beings like everyone else—"they didn't carry around flesh of a different sort from what you do," Augustine preached[8]—nonetheless, it was the specifically physical dimension of their endurance of often grotesque suffering that was highlighted as a mark of divinity working through them. Narrative elaborations of those sufferings, both in the genre of the *passio* as well as in sermons, focused attention on the bodies of the martyrs with graphic descriptive detail.

Basil of Caesarea's sermon on the Forty Martyrs is a particularly stark example of this focus on the grisly physical ordeal of torture:

The body that has been exposed to cold first becomes all livid as the blood freezes. Then it shakes and seethes, as the teeth chatter, the muscles are convulsed, and the whole mass is involuntarily contracted. A sharp pain and an unspeakable agony reaches into the marrows and causes a freezing sensation that is impossible to bear. Then the extremities of the body are mutilated, as they are burned [by the frost] as if by fire. For the heat is driven from the extremities of the body and flees to the interior; it leaves the parts that it has abandoned dead, and tortures those into which it is compressed, as little by little death comes on by freezing.[9]

Such intense descriptions, especially when read aloud during the martyrs' festal days, gave "a vivid, momentary face to the invisible *praesentia* of the saint," as Peter Brown has argued; from his perspective, "the public reading of the *passio* was, in itself, a *psychodrame* that mobilized in the hearer those strong fantasies of disintegration and reintegration which lurked in the back of the mind of ancient men."[10]

Yet focus on the suffering body alone was not enough to effect the spiritual transformation of body parts into relics. Such a focus carried a danger that was made explicit in Vigilantius's outright charge of idolatry, as we have already seen at the end of the last chapter. Jerome, who supported the cult of relics and did not appreciate being called an "ashman [*cinerarios*] and idolater who venerates dead men's bones," quoted Vigilantius as asking, "Why do you kiss and adore a piece of dust wrapped in a linen cloth?"[11] The danger was well recognized also by Augustine, who worried that actual worship rather than simple veneration was taking place at the martyrs' shrines and advised his parishioners in no uncertain terms not to behave toward martyrs as pagans behaved toward their gods.[12]

Even when Augustine did say an appreciative word about the presence of a martyr's literal body, he did so with a pun. In one of his sermons devoted to Saint Cyprian, Augustine remarked: "Many people everywhere have the great corpus of his works. But let us, here [in the Mappalia Basilica in Carthage], give more thanks than ever to God, because we have been found worthy to have with us the holy corpus of his body";[13] the wordplay on "corpus" that conflates Cyprian's body with his texts works to divert an overly literal focus on the body by introducing a complicating transfer of meaning. This form of rhetorical play, which we will see presently in a more elaborate form in Prudentius's ekphrases, was one dimension of the aesthetic style that vested in bones a signifying capacity that marked their emergence as relics; as noted earlier, this was a style that dissipated the material opacity (and so also the danger of idolatry) without betraying the substance.

Despite—or perhaps because of—their awareness that the specter of idolatry was a menace to be taken seriously, those who participated in the veneration of relics recognized that they brought a necessarily imaginative mindset to their participation in this form of worship. Christian celebration of material expressions of divinity demanded the cultivation of new forms of apprehension. For example, Victricius of Rouen defended his view of the ability of a bodily fragment to contain "the truth of the whole corporeal passion [of the martyr]" by arguing that an understanding of relics required an alternative hermeneutic based on a metaphoric sense of language. Only imaginal interpretation, with "the eyes of the heart," can see a drop of martyr's blood for what it truly is, a fragment of matter shot through with the fiery sheen of the divine.[14] Victricius seems to have known that the material piety associated with relics demanded vividly sensory expression in images that conveyed the tangible, palpable aspects of relic veneration.

Augustine too was moved by a similar imaginative dynamic, creating a virtual theater of the mind in which to place the martyrs, and, by extension, their relics. In one sermon, he wrote that hearing a martyr's passion read was simultaneously to see it, as if watching the performance of a mime or pantomime.[15] Wishing to redirect his parishioners' "lust of the eyes" away from actual dramatic spectacles, he presented the memorializing of martyrs as a holy festival in which one sings and dances the moral life in imitation of them.[16] In the martyrial theater, delight is an "embrace with the arms of the mind," and celebration is a "holy drunkenness" rather than a literal one.[17]

Like Gregory of Nyssa, Augustine knew that the aesthetically wrought mediums in which martyrs' bones became relics—that is, the shrines with their paintings and mosaics, the candle-lit festal vigils, as well as the emotionally charged rhetoric heard there—aroused the affective responses of the participants. As we have seen, Gregory was quite positive about the role of such expressiveness in the presence of relics: after describing the visual splendor of Saint Theodore's martyrium with its walls "colored with the flowers of art," he evokes an image of the venerators, who "embrace [the relics] as though they were alive, approaching them with eyes, mouth, ears—all the senses."[18]

Augustine, however, was not so sure about such engagement of the senses. He roundly condemned those who danced, sang, and drank at the shrines of the martyrs;[19] such "pestilential rowdiness" was not appropriate at "such a holy place as this [the Mappalia Basilica], where the body lies of such a holy martyr [Saint Cyprian]."[20] While not denying emotion—he himself had exclaimed in a sermon, "Look, here am I, watching Cyprian; I'm crazy about Cyprian . . . I'm delighted by him . . . I rejoice when he wins"[21]—he endeavored to engage his parishioners' cognitive skills by teaching them how to participate in the cult of relics with a spiritualized fervor, turning the singing and dancing inward as well as making such celebratory activities ritually more chaste. Thus during the vigils at the *memoria* of the martyrs, those who are the true "children of the martyrs praise them," he wrote, while "their persecutors dance; the children sing hymns, the others organize parties."[22]

Just as Augustine attempted to redirect the physical intensity attendant upon the cult of relics with a rhetorical aesthetic, constructing a kind of spiritual theater of the mind in which ethical mimesis of martyrs was paramount, so also his contemporary in Italy, Paulinus of Nola, appealed to an aesthetic medium, art, to achieve a similar form of instruction in how to engage this form of worship. Writing about the paintings that decorated the basilicas dedicated to Saint Felix at Nola, Paulinus explained that the reason for their existence was twofold.[23] Briefly, he noted that many in his congregation were unlettered; thus the paintings functioned as a visual "text" or artistic primer. More important to Paulinus, given the number of lines he devotes to this second reason, was the hope that the paintings would disengage his congregation from their habit of celebrating the vigils devoted to Felix with too much drink, dousing not only themselves but also the tomb with "reeking wine." Where once, as pagans, "their God was their belly," now their sensuous pleasures would be moved to another register: so forcefully would the minds of these rustics be struck by the many-colored spectacle of the paintings that the art would "beguile their hunger."[24] The polychromy on the walls, he hoped, would induce a similarly diversified, more spiritual mode of perception, not to mention a remaking of the body and its desires.

How might this beguiling reeducation of the senses happen? Paulinus chose a telling verb to describe the effect of the paintings in Felix's basilicas: "it seemed useful to us to enliven [*ludere*] the houses of Felix with sacred pictures."[25] By his choice of the verb *ludo*, he seemed to be suggesting that art effects a kind of play with interpretive possibilities: "the person who looks at these [paintings] and acknowledges the truth within these empty figures [*vacuis figuris*] nurtures his believing mind with representations by no means empty."[26] The irony of Paulinus's pun on the word "empty" is important to note here, because these empty representations that are nonetheless full did not refer literally to the relics of Saint Felix, about whose proper veneration Paulinus was so concerned. Representing instead scenes and persons from the Old and New Testaments as well as several notable martyrs, these paintings created a religio-aesthetic environment within which the relics of Saint Felix could be properly understood and celebrated. Like Victricius's "eyes of the heart," art offered a spiritual hermeneutic that instructed Felix's devotees in a more sophisticated form of devotion.

Relics and Literary "Art"

The role of art as a visual stimulant for engaging the active interpretive imagination of participants in the cult of relics was also present in a literary form in the ekphrasis, one of the main rhetorical devices used by such relic-minded authors as Paulinus, Gregory of Nyssa, Prudentius, and Asterius of Amaseia to evoke the "wrap-around environment" in which bones became relics.[27] Ekphrasis was one of the writing techniques practiced in the study of rhetoric; it was defined in the rhetorical handbooks used by late ancient authors as "a descriptive speech bringing the thing shown vividly before the eyes," thereby turning listeners into spectators.[28] Since, as Liz James and Ruth Webb have pointed out, "the subjects suggested for such visual presentation are persons, places, times, and events . . . the modern definition of ekphrasis as first and foremost 'a description of a work of art' has no foundation in classical rhetorical theory."[29]

For my purposes, the key term in this disclaimer is "description," since the subject-matter of many ekphrases in late antiquity was, of course, art.[30] However, when ekphrases presented paintings, mosaics, and buildings, they were not technical art-historical descriptions. Rather, to continue James and Webb's argument, "they represent a living response to works of art," conveying emotional response, not objective observation, and rivaling art in their ability to bring the subject alive.[31] A good example of these evocative qualities is the following excerpt from the *Ekphraseis* of Callistratus that describes a statue of Narcissus: "He gave out as it were a radiance of lightning from the very beauty of his body. . . . A white mantle, of the same color as the marble of which he was made, encircled him. . . . It was so delicate and imitated a mantle so closely that the color of his body shone through, the whiteness of the drapery permitting the gleam of the limbs to come out."[32] As one interpreter has noted, "the statue struggles to be more than marble, to be real flesh."[33] This enlivening effect is characteristic of ekphrasis as a literary form; the reader becomes a viewer who is "taken into a visionary world beyond objects" and experiences that uncanny moment of intensity in which "the ontological difference between artists' imitations and their objects" is erased.[34]

It is in this moment of the effacement of the boundary between an opaque object and a living body that I wish to situate the artistry that produced a poetics of the body in the early Christian cult of relics. Consider, for example, Asterius of Amaseia's *Ekphrasis on Saint Euphemia*. While out for a walk, Asterius had come upon a painting of the martyrdom of this saint and wrote an ekphrasis in order to capture the colors of the painting in words, since "we writers possess colors no worse than those of painters."[35] The artist, as Asterius points out, had placed his painting, a "holy spectacle,"[36] in proximity to Euphemia's tomb, suggesting that there was a close relationship between the art and the saint's remains.

In Asterius's opinion, the painting brought the dead body to life in a series of narrative scenes that were alarmingly lifelike, even "animated" (ἐμψύχους), so that, for example, when during torture Euphemia's teeth are pulled out, "drops of blood seem really to be trickling from her mouth."[37] He credited the painter with "having instilled feeling into his colors" and understood this subjective tone of the painting as warrant for the viewer's own exercise of interpretive license: thus he noted that, while the artist's intention was to portray Euphemia as literally beautiful, what Asterius himself saw was "her soul beautified by virtues."[38]

At the end of his ekphrasis, Asterius asked the reader to do some interpretation of her own, but with an interestingly ambiguous invitation: "Now it is time for you, if you wish, to complete the painting so that you can decide with accuracy whether I have fallen short of it in my interpretation."[39] What exactly is the reader being invited to do here? Ambiguities in two of the words in this sentence, τελέσαι ("complete" or "perfect") and γραφή ("writing" or "painting") suggest at the very least that this is an ekphrasis that has no end: in what sense can the reader "complete" the "painting"? Is it necessary to go see it, and in what sense might the viewer then "perfect" what the author has written or himself seen? Or, is the reader being challenged to fulfill—that is, to bring to a conclusion—what the author has written (or seen), since γραφή can mean both painting and writing?[40] Whatever answer to these questions one chooses, it seems that the reader is being positioned as an active participant in the creation of an aesthetics of relics as he is placed in the complicated space of the painting/writing of Asterius at Euphemia's tomb.

A Poetics of Relics: Prudentius

To move more deeply into the phenomenon of the poetizing, that is, the aesthetic fashioning of *both* venerator *and* relic, I turn to one of the more surreal spaces created by Prudentius for situating relics, surreal because of the stark oppositions that this passage from the *Peristephanon* both evokes and elides. It will become clear that Prudentius drew upon an ekphrastic technique in which words and pictures—and words *as* pictures—collaborate "to produce a hyper-real, sensuously intense experience that goes beyond the limits of both pictures and words."[41] The "surreal space" is Prudentius's depiction of the underground shrine of the martyr Hippolytus; it is here that one can experience the full impact of what Jacques Fontaine described as "the power [of Prudentius's] visual imagination," carried in part by "an alliance of the horrible and the graceful" that produces "sensuous riches."[42]

Accompanying Prudentius on his journey downward into the catacombs of the Via Tiburtina, one is presented with the following ekphrasis of a fresco on the wall above the tomb containing Hippolytus's relics:

The wall holds a painted representation of the crime, on which pigments of many colors set out the whole outrage. Above the tomb a likeness is depicted, powerful in its clear images, delineating the bleeding limbs of the man dragged to his death. The jagged rock tips dripped blood, dear bishop. I saw them, and read the crimson signs imprinted on the bushes. A hand skilled in imitating green vegetation had also portrayed the red blood with vermillion dye. You could see the torn frame and limbs scattered and lying randomly in unpredictable locations. Later, the artist added the loyal friends following with tearful footsteps where his erratic course traced its fractured path. Stunned with sorrow, they went along with searching eyes, filling the folds of their tunics with his ravaged guts. . . . And if any blood from the hot shower settles on the branches, they press a sponge to it and carry it all away.[43]

Typically, such ekphrases are literary devices that *interrupt* a narrative in order to present a work of art.[44] What has intrigued contemporary readers of this ekphrasis, however, is that it is not a digression; instead, as Martha Malamud has explained, Prudentius's ekphrasis on the painting in Hippolytus's shrine "dissolves its own frame, erasing the distinction between the painting being described and the poem describing it."[45] Similarly, Gabriel Bertonière has remarked that "it is . . . curious that the description of the painting is not only mentioned in the context of the narration, but serves as part of the narration itself, particularly in the part which describes the gathering of the martyr's members. In fact, one is not sure where the description of the painting ends and the thread of the story is taken up again."[46]

Malamud's conclusion regarding the "sensuous riches" of this aspect of Prudentius's literary art is worth quoting in full: "By refusing to close the frame of the ekphrasis, Prudentius creates the impression that the painting contains everything in the rest of the poem, including the saint's tomb and even the poet himself, who later appears as a character contemplating the mirrored shrine in the center of the tomb."[47] Further, as though to advertise the ambiguous shimmer of this poetic construction, Prudentius includes a pun on the verb *legere* when he describes the saint's followers gathering his body parts: "Another collects [*legit*] shoulders, mutilated hands, forearms and elbows, knees and bare fragments of legs."[48] As they collect, they also "read" Hippolytus's body, making it into a coherent whole once more, just as Prudentius the poet transforms the painting into a legible whole for his reader, who reads just as the painted followers do and thus enters the painting as a participant.

This, however, is only the beginning of the poetizing of the reader as

venerator as Prudentius's corporeal imagination intensifies in its affective, ocular appeal. Continuing the ekphrasis, Prudentius writes that the
saint's followers, having gathered all of the martyr's body parts, now
must find a place for his tomb. They go to the catacombs in Rome,
where they find the following:

A crypt opens up descending to hidden depths. Into its obscurity a path leads
downward with curving steps, and shows the way through the windings with fugi-
tive light. For the brightness of day enters the first doorway as far as the top of
the chamber's mouth and illuminates the threshold of the entrance chamber.
From there it is an easy progression to where the dark night of the place seems
to grow blacker in the indistinct cavern; where apertures let into the lofty ceiling
shed bright rays over the cave. Though indeterminate alcoves swathe on either
side the confined halls under shadowy galleries, yet within the hollow belly of
the carved-out mountain frequent shafts of light penetrate from the openings in
the vault. So it is possible to see and enjoy the radiancy of bright light even below
the earth where there is no sun. Such was the chamber Hippolytus' body was
entrusted to, and nearby was positioned an altar dedicated to God.[49]

Thus begins an ekphrasis-within-the-ekphrasis, as Prudentius takes the
reader down into the labyrinthine depths where Hippolytus's body will
be buried in a shrine that receives an elaborate description. Of course,
the reader has already been positioned in this underground space, since
this is where the multicolored painting of the gruesome martyrdom of
Hippolytus is located. Yet it is this second ekphrastic journey to the
shrine that allows Prudentius both to align the horror of the painting
with the grace of the shrine itself and to pull the reader more fully into
the experience of veneration that the relics provide.

As Prudentius constructs this space for a second time, the reader's
gaze is shifted from the vermillion glimmer of the martyr's blood to a
play of light that is explicitly presented as a sensuous pleasure: one perceives and enjoys (*frui*) the glitter of bright light, even though the sun is
absent.[50] The term used to describe the quality of the light in the darkness of the catacomb—*fulgor*, literally, a "flash of lightning"—recurs in
the ekphrasis-within-the-ekphrasis that describes the shrine containing
Hippolytus's relics and sets up a dizzying interplay of reflections of light.
As with the artistry of the photographer from Arkansas, here is one of
those moments when everyday flesh catches fire.

Prudentius's description of the shrine is brief: "The shrine itself,
which holds the sheddings of his soul, glitters, made from solid silver. A
wealthy hand covered it with smoothly polished bright tablets, which
reflect like a concave mirror."[51] Although they have opposite aesthetic
tones, the one filled with beauty, the other with horror, the mirrored
reliquary and the painting above it have much in common. Both collapse the distinction between art and writing. As indicated earlier, the

ekphrasis that presents the painting never ends, so that the distinction between the painting and the poem describing it is effaced; furthermore, the saint's friends collect *and* "read" his dispersed members, putting him back together again just as the poem and the painting do.

So also with the reliquary: the wealthy "hand"—*manus*—of a benefactor has covered it with silver plating—*tabulae*—concave surfaces that are also in some sense "writing tablets." Furthermore, the mirrored shrine is an artistic object that contains the martyr, just as the painting does; however, in the shrine the dismembered parts of the martyr's body have become relics. Just as the juxtaposition of painting and shrine collapses the temporal and spatial distinctions between earth and heaven, so also the boundary between the horrible and the graceful is dissolved as the tortured body and the beatific body become an aesthetic whole.[52] This is so because the reliquary, covered with silver surfaces that catch the flash of the light in the cavern, reflects everything around it, including the painting and the poet who is both looking and writing.

The intensity of the aesthetic interplay induced by the mirrored shrine has been insightfully described as follows:

A sense of endless circularity and repetition is suggested by the object at the center of the tomb. . . . The shrine . . . is covered with polished metal plates that act as mirrors. Instead of revealing its contents, the shrine reflects its surroundings, becoming a distorted repetition of the tomb/labyrinth itself. . . . The shrine is covered with hollow—that is, concave—mirrors, which not only reverse the image reflected in them, but also turn it upside down. We must marvel at the complexity of Prudentius' construction in this passage: not only do the mirrors, in a sense, contain the entire labyrinth that surrounds them, but the tomb itself and all its contents are themselves contained by the painting Prudentius describes in the open-ended ekphrasis.[53]

If the martyr's body thus "catches fire" in the constant interplay of these reflections, what of the venerator?

There is one more dimension of this chamber, one that implicates the body of the beholder in this aesthetics of incandescence. Just before describing the mirrored reliquary, Prudentius situates himself in front of it, praying; after his description, he pictures other venerators: "they imprint kisses on the clear metal."[54] Here again is another repetition of the metaphor of writing, as the worshippers' kisses are "imprinted" or "engraved" (*impressa*) on the reflecting metal, the *tabulae*, thus involving them in the complicated poetics of the space in which they are located.

Even more striking, however, is the fact that, in the act of kissing, the venerators are themselves reflected on the surface of the reliquary; that is, their bodies become part of the radiant reflecting that the space of the martyr's relics sets in motion. In the spiritual art of Prudentius's poetry, every body is a poetic body, caught up in that moment when intensity becomes something incandescent. Indeed, as Malamud points out, when one looks into a concave mirror, the image is not literal but rather upside down and reversed, a fact that suggests that the kind of looking appropriate to the cult of relics is a particular kind of vision, "a vision of a world of deformed forms"[55] whose imaginative operation depends upon a deformation of perception in order to induce poetic apprehension.

Relics, Flowers, and Blood

Prudentius was not the only participant in the cult of relics to implicate both the bones of the martyrs and the body of the venerator in the kind of sensuous aesthetic that I have been describing. In the signifying field that early Christian writers and artists created for relics, there was a particular cluster of images that recurred repeatedly, especially in ekphrases in the writings of Prudentius, Victricius of Rouen, Paulinus of Nola, and Gregory of Nyssa. This cluster of images, consisting of flowers, blood, and relics, situated martyrs' bones in an aesthetic style that pervaded the arts in late antiquity.

With ποικιλία and *variatio* as key terms, this style drew on an aesthetic sensibility that valued diversity imagined as polychrome patterning, whether metaphorically in terms of the "verbal dazzle" of literary composition or literally in terms of the play of color and light in mosaics and painting.[56] Individual words in a poem, for example, could be compared with flowers, gems, and the many-colored brilliance that they evoked.[57] Such appeals to metaphors of color and light for characterizing rhetorical embellishments aligned poetry with other forms of art; thus "the art of the poet was akin to that of the jeweler—to manipulate brilliant pieces," and words could be imagined as "the equivalent of colors in a painter's palette."[58]

Art too was valued for its (literal) "dazzle." Mosaics, like poems, were described as "meadows bright with springtime flowers" because of the brilliance and variety of their individual colors.[59] Indeed, as Dominic Janes has observed, "the late Antique enthusiasm for flowers and bright colours was for the massed effect of coruscating brilliance that dazzled the eye as it did the mind with associations of power, abundance and goodness."[60] This cultural taste for color and brilliance was one of the contexts in which martyrs' bones became relics. What was new in the Christian appropriation of this aesthetic in the cult of relics was an association of flowers with blood, which introduced yet another register of meaning to an already rich fabric of metaphorical relationships.

The Christian addition of blood to the flowery aesthetic just described was itself indebted to a rich cultural tradition in which flowers with a "bloody" hue were associated with death and rebirth. In Rome, the flower of choice was the rose.[61] By the fourth century C.E., the *Rosalia* associated with the rebirth of the earth in the Spring was an immensely popular public holiday, celebrated with games and theatrical performances.[62] Roses also served a commemorative and possibly a propitiatory function as well: the *dies rosationis* were Springtime rituals during which family members decorated the graves of their dead with roses (though other blood-colored flowers, notably the violet—hence *dies violares*— were also used for this purpose).[63] In the context of relics, Paulinus of Nola appears to have reimagined traditions associated with the *Rosalia* for Christian use. In the third of his *natalicia* in honor of Saint Felix (ironically, celebrated not in the Spring but on January 14), he wrote: "Sprinkle the ground with flowers, adorn the doorways with garlands. Let winter breathe forth the purple beauty [*purpureum*] of Spring; let the year be in flower before its time, and let nature submit to the holy day. For you also, earth, owe wreaths to the martyr's tomb. But the holy glory of the doorway to the heavens encircles him, flowering with the twin wreaths of war and peace."[64] In a later *natalicium*, Saint Felix is himself imagined as a "fertile field" in which "new flowers have emerged" in the form of converts to the ascetic life.[65] Here the *praesentia* of the saint as indicated by his relics ("You are here at Nola as well as in heaven" he says to Felix elsewhere)[66] is extended metaphorically by an organic image of chaste fecundity that links presence with productive power.

These transformative associations of flowers with rejuvenation, whether in memory, as in the *dies rosationes*, or in images of rebirth, were also common in cultic practice and in myth. The best-known use of flowers—again, the rose—was in the cult of Isis, where the *rosea corona*, the wreath of victory of Isis's consort Osiris, was connected with resurrection and also used to decorate statues of Isis herself.[67] And of course there was Apuleius's hero Lucius, transformed into a chastened, and finally religiously chaste, human being by eating roses.[68]

Associations of blood, flowers, and those metamorphoses to which the life of the body is subject had a long history in Graeco-Roman myth as well. A complicated myth connected with the cult of Cybele is devoted to her youthful consort Attis, who castrated himself (in one variant, he was induced to perform this act to prevent his marriage, thus preserving his "virginity"); from his blood there grew a violet-colored flower.[69] Ovid told the story of Adonis, the young lover of Aphrodite; when he was mortally wounded by a boar, the goddess used his blood to create a flower, the anemone.[70] In the Gnostic text *On the Origin of the World*, the blood that flows from Psyche following her sexual union with the god Eros mixes with earth, and from this mixture there grows the first flower, a rose.[71] Finally, there is the Cupid of Ausonius's poem *Cupido cruciatus*, whom the poet places in the underworld, being beaten by lovelorn goddesses; the blood from his wounds produces roses.[72] These stories make clear the transformative implications of an imaginal complex that became prominent in the Christian cult of relics.

The connection between relics and flowers may also be related to an early martyrological tradition that envisioned the heavenly home of martyrs as a paradisal *locus amoenus*, as in Saturus's dream in the *Passio Perpetuae et Felicitatis*, where paradise is pictured as a garden filled with rose bushes and flowers. Similarly, in a dream of the heavenly banquet in the *Passio Mariani et Iacobi*, a martyr appears wearing a garland of roses (*corona rosea*).[73] Eventually, martyrs themselves became flowers: Prudentius, for example, refers to the Holy Innocents killed by Herod as "flowers of martyrdom" (*flores martyrum*) who were crushed "like rosebuds" (*nascentes rosas*).[74]

Female virgin-martyrs, in particular, were presented as flowers, in literature as well as in art.[75] A fresco from a martyrium near Alexandria, reproduced by André Grabar in his *Martyrium* (fig. 7),[76] shows a female martyr as a flower blooming in a flower-strewn field. As Jill Ross has observed, this martyr-flower "is surrounded by other flowers, some of which bear the symbol of the cross, suggesting that their martyred bodies have become flowers in paradise."[77] In this fresco, the aesthetic complex of martyrs, flowers, and blood (suggested by the crosses) is graphically represented; it provided a way of seeing the meaning of the entombed remains whose space it shared.

Given the long history of the use of flowers to evoke paradise in the early Christian imagination,[78] it is not difficult to imagine that the association of relics with flowers can be read as a means for signifying the paradisal "home" of the "person" whose bones remain on earth. However, the insistence on retaining blood as part of the metaphorizing of relics by flowers suggests a desire to preserve a certain earthy dimension in this spiritual aesthetics. In the cult of relics, "flowers" were never far from "the weight of blood and bones," to recall the description of the photographer Disfarmer's technique.

In the rhetoric of the cult of relics, one has only to remember Prudentius's Eulalia. Her young, virginal body is described metaphorically as a "tender flower"; but, as Ross has shown, "this is an ironic foreshadowing of her actual transformation into a flower since she will not only become a flower in the Church's garland of martyrs, but the wounds her body receives will undergo a miraculous metamorphosis and will reappear as blood-red flowers."[79] In Prudentius's words, the flow of her "red blood" (*purpura sanguinis*) will reappear in the *purpureas violas sanguinesoque crocos*—the purple violets and blood-colored crocuses offered at

Figure 7. Fresco, Anonymous Martyr. Oratory at Abou-Girgeh, Egypt. From André Grabar, *Martyrium*, 2 vols. (Paris: Collège de France, 1946), vol. 2, plate LX.3. Photo: David Broda, Syracuse University.

the basilica containing her relics—as well as on the basilica's mosaic floor, decorated with multicolored marble "so that you imagine rose-colored meadows, reddening with many kinds of flowers" (*floribus ut rosulenta putes/prata rubescere multimodis*), flowers that are, finally, Prudentius's own verses, as he says explicitly.[80]

The imaginative operation of such texts depended upon the perceptual artistry associated with *variatio* and ποικιλία, since a relic is not literally a flower, nor are flowers bloody. By bringing this aesthetic style to bear on martyrs' bones, Christians created a "many-colored" form of imagination—that is, a diverse signifying ground—for this form of veneration. What I will call a "polychromatic poetics" operated as well in the spaces in which relics were placed. Thus Paulinus, describing a painting in the basilica at Fundi that contained relics of many martyrs, wrote: "Beneath a bloody cross Christ stands as a snow-white lamb in the midst of the heavenly grove of flowery paradise."[81]

Many late ancient Christian authors brought this polychromatic poetics to bear on relics, thus extending to the human body the kind of aesthetic pleasure found in the words of poets and the paints of artists. In his ekphrasis on the paintings in the martyrium of Saint Theodore, for example, Gregory of Nyssa wrote that "the painter has colored the walls with the flowers of his art," representing the martyr's torture and death; "he depicted the martyr's struggles clearly and ornamented the church like a magnificent meadow."[82] A passage from Victricius of Rouen's oration in praise of martyrs brought relics, flowers and their jeweled counterparts, and blood together in a strikingly intense way: the crowns of the martyrs, wrote Victricius, are "adorned with the varied lights of the jewels" of various virtues (*diademata variis gemmarum distincta luminibus*), and Christ is the artist (*artifex*) who has decorated the crowns with "spiritual jewels" (*spiritalibus gemmis*); these jewels, he continues, "bloom in beauty more and more" [*magis ac magis in specie florescunt*]; "even the blood shows that they are presented as signs of eternity, the blood which is still the sign of the fire of the Holy Spirit in the very bodies and relics of the limbs."[83]

This was not merely "verbal dazzle."[84] When Augustine wrote about the relics of Saint Stephen that "his body has brought light to the whole world," he meant something quite specific, healing.[85] In a passage in *The City of God* that narrates the arrival of the relics of Saint Stephen at Aquae Tibilitanae, Augustine tells the story of the healing of a blind woman by a flower—a flower held by the bishop who was also carrying Stephen's bones.[86] One function of the paradox of the sensuous relic was to span the vertical gap between the martyr's bones on earth and the saint in heaven, blunting the spatial distinction between here and there.[87] Only a poetic body could mediate the spiritual healing power sought by so many at the shrines of martyrs.[88]

Relics and Incandescence

The brilliant polychromy that characterized much of the literature of the cult of relics was thus not merely verbal *dazzle*, nor was it merely *verbal* dazzle. In Milan, not long after the death of Ambrose in C.E. 397, a martyr-chapel that housed the relics of Saint Victor was decorated with mosaics that included a portrait in tesserae of the saint himself (fig. 8).[89] The position of the image "high in the center of the dome echoe[d] the position of the loculus where his bones lay, more than fourteen meters below,"[90] a verticality both spatial and visual that the centripetal arrangement of the chapel both establishes and bridges. His portrait, encircled by a flowery wreath tied with a red ribbon, has at its top "a flame-like jewel set in an oval frame right above the head of the saint. The jewel, which seems to burn with a white heat at the center and is shaded to red, is clearly shown within the aureole of light, framed in gold."[91] A

Figure 8. Sacellum of Saint Victor in Ciel d'Oro: Dome—detail (bust of Saint Victor). Mosaic. S. Ambrogio, Milan, Italy. Photo: Scala/Art Resource, NY.

small jeweled crown with another red ribbon, a visual metonym of the flowery wreath, is held over the saint's head by a hand reaching downward, presumably the hand of God.

In the aesthetic context of relics that I have been exploring, this mosaic can be seen as a visual analog to the cluster of images that attempted to convey the spiritual fire of the blood and bones of relics by aligning them with the brilliant play of light associated with flowers and gems.[92] High above the dead body of the martyr, the portrait shows the human body meditated to the point of incandescence. In a meditation on the vertical imagination in European literature that seems appropriate also in this late ancient context, the philosopher Gaston Bachelard wrote the following: "The flame is an inhabited verticality. Everyone who dreams of a flame knows that the flame is alive. . . . The stem of the flame is so straight and so frail that the flame is a flower. . . . Everything that is vertical in the cosmos is a flame. . . . The fire flowers and the flower lights up. These two corollaries could be developed endlessly: color is an epiphany of fire and the flower is an ontophany of light."[93]

No one knew better than Paulinus that, in the cult of relics, one was placed in a visionary world such as this, a world in which the boundary between body and spirit, death and life, is dissolved—even if fleetingly—in a shimmer of light. In one of his poems, he gives a description of the atmosphere in the basilica that housed Felix's relics that is dazzling in its aesthetic intensity. Here is his ekphrasis:

In the middle of the basilica hang hollow lamps, fixed by bronze chains to the high ceiling panels. They have the appearance of trees throwing forth arms like vine-shoots, and at their very tips these boughs bear glass cups as their fruit. Spring blossoms, so to speak, flower in the light kindled in them. With their abundant, radiating flames they resemble densely-packed stars, and they punctuate the heavy darkness with numerous flashes. They color the delicate air with little fiery flowers, and as they shake their bright foliage and flash repeatedly, they disperse the gloom of night with everlasting flames. Their flickering appearance intermingles light and shadows, and they trouble the uncertain air with their tremulous appearance.[94]

This is what I mean by incandescence. As he fills the air with flickering fire-buds, Paulinus brings polychromatic effects of color and light associated with the art of ποικιλία to bear on the space occupied by relics, and in doing so he enacts the kind of perception appropriate to it. As in the mirrored shrine of Prudentius's imagination, here too the concave lamps set off ceaseless vibrations of light, an interplay of reflections that signals the aesthetic polyvalence in which the cult of relics was necessarily situated. I say "necessarily," because the real "substance" of material objects like a dead person's bones—that is, their ability to signify—can only be released by a strong form of imagination; otherwise they remain simply opaque.

I think Paulinus knew that this form of imagination was not romantic, not merely "airy" and sentimental, since he goes to some lengths to emphasize the "*flickering*" intermingling of light *and* shadows as the lamps "*trouble* the *uncertain* air with their *tremulous* appearance." By emphasizing the sensuous ambiguity of the aesthetic environment in which he imagined relics, Paulinus was disallowing the possibility that they might be evaporated by a spirituality devoid of earthy contact or objectified by an idolatrous materialism.

As relics, the bodies of martyrs were neither opaque nor transparent; they were poetic. The early Christian writers who achieved what I called earlier in this chapter a "vision of a world of deformed forms"[95] engaged a particular function of the imagination that Bachelard described as follows:

> We always think of the imagination as the faculty that *forms* images. On the contrary, it *deforms* what we perceive; it is, above all, the faculty that frees us from immediate images and *changes* them. If there is no change, or unexpected fusion of images, there is no imagination; there is no *imaginative act*. If the image that is *present* does not make us think of one that is *absent*, if an image does not determine an abundance—an explosion—of unusual images, then there is no imagination. There is only perception, . . . an habitual way of viewing form and color.[96]

Deforming, imagination creates. This view of the metamorphosing qualities of aesthetics is a most unromantic one, which is all the more interesting in Bachelard's case because, in one of his works on images of fire, the early Romantic poet Novalis figures prominently. Besides poetry, Novalis also wrote a novel, *Heinrich von Ofterdingen*, whose central image, the famous blue flower, was adopted by his fellow Romantics as a symbol of Romantic longing, beauty, and innocence. If one actually reads the novel, however, one finds that the blue flower is actually a transgressive object of desire, "a highly mobile object whose shape shifts throughout the novel,"[97] and that it functions as a symbol for the incandescence of poetic images.[98] Bachelard quotes from the novel: "'I need . . . flowers that have grown in the fire,' cried the King. . . . The gardener fetched a pot filled with flames and sowed in it a shining seed. It was not long before the flowers sprang forth," and ends his discussion of Novalis with these words: "You may object that Novalis is the poet of 'the little blue flower,' the poet of the forget-me-not tossed as a pledge of imperishable memory over the edge of the precipice in the very shadow of death. But go down into the depths . . . and find there with the poet the primitive dream and you will clearly see the truth: the little blue flower is red!"[99]

The little blue flower is red because it is on fire, as it were, with the poet's imaginative vision. It was this kind of vision that was needed for perceiving the extra-human value in martyrs' bones that transformed them into relics. The next chapter continues this exploration of ways in which those devoted to the veneration of relics achieved the transfigured eye so crucial to this aspect of ancient Christian practice and belief.

In particular, it analyzes how several relic-minded Christians attempted a re-formation of their audiences' habitual modes of perception by modeling various kinds of imaginative visualization, both of martyrs and the bones they left behind. The dazzle will continue, but in the form of mental spectacles and visionary storytelling.

Chapter Four

Bodies and Spectacles

A poetics of material substance, as Daniel Tiffany has written, calls for materialization of the invisible world.[1] As his use of the word "poetics" suggests, the invisible world is materialized in images, that is to say, in figurative language or word-pictures that are crucial for knowledge, since what is considered to be "real" is a function of the pictorial imagination.[2] In late ancient Christianity, the success of the material turn insofar as it was devoted to the paradox of spiritual bodies—in this chapter, martyrial bodies and their relics—was due in large part to its cultivation of an inner visual imagination that was sensuously intense.

In the literature about martyrs that arose in conjunction with the cult of relics, martyrs' bodies and their dramatic stories were often accorded the same kind of rhetorical dazzle that was accorded to their relics. The martyrs themselves, it seems, became visionary spectacles in order to bolster the belief that their relics were conduits of divine power. But because they were dead and so in the literal sense gone, martyrs were situated at the farthest reaches of sensual apprehension where memory turns to imagination.[3] Thus in order to animate the martyrial dead, authors such as Augustine and Prudentius relied on a certain pictorial theatricality that made the invisible visible in the form of mental spectacles and of visionary stories that collapsed past and present to create hyperreal dramas, while authors such as Victricius relied on striking metaphors in order to cultivate the transfigured eye so necessary to this romance of matter.

To open this analysis of the ways in which martyrs became sensuous and indeed emotionally charged spectacles, there is no better performance of the rhetorical sensibility in question than the following remarks of John Chrysostom: "What can I say? What shall I speak? I'm jumping with excitement and aflame with a frenzy that is better than common sense. I'm flying and dancing and floating on air and, for the rest, drunk under the influence of spiritual pleasure."[4] Thus did John Chrysostom open a homily devoted in part to martyrs and their relics in about 401 C.E. in a martyrium outside Constantinople.[5] His emotion is palpable. Indeed, in another homily, also delivered in the presence of relics, Chrysostom indicated that the spectacle of viewing that occurred in martyria ought to have a visible effect on the body of the venerator, producing more than "spiritual" acrobatics as in the passage above.

My point is that in the same way that those who descend from the theaters reveal to all that they've been thrown into turmoil, confused, enervated through the images they bear of everything that took place there, the person returning from viewing martyrs should be recognizable to all—through their gaze, their appearance, their gait, their compunction, their composed thoughts. [They should be] breathing fire, restrained, contrite, sober, vigilant—announcing the spiritual life within through the movements of their body. . . . Let's always return from martyrs, from spiritual incense, from heavenly meadows, from new and wonderful spectacles (θεαμάτων καινῶν καὶ παραδόξων) in this way.[6]

Indicating by his negative contrast with the effects of secular theater-going that the seeing connected with relics is a new—chaste—theater, Chrysostom credited the Christian spectacle with a remarkable, and very physical, transformative power.[7] So great is that power—"the grace of the Spirit . . . accompanies these bones"—that it affects not only the bodies of venerators, but also their clothing, shoes, and even their shadows![8]

What kind of seeing produced so dramatic an effect? In these two homilies preached at the tombs of martyrs, Chrysostom briefly implied that there were the following two kinds of seeing. On the one hand, while urging his audience to "stay beside the tomb of the martyr," he advised them at the same time to "immerse yourself perpetually in the stories of his struggles."[9] This suggests that the "spectacle" was a form of visionary storytelling in which the drama signified by the martyr's bones was enacted in the beholder's mind. On the other hand, Chrysostom used metaphors of light to indicate the power of the spectacle: in the tomb are "bones that reflect the very rays of the sun. No, rather they release flashes of light that are more brilliant. . . . So great even is the power of the ashes of the saints that it doesn't just sit inside the remains, but extends beyond them," repelling demons and sanctifying the faithful.[10] By engaging in this sort of rhetorical dazzle, Chrysostom tried to capture what was visually intractable, the spiritual power flowing from bones and ashes.

In a remarkable passage in his *Discourse on the Blessed Babylas*, Chrysostom brought out the full import of the connection between relics and vision by describing "the power that they have to excite a similar zeal in the souls of those who behold them." Here is the whole passage:

If anyone approaches such a tomb, he immediately receives a distinct impression of this energy. For the sight of the coffin, entering the soul, acts upon it and affects it in such a way that it feels as if it sees the one who lies there joining in prayer and drawing nigh. Afterwards, one who has had this experience returns from there filled with great zeal and [is] a changed person. . . . This vision [φαν-τασία] of the dead enters the souls of the living . . . as if they saw instead of the tomb those who lie in the tomb standing up. . . . And why speak of the location of a grave? Many times, in fact, the sight of a garment alone and the recollection of a word of the dead move the soul and restore the failing memory. For this reason God has left us the relics of the saints.[11]

Chrysostom was inhabiting a moment when memory turns to imagination. In one of his catechetical sermons, Chrysostom had remarked that faith consists in seeing the invisible as if it were visible, and this indeed is the perspective that underlies the passage above.[12] As Mary Carruthers has observed about Chrysostom's view of spiritual seeing, "the crucial power of the saint lies in the ability of his site/sight to enter the soul (through the eye), affect it and so cause one to feel as if one sees the saint himself—both in the mind's eye and heartfully."[13] Although Chrysostom sometimes distinguished between the "eyes of the flesh" and the "eyes of faith," in this passage physical sight cooperates in endowing the soul with a set of mental spectacles, as it were, with which to envision the saint, and the fleshly eye ("at the sight of a garment alone") also cooperates in bringing back to mind the storytelling spectacle, an experience that seems crucial to Chrysostom's view of this form of insight.[14]

Chrysostom's reflections suggest that being in martyria, in the presence of relics, provided visual stimulants for engaging an active theological imagination. His presentation of the veneration of martyrs and their relics as a spectacle was not idiosyncratic, nor was his rhetorical enhancement of ritual practice confined to Christianity in the Greek-speaking eastern empire. In the late fourth and early fifth centuries, authors writing in Latin as well as in Greek elaborated a set of culturally shared ideas and practices with regard to the cult of relics that cut across linguistic and regional difference. This chapter is devoted to a group of Christian authors writing in Latin whose ideas about martyrs, relics, and the ritual practices associated with them were remarkably consonant with those of Chrysostom. Thus I have structured my presentation of these authors' views by aligning them with three features of Chrysostom's martyr-discourse, so succinct and expressive of the ingredients that combined to produce the visionary atmosphere that was central to the cult of relics in late ancient Christianity.

Those three features of Chrysostom's writing on martyrs—theatrical rhetoric, the insertion of the venerator into the martyrial narrative, and the use of metaphors of light—will be used to explore the contributions of Augustine of Hippo, Prudentius of Calahorra, and Victricius of Rouen, all major players, with Chrysostom, in the development of the visionary literature that evoked the spiritual power of saints at the sites of their relics. First, theatrical rhetoric as well as an understanding of relic-veneration as mental theater will be the point of entry for engaging Augustine's position, concentrating primarily on his sermons on martyrs. Second, the view that the venerator at the shrine becomes part of the text, as it were, of the martyrial narrative, not only by being invaded by a vision of the dead but also by turning a physical landscape into a spiritual one, will be the point of entry for discussing Prudentius's *Peristephanon*. And third, a reliance on metaphors of light to evoke the power and presence of the saint in and around his relics will be the point of entry for considering the views of Victricius in his sermon *De laude sanctorum*. In their own ways, all three of these authors were, in effect, theorists as well as participants in the cult of relics, and all three "saw" the invisible by using verbal imagery to express an abstraction, that is, the belief that relics were conduits of divine power.

Augustine and Mental Theater

Augustine was shocked by the sensuous ambiance that often characterized celebrations of the feast days of martyrs. He found the drinking offensive, referring sarcastically in a sermon on the martyr Lawrence to those who, having had their bottles blessed at the martyrium, came back "soaked from the memorials of the martyrs"; in Augustine's view, such people were persecutors rather than venerators.[15] But he seems to have been especially annoyed by the dancing. In a sermon given in the Mappalia basilica in Carthage, he spoke against "the pestilential rowdiness of dancers" (as well as their "impious singing") that had profaned "such a holy place as this, where the body lies of such a holy martyr" (Cyprian).[16] Since, in Augustine's view, body and soul were a "coherent composite," these physical actions bespoke a misguided inner disposition toward the martyr and his relics.[17]

Such rowdiness, Augustine went on to note thankfully, no longer occurred but, as though anticipating a rebuke from Scripture, he quoted and then reinterpreted a version of Matthew 11.17 ("We have sung to you, and you have not danced?"). The non-dancers in this verse, as Augustine correctly noted, are being rebuked by the singers; what then is the proper song, and how shall one dance in honor of the martyr? "Our song," Augustine preached, is an ascetic song, and he quoted 1 John 2.15–17, a passage that condemns love of the world, and particularly "the lust of the flesh [*concupiscentia carnis*] and the lust of the eyes [*concupiscentia oculorum*]".[18] Here is the form of dancing that he recommended: "What a song that is, my brothers and sisters! You've heard me singing it, let me hear you dancing to it; see that you all do, by keeping time with your morals, what dancers do by keeping time with their bod-

ies and their feet. Do this inwardly [*intus hoc agite*]; let your moral attitudes match that song. Let cupidity, greed, be uprooted, charity, love
planted."[19] Augustine's solution for the problem of riotous celebration
is to direct the celebration inward, so that the rhythm of physical movement becomes the beat of a virtuous disposition. This involved more
than a rhetorical sleight of hand on Augustine's part: he was engaged in
retraining the senses to apprehend the meaning of martyrs and their
relics.

Redirecting what Augustine called, as above, "the lust of the eyes" was
of paramount importance in this endeavor. Like many others in antiquity, Augustine thought that the eye was active rather than passive. He
described the mechanics of seeing, now called the theory of extramission, as follows: "In this very body which we carry around with us, I can
find something whose inexpressible swiftness astonishes me; the ray
from our eye, with which we touch whatever we behold. What you see,
after all, is what you touch with the ray from your eye."[20] Seeing was thus
connective and embodied: there was "a certain participatory dimension
in the visual process, a potential intertwining of viewer and viewed."[21]
This kind of seeing, however, could be intrusive and dangerous: in
Graeco-Roman culture, seeing could be doing, because the eye could
wither, devour, and de-soul the object of its gaze.[22] Indeed, in the myth
of Narcissus, the eye could even consume the self, and Plutarch discussed the self-bewitching capacity of the gaze.[23]

If, by virtue of the eye's touch, the act of seeing was performative, as
Robert Nelson has argued, one had to be careful where one directed
one's gaze.[24] Like John Chrysostom, Augustine engaged the problem of
the lust of the eyes precisely on the topic of performance. In a sermon
preached in Carthage at the table of Saint Cyprian (the shrine erected
at the spot where he was executed), Augustine admonished his audience
as follows:

What evils vulgar, shameless curiosity is the cause of, the lust of the eyes, the
avid craving for frivolous shows and spectacles, the madness of the stadiums, the
fighting of contests for no reward! . . . Is this the way it is, then, that vile baseness
delights the decent man? You can also change your consuming addiction to
shows and spectacles; the Church is offering your mind more honest and venerable spectacles. Just now the passion of the blessed Cyprian was being read. We
were listening with our ears, observing it all with our minds; we could see him
competing, somehow or other we felt afraid for him in his deadly peril, but we
were hoping God would help him.[25]

In the course of condemning the base delight and the self-consuming
addiction that characterized watching secular performances, Augustine
also referred briefly to martyr-narratives as spectacles in their own right;
they differ from the other kind of spectacle in that the eye is directed

inward, where the drama is played out in the mind's eye. As Augustine went on to say, the real difference between the two kinds of spectacles revolves around mimesis. Seeing is doing: no one, he argued, would be crazy enough to want to imitate actors that they see in the theater, especially since the disrepute of the actors would contaminate the gazer.[26] But those with "a sound and healthy mind would love to imitate the martyrs."[27]

In emotionally charged rhetoric, Augustine immediately modeled how both the inner spectacle and the imitation take place: "Look, here am I, watching Cyprian; I'm crazy about Cyprian. . . . I'm watching him, I'm delighted by him, as far as I can I embrace him with the arms of my mind; I see him competing, I rejoice when he wins . . . Say to me, 'May you be like him!' See if I don't jump at the idea, see if I don't choose to be so, see if I don't long to be so."[28] Augustine was quite adamant in his conviction that martyr-narratives were a form of spiritual theater. In yet another sermon on martyrs, he exclaimed: "I love the martyrs, I go and watch the martyrs; when the Passions of the martyrs are read, I am a spectator, watching them."[29]

The kind of spectacle that Augustine was talking about could not be seen literally: speaking at a *memoria* of the martyrs Protasius and Gervasius, he urged his listeners, "Shake up your faith, bring the eyes of your heart [*oculos cordis*] to bear, not your human eyes. You have other ones inside, after all, which God made for you. He opened the eyes of your heart, when he gave you faith."[30] This was a spiritual theater of the mind—as Augustine told one audience, each one's heart is a stage (*theatro pectoris*) and "God is watching" (*deus spectat*)—and that inner stage was where he thought that the stories that infused the cult of relics with meaning were most truly performed, since that "theater" was where the ethical transformation provoked by the example of the saints took place.[31]

Underlying Augustine's notion of mental theater as the proper place for the Christian gaze lay the ancient rhetorical practice of *enargeia*, a type of composition that consisted of "vivid, sensuous word-painting" or "words that paint our thoughts" such that the mind's eye of the listener or reader could see what was being described.[32] The visionary aspect of this form of rhetorical exercise has been succinctly characterized as follows: "From well-established rhetorical practice Romans were accustomed to visualize the unseen, as if it were actually present. Visions (*visiones*), induced by powerful verbal representations, so stirred the emotions and stimulated the imagination that complex scenes could manifest themselves with convincing, vivid immediacy before the mind's eye."[33] This was, in effect, what Augustine was both modeling and recommending to his listeners as they stood at tombs hearing the martyrs' passions read.

Equally important was Augustine's theory about the three kinds of vision. In his *Literal Commentary on Genesis*, Augustine explained them as follows: one kind of vision occurs through the eyes, by which the soul perceives corporeal objects by means of the body; the second kind of vision occurs in the imagination, where the soul sees likenesses of corporeal things that are absent; in the third kind, vision occurs "through an intuition of the mind," where "the soul understands those realities that are neither bodies nor the likenesses of bodies."[34] Further, the three kinds of vision—corporeal, pictomorphic, and conceptual—are mutually implicated and hierarchically ordered. Corporeal vision supplies the impressions that the imaginative part of the soul uses to create signs, those "images and likenesses of things," some of which "demand an intuition of the mind to be understood."[35] In Augustine's ordering of these kinds of vision, "imaginal vision is more excellent than corporeal, and intellectual vision more excellent than imaginal."[36]

The following extended passage, in which Augustine gave a differentiated sense of his notion of the imagination, is crucial for understanding the "mental theater" that he connected with the veneration of martyrs and their relics.

For it is not the body that perceives, but the soul by means of the body; and the soul uses the body as a sort of messenger in order to form within itself the object that is called to its attention from the outside world. Hence corporeal vision cannot take place unless there is a concomitant imaginal vision; but no distinction is made between the two until the bodily sensation has passed and the object perceived by means of the body is found in the imagination. On the other hand, there can be imaginal vision without corporeal vision, namely, when the likenesses of absent bodies appear in the imagination, and when many such images are fashioned by the free activity of the soul or are presented to it in spite of itself. Moreover, imaginal vision needs intellectual vision if a judgment is to be made upon its contents, but intellectual vision does not need imaginal, which is of a lower order.[37]

The first feature of this passage to note is that two kinds of images can be present in the imagination; elsewhere, Augustine had specified these as the "true image" (*phantasia*), one that represents a corporeal object seen and stored in the memory, and the "fictitious image" (*phantasma*), one that is "fashioned by the power of thought."[38] In the commentary on Genesis, he gave as examples his mental image of Carthage, a place that he had seen, and of Alexandria, which he had only heard described.[39]

This understanding of the fictitious image, one that does not correspond to an object actually seen but stems sheerly from the soul's activity, constitutes the psychological underpinning of the rhetorical exercise of *enargeia*, in which absent (and sometimes nonexistent) objects were vividly conjured up in the hearer's mind.[40] And it also functions as a theoretical explanation for Augustine's promotion of the experience of martyrs' stories as spiritual theater, since those stories in the inner eye were surely "imaginal visions without corporeal vision" in which "likenesses of absent bodies" enacted their dramas.[41] These phantasmal performances brought the dead alive, making the invisible visible.

The other feature of the passage above that deserves attention is Augustine's statement that "imaginal vision needs intellectual vision if a judgment is to be made upon its contents." For it was not enough, in his view, to construct these visual tableaus as ends in themselves; judgment was called for. As Augustine explained elsewhere, when one reads or listens to what the apostle Paul wrote or to what Christ said or did, it is natural to fashion an image of that person in the mind. Furthermore, it makes no difference whether the image is true to reality or not; what matters is that "it is useful for some other purpose"—knowledge.[42] In his words, "But for our faith in the Lord Jesus Christ, it is not the image which the mind forms for itself [to use for thinking] (which may perhaps be far different from what he actually looked like) that leads us to salvation, but, according to our mental representations, what [sorts of thoughts we have] about his humankind [*quod secundum speciem de homine cogitamus*]."[43] What matters, in others words, is the process of conceptualization and religious judgment that accompanies such imaging.

The same need for conceptual knowledge and judgment can be seen in Augustine's position on constructing visual tableaus of martyrs. Their function as vehicles of moral reform and transformation has already been noted. But there is one more conceptual aspect of this mental picturing, which is the belief in the presence and power of saints in their relics, and it is in this context that Augustine's frequent preaching in the very presence of relics is significant. At a *memoria* dedicated to the martyrs Protasius and Gervasius, Augustine remarked, "[the martyrs] have asserted Christ's cause more effectively when dead than when they were alive. They assert it today, they preach him today."[44] Similarly, at the dedication of the shrine containing relics of Saint Stephen in Hippo Regius, he remarked, "His body lay hidden such a long time, it came to light when God willed, it shed its light on many lands, worked many miracles. Being dead, he brings the dead to life, because he isn't in fact dead."[45] Defining relics as "lifeless flesh adorned with such a powerful mark of divinity" (*caro exanimis tanto effectu divinitatis ornatur*), Augustine thought that they "bore witness to the truth that what dies does not perish."[46]

The kinds of judgment and conceptualization called for in the cult of relics thus entailed an understanding of the spiritual power of material objects like relics: they work miracles and they are active presences, testifying to Christian truth "today." And those spiritually charged objects also provide knowledge about such central Christian concepts as resurrection and the life of the soul with Christist.[47] In the spiritual theater of the mind that Augustine created for martyrs, pictomorphic vision was crucial, but the form of storytelling knowledge that it produced was not spectacle for its own sake. Rather, it was a vehicle for the kinds of ethical judgment and conceptual understanding of central Christian beliefs that underlay the cult of martyrs and their relics.[48] Thus the imaginal seeing of phantasmal martyrs-in-action played an important role in Augustine's understanding of Christian education, especially with regard to relics: what one really feels when one looks at the martyr with the eyes of faith is love "for his total and invisible beauty."[49]

Prudentius and Spiritual Landscapes

Referring to Prudentius's narrative poetry about martyrs in his *Liber Peristephanon* as both a "spiritual art" and a "spiritual exercise," Jacques Fontaine noted that this poetry was also full of "sensuous riches." He emphasized "the power of the visual imagination" at work in the poems—an "alliance of the horrible and the graceful" that combines richly varied descriptions of place with gruesomely detailed descriptions of torture, suffering, and death.[50] Like Augustine, Prudentius used a technique of visualization in order to make the martyrs present in the reader's eye.[51] Also like Augustine, he associated martyrdom with spiritual combat and, as Michael Roberts has pointed out, with the "conquest of sin and temptation in the everyday experience of the individual Christian"; further, he sometimes "emphasized that the emotional force of veneration at a martyr's shrine depends on sympathetic identification between devotee and saint," as Augustine had as well.[52]

Prudentius's distinctive contribution to the notion of martyrs' narratives as mental spectacles was his presentation of the poems as pilgrimages to physical landscapes that are also spiritual landscapes.[53] If the presence of the saints at the sites of their relics is palpable in Prudentius's text, it is due in part to the fact that, unlike Augustine, he made the martyrs' power of intercession a major theme of his narratives. Augustine also believed that the martyrs' souls, already with Christ in heaven, interceded for the faithful, especially by their prayers, and he mentioned intercession in his sermons on the martyrs.[54] But the motif of imitation of the saintly martyrs is much more prominent in the sermons, and in any case he was more cautious on the topic of intercession than Prudentius was, declaring that he couldn't say for sure exactly how it happened.[55] Prudentius, however, had no such scruples or doubts; again and again, he referred to martyrs as advocates who not only hear prayers but immediately take them to the ear of Christ.[56] The physical place of the tomb is the site of spiritual conversations.

Palpable presence is also conveyed by Prudentius's gritty, physical descriptions of the martyrs' combat and triumph, which are much longer than any of Augustine's evocations of martyrs' stories. These descriptions give his text a gripping realism: his poems situate the reader or hearer in a place "where blood is spilled, teeth and bones are shattered, and bodily parts are cut off with abandon."[57] This is of course *figural* realism, since Prudentius interwove myth with legends of the martyrs, and in any case much of his material cannot be verified historically; as one interpreter has wryly noted, "Prudence n'est pas un historien, c'est un poète."[58] As his poetic evocations of martyrs' stories unfold, the reader is taken on a journey that seems not only grippingly real, but often surreal, and it is in those moments that the physical landscape becomes a spiritual one.

Prudentius needed surreal imagery in order to make "visible" the nexus of physical with spiritual reality because intercession is a theological idea; it cannot be "seen," but it can be invoked by using imagery that encourages identification with the figure through whom that power is thought to flow.[59] In one sense, the devotee as presented by Prudentius was more passive than Augustine's, since Augustine encouraged active cultivation of virtue and ethical transformation when he recommended imitation of the martyrs, whereas Prudentius emphasized the stance of the devotee as petitioner, as one in need of forgiveness and succor. From that perspective, seeing was not doing but rather being acted upon. In another sense, however, Prudentius's devotee (including especially the poet himself) was *more* active than Augustine's venerator, since Prudentius emphasized the coincidence of physical with spiritual sight and often envisioned the devotee as actively engaged in ritual performance at the site of the martyrs' relics. Whereas Augustine emphasized the *inner* eye at the expense of corporeal vision, Prudentius, like Chrysostom, thought that the visual surround in a martyrium was an important stimulus for the process of visionary storytelling.

In order to animate the dead, Prudentius wrote mini-dramas of cruelty and pain that act directly on the readers' physical and emotional sensibilities, inducing an empathic response that opens the devotee to the martyr's passion and spiritual power. One of the most striking examples is his depiction of the martyr Cassian. As a character in his own text, Prudentius positions himself in the ritual act of prostration at Cassian's tomb. Weeping and reflecting on his sins, he looks up and sees a painting of Cassian's martyrdom, a particularly gruesome one in which the students of Cassian, a teacher, prick him all over with their pointed *styli* once he has been exposed as a Christian, and he bleeds to death. In this word-picture, Prudentius lingered, as was his wont, on the details of torture, making them seem so real that the reader cannot help but imagine it in a visceral way: "Some hurl their writing tablets at him, and they shatter against his face, and flying wooden splinters pierce his forehead. Loudly the wax-covered boxwood breaks on his cheeks all bloodied, and from the blow the page is wet with red ink."[60] Emotion is not lacking either, as Prudentius pictured himself as not only weeping but also embracing and kissing the tomb so that it became warm from his physical contact with it.[61]

The surreal moment of conjunction between physical and spiritual seeing occurs in the final line of this passage, in which the students' assault produces a "page wet with red ink."[62] Is Prudentius describing Cassian's body as a page, or is the blood-soaked page his own text? Given Prudentius's tendency to equate wounds with words, as well as his intensification of "the artistic convention of equating a martyr with a written text,"[63] the answer to the question would seem to be: both. As poet, Prudentius wrote with the martyr's blood, and he also identified with the martyr's wounds, since he referred to his own "mental wounds" (*mea vulnera*) and "pinpricks of sufferings" (*dolorum acumina*) that had brought him to Cassian's tomb in the first place.[64] Furthermore, identification brings intercession. As Jill Ross has argued, "It is not enough that the martyrs' bodies bear redemptive wounds, since what is required is a participation in their suffering made possible by the transformation of their bodies into texts. To share actively in their martyrdom one must read the marks on their bodies before salvation can be conferred."[65] And "salvation" does occur in this text: having surveyed (*percenseo*) all of his hidden anxieties—a mental narrative drama analogous to the one he wrote about Cassian—Prudentius was heard, and his pilgrimage to Rome was a success.[66]

The process of identifying with the martyr was Prudentius's version of Chrysostom's experience of a vision of the dead entering the soul of the venerator. Perhaps the most pointed example of this process is in his account of the martyr Romanus. When brought to trial because of his profession of the Christian faith, Romanus delivered a long anti-pagan diatribe. Irked by this, the judge ordered that Romanus's tongue be cut out; surreally, he continued to speak ("a tongue has never failed the man who speaks of Christ") until he was finally killed.[67] Exploiting the double meaning of *lingua* as both tongue and language, Prudentius makes it clear that the martyr's "tongue" is also *his* tongue. He opens the poem on Romanus by petitioning the martyr to make his "silent tongue vibrate" within his own mouth; calling himself "mute," Prudentius then says, "I stammer out my halting words with feeble tongue . . . but if you [Romanus] will sprinkle heavenly dew on my heart, my grating voice will then breathe sweet harmonies."[68] A few verses later, Prudentius writes, "I myself am mute, but Christ, with powerful eloquence, will be my tongue" and will enable him to speak clearly.[69] Not only are poet and martyr linked through the tongue, but the poet's language—his text—is divinely inspired. These surreal linkages, which are physical and spiritual at once, are surely an "alliance of the horrible and the graceful," but they also demonstrate how Prudentius's visualizing of the invisible depends upon identification with the martyr, such that temporal distinctions between the martyr's past and the venerator's present are annulled.[70]

This simultaneity of saintly and human experience also characterizes the way in which Prudentius as author converts a physical into a spiritual landscape. As Malamud has observed, Prudentius's poems "tend to progress by a series of dislocations, jumps that move the characters and the reader from one order of experience to another."[71] Just as identification with the martyr by a living person collapses temporal distinctions, so also the placement of martyrs both on earth as relics and in heaven as souls collapses spatial distinctions.[72] Prudentius, however, took the convention of the martyrs' simultaneous presence in two spatial realms a step further when he artfully depicted the transformation of physical into spiritual landscape while the martyrs are still alive, thus moving the reader's gaze from the drama of torment to its underlying theological significance, that is, from one order of experience (empathic response to pain) to another (conceptual knowledge of salvation).

In the story of the martyr Eulalia of Merida, for example, Prudentius depicted her nocturnal escape from her protective mother as she ran for miles to the magistrate's court in order to testify for the faith.[73] As the reader follows her "circuitous course over thorn bushes that lacerate her feet," the scene changes eerily as Prudentius notes the choir of angels that accompany her and the guide that lights her path, a reference that points forward to the path that her soul will take after her death, "winging its way to celestial heights."[74] This overlay of a spiritual journey on a physical one becomes even eerier as Prudentius abruptly compares the light that guides Eulalia with the pillar of light that guided the Israelites out of Egypt.[75] As the Israelites fled from Egypt to freedom in the promised land, so Eulalia's journey through Merida/Egypt will gain her freedom, too, since, as Roberts remarks, Prudentius describes her "both as fleeing from Egypt and on her way to heaven."[76] The physical landscape of Merida has become a spiritual landscape of religious liberation and salvation. In a manner analogous to Augustine's use of mental theater to provoke conceptual knowledge about such Christian doctrines as resurrection, Prudentius elided physical with spiritual landscapes to teach his readers about the theology underlying martyrs' journeys.

By animating the martyrs in his mini-dramas, Prudentius not only made them and their spiritual power visible, but he also gave another kind of "invisibility," the conceptual grasp of Christian truths, tangible expression. A final example from the *Peristephanon* will show how he accomplished these forms of animation by converting physical into spiritual location. In Prudentius's story of Vincent, the martyr refuses to worship pagan gods and lectures his pagan foe Datian about the stupidity of his beliefs; when torture proves to be to no avail, Datian throws Vincent into prison, described as a pit "blacker than darkness itself," which immediately becomes an image of hell ("this terrible prison, it is said, had an underworld [*inferos*] of its own").[77] As Roberts notes, "physical reality is here dematerialized into spiritual 'landscape'" as Vincent's story becomes one with Christ's descent into hell.[78]

But that downward journey is not the end of this overlay of the physical by the spiritual. Next, the saint's feet are put in stocks, and his tormentor also orders that the floor of the prison be strewn with sharp, jagged pieces of broken pots. As Vincent lies there in torment, the dark cell begins to glow and, as the stocks that bind his legs spring open, he realizes that "Christ, the giver of light," is present.[79] Immediately Vincent sees that the pieces of broken pots have been covered with "tender flowers" that are redolent of nectar, and angels surround him, inviting him to join their company.[80] Hell has become Paradise; Prudentius here draws on the conventional depiction of Paradise as a flowery *locus amoenus* in order to make visible the spiritual landscape that has merged with Vincent's physical prison.[81] In the surreal moment when the jagged potsherds—instruments of torture—begin to bloom with delicate flowers, the full significance of the spiritual landscape is realized: like Christ, Vincent will ascend to heaven. What the reader finally "sees," then, is not only the martyr's literal drama but also a paradigm of Christian redemption.

Unlike Augustine, Prudentius did not draw on images of theatrical spectacles in order to visualize the invisible (though the martyrial bodies that he conjured up were no less "spectacular" than those of Augustine). Instead, he employed a rhetoric that depended upon images of the human body in pain.[82] As Malamud has pointed out, however, those images of "dissolution, amputation, and dismemberment are offset by more positive images of liberation and freedom."[83] A rhetoric of gore yields to a rhetoric of liberation.[84] By giving the martyrs' stories detailed narrative life, and by undercutting the surface realism of the narratives with surreal images of spiritual intrusion into human life, Prudentius gave visual immediacy not only to a dead person's life but also to the religious ideas that gave that life meaning.

Two ideas are particularly prominent in his poems: first, that martyrs' lives and deaths embody the Christian belief in resurrection, and second, that because of their triumph, martyrs' remains are conduits of spiritual power, especially intercession for the forgiveness of human sinfulness. Resurrection and intercession are ideas, and one cannot "see" ideas, but powerful rhetoric such as Prudentius's gives them a presence that seems palpable. Finally, it is significant that Prudentius chose the framing device of pilgrimage to relic-shrines for his poems. As Georgia Frank has pointed out, "the journey remains an enduring metaphor for the spiritual life."[85] Prudentius's own physical pilgrimage was also a spiritual journey; this is clear from the endings of so many of his poems, in which he cries out for forgiveness, grace, and redemption. His own journey, that is, replicates the conflating of physical with spiritual planes of reality that marks the stories of the martyrs that he wrote about. For the "armchair pilgrims" who heard or read his narratives, the poems provided a double vision of the spiritual life.[86]

Victricius and Metaphors of Light

As noted in Chapter 1, Victricius was, like Augustine and Prudentius, an enthusiast of the cult of relics.[87] When, late in the fourth century, he received relics sent by Ambrose of Milan as a gift for his church in Rouen, he preached a sermon, *De laude sanctorum*, which offered a sustained theoretical explanation of relics.[88] With Victricius, one does not have to infer the means by which a material object like a relic—a dead body part—can be a conduit of spiritual power; his theological reasoning is overt.

Basically, the concern that underlay Victricius's view of relics was one that lay at the core of late ancient Christian asceticism: how can the human body be a locus of sanctity? More particularly, Victricius was interested in articulating the very nature of the sanctity of the body parts that were relics by showing how the spirit of the martyrs and even divinity itself were present in them.[89] The bulk of Victricius's treatise is thus devoted to two issues: the fullness of divine power in relics, and the wholeness of those fragments, that is, the idea that the saint's power is completely present in every corporeal bit. He argued that, "if God, the author of all things, put together this spiritual vessel and members out of nothing, why could he not convert an animate body [*animatum corpus*], formed (so to speak) by the leaven of blood, into the substance of his light [*ad sui luminis transferre substantiam*]?"[90] Victricius went much further than did either Augustine or Prudentius in developing a "radically incarnational" understanding of relics that viewed them not simply as conduits of divine power, but as virtually identical with that power.[91]

To the issue of the fullness of divine power in relics, Victricius based his reasoning on the premise that all human beings share the same corporeal nature; further, Christians, by virtue of the sacrament of baptism, are also one "body" spiritually: "for those who live in Christ and the church there is one substance of flesh and blood and spirit, by the gift of adoption." Finally, martyrs, who have imitated Christ's passion and so have a closer bond, "are entirely with the Savior in his entirety. For those who have nothing that differs in their profession [of faith] have everything in common in the truth of the godhead."[92] This union between martyrs and the godhead is physical as well as spiritual. Victricius argued, using human blood as the essence of corporeality, that "blood, after martyrdom, is on fire with the reward of divinity."[93] As Gillian Clark has succinctly remarked, "God, being complete and perfect, cannot somehow have saints added on: so after martyrdom the saints (flesh, blood, and spirit) are wholly united with divinity."[94]

The solution to the second issue—the complete presence of martyrs in the fragments of their "dead" bodies—follows logically from this view of the ontological union between martyrs and God (even if that union is "by adoption, not by nature").[95] If the martyrs are united with God, and God cannot be divided, therefore neither can the martyrs: the whole is completely present in the part. As Victricius expressed it, "the truth of the whole corporeal passion is present in fragments of the righteous."[96] Not only the bodies of the martyrs, but also their spirits, have "taken on the fiery heat of the word"; thus "there is nothing in relics which is not complete."[97] With abstract arguments such as these, Victricius did not really make the invisible visible so much as explain how the spirit could in principle be material; relics, the "first fruits of the resurrection," had breached the boundary between heaven and earth in a way that no mental spectacle ever could.[98]

Yet even Victricius, for all his heady theological conviction that divine spirit was materialized before his very eyes, felt the need to retrain—and restrain—the vision of his audience. At one point in his sermon, he contrasts the "confusion of the eyes" with the clearer "vision of reason":

If we said that relics were divided from the spirit, we would be right to look for all the connection and solidity of body parts. But when we realize that the substance is united, it follows that we are searching for the whole in the whole. . . . This confusion is of the eyes: the vision of reason is clearer. We see small relics and a little blood. But truth perceives that these tiny things are brighter than the sun, for the Lord says in the gospel, "My saints shall shine like the sun in the kingdom of the Father" [Matt. 13.43].[99]

In this passage, Victricius seems to be suggesting that, as material objects, relics are more ambiguously corporeal that he has argued elsewhere. The literal gaze wants to see the connection and solidity; perhaps it even wants to see a whole body, not realizing the truth of the argument about the whole inhering in the part (which is also a whole!).[100] The point is that relics are precisely *spiritual* objects, and as such, to look at or touch them requires, so Victricius will argue, a metaphorical sensibility.[101] Only thus could he preserve the necessary ambiguity of his ontology of relics, and only thus could he be as faithful to the matter of the relic as to its spirit. ,

In the passage just quoted, Victricius has risked dissolving the materiality of relics in the brilliance of their spiritual power. These "animate substances" are not, after all, so easy to "see." Just prior to his comment about the "confusion of the eyes," Victricius had used a semiotic argument to help his audience apprehend the meaning of relics properly: "Why, then, do we call them 'relics'? Because words are images and signs of things. Before our eyes are blood and clay. We impress on them the name of 'relics' because we cannot do otherwise, with (so to speak) the seal of living language. But now, by uttering the whole in the part, we open the eyes of the heart, not the barriers of our bodily sight."[102] Victricius has contrasted two kinds of eyes, much as Augustine had, and even though he saw "more" with the eyes of faith than did Augustine, he agreed that "seeing" relics demanded an imaginative approach.[103] His distinctive version of mental spectacle, in contrast with those of Chrysostom and Augustine, did not use the rhetoric of contemporary theater; rather, his images for relics depended upon the widespread late ancient rhetorical convention that evoked the holy by using metaphors of light, color, and jewels.[104]

Like others who wrote to create a meaningful ambiance in which relics could signify holiness, Victricius relied in part upon an aesthetics of light and brilliance in order to induce a "seeing" of relics that would not confuse the eyes.[105] In order to make spiritual sense of the sight of body fragments—that is to say, in order to evoke the whole in the part—he needed a metaphor that was powerful enough to rival an actual body. He found it in the metaphor of light, which appears in a variety of guises in his sermon: as the radiance of fire, the brightness of the sun, and the sparkle of jewels. Here the Christian taste for brilliance in the arts assumed literary form, and Victricius utilized this rhetorical dazzle in order to picture what his theological abstractions could not picture, a fusion of matter and spirit, an animate body converted into the substance of God's light.[106]

Perhaps because he thought of the saints and their relics as "renowned celestial powers," Victricius used the metaphor of the sun and heavenly light to depict their spiritual force.[107] Remarking twice that martyrs and relics are "brighter than the sun," he found a forceful metaphor to capture their immaterial materiality (for to look at the sun is blinding, not to mention something even brighter than the sun) and also to depict their presence in the Christian community: "heavenly brilliance is not cheated out of any place on earth," and "before the day of judgment the radiance of the righteous pours into all basilicas, all churches, the hearts of the faithful."[108] In the late ancient Christian imagination, gold, the color of the sun, had an ethical import. Gold was the most splendid form of heavenly light materialized, and when ancient viewers looked at gold, they saw the radiance of divine goodness.[109] In Victricius's literary appropriation of sunlight as a metaphor for relics, there is a distinctive ethics, and it is akin to that of Prudentius's sense of identity with martyrs and with Chrysostom's notion of being invaded by visions of the dead. For Victricius, the heart of the venerator is flooded by the radiance of the righteous.

The ethical significance of light is elsewhere overt in the sermon. Having connected the martyrs and their relics with light again and again, Victricius wrote, "sins are darkness, innocent is light."[110] Further, referring to the blazing quality of the sun, he imagined relics as having "fiery rays of light in themselves,"[111] and by that light the martyrs teach ascetic virtues to their venerators: "See, the righteous show us the path of truth, as if they carried before us the light of their relics. They teach reverence, faith, wisdom, righteousness, courage, concord, self-control, chastity, while in our besieged bodies they punish that which is opposed to these and remove the stains of vice."[112] Because their very blood is "mixed with supernal fire" and because they have "taken on the fiery heat of the Word," relics are divine pedagogues.[113] Victricius's fiery metaphors gave pictorial force to the moral understanding of brightness that he developed in passages such as this.

Finally, there are the metaphors of jewels, which convey straightforwardly the specifically ascetic form of conduct with which the veneration of relics was associated in Victricius's view. Although Augustine certainly encouraged his audiences to imitate the virtues of the martyrs, he did not make as close a connection as Victricius did with veneration of relics and a stringent form of ascetic practice. As David Hunter has pointed out, in late fourth-century Gaul "it was the advocates of ascetic renunciation who seem to have been most zealous in propagating the cult of the apostles and martyrs," and with it the cult of their relics.[114] Victricius first mentioned jewels precisely in the context of the participation of ascetic Christians in the veneration of relics. Early on in his treatise, he used imagery drawn from the imperial *adventus* to picture the entry into Rouen of the relics sent by Ambrose.[115] He described the crowd almost completely in terms of various kinds of renunciation: "throngs of monks refined by fasting," a "chorus of devout and untouched virgins," "multitudes of celibates and widows," and married women who have "condemned intercourse."[116]

After introducing this chaste group and noting that, unlike the crowd at an imperial *adventus*, none of them wears clothing marked with purple or jewelry, he then concentrates on envisioning the procession of the women: "These women advance resplendent, radiant with the intoxication of chastity. They advance decked with divine gifts as ornaments. Their breasts are filled with the riches of psalms. There is no night of vigils in which this jewel does not gleam."[117] In this passage, literal jewels have become metaphors for the spiritual gifts that are the prized possession of ascetics. Furthermore, these women have even taken on a bit of the light of relics, "radiant" as they are in their embrace of chastity. Victricius's description of their piety as a gleaming jewel is a rhetorical flourish, to be sure, but it gives visual immediacy to the ethical import of both asceticism and the veneration of relics.

There is more to the metaphor of jewels than evoking piety, however. Early on in the sermon, Victricius had called the martyrs "dwellers in our hearts" (*habitatores pectoris nostri*).[118] Toward the end, he returned to the close connection between relic-venerators and martyrs, this time drawing on imperial *adventus*-imagery in order to describe the martyrs rather than participants in their cult:

In place of the royal cloak, here is the garment of eternal light. The togas of the saints have absorbed this purple. Here are diadems adorned with the varied lights of the jewels of wisdom, intellect, knowledge, truth, good counsel, courage, endurance, self-control, justice, good sense, patience, chastity. These virtues are expressed and inscribed each in its own stone. Here the Savior-craftsman has adorned the crowns of the martyrs with spiritual jewels. Let us set the sails of our souls towards these gems.[119]

Here Victricius repeats the connection between martyrs and the virtues made earlier in the sermon. This time, however, the virtues are pictured as "spiritual jewels" in the martyrs' crowns. This second use of the metaphor of the jewel connects martyrs directly with the "radiant" ascetic women, ornamented with spiritual blessing, whose piety is a jewel that gleams. Through this metaphorical connection, it would seem that ascetics, too, are martyrs. In a manner analogous to Prudentius's version of identifying with martyrs by assimilating their attributes to his endeavors as poet (the "page wet with blood" as Cassian's body/text and Romanus's tongue/language), Victricius has at least implied a kind of identity by his use of the metaphor of the spiritual jewel.

Of course the identity is not complete; martyrs may dwell in our hearts, but they are also those gems *toward* which our souls travel. And living ascetic "martyrs" are not relics, however radiant with virtue they may be. The light that flashes from the relics is blinding and induces another kind of seeing that is of the heart, not the literal eyes. By consistently interpreting relics with metaphors of light-in-action—gleaming, shining brilliantly, sending out fiery rays—Victricius endowed them with a scintillating energy that his abstract theology about their divinity could point to but not embody. Victricius's theological construction of relics as ambiguously corporeal—as both immaterially material and materially immaterial—did indeed make them difficult to visualize. He needed metaphor, and he developed an aesthetics of relics that was no less a spectacle, an appeal to the inner eye, than those of his relic-minded companions Augustine and Prudentius.

Visual Desperation?

The literature that arose in the late fourth and early fifth centuries in the context of the cult of the martyrs and their relics was a literature characterized by bold imagination. Driven by a persistent and heartfelt urge to explain how a fragment of a dead body could be a conduit of spiritual presence, all three of the authors discussed in this chapter relied on imagery to make the invisible visible. Although their images were different—Augustine's spiritual theater of the mind, Prudentius's spiritual landscapes, Victricius's metaphors of light—their writings imply a conviction that a relic needed aesthetic enhancement in order to signify. Whether that enhancement was in the form of mental acting-out of the martyr's drama, as in the case of Augustine, or storytelling, as in the case of Prudentius, or the glossing of theological argument with rhetorical dazzle, as in the case of Victricius, all three authors were engaged in the delicate and difficult task of integrating a fairly new form of spirituality into Christian ritual and ethics.

Seeing the invisible as though it were visible involved different kinds of invisibility. On the one hand, it involved ideas. The belief that spiritual power was operative in relics, for example, was an abstract idea, something "invisible," as it were, that needed sensory expression in the form of lively mental images to make it tangible. On the other hand, the martyrs themselves were also "invisible" (even if fragments of their bodies were on display). Their valiant lives had to be re-created in such a way that their past was the venerator's present, especially when the virtues that they exemplified were at issue. Although their techniques differed, all three authors discussed here collapsed the past into the present: Augustine by modeling how to imitate a martyr, Prudentius by making the physical landscape of the martyr coincide with his own spiritual landscape, and Victricius by positioning martyrs as indwelling figures.

Invisibility, however, was not the only problem that these interpreters faced. The fact is that they were faced with developing "strategies for retrieving visually intractable forms," to borrow a phrase from art historian James Elkins.[120] Relics were "visually intractable" because they were not whole bodies; their humanness, and especially their human wholeness, was something that had to be inferred. In situations such as the cult of relics provided, when one encounters (or sees with the imagining eye) a body that is not quite a body and so cannot be easily categorized, Elkins argues that understanding "depends on finding workable analogies."[121] His name for the attempt to find workable analogies is "visual desperation": "'Visual desperation' is a name for a peculiarly strained and anxious seeing that casts about, trying to construct analogies and retrieve an unknown form into the fold of vision. When it succeeds, we complacently classify what we've seen as human, animal, plant, or fabulous beast. When it fails, we become blind—we see only chaos or trackless monstrosity."[122] To attribute a case of "visual desperation" to Augustine, Prudentius, and Victricius may seem like a rhetorical flourish on my own part, but, as Peter Brown has pointed out, anxieties about death, physical disintegration, and bodily reintegration lay close to the surface of late ancient thinking about martyrs and the cult of relics.[123] For interpreters, there was a real problem in trying to deal at once with the horror of dismemberment and the belief in restored integrity. The dramatic and forceful imagery of evocations of the meaning of relics suggests that relics were indeed fearfully odd—fragments that were no longer quite recognizable and so both like and unlike the reality of the living—and that they needed elaborate analogies in order to bring them alive. In my view, the pictorial strategies of the authors discussed in this chapter were successful resolutions of the particular form of visual desperation that pertained to the cult of relics.

Chapter Five
Ambiguous Bodies

Relics were not the only objects that became "things" when they were endowed with surplus value. And they were also not the only things that were difficult to visualize because, as noted in the previous chapter, they were ambiguously corporeal, both immaterially material and materially immaterial. Like relics, saintly bodies were corporeal objects that demanded a strong form of imagination in order to make their spirited presence intelligible in human life. Late ancient hagiographers were confronted with a problem similar to the one faced by Victricius in regard to relics, namely, how to portray the ongoing liveliness of a sainted, but dead, human being. Taking the phrase "ambiguous corporeality" seriously, this chapter explores hagiographic texts' use of sensory realism, especially in terms of sight and touch, in order to articulate how the holy could be present in the world in the form of an intangibly tangible saintly body.

As objects of the late ancient Christian hagiographical imagination, saintly bodies were subject to what I call "visceral seeing," a form of interpretation that achieved a transfigured gaze such that saintly bodies emerged in hagiographies as presences that were both ephemeral and tangible at once. As part of the new enthusiasm for the presence of the holy in everyday life, saints signaled a relation of the human subject to the sanctifying potential of human physicality as locus and mediator of spiritual presence and power. As noted in the Introduction, however, the phenomenon of the saintly body raised the issue of reifying the holy in the human. How was it possible to present human corporeality as a vehicle of transcendence without losing the mediating sense of "vehicle" and simply collapsing matter and spirit into each other? The form of imaginative visualization denoted by the phrase "visceral seeing," which produced the ambiguously corporeal bodies of the saints, was hagiography's answer to this question. Hagiography's crafting of ocular, affective images of the bodies of the saints materialized their invisible but real presence in the world in a rhetorically compelling fashion. As with aspects of the jeweled style discussed in earlier chapters, visceral seeing contributed to the sensuous intensity of the material turn precisely by joining the traditionally privileged sense of sight with other senses, especially touch: hence *visceral* seeing—the endowing of the ocular with affect.

Saint Augustine, who was no stranger to visceral seeing, will set the stage for the discussion of hagiographical images of the saints that follows. In a passage in *De doctrina christiana*, Augustine asks the reader to think of the Church as the Bride in the Song of Songs, pointing in particular to the line in which her teeth are compared to sheep. The context for his discussion of this image is his view of the greater pedagogical usefulness of figurative expressions when compared with prosaic language. He uses an explanation of the role of the saints in the church as an example. If one were to explain the role of the saints in nonfigurative language, Augustine writes, one would simply say that the church uses the exemplary lives of saints as disciplinary tools to correct improper behavior and belief. But, Augustine asks, "Why is it that if anyone says this he delights his hearers less than if he had said the same thing by expounding the passage in the Song of Songs where it is said of the church, as she is being praised as a beautiful woman, 'Thy teeth are as flocks of sheep that are shorn, which come up from the washing, all with twins, and there is none barren among them'? Does one learn anything else besides what he learns when he hears the same thought expressed in plain words without this similitude?"[1] "Nevertheless," he continues, "in a strange way, I contemplate the saints more pleasantly when I envisage them as the teeth of the church cutting off men from their errors and transferring them to her body after their hardness has been softened as if by being bitten and chewed."[2] What Augustine apparently means here is that striking images, being inherently affective, make their point more efficiently than matter-of-fact statements do.

But, however pleasant Augustine may have found it, this is a physically gruesome similitude, and its effect is surely visceral. Readers are drawn into the image by virtue of their very bodies, and are forced by the text to imagine saints as teeth in a presumably very large mouth, where the wayward are bitten, chewed, and digested into the body of the church. What interests me about such images of the body is their sheer appeal to the physical while retaining their figurative quality. This is the kind of image appropriate to the material turn in late ancient Christianity, which, as described in the Introduction, points to a shift in the late ancient religious sensibility regarding the signifying potential of the material world, a shift that reconfigured the relation between materiality and meaning in a positive direction.[3] Within this larger topic of late ancient appreciation for the role of both "things" and the material imagination, this chapter will focus on holy bodies in lives and miracles of the saints, and the term "hagiography" will be used broadly to designate written representations of holiness rather than a discrete literary genre.[4]

Visceral Seeing

The subject matter of this chapter is drawn from hagiographical texts from the late fourth through the seventh centuries that present the holy body of the saint as ambiguously corporeal, bodies, that is, whose visionary appearances are nonetheless tangible, or whose fragments are nonetheless whole.[5] Such texts, I will argue, draw much of their power from their insistence on "visceral seeing," defined by art historian James Elkins in his *Pictures of the Body* as "a peculiar kind of response to depicted bodies that puts in question the traditional distinction between viewer and viewed."[6] Extending Elkins's definition, I will also argue that "visceral seeing" includes not only the viewer's response to images of the body but also the particular kind of image that is capable of provoking such a response. Hagiographical writing about saintly bodies attests to the "intrinsic role of pictures in shaping knowledge of material substance"; hence I will entertain the view that corporeality, and material substance itself, is a medium "that is inescapably informed by the pictures we compose of it."[7] Late ancient hagiography, I will wager, formed an intriguing chapter in the history of "the inherently figurative character" of Western thinking about the material realm.[8]

First, then, visceral seeing refers to corporeal responses to word-pictures of the body, responses that implicate the reader in such a way that the boundary between text and reader begins to weaken, as the reader's reality is invaded by a surreal presence. A striking example of this weakening of the divide between text and reader is the *Ekphrasis on Saint Euphemia* by Asterius, bishop of Amaseia in Pontus.[9] Written toward the end of the fourth century, this text is a word-picture of a painting of Euphemia's martyrdom, a verbal rival, as Asterius says, of a work of art.[10] The conceit of the text is that the painting really existed, a conceit I will accept since for my purposes what matters is not the reality of the painting but the way in which Asterius, as a character in his own text, teaches the reader how to see.

Asterius credits the painting with possessing remarkable affect, the painter having "instilled feeling into his colors" so much so that the narrative scenes were "animated" (ἐμψύχους).[11] In the climactic scene of torture, men with hammers knock out the saint's teeth. Asterius comments: "From this point, I weep and the suffering cut short my discourse. For the painter had smeared drops of blood so vividly that they seem really to be trickling from her mouth."[12] For Asterius, seeing was connective and embodied: as Stephen Davis has observed, "the sight of the drops of blood trickling like tears down the martyr's face brings tears to the writer's own eyes—tears not only of sympathy, but also of mute imitation."[13] In this mimetic moment, the boundary between viewer and viewed begins to weaken. It is this kind of connective and embodied viewing that Asterius models for his reader; the holy body of Euphemia is not a passive spectacle but rather a kinetic presence. And it is not only Asterius as character whose own body is implicated by the body of the saint, tears responding and corresponding to drops of blood. At the end of his *ekphrasis*, he makes a direct appeal to the reader: "Now it is time for you, if you wish, to complete the picture (or the text: γραφή) so that you can decide with accuracy whether I have fallen short of it in my interpretation."[14] The ambiguous referent of γραφή in this direct address to the reader pulls the reader into both the text and the painting, as Asterius finally erases the boundary between viewer and viewed and involves the reader too in a kind of seeing that is performative.[15]

According to Elkins, images such as the one just considered have a cognitive function: "pictured bodies are expressive in two largely opposite modes: some act principally on the beholder's body, forcing thoughts about sensation, pain, and ultimately death; and others act more on the beholder's mind, conjuring thoughts of painless projection, transformation, and ultimately metamorphosis."[16] He admits that this binary opposition of the two modes of expression ultimately breaks down because depicted bodies are "intractable" and "escape all categories"; they are, in short, ambiguously corporeal.[17] And this kind of binary structure certainly does not pertain in the case of Christian images such as that of Euphemia, which acts both on the body, by conjuring thoughts of pain and death, and on the mind, by holding out the hope of transformation to life in another world, as Asterius explicitly says toward the end of his text.[18] The appeal of hagiographical images *both* to sense *and* to intellect was an important facet of their depictions of holy bodies.

Although my discussion focuses on the perception-transforming power of hagiographic imagery, some attention to the reader or beholder of such imagery is in order here. If hagiographic imagery had a double appeal that integrated sense and intellect, so too the one that read—or beheld or imagined such imagery—was not simply a mind thinking. Late ancient beholders such as Asterius were not committed to what would today be called Cartesian dualism. Indeed, as this exploration of hagiographic images proceeds, it will become apparent that the objects of hagiographic perception, those ambiguously corporeal saintly bodies, induced and also created a stance for the beholder to occupy, a stance in which the senses had cognitive status, and in which the intellect was materially engaged. This kind of embodied thoughtfulness was crucial to the experiential engagement of the beholder or reader with images of the saintly body.

Visceral Writing

The starkly physical and interactive qualities of depicted holy bodies became even more prominent in later hagiographical writing about the lives of saints. Along with the boom in written *vitae* celebrating their heroes' ascetic exploits in the wake of Athanasius's *Life of St. Antony*, there was, in Averil Cameron's words, "a mushrooming of collections of miracle stories" that conveyed a new sense of what counted as religious knowledge.[19] In such texts—for example, the *Life and Miracles of St. Thekla* in the mid-fifth century, the *Life of St. Symeon the Stylite the Younger* in the late sixth century, and *The Miracles of St. Artemios* in the mid-seventh century—the life of the saint, whether presented as living as in the case of Symeon or dead as in the case of Thekla and Artemios, is a prelude or preface to the explosion of the saint into action, as miracle succeeds miracle in rapid-fire, almost incantatory fashion.[20] And then, having dazzled the reader with an ancient version of overkill, the texts simply end. Whether in wonder or authorial exhaustion, the authors of these texts typically apologize for lack of completeness by saying that the saints' miracles are too numerous to recount, being like grains of sand in the sea.[21] Conventional narrative closure, however, is simply not possible in such texts because their point is not to present the reader with a complete picture of an imitable saintly life as in narratives devoted to earlier ascetic heroes; their point is rather to teach the reader how to see that everyday life is saturated with palpable saintly presence.

The visceral seeing in these texts is very powerful. Unlike such earlier saints as Macrina and Antony, who healed primarily by prayer, later saints were much more interactive physically; as Georgia Frank has pointed out, late ancient and early Byzantine Christians "cultivated a religious epistemology that combined the noblest of the senses, sight, with the most animalistic one, touch."[22] Saint Thekla, for example, is said by the anonymous author of her *Miracles* to have a piercing divine gaze; not only does her eye know no obstacles, but it is always open.[23] Ocular intensity characterizes not only Thekla herself but also a series of her miraculous cures.[24] Of particular interest in regard to the conjunction of sight and the saint's curative touch is *Mir.* 24. In this story, the saint is "present," as it were, in the form of one of the consecrated birds kept on the sanctuary grounds with which a child with an affliction of the eye has been playing. Because the child has prevented the bird from eating—or, as the text next explains, at the order of the saint herself—one of the birds, a crane, pecks at the child's diseased eye with its beak, and the eye is healed.[25]

Being in Thekla's sight can be painful, for, as in the case of the crane's pecking, her miraculously curative touch is often violent. One such miracle is as follows: an artisan who worked in marble was standing on a scaffold putting slabs on the upper portion of a wall when the scaffold collapsed, causing an injury to his leg so severe that he couldn't walk; having been taken to Thekla's church, the man was asleep when the saint approached and, saying nothing and indeed not even showing herself, she stomped on the foot of his injured leg, causing him such pain that he leaped up—and was cured.[26]

Here the saint's body, invisible but quite physical nonetheless, touches both the man in the story and the reader, for who could read this story without a visceral response, empathically sharing the injured man's pain? The image acts on the body but also on the mind, since the pain is a moment of cognition, a realization that transformation is possible. The visual and tactile immediacy of this kind of image—not to mention its sensory realism—is one way in which hagiographical writing addressed the issue of saintly materiality through the aesthetic medium of the visceral imagination.

The violent but curative touch as well as an emphasis on seeing are even more prominent in the later *Miracles of St. Artemios.*[27] The relics of Saint Artemios were preserved in the Church of St. John the Forerunner in Constantinople; like Saint Thekla's compound in Seleucia, this church was a healing center where incubation was practiced, and it was there that Artemios made his appearances although, again like Thekla, Artemios sometimes appeared in dreams, and sometimes as, so to speak, himself.[28] As a healer, Thekla was a general practitioner, curing different kinds of ailments, but Artemios was a specialist, focusing primarily on hernias of the testicles and other genital diseases. Many of his miracles follow a formulaic narrative pattern: an afflicted man joins other incubants in the church; Artemios appears to him and asks what the problem is; when told, Artemios says, "Let me see," whereupon, as the narrative continues, the man undresses and the saint touches his testicles and sometimes gives them a hard squeeze. Yelping with pain, the patient examines himself, finds that he is healed, and often shows his healed body to others gathered in the sanctuary.[29] This is visceral seeing at its most intense, not only because of the image's sensate effect on the reader but also because the saint's gaze invites the reader's eye to look at body parts that would normally be taboo. The affective quality of this image, especially when it is repeated over and over again, not only brings materiality and meaning very close together, it also demonstrates the close alignment of insistent physicality and equally insistent looking that characterized late ancient constructions of the holy body.

Artemios is often presented as a trickster, and this may be part of the teasing voyeurism that is present in so many of his miracles and even—despite the pain—gives them a rather comical tone.[30] Other hagiographies, however, also feature anecdotes in which the voyeuristic gaze is prominent, and I want to pause for a moment to consider what role this kind of gaze played in animating the "matter," so to speak, of the holy body.

The Ocular Imagination

A stock motif in the late ancient literature that grew up around the figure of the transvestite saint, that is, a woman disguised as a male monk, was the discovery of her true identity as female after her death.[31] In anecdotes from the *Apophthegmata patrum*, dated roughly from the fourth through the sixth centuries, as well as in John Moschus's *Spiritual Meadow* of the late sixth or early seventh century, the narration of this discovery is quite spare: male monks come upon a dead brother, prepare the body for burial, discover that "he" is really "she," praise God, and bury her.[32]

In full-blown *vitae* of such saints from the sixth and seventh centuries, however, the motif of looking at the woman's naked body became more prominent. In the *Life of St. Pelagia of Antioch*, the monks who discover that the dead Pelagius is really Pelagia try to keep it a secret but are prevented from doing so by "crowds of people thronging around," who presumably have looked at her.[33] In the *Life of Mary Who Changed Her Name to Marinos*, this scene of the gaze is repeated three times: first, when his fellow monks find that Marinos has died, they prepare his body for burial and discover the truth: "shrieking, they all began to cry out in a single voice, 'Lord, have mercy'"; next they report to their superior that "Brother Marinos is a woman," and *he* goes to see for himself; finally, the superior goes to the innkeeper whose daughter had accused Marinos of seducing her, and *he* looks as well.[34] A final example of insistent and voyeuristic looking from the transvestite literature is about a living woman rather than a dead one: in the *Life of Eugenia*, the heroine converts to the ascetic life, renames herself Eugenius, and is given the gift of healing; when Eugenius is falsely accused of seduction by a woman whom he had healed, he and his fellow monks are arrested and taken to court where they are "made to stand up in the sight of all the people" of Alexandria. In defense of herself and her monastic community, Eugenia theatrically rips open her clothing "from the top as far as her girdle," exposing her bare breasts and thus, of course, her female identity.[35]

This motif of exposure and mass looking at women's bodies was not limited to literature about transvestite saints. In the *Life of St. Symeon the Stylite the Younger*, for example, a group of women approaches the saint because they are unable to lactate. The saint touches their breasts and smears them with his saliva, and immediately their milk begins to flow. Then the saint orders the women "to squeeze their breasts in front of all the people"—and no milk comes out. Next, "he prayed over them, and seizing their breasts with his own hand, he squeezed them, and with the milk that flowed out he sprinkled the eyes of the spectators."[36] This is quite an elaborate performance, but no different in its specular display from the stories about Artemios's exposure of men's bodies. And, I would add, this anecdote is quite overt in its appeal to the transformed eye, anointed as it is with the physical results of saintly power.

On the evidence of such images, one certainly cannot accuse late ancient Christians of losing the body in a haze of abstractions. Like the images involving touch and pain discussed above, these voyeuristic scenes of manifest realism bridge the divide between reader and text. Further, the ocular and affective qualities of these images are appeals to the sensory imagination of the reader, and their visual and emotional intensity aid in naturalizing the fictive—because textual—world of which they are a part.[37] They are figuratively real—that is, they are narrative pictorial strategies that seduce the reader into forgetting that these are images in texts. Further, the visceral poetics of the body in these hagiographies aids in changing habituated modes of perception so that the transfigured eye needed to "see" the saints can be realized.

Discourse, Materiality, and Meaning

This kind of hagiographical writing is an example of what Judith Butler has called "performativity," defined as "the power of discourse to materialize its effects."[38] What is materialized in this discourse, that is, what is objectified and made tangible, and what we as readers are being exhorted to see in the strongest possible form, is a belief system based on the view that spiritual beings are corporeally present in human life, and that the human body is a locus of spirituality. These are not simple pictures. Rather, they are plausible visions that shape human behavior, most notably here in terms of the role of the senses in apprehending spiritual reality. Sensory form and vision go together, as do visual experience and interpretation.[39]

The material orientation of the spiritualizing and ascetic culture of late ancient Christianity has been well noted in recent patristic scholarship, particularly in terms of the growing importance, from the fourth century onward, of the holiness of place and the practice of pilgrimage, of sensuous ritual and expressive art, and of course in terms of the presence of the divine in the living bodies of holy men and also in their relics.[40] At just the moment when the Christian body had been so rigorously disciplined by ascetic discourses of several kinds—treatises on virginity, sermons on chaste love between spouses, the promotion of desert asceticism as an ideal, and so on—at just this moment the religious importance of materiality became a prominent feature of both discourse and practice, as did a new emphasis on sensuous apprehension. There was more involved in this process than a Freudian return of the repressed body as sign, given, on the one hand, the material objectification of the saints' presence in relics and amulets, and on the other, the theatricalization of the saints' physical interaction with ordinary human beings as discussed above. These bodies are not simply signs or symbols, and their depiction as corporeally real points to what I see as one of the urgent issues in late ancient Christian thought and practice, namely, to determine the means to articulate how the holy could be present in the contingent order nonidolatrously.[41]

The problem of idolatry, understood as investing the material realm with too much meaning, dogged the cult of relics from early on. In part this was due to the fact that it was the specifically physical aspect of the martyrs' endurance of suffering that was highlighted as a mark of divinity working through them, and later through their body parts.[42] The notion of relics as spiritual objects was trenchantly criticized in the late fourth century by the Gallic churchman Vigilantius, and Augustine also suspected that relics were eliciting worship rather than veneration.[43] Optatus of Milevis, reporting about a certain Lucilla's habit of kissing a martyr's bone before taking the Eucharist, remarked disparagingly that "she preferred to the saving cup the bone of some dead man."[44]

And it is true that enthusiasts of the cult could go a bit far in their willingness to endow relics with a touch of transcendence. Basil of Caesarea, for example, thought that "grace" was present in relics, while Cyril of Jerusalem believed that the "power" that resided in relics was what remained of the just soul that once inhabited the saint's body.[45] Most striking of all, as we have seen, were the ontological claims made on behalf of relics by Victricius of Rouen, a contemporary of Vigilantius in Gaul, in his sermon, *De laude sanctorum*.[46] Recall that at one point in his treatise, he seems to realize that idolatry could be avoided only by deflecting attention from the starkly physical nature of relics: "Why, then, do we call them 'relics'? Because words are images and signs of things. Before our eyes are blood and clay. We impress on them the name of 'relics,' because we cannot do otherwise, with (so to speak) the seal of living language. But now, by uttering the whole in the part, we open the eyes of the heart, not the barriers of our bodily sight."[47] With this cautionary statement about privileging spiritual over physical seeing, Victricius betrayed, however unwittingly, a certain skittishness concerning the phenomenon of relics. Why insist on a retraining of physical sight if the view that human "matter" had been converted by God "into the substance of his light" (*ad sui luminis transferre substantiam*) did not carry a whiff of idolatry, at least as understood in traditional Christian discourse about it?[48]

For most of the rest of this sermon, however, Victricius seems to have forgotten his cautionary statement contrasting physical with spiritual seeing. After all, explaining the spiritual excess that body fragments such as relics harbored was the main thrust of his treatise's argument that the martyr is completely present in the relic and is united to God both materially and spiritually.[49] And even though Victricius is careful to qualify his point by noting that the martyr is the same as God "by gift and adoption, not by property and nature," he has surely flirted with erasing the difference between the spiritual and the material.[50]

The specter of idolatry that haunted this form of incarnational theology, which at the very least blurred the ontological distinction of divine and human, also presented itself as an anxiety in hagiographical thinking about the bodies of holy people: were they passive channels of divine activity, or was there an active synergy of human and divine at work in them, and if so, how was it to be pictured?[51] In his *Life of St. Antony*, Athanasius tried to chart something of a middle course. Although he was very wary of localizing the divine, whether in holy places such as Jerusalem or in relics, he was willing to portray the body of Antony, still vigorous and youthful after decades of ascetic practice and combat with demons, as a prefiguration of the incorruption that humans would enjoy in the resurrection.[52] Yet he emphasized that Antony achieved what he did, not by virtue of his own agency, but through Christ. As David Brakke has argued, "from Athanasius' perspective, it is correct to call Antony's body 'holy,' but only in the sense that it has been restored to its original (prefall) condition through the divinizing work of the incarnate Word. Antony's body is not holy in the sense that it transmits or mediates holiness to others."[53]

For later hagiographers, however, the problem of God's presence on earth, and particularly in the saints, had become more acute. Not far in the background lay the Christological debates of the fifth century, since Christ was the supreme instance of divinity enfleshed.[54] In the course of these debates, extreme care was taken not to compromise the transcendent divinity of Christ. However, as Peter Brown has put it, this elevation produced

a need to show that so high a God was truly implicated in human affairs. . . .
Often seeming to be tragically absent, Christ needed to be "represented" on
earth, and it was as "Christ-bearers," as those who imitated him and consequently carried his power within them, that holy persons—alive or in their
tomb—gave human density to the urge to find a joining of heaven and earth,
which the rise of monotheism, despite the Christian doctrine of the Incarnation,
had placed in jeopardy.[55]

It was this heightened view of human holiness that, I argue, helps
account for the development of new strategies for retrieving what was
visually intractable, the presence of divine power in an earthly object,
the human body, as well as for safeguarding against the attribution of
too much extra-human meaning to the saint.

Carnal Rhetoric and Transfiguration

The carnal rhetoric of the hagiographies I have been exploring was one
of those strategies, yet the problem of idolatry remained, as an interesting late sixth-century debate about the ontology of saintly appearances
shows. On one side of this debate, as reported by Eustratius of Constantinople, were those who effectively denied the cults of saints and relics by
arguing as follows: "human souls, after their departure from their bodies, are inactive . . . and cannot appear to the living in their own substance (οὐσία) or existence." According to this view, saintly apparitions
do occur, but by means of "divine power simulating their form (σχηματ-
ιξομένη) and appearing as the souls of various saints in states of
activity."[56]

Against this way of thinking, Eustratius, presbyter in the church of
Hagia Sophia in Constantinople, wrote his treatise *On the State of Souls
After Death*. Being both a hagiographer and a proponent of the cult of
relics, Eustratius objected to this theory of divine masquerade, arguing
that it turned the church into "a stage of mimes and jesters."[57] In a
recent article on this topic, Nicholas Constas has shown that Eustratius
"rejected the theory of divine visionary dissemblance as nothing more
than a sign system of real but ultimately absent objects" and argued
instead for "the union and cooperation of human and divine energies
in the activity of the saints," who were "even *more active* in death than in
life" because they had "transcended the spatial and temporal restric-
tions of the body."[58] For Eustratius, then, saintly appearances *did* have
ontological reality; they were, in Constas's phrase, "genuine epiphanies
of a transfigured human presence."[59]

By emphasizing the specifically *transfigured* quality of saintly presence,
Eustratius avoided the kind of sheer materialism that his opponents
seem to have feared. Ideas such as his about the coinherence of vision

and substance, which are refined theological parallels to Victricius's view
of the divinely illuminated matter of relics, can help explain a final feature of holy bodies such as those of Artemios, Thekla, and Symeon the
Stylite the Younger. As we have seen, the texts devoted to such figures
exhibit a virtual "romance of the ontology of pictures,"[60] as, with their
heightened affect, they produce a picture of the saints that is very corporeal indeed. But there is a counter-tendency to this romance of the
ontology of pictures. At the point when the reader is ready to be seduced
by the theatrical physicality of these images, she also notices that the
texts have an equally theatrical rendering of saintly bodies as "*enigmas* of
corporeal substance."[61] For, just as the texts insist on the saints' tangible
presence, they also insist on their visionary, almost ephemeral aspect,
making them figures of ambiguous corporeality, as I have mentioned
earlier in this chapter.

Two of these saints, Thekla and Artemios, are of course visionary from
the start, since in the context of incubation they sometimes appear in
and as dreams. But there is far more to their ambiguous corporeality
than this. Both of them are masters of disguise. Thekla, for example,
appears as a virgin in conventional monastic clothing, or as a chamber-
maid, or as a naked young woman; Artemios appears in disguise in fully
half of his miracles, and with striking changes in character, appearing
one time as a member of the Imperial Senate and on another occasion
as a sad-faced stranger in a latrine. Even Symeon the Stylite the Younger,
who is "alive" in his text rather than active post-mortem like the other
two, can appear to a blind man as a splendid, fur-cloaked grandee,
described as an apparition who yet gives the man a very tangible
embrace; in another anecdote he appears as a "spiritual image" (πνευ-
ματικὴ εἴκων) speaking with a human voice, and in yet another he is a
tangible apparition performing surgery.[62]

And, as if these motifs of disguise weren't enough to unsettle the reader's confidence in the solidity of these saints, there are the following textual indications that these saints are indeed subtle bodies.[63] Both
Artemios and Symeon the Stylite the Younger heal by giving to the sick
eulogiae, tokens of blessing made of wax or earth that were stamped with
the saints' images.[64] Artemios, in fact, even appears as a healing presence in one miracle in the guise of his own icon that hung in the church,
and icons of Symeon are said to work miracles.[65] Symeon, stunningly,
commands one man, who is begging to stay with him physically at his
column, to leave, and says about the *eulogia* that he has given him, "Take
the token made of my dust, leave, and when you look at the imprint of
our image, it is us that you will see."[66] Whatever one might say about
icon-piety in regard to this motif, the emphasis on the saint's image
deflects attention from his actual body and toward his status as a kind

of icon of corporeality, as though the text were forcing the reader to consider—and reconsider—the kind of pictures that it has devised to represent the nature of spiritual matter.[67]

The most subtle body of all, however, is that of Thekla. Two anecdotes will suffice. The first begins by introducing Dionysia, a woman who, having decided to live the ascetic life, has renounced husband, children, and home and has taken refuge at Thekla's sanctuary. To the great surprise of Dionysia's roommate Susanna, Thekla gets into bed with Dionysia and holds her in her arms all night long. Susanna keeps propping herself up on her elbow, wondering how a third person came to be in the room, and then to her even greater surprise, she watches as Thekla eventually rises up—"unlike an ordinary sleeper," as the text says—and flies out of the room.[68]

Of course Thekla had a special affection for women in her cult, but, as our somewhat narcissistic author assures us, she also liked men, especially men of letters, and of those especially himself![69] He tells the following story as one of her miracles. As he was in the process of writing the very book that the reader is reading, he says, he found himself becoming a bit lazy and, feeling overwhelmed by all he needed to collect and write, he was at the point of giving up the project. He writes: "I thought I saw with my eyes the martyr sitting next to me . . . and she took the book I was writing from my hands; she seemed to me to be reading . . . and to smile, indicating by her look that it pleased her and that I should not leave the work unfinished."[70] Full of fear and ardor following this "apparition," as he calls it (ὄψις), he takes up his pen once more.

Like her fellow saints, Thekla too is ambiguously corporeal, visionary and tangible at once. The authors of such textual images of holy bodies could not fix those bodies as simple objects of thought. The saintly body as locus of surplus value was too complicated for that. It should be clear by now that, in my view, hagiographical writing was based on more than naïve wonder and credulity. It was dealing with serious issues regarding the relation between the divine and material realms that had had a long history in Western philosophy and religion. Its means of expression by constructing word-pictures may seem somewhat alien to those of us who would prefer more abstract formulations, but as I have tried to show, the texts themselves are crafted in such a way as to train the eye of the reader to bring sense and intellect together. In its own imagistic way, hagiography articulated a kind of religious knowledge that dignifies bodily existence by giving the senses cognitive status. Whether violent or charming, the holy body solicits the very embodied thoughtfulness that it enacts in word-pictures. Neither wholly visionary nor wholly substantial, saintly images deny the dualistic position that splits matter from spirit, body from soul, nature from the divine. The body can be a locus of spirituality without compromising the divine.

Saintly bodies are neither real nor unreal; rather, they are effects of the hagiographical texts in which they appear. As effects of those texts, saintly bodies are enigmatic and, as materializations of an invisible world, they draw attention to the inherently figural character of the materialist turn in late ancient and early Byzantine Christianity. Why is this important? It seems to me that hagiographical insistence on the enigma of the holy body is this tradition's way of handling the problem of idolatry. Because they are figurally real, these bodies cannot be reified, just as the texts that they appear in cannot achieve narrative closure. And just as they avoid idolizing the material, they also deconstruct naïve notions of spiritual presence. Holy bodies are epiphanies of transfiguration that occupy a signifying space between transcendence and immanence. This is the premise of hagiography's version of figural realism. In my view, hagiographical writing was engaged in working out a theological poetics of material substance.

With its emphasis on the elaboration of a poetics of the saintly body in ancient Christian hagiography, especially insofar as those bodies are ambiguously corporeal, this chapter lays the groundwork for the four chapters that follow. The issue, again, will be the materialization of saintly presence in the world. Chapter 6 extends the focus on hagiographers' treatment of saintly bodies by introducing the concept of the subtracted self of the saint. The next two chapters narrow the focus by concentrating on anecdotes regarding icons that began to appear in hagiographies in the two centuries prior to iconoclasm; but they also broaden the focus by bringing icon theory into the discussion of spiritual objects. Finally, Chapter 9 considers how a mosaic icon achieved a representation of a saint whose body, as "immaterially material," was analogous to the bodies of saints in hagiographies. Overall, these chapters study the ways in which ancient Christian literature and art promoted a certain hesitation in regard to the spiritual animation of material objects, primarily by provoking uncertainty regarding how, exactly, a human body, an icon, or a mosaic portrait harbors saintly presence.

Chapter Six
Subtle Bodies

From the fourth through the seventh centuries, late ancient Christianity fostered the development of three remarkable movements—the cult of the saints, the cult of relics, and the production of iconic art—all of which were premised on the conviction that the material world, particularly in the form of the human body, was a locus of spiritual presence. As noted in the Introduction, the "tangible, palpable piety" that began to emerge in the fourth and fifth centuries was spurred in part by a theological position that emerged in the context of the Trinitarian and Christological controversies of those centuries, namely, that "at the incarnation the divine itself had entered into matter, sanctifying and renewing the whole of material existence. The elaboration of Christian piety in sensory terms was a further expression of this view."[1] This dignifying of "matter," however, raised what later became urgent issues: the problem of idolatry, understood as investing the material world with too much meaning, and the consequent need to articulate how the holy could be present in the contingent order in a nonidolatrous fashion.[2]

The focus of this chapter is on one of the most interesting features of ancient Christian representations of the bodies of the saints, namely, that they disrupt the conventional binary of transcendence and materiality in such a way that the material can "show" the holy without being completely identified with it. In a seventh-century ex-voto mosaic in the Church of Saint Demetrius in Thessaloniki, for example, the saint appears in living color in front of a petitioner—but his hands are rendered in silver, not in mosaic tiles. In a single image, this icon brings together the transcendent and material aspects of the saint, whose silver hands emphasize "the intimacy of touch yet also its supernatural quality."[3] This phenomenon of the saint as material apparition was part of a particular problematic in late ancient Christianity that developed in the course of the burgeoning of the cult of the saints in the fourth and fifth centuries: how might human holiness be depicted without either transgressing on the prerogatives of divinity or undermining the earthy humanity of the saint? The hagiographers whose saintly images are featured in the following discussion did not, of course, articulate this problematic as I have. Yet I argue that their crafting of these images can be read as pictorial strategies for conceptualizing transfiguration enacted on the human level.

Imagining Saintly Bodies

As the later iconoclastic controversy of the eighth and ninth centuries made very clear, the transfiguration of both Christ and human beings could be understood in two quite different ways: on the one hand, as the triumph of spirit over matter, and on the other, as the triumph of flesh over human fallenness. In art, the primary battleground of the iconoclastic controversy, these different understandings of transfiguration had direct implications for the representation of saints as exemplars of human holiness. In Marie-José Mondzain's succinct summary of the issue, the iconoclasts' position that transfiguration signaled a triumph of spirit over matter rendered "the portrayal of that triumphant and radiant immateriality useless and impious," while the iconophiles' understanding of transfiguration to mean "the triumph of the flesh over sin, suffering, and death" entailed an affirmation of art. "Portrayal [of saints as well as Christ] is therefore the *portrayal of life* itself."[4] The two sides of the debate could not be clearer: either the body is glorified, or else it is beside the point.

In the three centuries prior to the outbreak of the iconoclastic controversy—centuries that witnessed a "growth industry" in hagiographical literature as well as what Averil Cameron has termed an "extreme proliferation of religious imagery"[5]—the battle lines drawn between "radiant immateriality" and "the flesh" were not quite so stark, and yet there *were* indications that religious investment in human holiness carried certain risks. It was one thing for authors such as Basil of Caesarea to declare that even the tiniest plants and animals might offer a "faint reflection" of the grandeur of God[6]; but it was quite another to view certain people, or their relics, or their artistic portraits as somehow imbued with the holy. In part this was because embodying the holy in the form of saints posed a new problem in terms of imagining the relation between the human and the divine. For centuries, the Graeco-Roman cosmos in which Christianity developed had been densely populated with mediating spirit-beings (daimons, *genii*, guardian angels) that functioned as invisible friends and protectors of human beings. As described by Peter Brown, such a protector "was an invisible being entrusted with the care of the individual, in a manner so intimate that it was not only the constant companion of the individual; it was almost an upward extension of the individual."[7] Brown is correct to add "almost" here, since the personal spirit-guardian did not render the human being in its care "holy," nor did it enable that person to function as an intermediary between the divine and earthly realms. Contact with the divine was the province of a decidedly *im*material being.

The difference between this older model of divine-human relations and the newer one signified by the phenomenon of saints is striking: "to seek the face of a fellow human being where an earlier generation had wished to see the shimmering presence of a bodiless power is no small change."[8] It was in fact a momentous change, involving alterations both in notions of what was possible for an embodied self and also in possibilities for divine intervention in the world. Now a human being (or that person's body part or picture) could play an active role in the physical or spiritual salvation of a fellow human being: as a woman in need of a cure says of St. Symeon the Stylite the Younger, "if only I might see his face [ὁμοίωσιν: his painted likeness], I shall be saved."[9] As celebratory as the cult of the saints seems to have been in terms of dignifying the material realm with a touch of transcendence, it was also accompanied by a certain pause or holding back, and in that hesitance lies the phenomenon of the transcendent-but-material body as it applies to human holiness. In an essay about her favorite kind of poetry entitled "Disruption, Hesitation, Silence," the poet Louise Glück wrote, "I do not think that more information always makes a richer poem. I am attracted to ellipsis, to the unsaid, to suggestion, to eloquent, deliberate silence. The unsaid, for me, exerts great power: often I wish an entire poem could be made in this vocabulary. It is analogous to the unseen; for example, to the power of ruins, to works of art either damaged or incomplete. Such works inevitably allude to larger contexts; they haunt because they are not whole, though wholeness is implied."[10] As I will argue, this particular kind of commitment to "less is more" was characteristic of late ancient Christian constructions of what I will eventually designate as the "subtracted self" of the saints. Using a variety of strategies when they wrote about and depicted saints, hagiographical authors (and artists, as we shall see in the final chapter) relied not so much on the "unsaid" as on what Michael Sells calls an apophatic "speaking away."[11] Ellipsis, then, and suggestion and allusion to the hauntings of (un)wholeness: these are modern ways of describing the ancient presentation of the ephemeral solidity of the saints.

Ephemeral Corporeality

In this chapter, I will treat hagiography not as a discrete genre limited to literary lives of saints but rather as a set of discursive strategies for presenting sainthood.[12] Hence anecdotes in collective biographies of desert ascetics and miracle stories in full-fledged saintly *vitae* will all fall under the purview of late ancient hagiography, whose primary purpose lay in the materialization (and not simply the memorialization) of saintly presence in the world. Because saints were *a*—if not *the*—major conduit for the activity of the divine in everyday life, strategies for understanding the sensible world as sustaining, however subtly, traces of holiness, of the suprasensible, were crucial to Christian religious sensibility.

As necessary as they were, however, such strategies were also delicate—delicate because collapsing the transcendent into the immanent, as compared with maintaining a tensive relation between them, would be idolatrous. As their literary constructions of saintliness attest, late ancient Christians were cautious about investing the material world, including the human bodies that once or still inhabited that world, with too much spirit. At the same time, however, they thought the material world to be saturated with divine presence. A good example of this perspective is the following passage from a late fourth- or early fifth-century sermon by Maximus of Turin: "As the result of Christ's resurrection the air is healthier, the sun warmer, and the earth more fertile. As a result of it the young branch comes into leaf, the green stalks grow into fruit, and the vine ripens into vine sprouts. If all things, then, are clothed in flowers when the flesh of Christ blossoms anew, then it must be the case that when it bears fruit, everything else must bear fruit as well."[13] Human beings were of course part of this blossoming and fruit-bearing world: convictions that the human body could be a locus of sanctity were central to the late ancient Christian mindset.[14] Hence the need, when representing human holiness, to tread lightly, avoiding both a spirituality devoid of earthy substance and sheer materialism.

Approaching this problematic with a more contemporary vocabulary, one might say that, in the process of materializing saintly presence, Christian hagiography developed techniques for the animation of lifeless objects.[15] Saints might be considered to be "lifeless objects" because they were, of course, physically dead. Yet, when the hagiographical tradition sought to convey the spiritual aliveness of the saints, it did so not by emphasizing their immaterial presence but by endowing them with bodies that flirted with material substance without quite achieving corporeal solidity.

An example of this "speaking away" of literal physicality without losing the body is the following anecdote from a seventh-century hagiography, the *Life of Saint Theodore of Sykeon*. Returning to his monastery after performing miracles in local villages and successfully routing an evil sorcerer, Saint Theodore falls ill and lies weeping underneath an icon of Saints Cosmas and Damian. Eerily, the saints emerge from the icon "looking just like they did" in the painted image. Coming close to him "like doctors do," they take Saint Theodore's pulse, determine that he is indeed desperately ill, ask the saint a series of questions, and finally offer to go to heaven to plead with Christ on Theodore's behalf. Returning, they announce that his life has been extended, and vanish—presumably back into the icon whence they came.[16] In the uncanny moment when Saints Cosmas and Damian emerge from their own iconic portrait as animate presences in the life of Saint Theodore, the reader experiences what material-culture theorist Bill Brown describes as ontological instability: are these saints somehow "inside" their own portrait, or is it just a picture? Can bodiless saints really take someone's pulse? What is the status of these figures who seem to have a privileged relation to divine power?

In one of his studies of "things," Brown has analyzed the "ontological ambiguity" of animated objects: human or thing?[17] What interests Brown is the "ontological instability" of such artifacts, namely, their "oscillation between animate and inanimate, subject and object, human and thing."[18] According to Brown's analysis, this oscillation is what makes such artifacts uncanny, uncanny in the sense developed by psychologist Ernst Jentsch, who linked uncanniness with intellectual uncertainty about "whether an apparently animate being is in fact alive; or, conversely, whether a lifeless object might not in fact be animate."[19] The hagiography devoted to Saint Theodore certainly does present the reader with a form of intellectual uncertainty. Indeed, I would suggest that this text is playing with—perhaps even intentionally straining—the reader's credulity for a pedagogical purpose: to teach the reader how to "see" or apprehend that saintly presence does (not quite) incarnate divinity.

The feature of Brown's argument that strikes me as most relevant to hagiographical representation is the phenomenon of ontological instability and the uncanny oscillation that it produces. Consider another anecdote from the *Life of Saint Theodore of Sykeon*. While visiting a monastery in Constantinople, Theodore is subjected to the following ruse: unbeknownst to him, the monks and their abbot, desiring to have a memorial of the saint's stay with them, hire an artist to paint Theodore's portrait. On the sly, the artist produces a good likeness, and one of the monks shows Theodore the portrait and asks him to bless it. Smiling, Theodore says, "You are a fine thief, what are you doing here? We must see to it that you don't run off with something."[20] As Robin Cormack has observed, "with his remark [Theodore] had betrayed a belief that an icon which copied a person could somehow take away something of the original and have a reality of its own in his image," the implication being that "the icon might function independently of Theodore."[21] Yet Theodore made his remark with a smile—was he joking about the theft of his own "substance," or was he dead serious? Which is the real Theodore, and what kind of body does he have?

The fact that this anecdote (and many more like it) raises such questions is not, I think, an accident. This form of subtle embodiment, which refuses to take a final stand on the reality—the concrete solidity—of the saintly body, had theological warrant, because only an ephemerally solid body could allude to the larger context of Christic power without in effect replacing it or claiming identification with it. As Rowan Williams has explained, "only in Christ is the flesh fully and lastingly saturated with the indwelling divine power," and he notes the development, beginning in the fourth century, of "a picture of holiness that is wary of anything like a fusion between the fully and unambiguously holy on the one hand and the created human agent on the other."[22] This development did not, however, simplify the hagiographical task of constructing images of human holiness that supported a "dialectic of immanence and transcendence,"[23] such that hagiographical representations matched the delicate balance of human and divine in the saints themselves.

Rhetoric of the Holy Body: Collective Hagiography

How then can one have a truly material (because humanly physical) sign of the presence of the spiritual world in this earthly world without reifying the holy? The beginning of the early Christian journey toward answers to this question can be found in the hagiographical literature of the late fourth to the sixth century devoted to desert asceticism. Much of this literature was written in the form of collective biographies (or, more appropriately, collective hagiographies), compendia of anecdotes compiled by admirers who had gone out into the deserts of Egypt and Syria to observe the lifestyles of the men (and a few women) who practiced an austere form of Christian devotion there.[24] One of the striking features of these hagiographies is their presentation of the ascetic practitioners' emaciated and mutilated bodies as angelic bodies full of light.[25] The literature of desert asceticism, that is to say, developed a rhetoric of the holy body that focused the reader's attention on the vulnerable physicality of the saint while deflecting attention away from it at the same time.

Although one might think that the angelic body would eclipse the human one, there is no doubt about the insistent physicality of the phenomenon of desert asceticism and the reportage about it. This hagiographical literature is dominated by reports of practices of extreme fasting, repetitive praying and singing, wrapping the body with chains and ropes, and so forth.[26] What might seem, to a modern sensibility, as

negative results of such practices—the ulcerated feet of Symeon the Stylite, the sun-blackened body of Saint Mary of Egypt, the sunken eyes of
Saint Pelagia of Antioch—were positioned by hagiographers as positive
signs of spiritual transformation.[27] As Peter Brown has argued, it was in
the desert that the transformative implications of the Incarnation for
human beings were put into practice: "Through the Incarnation of
Christ, the Highest God had reached down to make even the body capable of transformation."[28]

And transformed their bodies surely were, especially given their practices of eating (or not). Fasting produces a body that looks different
from conventional bodies, that is, bodies marked by their ties to normal
social and domestic contexts. Yet, despite the obsession of such collective hagiographies as the *Historia monachorum* with ascetic bodily practices like fasting, there is very little actual physical description. On the
basis of such texts, one cannot visualize those desert saints who had
"attained a Godlike state of fulfillment by their inspired and wonderful
and virtuous way of life."[29] Instead, hagiographers used metaphors of
light to describe these exemplars of the saintly self. According to the
Apophthegmata Patrum, for example, the face of Abba Pambo shone like
lightning, and Abba Sisoes's face shone like the sun.[30] The author of the
Historia monachorum observed that Abba Or "looked just like an angel,
and his face was so radiant that the sight of him alone filled one with
awe."[31] The entire body of Abba Silvanus shone like an angel, while
another old man appeared "entirely like a flame."[32]

These metaphors of light were useful for evoking the subtle bodies of
the desert saints because they allowed hagiographers to materialize the
holiness of the saint without reifying it. One cannot, after all, "see"
light. In these texts, there is a "speaking away" of literal physicality without losing the human body, which persists alongside the shining angelic
body as the disfigured ascetic body—"the disfigured [that] was figured
as desirable," as Geoffrey Galt Harpham has argued.[33] By aligning
images of mutilation and disfigurement with images of light, hagiographers of desert ascetics maintained their subjects in a tensive perch
between transcendence and materiality.

It was apparently difficult, however, to be hesitant about the spiritual
excess that made these saints magnets of attraction,[34] for these texts constantly strain after inferences to wholeness or spiritual completeness.
Along with their emphasis on ascetic practices, collective hagiographies
prominently feature the various charisms granted to the denizens of the
desert on the basis of their ascetic efforts. Many of these spiritual gifts
are decidedly Christomimetic: exorcising demons, healing the sick, even
raising the dead and walking on water.[35] And in addition to tales about
spiritual gifts, there are the stories about ascetics whose bodies negotiate

the spirit/human divide with astonishing ease. For example, one old man, Patermuthius, flies through the air, passes through closed doors, and was once "transported physically to paradise," whence he brought back "a large choice fig" as proof of his journey.[36] For three years another monk, Abba Or, ate only heavenly food, which was placed in his mouth by an angel.[37]

Such textual representations of desert saints gave human materiality a hefty push toward transcendence, indeed toward what Harpham has called the most insidious temptation of the ascetic life: "the illusion that one had reached an ideal or perfect identification with Christ the Word."[38] Even the literary form of such collective hagiographies as the *Historia monachorum* and Theodoret's *Historia religiosa* supports the divinizing tendencies just noted. The stories that form these collections are not full, chronologically organized biographies that situate their subjects in richly detailed sociocultural contexts. Instead, they are rapid, staccato-like accounts of the saints in action, taking the form of snapshots endlessly repeated. The collections thus place the desert saints in an extended "middle" that, by subverting conventional biographical narrativity and hence depriving their ascetic characters of history, helps accentuate their heavenly status.

But there is in these hagiographies a countermove to this tendency to allow the embodiment of desert saints to slip wholly into the luminosity of the saints' holiness, and herein lies another kind of "hesitance," one that curbs the divinizing tendency of these portrayals of human holiness. For, in order to maintain a tensive balance between divinity and humanity, the kind of "speaking away" referred to earlier must "unsay" transcendence as well as materiality. In this regard there is the stunning story about the monk Macarius, who "asked God to show him the paradise which Jannes and Jambres [Egyptian magicians] had planted in the desert in their desire to make a copy of the true paradise."[39] After much wandering in the desert, an angel sets him near the garden, inside which Macarius encounters two holy men. After partaking of marvelously large fruit, "they said to each other, 'How good it would be if all the monks were here.'"[40] Macarius decides to go back home and lead his fellow monks to this paradise, but the two holy men caution him against this, warning about the demon-filled desert in which many monks had perished. Ignoring this advice, Macarius sets forth. The rest of the story deserves quoting in full:

He set off in haste for the settled region, carrying some of the fruit as proof. And taking with him a large bundle of palm branches, he planted them as markers in the desert so that he should not lose his way when he came back. Then he slept for a while in the desert, and when he woke up he found that all the palm branches had been gathered up by the demons and placed by his head. Then getting up, he said to them, "If it is the will of God, you cannot prevent us from entering the garden." When he arrived at the settled region, he kept showing the fruit to the monks to persuade them to come away to the paradise. Many fathers gathered around him and said to him, "Could it not be that this paradise has come into being for the destruction of our souls? For if we were to enjoy it in this life, we should have received our portion of good things while still on earth. What reward would we have afterwards when we come into the presence of God? For what kind of virtue shall we be recompensed?" And they persuaded Macarius not to return.[41]

Clearly it was not "the will of God" that monks should enjoy paradisal life in the here-and-now and, despite Macarius's enthusiasm, the text suggests that this "paradise" was a sham, a magical simulacrum that induced dangerous fantasies of attaining transcendence on earth.

Another strategy that texts such as the *Historia monachorum* used to avoid the blasphemy of complete identification of their saints with the ultimately holy, Christ, was the presentation of ascetics as constantly in motion. This is the other side of the staccato-like format of these texts, most of whose anecdotes present their subjects performing one ascetic feat after the other. As Harpham argues, this kind of restless activity is one of the central features of asceticism, defined as "a quest for a goal that cannot and must not be reached, a quest with a sharp caveat: 'seek but do not find.' "[42] Living out a Christomimetic dynamic in which he is "constantly progressing but never arrives," the ascetic may be defined as an "emergent person" or an "evolving subject" ever in motion toward a divine paradigm.[43] As Abba Poemen said about Abba Pior, "Every day he made a new beginning."[44] Thus is the saint subjected to the hesitance that even the exuberance of this kind of incarnational thinking cannot dispel.[45]

Collective hagiographies were among the earliest Christian attempts to imagine the (near) triumph of flesh over human fallenness. Their version of the "subtracted selves" of the saints, inhabiting bodies radiant and ravaged at once, displays the difficulty of bringing human and divine together by the way in which their representations of the desert ascetics veer from one pole of the transcendence/materiality binary to the other.

This kind of textual anxiety over endowing human beings with too much divinity was not limited to collective biographies of saints. Hagiographies devoted to single figures also exhibit a degree of vacillation concerning how to present the relation between the spiritual and the material: what degree of under- (or over-) statement was appropriate for picturing a holy self?

Picturing Macrina

A good example of such a hagiography, one roughly contemporary with the collective hagiographies just discussed, is Gregory of Nyssa's *vita* of his sister. In his *Life of Saint Macrina,* Gregory characterized Macrina as a person poised on the boundary between human life and bodiless nature: "It was as if an angel," he wrote, "had providentially taken human form, an angel with no attachment to or affinity to life in the flesh."[46] Although Gregory declares the "as if" quality of Macrina's angelic status, his account of his sister strains against this qualification of her holiness. As Derek Krueger has observed, "the act of biography that grounds her story in time and place also subtly 'loosens her from the chains of the body.'"[47] It does so, as Krueger has shown, by attributing to Macrina two autobiographical discourses, both of which contribute to a spiritualizing portrayal. The first discourse is one in which "Gregory relates that Macrina recalled with thanksgiving the religious history of her family," emphasizing the acts of God in her and her family's life.[48] As Krueger remarks, "A Christian narrative is also the story of God."[49] Less subtle is the second discourse, the dying Macrina's final "prayerful offering" that includes a narration both of "a history of God" as well as of Macrina's past, "a narrative gesture that ultimately inscribes Macrina's story in God's."[50] This inscription of the human in the divine—surely a qualification of Gregory's initial "as if"—is accomplished by a Christomimetic gesture whereby "Macrina merges her own narrative with that of Christ" by remembering her participation in his passion as well as by presenting herself as an incense offering, a sacrificial gift.[51]

Gregory's sacramentalizing portrait of his sister veers decidedly in the direction of a view of the saint as a self so "subtracted" that it is difficult to detect the human element. This view would seem to be supported in the two passages in which Gregory pictures his sister's body. In these stunning images, Macrina appears as the brilliantly gleaming relics of the dream that Gregory recounts having prior to his visit, and as the radiant corpse of his depiction of her death: "She shone even in the dark mantle; God's power, I think, added even such grace to her body that, exactly as in the vision [of gleaming relics] I had while dreaming, rays of light seemed to shine out from her beauty."[52] Macrina's deathbed scene is appropriate to Gregory's construction of her as a near angel, and it is difficult to recognize her as a self with an identity in any conventional sense. But perhaps that is just the point: hagiographic images work to destabilize conventional identity because the saintly self, perched between materiality and transcendence, is refractory to representation.

While Gregory's images of Macrina attempt to occupy the boundary between the human and the spiritual, his insistence on objectifying her—as glowing martyr's relics, for example—comes close to erasing that boundary by denying her humanness. Nonetheless, the images remain equivocal, since Macrina's body does not disappear in a flash of glory but remains as a tangible sign of her humanity. As Virginia Burrus has noted about this portrayal, "In the theology of incarnation conveyed by this vita, flesh is not transformed into spirit, it is not even redeemed by (or simply 'married to') spirit. . . . Flesh is itself the mirroring of spirit. . . . By the same token, spirit is itself the reflection, the mark (the sign), of the flesh."[53]

In his composite image of Macrina, Gregory's text depicts transfiguration enacted on a human level. A final, remarkable, example of this comes in the form of one of the biography's flashbacks, which all occur in the narrative after Macrina has died and which present her as alive again. The setting of the particular flashback to which I refer is the moment when Gregory must wrap his sister's body in a funeral robe.[54] One of Macrina's deaconesses shows him a scar on Macrina's breast and relates the anecdote regarding her cancerous tumor and its miraculous healing. Yet the scar remains, even if it is a "reminder of God's visitation."[55] The narrative that brings Macrina to life once again, arguing with her mother about going to a doctor and weeping all night in church, forms one of the longest anecdotes in the vita; strikingly, it is immediately followed by Gregory's description of the dead Macrina's body as shining in her dark mantle. It is a jolting narrative juxtaposition not only of life and death but also of human and angelic bodies.

By relying on an overlay of different planes of perception—the scarred human body juxtaposed with the glowing body touched by transcendence—Gregory does represent a saintly persona. However, Macrina is not finally endowed with the kind of "subtracted self" that characterized later hagiographical portraits of saints. Gregory's presentation of Macrina's saintly self was based more on her ascetic heroism than on her role as intercessor or vehicle of the holy spirit's action in the world. This is suggested not only by his straightforward connecting of her ascetic practice and spirituality with the angelic life,[56] but also by his placement of the miracles attributed to her at the very end of the vita, seemingly as an afterthought, and further by his deeming it "not advisable" to detail such miracles due to the strain they would put on the credulity of "those who have too little faith."[57] But as the cult of the saints developed more fully in later centuries, intercession and miracles came to dominate the conception of saints, and hagiographers were faced with the problem of representing human beings who were more powerfully holy.

Saints as Subtracted Selves

A point that I have made elsewhere in this volume bears repeating here: for hagiographers of later centuries, the problem of God's presence on earth, and particularly in the saints, had been thrown into sharper relief than for hagiographers of earlier centuries.[58] Contributory to this problem were the Christological debates of the fifth century, since Christ was the supreme instance of divinity enfleshed.[59] In the anti-Arian theology of Christ's person that emerged from these debates, extreme care was taken not to compromise his transcendent divinity. However, as Peter Brown has put it, this elevation produced "a need to show that so high a God was truly implicated in human affairs. . . . Often seeming to be tragically absent, Christ needed to be 'represented' on earth, and it was as 'Christ-bearers,' as those who imitated him and consequently carried his power within them, that holy persons—alive or in their tomb—gave human density to the urge to find a joining of heaven and earth, which the rise of monotheism, despite the Christian doctrine of the Incarnation, had placed in jeopardy."[60] This way of thinking about human holiness prompted the development of new hagiographical strategies for materializing the presence of the holy in human bodies.

As noted in the previous chapter, in the hagiographical literature devoted to individual saints that developed in the late fifth through the seventh centuries, a brief biography of the saint often functions simply to launch the saint into action, as miracle after miracle is narrated at a very quick pace.[61] Here again is the staccato-like format as in collective hagiographies, yet in these (mostly later) *vitae* that are essentially collections of miracles, the saint is not presented as an "emergent person" or "evolving subject." The goal of later hagiographies, such as the *Life of Saint Theodore of Sykeon* discussed above, is not to present the reader with a snapshot of an imitable "angelic" life, as in the literature on the desert ascetics or in Gregory's *Life of Saint Macrina*. In later hagiographies, saints are not aligned with angels; rather, they are themselves theophanic vehicles of the highest degree. Hence the task of these texts is to teach the reader not only to see *that* the earthly realm is home to the real presence of the holy, but also *how* to conceptualize these material interactions with the saints properly.

Because Christ had become more remote as intercessor between heaven and earth, there was an urgent need for figures that could mediate divine presence.[62] Hagiography satisfied this need by fashioning the bodies of the saints as transcendent bodies, their "matter" charged with religious power. Instead of being exemplars of spiritual progress like the desert ascetics, these later saints' lives are stages for the display of divine action in the world. Understandably, the theological pressure that the idea of intercession placed on saints posed a problem for conceptualizing and then narrating their embodiment. What exactly was the difference between the human and the divine? In other words, how might one portray spiritual presence in the saint without idolizing the human and circumscribing divinity?

Hagiographies such as the *Life of Saint Symeon the Stylite the Younger* developed what I discern to be techniques for rematerializing the saint as a substracted self, an "enigma of corporeal substance."[63] We have already, in fact, seen an example of such enigmas in the ephemerally solid bodies of Saints Cosmas and Damian as they interact with the ailing Saint Theodore of Sykeon. Mediation of the divine by a human body requires not *de*materialization, but precisely *re*materialization in verbal images that convey how a body touched by transcendence can be palpably present in the world.[64] To construct a truly *material* sign of the presence of the spiritual realm in the here and now, the hagiographer could not overemphasize the indwelling of spirit in the saint for fear of erasing the humanness of the saintly *persona* as intercessor. On the other hand, overemphasis on the humanness of the saint would detract from the status of the saint as a genuine epiphany of a specifically *transfigured* human presence.[65]

One of the most interesting hagiographical techniques for keeping saints in such a tensive balance between two worlds was the *dis*placement of the reality of saintly presence and power onto images. As with the (near) identity of Saints Cosmas and Damian with their own icon, such animated images may, like apophasis, accomplish a "momentary liberation from referential delimitation," which is precisely what the phenomenon of saintly flesh demands.[66] An apt example of this technique is in the late sixth-century *Life of Saint Symeon the Stylite the Younger*, which is one of those hagiographies marked by a profusion of miracle stories. In Miracle 231 (!), a priest has brought his ailing son to the foot of Symeon's column for healing. Having blessed the son, Symeon tells the priest and his son to go home. The priest begs that they be allowed to stay in Symeon's vicinity, since "being close to you will guarantee us a complete cure." As Charles Barber remarks, Symeon's next move is to "extend the notion of his presence": "The power of God is effective everywhere," says the saint. He continues: "So take this *eulogia* [token] made of my dust (τῆς κόνεως μου), depart, and when you look at the imprint of our image, it is us that you will see."[67]

Not only does Symeon extend his presence, but he also extends his body by scattering it in the form of clay tokens imprinted with his physical likeness. Yet the dust has an ambiguous referent: is it some actual shedding from the saint's real body (an allusion, perhaps, to the creation of human beings from the dust of the earth in Genesis), or is it the dust from around the saint's column, rendered holy due to its contact with Symeon's body and to its use as image-bearing token? And what of the priestly petitioner? It would seem that Symeon's gift of the *eulogia* and his command to depart are intended to deprive the priest of an idolatrous attachment to the saint's very flesh—except that the dusty token *is* (possibly) his flesh. The saintly body has a persistent vitality that defies categorization: is it an entity, or an event?[68]

Stories such as this one are full of deflections and oscillations. Symeon's location seems truly undecidable. At the very least, the displacement of Symeon's powerful presence onto his material artistic image dignifies the "matter" of the world as a site of the working of divinity, but at the same time this displacement disrupts the reader's (and the priest's) singular focus on the saint's body. Yet, while seeming to opt for a two-dimensional Symeon, simply a figured seal on a clay token, the text is also a powerful affirmation of the saint's holy touch. Is he a figure in the round, or not? Like the icon of Saints Cosmas and Damian, Symeon's figured token partakes of that ontological instability, an oscillation between subject and object, human and thing, that teaches the reader to exercise a certain hesitance in regard to the phenomenon of human holiness.

In fact, this sort of hesitance—a disruption of expectations of divinity straightforwardly embodied—seems built into the saintly bodies of the later hagiographical tradition. As Sells argues, at the heart of "unsaying" is a dialectic of transcendence and immanence. One of the results of this dialectic is that, "when the transcendent realizes itself as immanent, the subject of the act is neither divine nor human, neither self nor other."[69] We have just seen Symeon's identity turn on an imaginal displacement or disruption of his presence. This "neither-nor" (which is also a "both-and") seems characteristic of the hagiographical presentation of saintly bodies, especially when the corporeal solidity or wholeness of the saint is implied, and then questioned. Paraphrasing Glück, one might say that such hagiographical constructions of holy bodies "allude to larger [heavenly] contexts"—but "they haunt because they are not whole, though wholeness is implied."[70]

A final hagiographical technique pertains precisely to this "haunting" whereby the saint's textually reconstituted body flits in and out of focus, tantalizing the reader with intimations of complete divine-human synergy. My exemplary text is the fifth-century *Life and Miracles of St. Thekla*, which presents the holy body of its saint as ambiguously corporeal.[71] Saint Thekla's body is a visionary appearance that is nonetheless tangible, as in the following anecdote. In Miracle 38, Thekla, described as a great friend of the literary arts, decides to help a gravely ill scholar named Alypius, who has come to her compound seeking a curative dream. She visits him (in the form of a dream) at night; but the text, instead of emphasizing the saint's phantom-like appearance, insists that "she showed herself in her real form." This tangible wraith then asks the scholar what ails him, and he replies with a Homeric tag. Charmed by the appropriateness of the verse to the situation, "the martyr [Thekla] smiled and gave the man a pebble," which she ordered him to attach to his neck, saying that it would cure him. When the scholar woke up, the pebble had vanished, and he was still ill. Meanwhile his son, on the way to visit his father, came upon the pebble lying in the road and, "seduced by its beauty," picked it up, took it to his father and placed it in his hands, and he was immediately cured.[72] According to the author of the *Miracles of Saint Thekla,* the pebble had such great beauty and power because the saint had touched it—another indication of the palpable presence accorded to the visionary substance of such saints.

This is a holy body that is both starkly physical and utterly phantasmal, as is the pebble that she proffers. Materiality is inflected with divinity, but uncannily so. Stories like this one abound in the hagiographical tradition, although they are especially striking in the case of Saint Thekla who, for another example, once spent an entire night with her arms wrapped around an emotionally fragile female suppliant and then, at evening's end (and as observed by the suppliant's roommate), flew out of the room.[73] Interestingly, even though Thekla tends to interact physically with her venerators, the most commonly used verb to describe her appearances (ἐπιφοιτάω) means to visit or to haunt.[74] Thekla's haunting presence implies wholeness but does not reify it. Literally "fleeting"—indeed, flying was her usual mode of locomotion—this ambiguously corporeal body of the saint enacts the "referential openness" that a transcendently material body needs in order to preserve its enigmatic character.[75]

In light of such images, I think it is fair to say that late ancient hagiography accomplished the transformation of the literal body into a deeper truth. Holy bodies such as Saint Thekla's are epiphanies of transfiguration that occupy a signifying space between transcendence and immanence; and just as they avoid idolizing the material, so they also deconstruct naïve or insipid notions of spiritual presence in the world. Theophanic and human at the same time, the subtle embodiments of late ancient hagiography were supremely indirect, and in that indirectness lies their unsaying, their sidestepping, in short, their achievement of the subtracted self of the saints.

Chapter Seven

Animated Bodies and Icons

Depicting the relation between a saint and his icon required as subtle a touch as depicting the saintly body itself. This chapter begins a discussion of the role that hagiographical word-pictures played in "showing," as it were, the ephemeral-but-tangible materialization of a saint in an icon. Like relics, icons were an important part of the material turn in late ancient Christianity, a perspectival shift that fostered reverence for those objects that gave palpable reality to religious ideas like saintly intercession. Also like relics, icons raised the problem of the overinvestment of matter with meaning, particularly to the extent that their status as painted portraits was thought to present, and not merely to represent, saintly presence and power. Icons were just as much "things," in Bill Brown's sense of the term in his "thing theory," as relics: they were objects whose surplus value made them magnets of attraction, and their force was sensuous (material) and metaphysical (theological) at once.[1]

My argument in this chapter and the next is that certain anecdotes about icons in late ancient hagiographies betray an awareness of the delicacy involved in dealing with the spiritual objects that were icons. Of particular interest are anecdotes whose narrative oddities provoke uncertainty about how, exactly, an icon harbors saintly presence. The way in which these brief narratives are crafted curbs the tendency toward idolatry that was endemic to this form of Christian expression in its early stages. This taming of the idolatrous impulse was achieved by dissipating the material opacity of the icon without betraying its substance as mediator of the holy, thus rendering icons as objects that are neither wholly material nor wholly spiritual—or perhaps better said, as objects that are both at once without, however, equating them. Like the phenomenon of relics, the phenomenon of icons was both the sign and the carrier of a complicated relation between materiality and spirituality.

In the two centuries prior to the outbreak of iconoclasm, anecdotes about icons began to appear in hagiographies. One such anecdote, contained in the seventh-century collection of the miracles of Saints Cosmas and Damian, tells the story of a woman who had been healed of various physical afflictions at the saints' shrine on the Golden Horn just outside

Constantinople. Upon her return home, the woman painted images of the saints "on all the walls of her house, being, as she was, insatiable in her desire to see them." One night, the text continues, while alone in her house, the woman came down with an acute stomachache. "Perceiving herself to be in danger, she crawled out of bed and, upon reaching the place where these most wise saints were depicted on the wall, she stood up leaning on her faith as upon a stick and scraped off some plaster with her fingernails. She put the plaster into water and, after drinking the mixture, she was immediately cured of her pains by the visitation [ἐπιφοίτησις] of the Saints."[2]

What is one to make of such a story? At the very least, and on the surface, this seems to be a portrayal of iconophilia run amok, as the woman indulges herself in decorative overkill for the sake of piety. But not only does she plaster her house with images of these saints, she eats their portraits, treating the material substance of the pictures as though it carried the curative presence of Cosmas and Damian themselves. Has this woman passed beyond simple iconophilia to outright idolatry by equating the stuff of a painted image with divine power? From the perspective of an eighth- or ninth-century iconoclastic reader, this story would certainly seem to flirt with idolatry, understood as investing the material world with too much extrahuman meaning and power.

In this chapter, I want to view the flirtation positively as a narrative technique for negotiating the delicate dynamic of saintly presence and absence in images. Consider, first, how the woman is depicted: situated on the knife edge of desire, she yearns for presence. Her longing to see the saints is described as "insatiable" (ἀκόρεστος). What her desirous gaze sees, however, is not the saints themselves, but their artistic representation. Nonetheless, the saints *are* somehow present, since the stuff of their portrayal heals. Insofar as images, like iconic portraits, do not sheerly present but *re*present, they draw on the power of longing to overcome absence; the dead saints come alive not only in memory but also in art. Equally important, second, is the *manner* in which Cosmas and Damian are present. The saints are also on an edge, not of desire but of ontological uncertainty regarding the quality of their presence. The text says that the woman was cured of her pains by the visitation of the saints. The word used for visitation—ἐπιφοίτησις—does indeed carry the sense of divine visitation, but it can also mean a haunting or inspiration.[3] Saintly presence is neither fully material nor fully ethereal but something in between. It inhabits an edge that keeps human saint and spiritual power in a tensive relationship.

By affirming the flirtation in this way, I will develop a reading of certain hagiographical images as constituting a form of "picture theory" that teaches the reader how to engage with icons and how to imagine saintly presence.[4] Reading backwards from the overt theorizing about images during the iconoclastic controversy, I am arguing that the hagiographical enterprise that preceded iconoclasm developed discursive strategies for advertising the importance of representation, of imaging, as a means for embracing the saints without idolizing them. In my view, hagiography's verbal pictures of icons can be read as anticipations of later defenses of icons. That is, they are ideological tools that speak, in narrative pictures, on behalf of the role of images in the religious imagination of late ancient Christianity.[5]

Images and Ideology

Of course, wielding images in the service of religious ideology was nothing new in late antiquity. A striking example is this gold coin minted early in c.e. 313, just a few months after Constantine's victory over Maxentius at the Milvian Bridge (fig. 9). Here Constantine is shown in twin profile with the god Apollo, whose radiate crown assimilates him to Sol Invictus, the "Unconquered Sun" who was Constantine's special divine *comes*, or companion, from as early as c.e. 308.[6] This image not only situates the human Constantine as the near-double of the god but, through the medium of the rayed crown, it also links him to Hellenistic conceptions of divine kingship with which the crown had long been associated.[7] Less obvious but no less important, the Apolline twin associates Constantine immediately with the first *princeps*, the emperor Augustus, who took Apollo as his special divinity, and this dynastic tie is further underscored by Constantine's lean face and "maturely youthful" air, both artistic attributes of Augustus.[8] As R. R. R. Smith has suggested, images such as this one "were not passive reflectors, but like texts and speakers, active participants in public discourse."[9] Not only does the image give Constantine a hallowed politico-religious lineage, it also shows that he has friends in high places.

Edging thus in the direction of divinity made good political sense and, perhaps not surprisingly, this form of imaging had a long history. As James Francis has pointed out,

Persons became symbols well before the Common Era. Hellenistic kings were often portrayed as incarnations of *logos*, living and effective representations of an abstract reality, while in more concrete fashion Roman *triumphators* were made up to resemble the statue of Jupiter Optimus Maximus in the Capitoline temple. The Roman example is indicative of the fascinating complexity which inheres in this topic, since the victorious general was himself an image of an image—a living man made to resemble a statue, the resemblance to which manifests likeness to the living god imaged in and by the statue.[10]

Figure 9. Gold medallion (nine-solidus piece). Constantine and Apollo in profile. Beistegui 233. Photo: Bibliothèque national de France.

Added to the complexity of images imaging images is the fact that the Constantinian artistic gesture in the direction of divinity cohered with the centuries-long tradition of imperial apotheosis. In this tradition, emperors were not, of course, declared to be *divus* until after death. However, as Simon Price has pointed out, "in the third century the reigning emperor was more closely associated with individual patron deities," and while the living emperor was not formally deified, his ties with the gods were made more explicit.[11]

This movement of the emperor closer to the godly end of the human-divine continuum continued in the imperial art of the Constantinian period, as can be seen in the following image of Constantine, a fourth-century bronze statuette (fig. 10). Whereas the doubled image of Con-

Figure 10. Bronze statuette of Constantine. Photo: Lennart Larsen, National Museum of Denmark.

stantine and Apollo on the gold *solidus* maintained a certain oscillation or tensive relationship between the two figures, here the association of the emperor with his patron deity has resulted in a virtual identification of the two. The tensive ambiguity of the image on the coin has vanished as one beholds a true imperial epiphany.[12] Given the radiant resplendence of this image, it is not surprising to read the report of the church historian Philostorgius that "in fifth-century Constantinople, people propitiated with sacrifices and lamps the image of Constantine set on a column, honored it with incense and uttered prayers as to a god."[13] As Archer St. Clair has remarked, in cases like this "the line between earthly respect and divine worship remained a thin one."[14]

From a Christian point of view, the crafting of images such as this for purposes of religious ideology—not to mention veneration—was a risky business. Even though the idea of a continuum between the human and the divine was present in late ancient Christianity in the form of the holy men of the desert and especially the cults of relics and saints, Christians were wary of representations such as the statuette of Constantine, since for them only one human being could claim to be divine. And even when that person, Christ, was represented in the form of a statue, there were defensive protestations against adoring something made of mere matter.[15] As we will see, hagiographers in particular were aware of the dangers inherent in evoking the holiness of human beings.

A major risk associated with images was their use in making the holy accessible to sensation: how can a material object have spiritual life, and how can that spirit be sensed? The anecdote about the frescoes of Saints Cosmas and Damian poses this problematic in stark fashion: the painted bodies of the saintly twins somehow come alive with their healing presence, a presence that is both visual and tactile. This idea that a representation of a holy body might be animate was in my view a continuation, with a Christian hagiographical twist, of an ancient Mediterranean culture-pattern, in which immobility and animation were paradoxically linked.

Animate Immobility

Immobility and animation came together most obviously in statues of the gods and special people such as emperors. Early intimations of divine habitation of statues can be found in the comedies of Aristophanes, in which people "greet a god's statue as their 'neighbor' and speak freely of a statue's hand as the hand of a god."[16] By the early imperial period, widespread testimony documents the belief that "the gods were present through their images," so much so that suppliants pinned petitions to their thighs and legs.[17] As Robin Lane Fox has pointed out, "the simple rustic was not the only person who identified a god with his image: Augustus, no less, showed his annoyance with Poseidon for a spell of bad weather by banishing his statue from a procession."[18]

Several centuries later, this mindset still prevailed. Libanius recorded the following incident involving a statue of the emperor Constantius: "In the city of Edessa, the inhabitants, resenting some treatment they had received, cast down his bronze statue, turned it face down, lifted it up, as they do with children in school, and administered a thrashing to the back and backside, commenting also that anyone visited with such a whipping was far removed from imperial dignity."[19] Like the statue of Poseidon in some way "standing in" for the god himself, here the statue of Constantius reiterates the emperor, who gets the spanking he deserved.[20] Striking a more serious tone, the emperor Julian explained this mindset straightforwardly: recalling the historic moment when the Phrygian goddess Cybele entered Rome in the form of a black stone, he wrote that the stone was "no human thing, but really divine, not lifeless clay but something having life and divinity."[21]

Not only could statues be treated and conceptualized as though they were, in some sense, divinely or humanly alive, the statues themselves were credited with movement and speech. In Graeco-Roman culture at large, statues of the gods had for centuries been said to smile, weep, walk, levitate, give oracles and more humble advice, even sweat. People in trouble could whisper requests in their ears and hope to get a response.[22] From the compassionate ear of the marketplace Hermes observed by Pausanias to the exalted lips of the statue of Serapis in Alexandria, kissed every day by the sun, these stones were more than mere matter insofar as they provided a place for the apprehension of a suprasensible world in this earthly one.[23]

The sense of an immobile statue's animated quality could be indicated by inscriptions on the statue's base. Sometimes these inscriptions took the form of the gods' own speech in answer to the petitionary prayers that had summoned them: "'I am come,' they say, 'standing always beside'" you, whether the "you" be "the citizens, the Emperor, or the men in the city's gymnasium."[24] Other times, the inscription would be in the form of a petition from a devotee "speaking," as it were, to the statue in the first person, as in the following example from the period of the early empire: "Great god, mighty Silvanus, most holy shepherd: . . . attend here favoring to me, holy one, and bring to bear your divine power, for I have offered you as you have deserved a likeness and an altar, which I made for the sake of my masters' and my own safekeeping, and that of my family too. . . . Stay close at hand as my supporter . . . and 'joyfully refresh yourself after your good service.'"[25] There was in fact a long tradition in Greek and Roman antiquity of dedications inscribed on objects given as gifts to gods that, in one way or another, brought the votive objects to life. As Kenneth Gross has observed, "Some [dedicatory inscriptions] describe the gift and the giver, ask a boon, thank the god for past favors, or ask the divinity to take delight in the votive itself. Rather than just describing the object, in other words, they help put it into play, or animate it, as the site of a ritual event. . . . It is perhaps as a reflection of this heightened investment that many of the texts lend a voice to the object itself, letting the statue, shield, mask, stone, or shell speak for its absent donor."[26] Eventually, Christians too participated in this verbal enlivening of images, as in the type of *eulogia* token picturing Saint Symeon the Stylite the Younger inscribed with the words, "Receive, O Saint, the incense, and heal all."[27] Whether the image itself was speaking or being spoken to, the text inscribed on the statue or incised figure was unambiguous in its conviction of comforting presence and power.

For purposes of divine intercession and epiphany, ritual, like inscription, could also animate the inanimate. Several of the spells in the Greek magical papyri are aimed at procuring a spiritual assistant, a πάρεδρος, for the practitioner in need of a lover, dreams, banquets, and other amenities of the good life.[28] Two of these spells, both directed centrally at procuring the affections of a loved one, involve the animation of a statuette of the god Eros. In the simpler of the two rituals, the magician is instructed to carve the statue out of mulberry wood: "He is made as a winged Eros . . . with his right foot lifted for a stride and with a hollow back." Thus fashioned for action, the statue is "endowed with soul" by a burnt offering and activated by the insertion into its hollow back of a gold leaf inscribed with the name of the beloved and a magical name.[29]

In the more elaborate of the two spells, a wax statue of a torch-bearing Eros is enlivened in rather grisly fashion as the magician gathers seven living birds and strangles them: "You are to take them [the birds] in hand and choke them, all the while holding them up to your Eros, until each of the creatures is suffocated and their breath enters him."[30] Thus ritually endowed with life, the statue is now ready to be used to deliver the magician's message. In both spells, the statue of Eros serves as the launching point for a vision of the god, who appears to the beloved in the "likeness of the god or daimon whom she worships."[31] The idea that a representation—here, a statue—might be the source of another representation—a visionary appearance—is a phenomenon that will recur in the context of Christian icons. As we shall see, the paradox of the visionary body had a long and interesting history.

In late Neoplatonic theurgy, another kind of animated statue provided the occasion not only for divine epiphany but also for a blurring of the boundary between the human self and its divine other. Best

known from the work of the fifth-century philosopher Proclus, the theurgical animation of statues of the gods was based on a view of the material world as theophany.[32] Divine power was immanent in the world in
the form of σύμβολα, which were tokens or traces of the divine sown in
the material world in the form of "godlike stones, herbs, animals, and
spices."[33] When the material σύμβολα proper to a specific god were
inserted into hollow cavities of the god's statue, the statue was animated
or activated by the divine power channeled through the levels of being
by those σύμβολα; the goal of this ritual procedure was the presencing
of the god in the form of oracles.[34] Rather than playing the dubious role
of intercessor for erotic gain, in this case the animate object allows the
human practitioner to tap into divine wisdom.

The epiphanic promise of the idea of animated statues was so alluring
that Proclus appropriated it as a metaphor for his definition of a human
being.[35] Aligning the human body with a statue, he observed that, just as
a theurgist attaches "certain symbols to statues [and] makes them better
able to participate in the higher powers, in the same way universal
Nature . . . made [human] bodies like statues of souls [and] she inseminates in each a particular aptitude to receive a particular kind of soul."[36]
Here human body and statue relate in the same way that the human
soul and divine σύμβολα do. In another passage, however, Proclus was
more direct: because the human soul is actually composed of divine
tokens (θεία σύμβολα), "we are statues of the unknowable signs
[συνθήματα]." Further declaring the human body to be an "icon" of
the spiritual world, Proclus used the metaphor of the statue to make the
inscrutable divinity of human beings manifest.[37]

Immobile Animation

In presenting the paradox of the animated object, it is easy to privilege
the liveliness of the material object rather than its immobility—that is,
its status as an inert object—because the culture-pattern that I have been
exploring was premised on the conviction that art can exceed the limitations of its material composition, limitations that are only apparent,
not real.[38] After all, we have seen statues listening, speaking, getting
spanked, sending visions. To be true to both elements of the paradox,
however, attention must also be given to immobility. In this sense, Proclus is a good transitional figure, since he assimilated the human body
to a statue, that is, to a material work of art, and his thought is also useful
for introducing a human inflection into the culture-pattern under discussion. That is, his iconizing of the living human body, declaring it to
be immobile as a statue, raises the question of the relation of the human
being to art. And it also raises the question of the degree of spiritual

animation that enlivens the human-as-artifact, a question that will be pertinent to Christian understandings of icons.

There were others besides Proclus in late antiquity who embraced the metaphor of the human body as immobile statue in order to convey human kinship with a transcendent realm, although they restricted the metaphor of the statue to holy men rather than using it, as Proclus did, to designate the human body per se. Some fifty years prior to Proclus's work, another Neoplatonist, Eunapius of Sardis, wrote his *Lives of the Philosophers and Sophists,* in which he presented two of his philosopher-heroes as statues. One of them was Antoninus, whose students "encountered a statue" when they asked him questions: "fixing his eyes and gazing up at the sky he would lie there speechless and unrelenting."[39] The other was Eunapius's teacher Prohaeresius: Eunapius reported that the crowds listening to him "licked the sophist's breast as though it were the statue of some god."[40] As Eunapius uses it, the metaphor of the statue indicates the stillness needed for contemplation of the divine realm as well as the wisdom of the philosopher, so towering that it links him with the gods.

This metaphorizing of the human as statuesque artifact can be found in the late ancient Christian conceptualizing of holy men as well, especially among ascetics. Indeed, as Peter Brown has observed, "the ideal holy man was thought of as immobile as a statue."[41] Thus in his *Eulogy on Basil of Caesarea,* Gregory of Nazianzus pictured Basil standing in church, "his body, his eyes, his mind unmoving, like a statue set up for God and his altar."[42] Interestingly enough, Basil himself had used the statue-metaphor in a letter to the same Gregory. "He who is anxious to make himself perfect in all the kinds of virtue," he wrote, "must gaze upon the lives of the saints as upon statues, so to speak, that move and act, and must make their excellence his own by imitation."[43]

These kinds of association between holiness and "statuesque" stillness were not only metaphorical. Among desert ascetics, as reported by their awe-struck observers, immobility seems to have been all the rage, as the multiple instances of the practice of standing attest.[44] Whether undertaken as a show of ascetic endurance or contemplative piety and communion with the divine, monks such as the fabled John stood—for three years!—thus withdrawing, as the author of the *Historia monachorum* remarked, from "sensible things."[45] That this practice of standing was directly connected with the motif of the body-as-statue is suggested by the tradition of the stylites on their columns, mimicking or even replacing pagan statues, as some have argued.[46] And an even more blatant linking of the practice of standing with the motif of the statue-body is the report about Saint Theodore of Sykeon, who is said to have "stood like an iron statue through the night and without sleeping continued in praise to God."[47]

Yet, despite the approbation of this phenomenon evident, for example, in Theodoret's celebration of his holy men as "living images and statues" (οἷον τινας εἰκόνας αὐτῶν ἐμψύχους καὶ στήλας) of the holy men of old, the practice of standing carried with it a risk of dehumanization.[48] In his *Lausiac History*, Palladius reported an anecdote about the visit of Macarius of Alexandria to the Pachomian monks at Tabennisi. Observing that some of these monks followed the Lenten penitential practice of standing all night, but getting some relief by sitting during the day, Macarius decided to go the extra mile, as it were. "He took his stand (*estē*) in a corner and stayed there—night and day, presumably—until Easter without kneeling or lying down. . . . The eventual result of this was loud complaint from the other monks about 'this fleshless one' (*ton asarkon*), who had to go or else they would all leave."[49] This anecdote suggests that the metaphor of the holy man as statue threatened to drain him of his human animation, rendering him too abstract and object-like, and perhaps too divine. Macarius is "fleshless" because his inhuman standing assimilates him, through his rigid statue-body, to the stability of the transcendent world, or so it apparently seemed to his fellow monks.[50] And it seemed that way to Macarius himself, at least according to Palladius's report of this monk's own account of another bout of standing:

Having successfully accomplished every form of activity which I had put my mind to, I then came upon another desire, namely, I wanted to spend five days with my mind totally undistracted from its concentration upon God. Having decided this, I shut up my cell and its hall, so that I might not answer anyone, and I stood still beginning at the second hour. I commanded my mind as follows: "Do not descend from heaven; there you have angels, archangels, the powers above, and the God of the universe. Do not descend from heaven!"[51]

In Macarius's mind, the immobile pose took him out of the human and into the divine realm, where he had angels and even God as his companions—a claim, as he notes, that could be subject to the charge of "vanity" or spiritual affectation (τῦφος).[52]

From the Christian point of view, then, finding the proper edge or balancing point between immobility and animation was difficult in terms of ascetic practice, and even more difficult when the issue was posed as the spiritual liveliness of art: there was a danger either of imbuing matter, in the form of a work of art, with too much divinity, as in the case of the animated statue, or of divinizing the human, as in the case of the metaphor of the holy man as statue. The aggressive stance of Christians toward actual statues of pagan gods from the fourth century onward was represented as a battle precisely against idolatry. Yet the fact that that stance was often also superstitiously fearful of the dangerously animated, because demon-infested, character of those same works of art shows that Christians were not only aware of the culture-pattern that I have outlined, but participant in it, even if negatively. Ironically, perhaps, as matter became central to Christian identity in late antiquity, first in the form of relics, and then in the form of icons, Christians would have to elaborate strategies for dealing with their own investment of matter with meaning, seen by some among them as idolatrous.[53] Although Christian artists largely eschewed illusionistic, three-dimensional art for representing their religious heroes,[54] opting instead for the flat, two-dimensional surfaces of painting and mosaics, that choice did not quell the specter of idolatry that I think necessarily accompanies the idea of artistic representations—that is to say, materializations—of the divine.[55]

Icons and Animation

Certain anecdotes in hagiographical literature in the centuries prior to the outbreak of iconoclasm demonstrate how to conceive of an animated image without (quite) idolizing it. I refer specifically to hagiographical images of icons—that is, verbal representations of artistic objects—that model for the reader how one might conceptualize such spirited objects. The context for this literary phenomenon is the "image-rich culture" of the late sixth and seventh centuries.[56] Especially but not only in Byzantium, this period saw a rapid increase in religious imagery both in literature—for example, the miracle-packed *vitae* of saints such as Symeon the Stylite the Younger and Artemios, where icons of the saints are associated with saintly intervention in human life—as well as in the rise of icons themselves and their use in domestic and institutional veneration of the saints whom they depicted.[57]

In both literature and art, icons of the saints were assuming a central role in Christian devotion, in large part because of their connection with miracles of healing and other kinds of intercession.[58] The sense of spiritual presence in icons was so strong that the author of the *vita* of Saint Symeon the Sylite the Younger could attribute the miracle-working power of his image to the fact that the Holy Spirit that dwelled in the saint had "overshadowed" [ἐπισκιάζοντος] his icon.[59] From God to saint to image: this attribution of real spiritual presence was succinctly stated by Leontius of Neapolis who, writing around 630 c.e., had this to say about icons:

When he received from his sons the many-colored coat of Joseph covered with blood, Jacob kissed it while weeping and pressed it to his eyes. He did this not because he loved or venerated the garment, but because by means of it he believed that he embraced Joseph and held him in his arms. In the same way, when we Christians physically [or in the flesh: τῇ σαρκί] hold and embrace an image [εἰκόνα] of Christ, an apostle, or a martyr, we believe that spiritually [τῇ ψυχῇ] it is Christ himself or his martyr whom we hold.[60]

Leontius managed to sidestep idolatry at the same time as he professed a view of icons as conveying spiritual presence.

It was this view of icons as material objects somehow saturated with divine presence that helped provoke the iconoclastic movement in the eighth century. Promoting "a spiritual Christianity over a material one," iconoclasts argued that "an idol of dead matter could not be considered an adequate likeness of a creature that has lived."[61] For them, such images were soul-less.[62] Further, using "the idea of likeness to critique visual representation," iconoclasts argued that likeness pertained only to appearance and hence drew "attention to the visible material creature rather than the invisible deity."[63] Images were thus partial and false, "unable to comprehend the invisible."[64] In response, iconophiles argued that icons were "matter transformed into a holy state."[65] They understood painting to be "a form of visual contact between copy and original"; the icon thus "maintains a trace of its origins in the act of representation."[66] As a major early theorist of icons, John of Damascus, argued, "an image is participatory in that which it represents"; therefore "an icon of Christ must be understood to participate in the divine essence."[67] By extension, an icon of a saint is participatory in the holy powers of the saint. Indeed, like Saint Symeon the Stylite the Younger's hagiographer before him, John of Damascus used the concept of spiritual overshadowing to explain the power of icons (and also why they deserved veneration).[68] Yet concepts such as participation, overshadowing, and trace do not constitute claims to absolute identity of image and spirit. Iconophiles viewed painted representations in terms of a *play* of identity and difference that attempted to avoid circumscribing or confining the subject in the art without forfeiting their ability to harbor the transcendent.

Picturing the Theory of Icons

In hagiographical literature prior to the eighth century, there are anecdotes about icons of saints that anticipate iconophile theory in the ways in which their verbal images of painted images are crafted. In effect, they exploit the paradoxical joining of artistic immobility and spiritual animation in order to convey how an icon of a saint is both limited and unlimited. In so doing, they address the phenomenon of representation as such and thus can be said to "picture theory." We have already seen one such anecdote that "pictures the theory" of nonconfining participation of the saint in the image. The anecdote on the first page of this chapter described the woman who decorated her walls with icons of Saints Cosmas and Damian in thrall to her desire to see them. When she got sick, she scraped off some of the plaster on which the icons were painted, mixed it with water, drank it, and was cured. On a first reading, this image of an icon seems to anticipate the iconophile position concerning the transcendent referent of the image by overstatement, taking participation to entail identity. Saintly curative power is fully and physically present in the matter of the artistic object.

But look again: the text is—intentionally?—ambiguous concerning the source of the cure: one is at first led to think that the iconic drink did the trick, but the text actually says that the woman was cured of her pains by the visitation of the saints. Where and how were they present? What does it mean that the saints are present as a visitation understood as a haunting, as indicated earlier? Although this image of an icon certainly petitions an overinvestment of meaning in matter, it hesitates fully to identify saintly subject with artistic object. Saints Cosmas and Damian, after all, only "visit"; nonetheless, their ephemeral bodies become quite tangible in the substance of their portraits. By thus suspending the reader's certainty about how saints are present in their icons, this image maintains a paradoxical relation of immobility and animation.

Other hagiographical images of icons are even more overt in modeling how to conceive of the conjunction of human and divine in a saintly icon. Consider again the following anecdote featuring Saints Cosmas and Damian, discussed briefly in the last chapter. From the perspective developed in this chapter, it is an anecdote that seeks to convey the animated quality of icons by showing the saints' uncanny (im)material presence in the painting, as in the previous example, but it does so by endowing the saints with a physical presence that seems to be materially substantive without ever quite achieving corporeal solidity. In this story from the *Life of Saint Theodore of Sykeon*, the saint, ill and tearful, lies beneath an icon of the sainted healing twins. Uncannily, the saints emerge from the icon, their appearances matching those in the painted image.[69] Taking Theodore's pulse, Cosmas and Damian determine that he is indeed desperately ill, ask the saint a series of questions, and finally offer to go to heaven to plead with Christ on Theodore's behalf. Returning, they announce that his life has been extended, and disappear—one supposes back into the icon.[70]

In this anecdote, the icon is certainly participatory in the holy powers of the saints; the image harbors healing power, but significantly does not circumscribe it, since Cosmas and Damian are free to flit about wherever they wish, even as high as heaven. And the precise relationship between saintly presence and artistic image is left unspecified: are these saints somehow "inside" their own portrait, or is it just a picture? How is one to understand these ephemeral bodies who nonetheless take a live human being's pulse? As a meditation on representation, this verbal image sets up an interesting illusionistic play between the three-dimensional saintly presences and their two-dimensional portrait, as though to sidestep the idolatrous stance that it comes close to by show-ing the discrepancy or incongruity between saintly presence and art.

Clearly Christian icons could be just as animated as pagan statues. The painting out of which the "living" presences of Cosmas and Damian emerge is very like the magical statue of Eros that sends out a similar visionary body. Icons were just as animated as statues, but more inscruta-bly so, and herein lies the hagiographical twist on the culture-pattern that brings immobility and animation together. In the eerie moment when Saints Cosmas and Damian emerge from their icon as animate beings in the presence of Saint Theodore, the reader experiences what material-culture theorist Bill Brown describes as the ontological insta-bility or ambiguity of animated objects, in which there is "an oscilla-tion between animate and inanimate, subject and object, human and thing."[71]

Ontological ambiguity was not, as far as I can discern, a feature in the pagan tradition of animated statues of the gods, since they do not seem to have provoked intellectual uncertainty about "whether an apparently animate being is in fact alive, or, conversely, whether a lifeless object might not in fact be animate."[72] But hagiographical images of iconic representation such as the one just discussed *do* provoke such intellec-tual uncertainty. And that uncertainty is productive, since it teaches the reader to imagine how a finite object operates in an infinite field of meaning. As Bill Brown might say, an icon is an object that has become a value, and as such it gives tangible reality to the idea of saintly presence and intercession in the real world.[73]

Furthermore, not only do icons contribute the phenomenon of onto-logical instability to the culture-pattern of animated objects; they fore-ground the ambiguity. That is to say, they advertise the flirtation with idolatry without giving into it. In the late sixth-century *Life of Saint Symeon the Stylite the Younger*, there is an anecdote about a clay *eulogia*, a token or blessing, that neatly captures this feature of hagiographical pictures of the theory of icons (fig. 11).[74] In this story, as we saw in the last chapter, a priest has brought his ill son to Symeon's column for heal-ing. Having blessed the son, Symeon tells the priest and his son to go home, but the priest begs that they be allowed to stay in Symeon's vicin-ity, since "being close to you will guarantee us a complete cure." Symeon's response is to rebuff this request: "The power of God is effec-

Figure 11. Eulogia with St. Symeon the Stylite the Younger. Menil Collection, Houston, 79–24.198 DJ. II.J.4 (IV A4). Photo: Menil Collection.

tive everywhere," says the saint. He continues: "So take this *eulogia* made of my dust [τῆς κόνεως μου], depart, and when you look at the imprint of our image, it is us that you will see."[75] By thus deflecting attachment to his person, Symeon directs the priest's, and our, attention to his icon (the imprinted token), an image now imbued with divine power. Yet to look at this image is to see Symeon. Perhaps the deflection has not really fended off the total divinizing of the piece of matter that is Symeon's body. On the other hand, after declaring that the token is made of "*my* dust," Symeon then says, "when you look at the imprint of *our* image, it is *us* that you will see." Who is this "we"? Might it be the overshadowing presence of the Holy Spirit? The text does not say, but the sudden appearance of the plural pronoun in the text unsettles the identification of Symeon, icon, and divine power that the text has put in motion, and then derailed.

Another oddity, noted in the last chapter, concerns that dust out of which the *eulogia* is made. Symeon is clear about ownership; it is "*my* dust." But what exactly is Symeon claiming about the composition of the token? Is it made from the substance of his very body, or from the dirt at the base of his column, dirt sanctified by contact with the saint through the mediation of his pillar? Symeon's location in terms of the *eulogia* with which he claims identity seems truly undecidable, just as the spiritual life of his iconic artifact seems somewhat inscrutable. As a picture of how pictures bring the human self of the saint together with the saint's divine other, this text is somewhat skittish. With its displacements *and* identifications, it seems to reach for a play of identity and difference that would sidestep the positing of the full presence of the invisible in the visible that so alarmed the later iconoclasts.

Given this foregrounding of ambiguity, all of these hagiographical images of icons seem to me to express caution in the face of the spiritual animation of material objects. Yet there is no doubt that these texts embrace iconophilia; they function as pictures of the theory that icons of saints participate in the holy powers of the transcendent realm with which the saints were in communion. They are also, finally, witness to the Christian chapter of a long cultural expectation that the boundary between human self and divine other was an edge that connects, rather than divides, the transcendent and earthly realms, and that the connection happens in a paradoxical conjunction of immobility and animation. That edge is thus double-edged: by exposing separation, it also momentarily effaces it, flirting with idolatry, yes, but unleashing all those visionary bodies to do their healing work. For healing—the assuaging of human anxiety and suffering—was the animating hope in the tradition that filled the material world with spiritual hauntings.

Chapter Eight

Saintly Bodies as Image-Flesh

This chapter continues the inquiry, begun in the previous chapter, into the relation between saints and their icons as portrayed in hagiographical anecdotes about them. Although the focus will continue to be on a poetics of saintly substance and its pedagogical value, more attention will be given to later icon-theory and hagiographies' anticipation of some of its major theses. Since this chapter deals more explicitly with the visual and with problems of representation in literature as well as in iconic art, I begin by introducing a set of terms that will shape the discussion that follows.

In his book *Picture Theory*, W. J. T. Mitchell coined the phrase "the pictorial turn," by which he meant "a postlinguistic, postsemiotic rediscovery of the picture as a complex interplay between visuality, apparatus, institutions, discourse, bodies, and figurality."[1] In a subsequent book, Mitchell returned to this phrase in order to correct the "fallacy" of understanding the postmodern pictorial turn as somehow unique or historically unprecedented, since readers apparently neglected to note his insistence that the turn is a *re*discovery. In that later book, entitled *What Do Pictures Want? The Lives and Loves of Images*, Mitchell wrote, "The pictorial or visual turn, then, is not unique to our time." Rather, "the pictorial turn is a *trope*, a figure of speech that has been repeated many times since antiquity." Further, "a critical and historical use of this figure would be as a diagnostic tool to analyze specific moments when a new medium, a technical invention, or a cultural practice erupts in symptoms of panic or euphoria (usually both) about 'the visual.'"[2]

In late ancient Christianity, there was such a pictorial turn in the "image-rich" culture of icon-veneration, especially in the eastern empire of the sixth and seventh centuries.[3] And this cultural practice certainly did erupt in symptoms of "panic"—the iconoclastic attack—and "euphoria"—the iconophile defense—in the course of the eighth and ninth centuries, as Christians debated the role of the visual in religious devotion. Prior to the overt theorizing about pictorial representation that characterized the iconoclastic controversy, hagiographies of the sixth and seventh centuries were registering symptoms, if not precisely of panic and euphoria, at least of awareness that the "new" medium of icons posed problems regarding the status of visual representation that required addressing.[4] This awareness is carried in hagiographical anecdotes regarding saints' relationships with their own icons. As noted in the last chapter, my argument is that these anecdotes are verbal portraits of the process of picturing; that is, they are a kind of theory in storytelling form that anticipates the later, more straightforwardly conceptual debates about images.[5] My focus in this chapter is on the odd doubling of saint and icon that occurs in these hagiographical anecdotes. Drawing on Mitchell's view of a picture as a complex interplay among (inter alia) visuality, bodies, discourse, and figurality, I will analyze hagiography's depiction of the saint-icon relationship as a meditation on the manner in which flesh enters the order of representation.

Image and Prototype

A straightforward example of the kind of doubling that is my focus is the following anecdote from John Moschus's *The Spiritual Meadow*, a late sixth-century compendium of mini-hagiographies similar to the *History of the Monks of Egypt* and other late ancient Christian collective hagiographies. According to John Moschus, a group of monks in the monastery of Skopelos in Cilicia told this story:

In our times a pious woman of the region of Apamea dug a well. She spent a great deal of money and went down to a great depth, but did not strike water. So she was despondent on account both of her toil and her expenditure. One day she sees [sic] a man in a vision [θεωρεῖ] who says to her: "Send for the likeness [ὁμοίωμα] of the monk Theodosius of Skopelos and, thanks to him, God will grant you water." Straightaway the woman sent two men to fetch the saint's image [εἰκόνα], and she lowered it into the well. And immediately the water came out so that half of the hole was filled. The men who had conveyed the image brought to us some of that water, and we drank it and gave praise to God.[6]

In this anecdote, the icon bearing the likeness of the saint performs a miracle, just as the saint would have done in person. The art-object is the doublet of the holy man, inanimate matter endowed with spiritual power.

As Averil Cameron has observed, in the two centuries prior to iconoclasm, icons were taken to be "material signs of the presence of the spiritual world"; "contemporaries did not doubt that [icons] were true representations of actual reality."[7] But what exactly constituted the "truth" of the representation? Ernst Kitzinger and others have noted a crucial tendency among adherents of the cult of images in the period under discussion here, a "tendency to break down the barrier between image and prototype," such that the subject—be it Christ or a saint—is "palpably present in his image."⁸ Lying behind this perspective may well be the veneration of imperial images as conceptualized by Basil of Caesarea in the fourth century. Using the relation between an emperor and his image as an analogy for explaining Trinitarian relations between Father and Son, Basil wrote:

> How, then, if these are one and one, are there not two Gods? Because we speak of the emperor and of the emperor's image [εἰκών], but not of two emperors. The majesty is not cleft in two, nor is the glory divided. The sovereignty over us is one, and so the acclamation we pay to it is not many but one, because the honor paid to the image passes on to the prototype. Now in the case of the image this is by reason of imitation [μιμητικῶς]; in the case of the Son it is by nature. And as in works of art the likeness [ὁμοίωσις] is dependent on the form [μορφὴν], so in the case of the divine and uncompounded nature the union consists in the communion of the Godhead.⁹

This passage posits a certain reciprocity between the human ruler and his artistic representation. Yet, as Peter Brown has cautioned, "Byzantines of the sixth, seventh and eighth centuries were getting from the icons what they never expected to get from an imperial image—they got the miracle of healing."¹⁰ The earlier analogy based on the imperial image, which emphasized imitation and honor, lacked the tactile physicality of presence and power that anecdotes such as the one from John Moschus's *Spiritual Meadow* convey.

On the other hand, as Charles Barber has argued, the emperor's portrait provided a model for a "very full sense of representation" because iconic painting was "understood as a form of visual contact between copy and original" and thus maintained "a trace of its origins in the act of representation." The icon "reiterates" the emperor, becoming the figure whom it represents in his absence.¹¹ A model for the power of iconic likeness had already been articulated in the fourth century by Athanasius of Alexandria, who like Basil of Caesarea had used the analogy of the emperor's icon to describe the theological image-relation of the Son to the Father:

> In the image [εἰκόνι] [of the emperor] there is the character [or appearance: εἶδος] and the form [μορφὴ] of the emperor, and in the emperor is that character which is in the image. For the emperor's likeness [ὁμοιότης] is exact in the image, so that the one gazing at the image sees the emperor in it, and again the one gazing at the emperor recognizes that he is the one in the image. And since the image does not at all differ, the image might say to one wishing to view the emperor after seeing the image: "I and the emperor are one; I am in him and he is in me. That which you see in me you behold in him, and what you look upon in him you behold in me." Therefore whoever adores [προσκυνῶν] the image also adores the emperor in it, for the image is his form and character.¹²

The ritual vocabulary of adoration (*proskynesis*), along with the view that between the painted likeness and the actual person depicted there is a fluid back-and-forth of identity, icon and emperor being somehow "in" each other, both carry the sense of full representation as argued by Barber. Like relics, images can effect presence in the face of absence.[13]

Nonetheless, Athanasius's sense of presence, carried by the visual vocabulary of *eidos* and *morphē*, is more formalist than it is material, at least in the sense that later hagiographers understood saintly presence in icons. A recent student of the economy of the icon has argued for "an understanding of icon doctrine in its powerful appeal to flesh and matter."[14] If palpable presence constitutes at least part of the truth of an icon's status as representation, a perspective more relevant than that derived from views of imperial images can be found in fragments from the work of the sole (extant) theorist of icons prior to the outbreak of the iconoclastic controversy, Leontius of Neapolis. Writing in the early seventh century in his *Fifth Discourse Against the Jews*, Leontius wrote that when he performs *proskynesis* before an icon of Christ, he is of course not worshipping the nature of the wood or the pigments.[15] Having thus absolved Christian ritual veneration of icons from the charge of idolatry—a defensiveness that permeates this treatise—Leontius then declared, "All Christians when in the flesh [τῇ σαρκί] we hold and embrace an icon of Christ or an apostle or a martyr, we believe that we hold in the spirit [τῇ ψυχῇ] Christ himself or his martyr."[16] As Vincent Déroche has observed, the heart of Leontius's argument lies in a theory based on "the necessity of material intermediaries in a genuine religion."[17]

According to Leontius, the icon makes present again what is absent through an affective medium; just as icons compensate for the absence of Christ and the saints, so they also serve as constant reminders of the true God.[18] Leontius has brought "the material icon to the center of an economy of remembrance."[19] However, flesh and spirit, body and figurality, are somewhat estranged from each other by Leontius's dual concern to protect Christians from the charge of idolatry—honoring the objects themselves—and to emphasize the memorial status of icons. That is, his presentation of the icon as aide-mémoire seems to be in tension with his view of the specifically *material* quality of the icon as mediator between flesh and spirit. On the other hand, his pairing of icons with relics brings matter to the fore by virtue of an insistence on touch as well as on the active power of those bones and pictures.

As Leontius argues, "relics and icons of the martyrs have often driven off demons." "Tell me," he says to his imagined interlocutor, "how many manifestations of saints' presence [ἐπισκιάσεις], how many gushings forth [of balm], often even of blood, have been produced by the

icons and relics of martyrs?"[20] Further, "If God does miracles by means
of bones, it is quite clear that he is also able to do the same by means of
icons, stones, and many other objects."[21] With statements such as these
that draw a parallel between icons and relics in terms of active spiritual
presence and power, Leontius takes a step toward viewing icons as transformed matter. Especially pertinent is his use of the term "ἐπισκιάσεις,"
literally "overshadowings," to describe saintly presence in icons and relics. Derived from the verb ἐπισκιάζω, this word suggests powerful transformative presence, given the verb's use to designate both the Holy
Spirit's "overshadowing" of Mary at the Annunciation, as well as the
bright cloud that "overshadows" the disciples after Jesus' transfiguration and out of which God speaks.[22] Leontius has brought matter (in the
form of icons and relics), human saint, and divine spirit into the same
intimate neighborhood.

Nonetheless, when Leontius looked at an icon, he did not see divine
energy in action as some of his contemporary hagiographers did. The
material itself is not imbued with the holy. As Barber has observed, "The
thread that runs through all of [Leontius's] responses is to claim that
the material's value is at best partial. The image is appropriate for man's
material nature; it has value when it maintains a formal relation to the
one it shows, and it engenders a symbolic relation to the one represented."[23] But at least the material has partial value.

Leontius's worry about idolatry in connection with icons was echoed
in the hagiographical topos, evident already in the fourth century in
Athanasius's *Life of Saint Antony*, whereby the saint's miraculous powers
of healing, discernment, and other charisms are attributed to Christ, the
saint being an intermediary for the manifestation of divine presence.
However, unlike Leontius, many sixth- and seventh-century hagiographical anecdotes about icons convey a notion of iconic representation that
is ontologically more radical than his adherence to an understanding of
the saint-icon relation as largely formal and symbolic. In anecdotes such
as the one above about the well-water-producing icon of the monk Theodore, the icon is a presentation as well as a representation of the monk;
in a sense, it is truly his double. In hagiographical discourse about icons,
the saintly body is not just a figure; it is what I will call "image-flesh," a
phenomenon in which the relation of likeness is transformed into one
of immanence.

Presentation and Representation in Icons

An example of "image-flesh" occurs in one of the eerie moments of
saint-image oscillation in the *Life of Saint Symeon the Stylite the Younger*. In
one of the miracle stories, a barren, demon-possessed woman takes ref-

uge near the saint's column. While at the column, the woman and the demon both hear "the spiritual icon of the saint which said with a human voice [τὴν πνευματικὴν αὐτοῦ εἰκόνα λέγουσαν ἀνθρωπίνη φωνῇ], 'Evil and impure spirit, I separate you from her, and she will return to her husband and a child will be born to them in the following year.' "[24] It is odd enough that an icon of the saint should be in the living saint's presence. It is even odder that it is the icon that speaks with a human voice. It really *is* Symeon's double, so much so that it can replace him . . . or can it? Immediately after the icon makes its pronouncement, the devil protests at some length. And then the text continues with the words, "*Symeon* said to him," with no mention of the icon.[25] Who is speaking? The matter of the icon and the body of the saint seem interchangeable; what they share is the voice of power. As image-flesh, Symeon and his icon are a duality, but at the same time a unity, like a double exposure on photographic film. But this double exposure is not a mistake; the superimposition of saint and artistic object makes it impossible to decide whether the image reflects the saint, or whether the saint reflects the image, and provides support for the paradoxical ontology of saintly icons.

As this miracle story continues, the icon is pulled back—somewhat—from the order of ontological presence and viewed as an artistic object in the order of representation. A child is born as promised, and the woman and her husband take their child to show Saint Symeon. Back home once again, the woman hangs an icon of Symeon in their house, where it performs miracles of exorcism and healing, "because the Holy Spirit that dwelled in [Symeon] overshadowed it [the icon]" [ἐπισκιά-ζοντος αὐτῇ τοῦ ἐνοικοῦντος αὐτῷ πνεύματος ἁγίου].[26] We have encountered this notion of an icon being overshadowed by the Holy Spirit earlier where, in Leontius's text, it functions to figure the very full representative power of icons.

Here, too, the idea of overshadowing places the icon squarely in the sphere of artistic representation and the power that such representations were thought to mediate—but it doesn't stay there for long. Or, perhaps better: the text presents the reader with a moment in which the "presentist" dimension of representation is exposed. That moment comes at the end of the section of the *Life of Saint Symeon the Stylite the Younger* that I have been discussing. Immediately following the hanging up of the icon of Symeon and the declaration of the Holy Spirit's over-shadowing, the text mentions a woman in the couple's community who had been bleeding for fifteen years: her faith led her to their house to look at the icon and she was healed, for she had said to herself before-hand, "If only I might look at his image [or face or likeness: ὁμοίωσιν], I will be saved."[27] This conviction that simply looking at an icon can heal brings out the full meaning of the gaze as touch at the same time as it shows the power of the icon as saintly double. It is an image, and more than an image, at once.

And there is a further doubling, since this act of healing is Christomimetic, repeating the act of Jesus in curing the hemorrhaging woman in Mk. 5:25–29 and conflating the Markan woman's reference to touch with the later woman's reference to sight.[28] Fullness of representation has become fullness of presence; Symeon's icon is image-flesh. So much was Symeon's image imbued with the saint himself that one type of blessing token available for pilgrims at his column featured the bust of the saint atop his column, with this prayer of direct address inscribed within the circular field of the token: "Receive, O Saint, the incense, and heal all."[29] One could address the image as though real, a phenomenon attested also for Saint Daniel the Stylite, to whom a group of grateful pilgrims dedicated a silver icon with the words, "O Father, beseech God to pardon our sins against thee."[30]

The secret of the image's vitality is its spirited surplus. One of the pedagogical lessons of such a view of icons may well be that representation entails metamorphosis, defined as "a process at once natural and unnatural, at once bringing the dead to life and yet transcending life, the real, and nature, in that very triumph."[31] And metamorphosis—or, in Christian terms, transfiguration—entails not only the transformation of the matter of the icon by a touch of the holy but also the transformation of the eye of the beholder. Only a transfigured eye can gaze at an icon and be healed; thus just as the saint and the icon double each other, so the one who gazes must cultivate double-vision, because icons as representations extend the boundaries of the observable, visible world, and when they move into their presentist mode, they invite a seeing of divine energy in action.

Tangible Visions, Uncanny Doubles

Making contact with a saint by means of his image seems to have been late antiquity's version of virtual reality, except that the visionary simulation had tangible and lasting effects. As Gary Vikan has pointed out, one function of icons was "to stimulate the epiphany" that was "critical for the saint's miraculous intervention."[32] For example, the seventh-century hagiographical collection, the *Miracles of Saint Artemios*, relates the following anecdote about a certain Sergios, a man suffering from a testicular hernia. While he was sleeping one night at the granary where he worked, Saint Artemios appeared to him in the guise of the granary's administrator and gave him a gold coin.

After Sergios woke up, he was pleased with the gift of the coin. For while still drowsy with sleep, he believed he actually held the gold coin. But when he opened his palm and fingers and found that he possessed a wax seal bearing an image [ἐκτύπωμα] of the saint, coming to his senses, he recognized the miracle that was worked upon him and that St. Artemios was the one who had appeared to him. Immediately softening the seal, he anointed his genitals and as soon as the softened wax of the seal touched him, instantly he became healthy and glorified God and the holy martyr.[33]

As Vikan notes, "the miracle is triggered by an iconic match between a midnight vision experienced by a suppliant . . . and the image stamped into the wax *eulogia* he wakes up with the next morning."[34] The vision, the image, and the healing wax of the token all double each other, and once again, sight and touch are complementary.

Vikan notes further about this anecdote that "the image brings the saint and the blessed substance—and not the icon itself—brings the cure."[35] Here I disagree, for how can one separate the icon (the wax token) from the image of the saint that is stamped in it? If anything, the icon *really* brings the cure, as the saint's image melts into the waxen substance, energizing it with healing power. From the perspective of the phenomenon of image-flesh, Vikan's statement does not go far enough in terms of the text's situating of Artemios's image as it shifts from representation to presentation and back again. I say "back again" to the order of representation, because one could also say that the image *disappears* as the token melts, thus preserving difference between the visionary presence of the saint and his icon. It is precisely this oscillation that the phenomenon of saintly doubling preserves. Matter can be transformed by the holy without becoming an idol.

Nonetheless, I agree with Vikan that, in anecdotes such as this, epiphany or visionary appearance is critical to saintly interaction. Yet, when visionary presence is paired with the saint's icon, there is an odd undecidability about identity that deserves to be underscored. As with Saint Symeon, so also with Saint Artemios: real presence and image seem sometimes interchangeable. In one anecdote in the *Miracles of Saint Artemios*, for example, a sailor named Isidore who had a genital disorder was lying in Artemios's church, a center where Christian incubation was practiced. One night "the saint in full view [ὀφθαλμοφανῶς] approached the man, while many others who were awaiting the cure looked on."[36]

Here the martyr-saint comes alive, not in a dream as he usually did, but as a real presence—"evident to the eye," visible not only to Isidore but to the others in the church.[37] Thus in full view, "the saint stood over him with an invisible force [ἀοράτῳ δυνάμει]. Isidore arose from his bed and ran toward the image [εἰκόνος], and holding up his outstretched hands, he hung suspended as though his hands were tied to chains, hovering one cubit above the floor and yelling loudly."[38] As with Saint Symeon, so in this anecdote there is an unexplained switching from the saint in full view to an icon. In the case of Saint Artemios, not only can the reader not discern for certainty the source of the power that suspends the man in the air, even the referent of "icon" is unclear. Is it the icon of Artemios himself, mentioned in Miracle 34, which also mentions icons of Christ and John the Baptist hanging in the church? Or is it the icon of Christ mentioned in Miracle 32? Furthermore, even the visionary presence of Artemios is doubled; when, after Isidore falls onto his mattress after being suspended, the crowd asks him what happened, he says that "some person wearing a cloak and a belt suspended" him, squeezed his afflicted genitals, and exorcised the demon that was the source of his problems. Only when he saw that he was healed did he realize that the vision in cloak and belt was Saint Artemios, who has now inexplicably vanished from the scene of action.[39]

Although Artemios may have been more metamorphic than most saints, still the point that this anecdote makes about iconic representation is clear. A dynamic surplus unites image and saint, but any final union is troubled by their odd doubling. Thus Artemios, for example, can be present as an immanence possessing an immovable power, but he can also be present as the icon toward which his patient reaches, an artistic object that exists inanimately as "swirls and eddies of paint on a flat plane, mere material."[40] The genius of the hagiographical storytelling is that it manages to bring saint and object together without ever—quite—equating them. They are uncanny doubles, and herein lies the significance of these anecdotes as a mode of thought rather than as simple, straightforward narratives of "true" miracles. Because these hagiographical anecdotes present the saint-icon relationship as a dynamic rather than a static one, they provide models for valuing the material, fleshly realm without idolizing it. They are, in short, verbal visualizations of what would later become iconophile theory.

Icon-Theory: John of Damascus

As anticipations of later theorizing about icons, these picture-concepts that I have been discussing can be read as meditations on the role of representation in religion. This was an issue that exercised the eighth-century theologian John of Damascus, whose arguments in favor of icons as divine images constituted the first wave of iconophile theory in reaction to iconoclasm. Writing in defense of representation, John famously based his position on the event of incarnation. The enfleshed god, visible in a human body, had dignified the material realm and, by extension, images crafted out of it. In one of his treatises "On the Divine Images," he wrote:

I do not venerate matter, I venerate the fashioner of matter, who became matter for my sake, and in matter made his abode, and through matter worked my salvation. "For the Word became flesh and dwelt among us." It is clear to all, that flesh is matter and is a creature. I reverence therefore matter and I hold in respect and venerate that through which my salvation has come about, I reverence it not as God, but as filled with divine energy and grace.[41]

The fact that the Word had a body made embodiment itself a site of religious meaning, "filled with divine energy and grace." This passage continues with an enumeration of physical objects and places (the cross, the tomb, the skins on which the Gospels were written, liturgical objects) that are all "matter" that can be included in the economy of divine energy that John is describing. This is surely an instance of the corporeal imagination at work and, in John's hands, situating icons in this broader context makes icons part of a theological discourse that celebrates a material over a spiritual Christianity.[42] Portrayal could be "the portrayal of life itself" because this form of Christian theology, centered on the Incarnation, celebrated "the triumph of flesh over sin, suffering, and death,"[43] whereas iconoclasts, rejecting iconophiles' embrace of icons as things that were "more carnal" [τὸ σωματικώτερον], "refused a value to the incarnate knowledge of the one God."[44]

John's view that the Incarnation had made matter capable of being filled with divine energy and grace was, of course, a direct answer to the charge of idolatry. While he recognized that the "uncircumscribable and invisible" God cannot be depicted in an image, he declared, "I am emboldened to depict the invisible God, not as invisible, but as he became visible for our sake, by participation in flesh and blood."[45] Furthermore, he argued, "When you see the bodiless become human for your sake, then you may accomplish the figure of a human form [τῆς ἀνθρωπίνης μορφῆς τὸ ἐκτύπωμα]; when the invisible becomes visible in the flesh, then you may depict the likeness [ὁμοίωμα] of something seen."[46] Thus the Incarnation had in effect abrogated the second commandment against the fashioning of idols. As Andrew Louth puts it, "When God became incarnate, he placed himself in the order of signs."[47]

Images were critical elements in John's view of cosmic harmony. They functioned to "establish relationships between realities: within the Trinity, between God and the providential ordering of the universe, between God and the inner reality of the human soul, between visible and invisible, between the past and the future, and the present and the past."[48] His enthusiasm for images no doubt accounts for his somewhat defensive tone in regard to the charge of idolatry—his repeated insistence that he does not venerate matter itself, for example, and his repeated affirmation that the incorporeal God cannot be shown in images. His (somewhat feeble) attempt at distinguishing between Christian icons and pagan "idols" further exposes his embrace of an economy of the image and the senses as crucial portals of religious knowledge, and his statement that "divine providence provides figures and shapes of what is without shape or figure" certainly underscores the positive aspects of images, and of icons in particular.[49]

Critical to John's view of icons is the concept of participation. As examples of the kind of matter that "participates in divine energy [ὕλην τῆς θείας ἐνεργείας μέτοχον],"[50] icons are a kind of image that is "participatory in that which it represents."[51] Teetering close to an identification of signifier and signified, John states (following his quotation of Basil of Caesarea cited above), "If the image of the emperor is the emperor, and the image of Christ is Christ, and the image of a saint is a saint, then the power is not divided nor the glory shared, but the glory of the image becomes that of the one depicted in the image."[52] Elsewhere, however, John pulls back from an unquestioned ontology of the image by introducing difference into his notion of identity: "An image is therefore a likeness and pattern and impression of something, showing in itself what is depicted; however, the image is certainly not like the archetype, that is, what is depicted, in every respect—for the image is one thing and what it depicts is another—and certainly a difference is seen between them, since they are not identical."[53] As he says in another passage, icons of saints are "overshadowed [ἐπισκιαξομένων] by the grace of the divine spirit."[54] In John's theory, the energy that activates icons participates in matter without being captured or circumscribed by it. He has broken the barrier between image and prototype—but not completely—thus allowing for a "showing" of participation that maintains difference.

In my view, the doubling that characterizes many hagiographical depictions of saints and their icons anticipates the later conceptualizing of artistic representation in Christianity, especially regarding theories about a play of identity and difference in the relation between saint and icon. In hagiography, icons are clearly the locus of divine performance; they show that "matter" (a picture) can harbor "spirit." Yet the repeated motif of the animated icon, which is premised on the ability of human beings to see divine energy in action, both reflects and attempts a negotiation of a religious conundrum regarding the mediating power of artistic objects. Because, in icons, flesh had entered the order of representation in a particularly bold way, devotees of icons were pressured to imagine how an object can mediate divine presence without circumscribing or limiting it or, worst of all, being identified with it.

Double Exposures

One hagiographical solution to this problem was the uncanny doubling of image and saint in anecdotes that draw the reader into a site of divine encounter that rests on the paradox of image-flesh, in which the visionary body of the saint is nonetheless real. The truth of the iconic representation of the saint lies in its ontological uncertainty, as in the following anecdote from the *Miracles of Saints Cosmas and Damian*, a collection of stories from the sixth and seventh centuries. This story concerns a soldier named Constantine, who was in the habit of taking an icon (ἐκτύπωμα) of the twin saints along with him whenever he was posted away from home. While abroad, he married a woman who became afflicted with pain in her jaw and, "forgetting that he had the icon with him, Constantine was at a loss what to do."[55] The story continues:

> The following night she fell asleep and saw these great and awesome physicians . . . Cosmas and Damian standing by her bed in the form in which they are depicted [ἐν ᾧ ἐκτυποῦνται σχήματι] and saying to her, "Why are you afflicted? Why are you causing distress to your husband? We are here with you. Do not worry. . . ." When she awoke, she questioned her husband, wishing to learn from him the appearance (τὰ σχήματα) of the glorious Saints Cosmas and Damian, i.e., how they are depicted and in what manner they manifest themselves to the sick. The husband explained to her their appearance and related the blessings they confer. . . . The story made him remember that he had in the wallet he carried under his arm a representation of the saints on an image [τὰ τῶν ἁγίων ἐν εἰκόνι ἐκτυπώματα] and, taking it out, he immediately showed it to his wife. When she saw it, she offered obeisance and realized that indeed the Saints were present with them as they had said.[56]

Here indeed is a portrayal of an icon as an image that is participatory what it represents, as John of Damascus would argue a century or so later. Depiction and manifestation of these two saints are doubles, and seeing is both artistic—looking at the icon—and visionary—dreaming saintly presence—at once. In fact, looking at the icon confirms the saints' visionary presence; there is likeness, but not identity, since a painting and a dream image are not the same. The representation is true, and the saints' presence is quasi-ontological; but the means by which saint and object relate is left unspecified. What matters is that the saints have become image-flesh.

A similar anecdote about these same saints is in the *Life of Saint Theodore of Sykeon*, which I present again in this chapter with the addition of part of the text not included in the discussion of it in Chapter 6. Recall that in this anecdote, Saint Theodore collapses in emotional and physical distress beneath an icon of Saints Cosmas and Damian. "These saints," according to the narrative, "were seen by him looking just as they did in that sacred icon and they came close to him, as doctors usually do; they felt his pulse and said to each other that he was in a desperate state." Following extensive conversation, the saints undertake a heavenly journey to plead for an extension of Saint Theodore's life, return and announce that his life has been spared by Christ. The angels who had been hovering around Theodore, waiting for his death, are told to depart by a mysterious young man who accompanies Saints Cosmas and Damian from heaven to Theodore's side. Next, the young man and the angels disappear from sight, "going up to heaven." The saints then announce to Theodore that his life has been spared, and "with these words they, too, vanished."[57]

In this anecdote, as in the previous one, there is the motif of visual likeness between saints and their icon. Here, however, saintly presence is more palpable, as Cosmas and Damian touch Saint Theodore by taking his pulse. The physicality of icons is a theme that occurs throughout Theodore's *vita*; twice he is cured by substances dribbling or bubbling over from icons.[58] Yet the theme of tangibility is matched by a mysterious ethereality; after they have done their work, Saints Cosmas and Damian simply "vanish"—where? Back into their icon? The text is tantalizingly silent. As Robin Cormack has commented about this anecdote, "Theodore, then, makes his contact with the 'other world' through the activity of the inhabitants of an icon. In this particular narrative there is a sense of passing, like Alice, into a looking-glass world. Icons are perceived as the means through which direct contact is to be made with the supernatural world."[59] Yes, but I would add that, in the realm of image-flesh, the looking-glass world is *this* world, seen with a transfigured eye.

The most spectacular instance of representation as metamorphosis occurs in the *Life of Saint Symeon the Stylite the Younger*, where the motif of icon-saint doubling betrays a skittishness about idolatry at the same time as it petitions the real presence of what John of Damascus called "divine energy" in matter. Here is Miracle 231 once more, but now with telling details that were not addressed in discussions of it in previous chapters. In this miracle, a priest and his ailing son visit Saint Symeon at his pillar on the Miraculous Mountain, seeking a cure. "Inspired by the Holy Spirit," Symeon prays over him: "In the name of our savior Jesus Christ, Son of God, who enlivens all things, be whole in your entire body." Upon hearing these words, the son senses a "force" (δυνάμιν) enter him, and is healed. The priest then finds that his second son is ill, and takes him also to the saint, who with his right hand marks him with the sign of the cross and tells the priest to go on their way. But the priest asks that they be allowed to stay for a few more days: "your hand will touch and bless us, for being near you will assure us of a complete cure." Symeon responds: "the power of God is effective everywhere. Take this token made of my dust, leave, and when you look at the imprint of our image, it is us that you will see" (Λαβὼν οὖν τῆς κόνεως μου τὴν εὐλογίαν, ἀπότρεχε καὶ ἐν τῇ σφραγῖδι τοῦ τύπου ἡμῶν βλέπων ἐκεῖνο βλέπεις ἡμᾶς). Testily, Symeon asks the priest which he finds more to his advantage, the blessing-token or his (that is, Symeon's) (literal) right hand, but he ends up extending both his right hand and the token anyway; that night, the priest's son is cured.

Some days later, the priest's third son falls ill, and he asks to be taken to the saint. But the priest, remembering Symeon's counsel to have faith, says: "Saint Symeon, my son, has the power to come visit you here, and you will be healed and live." Although the text does not say so, the logic of the story suggests that, at this point, the *eulogia* bearing Symeon's image is brought out. The boy, gasping with amazement, cries out, "Saint Symeon, have pity on me," and directs his father to "throw on incense and pray, for the servant of God, Saint Symeon, is [standing] before me."[60] As Gary Vikan remarks, "the conclusion is predictable; Symeon appears to the boy in a vision, attacks the demon that possesses him, and (with his blessed earth) restores the boy to good health."[61]

In this anecdote, the sense of representation is so very "full," to recall Barber's characterization, that it becomes presentation, yet the complicated doubling troubles any sense of absolute identity between saint and image. Consider, first, the *eulogia*, a pilgrim token of blessing made of red clay and stamped with the saint's likeness; icons in effect, dozens of these "Symeon souvenirs" have survived to the present. As Vikan has pointed out, a token such as the one in this story was not a mere memento but rather "a piece of portable, palpable sanctity which possessed and could convey spiritual power to its owner."[62] This is certainly an appropriate description of the *eulogia* made of Symeon's "dust." In fact, Symeon's dust, whether in token form or not, is presented in his *vita* as matter superabundantly impregnated with power: not only does it cure human illnesses, it also restores a sick donkey to health, calms a storm, and makes soured wine sweet again.[63]

If the referent of "dust" is the reddish earth at the base of Symeon's pillar, there would seem to be a chain of spiritual contamination, as it were, from the spirit-filled saint down the column to the dirt around it.[64] Charged with power by virtue of contact with the saint, the dust doubles for the saint himself. And there is a further doubling, since the dust is formed into an image, an iconic representation of Symeon that is a site of constant arrival, because whenever one looks at it, one will "see that it is" Symeon.[65] But is it only Symeon? He says, "Take this image of my dust, and when you look at the imprint of *our* image, you will see that it is *us*." These plural pronouns seem to imply a further doubling; could it be the Holy Spirit that dwells in Symeon, as the text says elsewhere, or even Christ, given the Christomimetic character of Symeon's holiness?[66]

The uncertainty about who is doubling whom, as well as the whereabouts of the saint's power, is reinforced by Symeon's irritated remark to the priest. When he asks the priest which he would prefer, the *eulogia* or the touch of his right hand, Symeon seems to imply (having, after all, just told the priest to leave his presence and go home) that the priest ought to prefer the token. Yet he gives the priest both the token and the touch of his hand anyway, as the text once again calls attention to the doubling whereby Symeon's presence is constantly displaced. Symeon's body seems to be everywhere, and nowhere, such that an idolatrous identification of flesh with spirit is simply impossible, a fact that receives further support from the saint's visionary appearance—out of the iconic token, perhaps?—at the end of the anecdote. Living saint, dust, icon, and vision come together in a dizzying doubling that affirms the performative power of both saint and icon at the same time as it defeats the view that representation collapses image and archetype. As archetype, Symeon is both present and absent, always on the move, an elusive ontological force.

What, finally, is the point of this doubling in hagiographical anecdotes about saintly icons? In large part, I think, it can be read as an attempt to defuse the very real anxieties about idolatry that the veneration of icons provoked, both during the period of the boom in icon veneration, as witnessed by Leontius of Neapolis, and later during the period of the iconoclastic controversy, as witnessed by John of Damascus.[67] Taking advantage both of what is visible and what is invisible in the image, hagiographers constructed an eerie ontology for icons by situating them in a play between presentation and representation. As with the story about Symeon, it becomes difficult to decide whether the image reflects the saint, or whether the saint reflects the image. One would like to ask the "real" Symeon to stand up, but in these hagiographical anecdotes, that is impossible, for as John of Damascus later argued, in religious representation, difference trumps identity, but not so as to cancel participation. As image-flesh, the saintly icon in hagiographical anecdotes was a form of picture-theory that drew on a complex interplay of visuality, discourse, bodies, and figurality in order to "show" how the spirit inflects the human world. With their complicated doublings, these anecdotes model the kind of double-vision needed to engage with the iconic presence of the saints.

Such was hagiography's contribution to theorizing about the role of

art in religion. In the final chapter, the subtle body of the saint in literature will give way to the subtle materialization of the saint in art. As we
will see, ephemeral tangibility was as much a part of artistic portrayal of
saints as it was of hagiographic portrayal. Wherever it appeared, it seems,
the saintly body was a poetic body.

Chapter Nine
Incongruous Bodies

The icons that figure in the hagiographical anecdotes discussed in the previous two chapters were in the main objects that could be hung on walls. But this form of icon does not exhaust the late ancient conception of icons: as Averil Cameron has pointed out, though "we tend to think of icons typically as portable images painted on wood, it is important to realize that it was neither the material nor its portability that made a picture into an icon."[1] She continues: "It is rather the subject and treatment of the picture that qualifies it for the term 'icon,'" as evidenced by the fact that "several of the images that would attract the hostility of the Iconoclasts in fact took the form of fixed decoration in churches, in mosaic or fresco."[2] One such fixed decoration, a mosaic portrait of Saint Agnes, will ultimately provide the focus of this chapter's analysis of an artistic style that re-materialized the once-living body of a saint in a concrete image so fashioned as to "show" the holiness of a special human being.

As noted in an earlier chapter, because they were dead and so literally gone, martyrs were situated at the farthest reaches of sensory apprehension where memory turns to imagination.[3] For the artist, crafting an image of a martyr in mosaic tiles was thus not only a material but also an imaginative practice, especially since martyrs such as Agnes had, as saints, become vehicles of intercession between the earthly and heavenly realms and so had been touched by transcendence. How one might use a material substance such as glass tesserae in order to represent a saintly body that could both disclose and mediate the power of an invisible spiritual world is the issue explored in what follows.

Icons and Agency

Attributing to icons the ability to disclose and mediate spiritual power suggests that icons have agency. As objects that, following Brown's "thing theory," have become things, loci of surplus value, icons have not only "force" as sensuous and metaphysical presences, but they also effect a change in the relation between object and human subject.[4] An

icon is not an ordinary picture, and to behold one, especially as a suppliant, is to undergo a change in one's "natural" perception of art. In his
book *What Do Pictures Want?* literary and art critic W. J. T. Mitchell has
trenchantly stated the obvious about the issue of iconic agency: "Iconophilia and iconophobia only make sense to people who think images
are alive."[5] As he goes on to observe, "[images] are phantasmatic, immaterial entities that, when incarnated in the world, seem to possess
agency, aura, a 'mind of their own.'"[6]

In early Byzantine hagiography, the idea that images possess agency,
aura, and a mind of their own functions well as a theoretical conceptualization of their concrete treatment of icons, expressing what hagiographers themselves did not explicitly say. For rather than theorizing about
the nature of artistic representations of the saints, as did later iconophiles such as John of Damascus, hagiographers instead wrote anecdotes
that showed icons in action—or perhaps better, in *inter*action with their
venerators. We have already seen, for example, the seventh-century *Life
of Saint Theodore of Sykeon*, which is punctuated by stories that narrate the
boons granted to Saint Theodore by icons. To mention just a few: as a
child, Theodore was cured of bubonic plague by drops of dew dripping
from an icon of Christ, and another icon of Christ, giving him in effect
a honeyed tongue, granted the boy the grace of a better memory for
learning the psalter by heart; as an adult, bubbling myrrh from an icon
of the Virgin Mary soothed an affliction of his eyes.[7] Of course the most
remarkable example of iconic agency in this *vita* is the anecdote in
which the painted image of Saints Cosmas and Damian comes alive, as
it were, with the saints' healing presence.[8] As Robin Cormack has
observed, Saint Theodore "owes his life to the concern of a supernatural
being in the form of an image"; indeed, the saint's recovery is "to be
attributed to the agency of God as icon."[9] When "incarnated," as it
were, in the matter of their icons, the saints—not to mention Christ and
his mother—did in fact possess agency according to the hagiographical
imagination.

I have already referred to the "image-rich culture" of the late sixth
and particularly the seventh century that was the context for the development of these animated icons, as well as the increasing use of icons in
domestic and ecclesiastical veneration.[10] Crucial to this development was
the belief in intercession. Peter Brown has put the issue bluntly: "If Byzantines had not believed that it was possible for created beings to sway
the will of God by their intercessions, then the rise of the holy man and
the rise of the icon would not have happened."[11] Belief in the intercessory efficacy of icons clearly necessitated granting these material objects
an aura of active presence since, having "minds of their own," they
made heavenly power available for human need. Whether fixed in apses

or painted on wooden panels, the function of icons was to memorialize or "recall" the saint depicted, and also to effect an exchange between the human beholder and the image whereby the spiritual power mediated by the image had a material impact on the beholder, usually in the form of some kind of healing.[12] Icons, then, had a double existence in terms of time, bringing together a human past and a spiritual present: as Hans Belting has observed, "icons of saints look backward at a human life as well as forward to a suprahuman reality."[13] Icons also led a double life as art objects: they were "visible images of invisible presence."[14] Due to this play of the visible and the invisible, icons were paradoxical because, as Belting puts it, they invest "the anthropomorphic figure with a meaning that its visibility cannot support: the idea of the invisible."[15]

In order to engage the paradox of icons as visible images of the invisible, Christian authors and artists developed strategies for encouraging what Cynthia Hahn has called "imaginative vision."[16] Among these strategies, the literary anecdotes about icons composed by hagiographers would seem to have had the upper hand in terms of a successful "showing" of the actuality of spiritual presence in icons. With little need to give physical descriptions of the icons (apart from assertions of the match between image and saintly prototype), hagiographical authors could concentrate on the liveliness of these material objects as they interacted with venerators—hence the dripping dew drops and bubbling myrrh and the leap into being of Saints Cosmas and Damian as seen above in the *Life of Saint Theodore of Sykeon*. Artists, however, could not appeal to the imagination of the viewer in quite the same way as writers did to readers. It is one thing for hagiographers to conjure up the ephemerally palpable presence of saints by capitalizing on the ability of narrative to describe the action in and around the saints' icons. But, given the very full sense of representation or reiteration that had been developed from the late sixth century onward, how could one capture this kind of spiritual presence and power in mosaic tiles or frescoes? In what way could an icon "show" that it was itself "matter transformed into a holy state," capable of taking action in the human realm?[17] In what way, in other words, could icons show the active quality of their status as "theology in colour"?[18]

Face and Focus in Icons

One aspect of icon art that is important in regard to these questions is the change in artistic representations of saints that occurred in the late fourth and fifth centuries. As Robin Jensen has noted, "in time the emphasis shifts away from narrative types, and the portrait becomes more prominent, with the saint's face rather than the saint's deeds as the focus of devotion. Thus *imago* begins to replace *historia* in Christian art, insofar as it invites veneration and prayer."[19] In Peter Brown's view, the shift to portrait art continued the "mechanism of focusing" that had been operative in suppliants' visits to living holy men: "A woman cured by St. Symeon the Younger carried his portrait back home with her. But the very mechanism of focusing, which had made possible the first cure in the face-to-face encounter with the living holy man, could be brought to bear equally efficaciously around the silent portrait. Another woman came to the icon, confident that 'if I can only see his face, I shall be saved.'"[20] Translating "the awesomely distant loving-kindness of God into the reassuring precision of a human face," the icon was the locus of an intimate rapport between venerator and intercessor.[21] And that rapport was channeled through the eyes, which in most icons were not gazing heavenward, but directly outward at the viewer. Perhaps it was the fact of eye contact between the human gazer and a figure so other-worldly yet personal that constituted in part the holiness of icons insofar as, through the mesmerizing power of the gaze, icons functioned "to forge certain mental and even physical attitudes toward believing."[22] That the intimate yet awesome power of the gaze made up part of what Hahn names "a visual rhetoric of sanctity" is suggested strongly by what Cormack has designated as "the regular grammar of the iconoclast": "the desecration of the eyes . . . to annihilate the power of the image."[23]

Icons could thus be said to "show" their holy status through their arresting gaze. Yet this focus on the portrait, the face, and the eyes was not the only means for artistic representations of the saints to proclaim their status as "holy matter," and the fact that icons represented a shift away from literal narrative art, such as portrayals of a martyr's ordeals in a relic-shrine, does not mean that there were no "narratives" inherent in iconic images. Indeed, the phrase characterizing icons quoted above—theology in color—suggests that icons provided a visual matrix for the expression of central tenets of Christian theology.

Icon-Art and Theology

There is another approach to the question of icons and spiritual power, that is, the question of "how the body of the saint, if not continually working miracles, could be shown to be holy,"[24] and it is this approach, one that emphasizes the connection between artistic style and theology, that I will examine at length before proposing an approach of my own. The approach in question, as formulated by the eminent art historian Ernst Kitzinger, notes the shift from narrative scene to portrait image but concentrates on a shift in artistic style. Focusing centrally on iconic figures in church apses notable for their "statuesque isolation,"[25] Kit-

Figure 12. Apse mosaic. Saint Agnes between two donors. S. Agnese fuori le mura, Rome, Italy. Photo: Scala/Art Resource, NY.

zinger's discussion of style is, in my view, deeply indebted to the theological narrative in which he sees them embedded.

To the question, then, of how an icon can "show" holiness, Kitzinger had an answer, which he termed a "major stylistic shift" involving "a bold reassertion of abstract principles of design" in mosaics from about C.E. 550 through the seventh century.[26] This was a "new order of geometric simplicity" in which "heads have shrunk, bodies have lost their weight and volume, and draperies are reduced to linear schemes."[27] This loss of "three-dimensional, organically built"[28] figures characterized art from Rome in the West to Nicaea in the East, as seen in two of the mosaics adduced by Kitzinger as evidence for his theory: the church of Sant'Agnese fuori le Mura in Rome, whose apse was decorated between C.E. 625 and 638 under Pope Honorius (fig. 12); and the Dormition Church in Nicaea, whose apse mosaic of the Virgin Mary and child is a ninth-century reconstruction of a seventh-century work (fig. 13).

Figure 13. Apse mosaic. Virgin and child. Dormition Church, Nicaea. From
Theodor Schmit, *Die Koimesis-Kirche von Nikaia* (Berlin: Walter de Gruyter, 1927),
Plate XX. Photo: David Broda, Syracuse University.

Although I agree with Kitzinger that this kind of art is best understood in the context of the "sharp upswing of the cult of images" from the second half of the sixth century onward, and although I agree that narrative sequences or tableaux have been replaced by an increasing tendency to situate saintly bodies "in statuesque isolation" in central areas of churches, in the end I find Kitzinger's analysis of this stylistic shift unsatisfactory.[29] In particular, I will argue that terms like "abstraction" and "extreme dematerialization" are inadequate as characterizations of these saintly portraits. Focusing on the mosaic figure of Saint Agnes, as does Kitzinger, I will briefly rehearse his art-historical and theological arguments and then suggest an alternative means of conceptualizing the "steady falling off of organic substance" in the art of this period.[30]

Kitzinger laid the basis for his observations about the dematerialization of the saintly image by arguing that the most important conceptual feature of the cult of images in the late sixth and seventh centuries was the "tendency to break down the barrier between image and prototype," so as to imbue the icon with the palpable presence of its heavenly subject.[31] One crucial ingredient in this divinizing of the icon was the view that the icon was a channel of communication between the earthly and spiritual realms, a view that developed in the wake of one aspect of the philosophy of Pseudo-Dionysius the Areopagite, namely, that visible symbols or images in the human world can lead the mind upward to contemplation of the divine.[32] The next step taken by image-apologists, also relying on a Neoplatonic concept of a "descending hierarchy of mirror reflections," was to claim "that the holy spirit which indwells the saint is reflected in the saint's image."[33] "The icon thus becomes a receptacle for the holy spirit" and is given an objective status of its own "in the divine order of the universe."[34]

According to Kitzinger, the "claim that the image stood in a transcendental relationship to the holy person it represents" is what accounts for "the thinness and transparency of these figures."[35] On his reading, mediation of the divine by a human body needs abstraction: "the artist is charged with the task of creating an image timeless and detached, in contact with heaven rather than humanity, an image capable of mirroring, as if by direct reflection, its divine or sainted prototype and, indeed, of serving as a vehicle for divine forces, as a receptacle for divine substance."[36] When Kitzinger looked at Saint Agnes, what he saw was "a shell, limp and meaningless in itself, ready to receive power from on high."[37] She is "gaunt and remote," a spectral "ghost of her former self," "anaemic and wraithlike."[38] He argued that a realistic style would have impeded the image's receptivity to the Holy Spirit: "the thinness and transparency of these figures are fully in keeping with their being conceived as receptacles for the Holy Ghost and as channels of communication with the Deity."[39] Hence the religio-aesthetic innovation of the abstract, weightless, dematerialized icons in the seventh century.

Theorizing Icons: Critique of Kitzinger's Position

While I agree that the artistic style of a figure like Saint Agnes does not attempt to depict an illusion of organic or three-dimensional lifelikeness, I disagree that she is wraithlike, dematerialized, in short, abstract to the point of being unintelligible apart from her role as vehicle for the transcendent. Kitzinger's reading of such icons as virtually collapsing the distinction between original and copy, prototype and picture, has curiously dehumanized the saint, neglecting the devotional, intercessory context that depended upon the phenomenon of the holy endowed with a specifically *human* face.[40] In my view, he has "over-read" the few sources he assembled as testimony to the transcendental status of such figures, noting but downplaying the "as if" in statements about icons such as one ascribed to Saint Symeon the Stylite the Younger: "when we see the invisible through the visible picture," Symeon reputedly said, "we honor [the saint] *as if* he were present" (ὁρῶντες τὸ ἀόρατον διὰ τῆς ὁρωμένης γραφῆς, ὡς παρόντα δοξάζομεν).[41] Taking seriously the "as if" dimension of this view of spiritual presence in icons both prevents the human element from being swallowed up by the divine and preserves the tensive play *between* human and divine that was a crucial feature of the paradoxical ontology of icons—their status as "image-flesh"—as I have argued.[42]

Along these same lines, Kitzinger relied too much on a statement by Leontius of Neapolis, who compared veneration of saintly icons to glorification of the "house"—that is, the body—indwelt by the Holy Ghost.[43] Leontius had written: "The image [εἰκὼν] of God is the human being who was made in the image [κατ' εἰκόνα] of God, and especially since the holy spirit has come to dwell in him. It is right therefore that I honor and adore the image [τὴν εἰκόνα] of the servants of God and that I glorify the house of the Holy Spirit."[44] Kitzinger's reading of this passage is as follows: "'God's servants' are the saints. It is they who have received 'the indwelling of the Holy Ghost' and therefore they are more especially 'images of God.' In worshipping their image the faithful glorifies the 'house of the Holy Ghost.' Granted, then, that what the artist depicts is only a shell, a 'house,' this shell is hallowed and transfigured by the Holy Ghost, at least in the case of the saint."[45]

Kitzinger's reading is problematic, first, because his insistence that this passage refers only to saints misses the ambiguous (and punning?) use of the term "image," with its reference to the creation of human beings in the book of Genesis as well as to the sanctification of the saints and their icons. This is a very full sense of "image," and Kitzinger's quick assumption that the icon as "house" is only a "shell" is certainly an unwarranted one. Reading image as shell is problematic also because it relies upon an overemphasis on the action of the Holy Spirit; this erases the role of the saintly *persona* as intercessor, and it also neglects one context of the very explosion of images that Kitzinger was so eager to bring to bear on the phenomenon of icons, namely the explosion of hagiography in this period, where saints are not gaunt and remote but "genuine epiphanies of a transfigured human presence"[46] active in the lives of ordinary people. Given the intercessory role of saints, it would make no sense to portray their bodies iconically as "detached" and "in contact with heaven rather than humanity."[47]

Finally, reading the bodies of the saints in art as mere shells—as abstract, anemic, and wraithlike vessels—led Kitzinger to view icons such as that of Saint Agnes as humanly unrealistic. Quoting the "hobby horse" of his fellow art historian Sir Ernst Gombrich ("the greater the wish to ride, the fewer may be the features that will do for a horse"), Kitzinger argued as follows: "By the same token, when the desire to pray, the urgency to communicate with Christ and his saints are great enough, there is no need to elaborate the physical features of the holy persons. In fact, too much realism can be an impediment."[48] The problem is that viewing icons as unrealistic portrayals flies in the face of what Byzantines themselves thought about these images. The stylistic shift in portraying the human body from three dimensions to two did not necessarily pro- duce a likeness that looked "remote" and "abstract." The opening of this chapter, after all, referred to Saints Cosmas and Damian, appearing "live and in the round" to Saint Theodore of Sykeon, "looking just like they did" in their portrait icon.[49] To my mind, the most succinct expla- nation of Byzantine viewing practices is that of Henry Maguire:

To the modern viewer, Byzantine portraits might seem to resemble children's drawings [i.e., stick figures] that may seem true to the children who produced them but not to the adult viewer. Such a perception of Byzantine icons, however, would be wrong, for the Byzantines were neither children nor naïve. The differ- ence between the present-day and the Byzantine viewer is not that of sophistica- tion as opposed to naiveté, for no people have ever been more sophisticated in their approaches to images than the Byzantines. Rather, the difference is one of expectation. When a modern viewer speaks of an image being "lifelike," the expectation is that it will be illusionistic, with realistic effects of lighting and per- spective, like a photograph. The Byzantines, however, did not seek optical illu- sionism in their portraits, but rather accuracy of definition.[50]

As Maguire goes on to say, the expectation of Byzantine viewers was that "the image should be sufficiently well defined to enable them to identify the holy figure represented, from a range of signs that included the clothing, the attributes, the portrait type, and the inscription."[51] These signs were what constituted the lifelikeness of the iconic portrait. A visitor to the church of Sant'Agnese fuori le Mura, for example, would have recognized the icon of Saint Agnes in the apse not only from the inscription of her name above her head but also from the fiery flames at her feet, an allusion to the means of her martyrdom.[52] Far from being a "triumph of geometry and abstraction," as Kitzinger describes her, the stately and bejeweled Agnes is a picture of the triumphant overcoming of suffering.[53]

It is difficult to tell whether the "high theology" of icons as indwelt by the Holy Spirit to which Kitzinger subscribed influenced the way in which he looked at icons such as the mosaic of Saint Agnes, or whether his discourse about stylistic change in figural art affected the way in which he read sixth- and seventh-century theological sources. But either way, his argument has the effect of dehumanizing icons, making it difficult to read them as "*material* signs of the presence of the spiritual world"—one might say, as paradoxes—and making the iconoclasts' charge of idolatry perfectly understandable because of the collapse of the human into the divine.[54] In Kitzinger's presentation, the image, however dematerialized, signifies too much about the saint's divinity and not enough about the saint's humanity. In his hands, Saint Agnes is an image, but she has no "flesh."

Icons and Incongruity

What Kitzinger did not take into account was the image-status of the icon *as image*, as a material sign that represents or even re-incarnates a being now nonmaterial. To be true to the character of saints as they were understood in this time period, icons had to be weighty *and* weightless, near *and* remote. In order to imagine Saint Agnes otherwise, I will position her icon as a form of visual hagiographical rhetoric that, like its contemporary literary counterparts, emphasizes the specifically transfigured quality of saintly presence, thus avoiding idolatry—the takeover of the human and her visual representation by the divine—by treading a fine line between the sheerly concrete and the sheerly transcendent. In my view, iconic representation was an acknowledgment of the "power of images to signify beyond the limits of the visible"[55] while retaining their significance as material signs available to human perception and interpretation. The context for this view is the work of Pseudo-Dionysius the Areopagite, whose semiotic theory was very influential in setting the cultural conditions of seeing, as well as reading, images from the sixth century onward.

In his *Celestial Hierarchies*, Pseudo-Dionysius argued that, as intelligible or invisible beings, angels are most appropriately represented by biblical images that are dissimilar, incongruous, even deformed or misshapen, since such images are least likely to be taken as literal representations of their referents.[56] Biblical authors were wise to use "incongruous dissimilarities [τὰς ἀπεμφαινούσας ἀνομοιότητας], for by doing this they took account of our inherent tendency toward the material."[57] Lowly images uplift: "the sheer crassness [δυσμορφία: misshapenness] of the signs is a goad so that even the materially inclined cannot accept that it could be permitted or true that the celestial and divine sights could be conveyed by such shameful things."[58] However, even images "drawn from the lowliest matter can be used, not unfittingly, with regard to heavenly beings" because matter owes its existence to God and "keeps, throughout its earthly ranks, some echo of intelligible beauty."[59]

By contrast, images that are "similar" by virtue of their beauty or elevated quality are dangerous because they might lead one to think that such images actually disclose the reality of the beings they purport to represent.[60] "Positive affirmations," he argues, "are always unfitting to the hiddenness of the inexpressible," so "one must be careful to use the similarities as dissimilarities to avoid one-to-one correspondences."[61] Yet, as he also argued, the similar and the dissimilar are not mutually exclusive categories of images, since every image, whether lofty or lowly, has a double character: "the very same things are both similar and dissimilar."[62] That is, every image is characterized by a simultaneity of lack and plenitude; all images are incongruous, but all are nonetheless epiphanic. Dionysius's recommendation was to read the dissimilar as similar, and also the reverse, to read the similar as dissimilar.

Pseudo-Dionysius was, of course, referring to verbal images in Scriptural texts. However, as Glenn Peers, Averil Cameron, and others have noted, his argument that images offer the primary means of access to the divine was appropriated by later Christians for the defense of visual images—a process facilitated by the fact of his frequent use of the term *eikōn* to designate written images, a term that can also designate an object of art.[63] As Andrew Louth puts it, "What the iconodules took from Dionysios was his insistence that the visible provides access to the invisible: 'truly visible things are manifest images of invisible things.'"[64]

In the present context, it is important to note that Dionysius was writing not about images of saints, but about images of angels. However, given his often-repeated position that the sensible world bears traces of the suprasensible world (recalling his words, "truly visible things are manifest images of the invisible"),[65] I think that his view of the dissembling quality of images can be used to understand the "look" of icons like that of Saint Agnes. Saints too were part of the invisible realm, and their images too were theophanic in terms of their intercessory function as vehicles for the manifestation of the power of the holy spirit in earthly life.[66] Certainly it is the case that later theorists of images like John of Damascus used Dionysius's position on images of angels to defend the use of images per se as essential to religious understanding.[67]

Unlike angels, who were never corporeal, saints once had material bodies. Picturing saints thus required some physical verisimilitude. Images of them could not be completely dissimilar to their once literally animate selves. On the other hand, given the saints' paradoxical status as dead and alive at once—that is, as physically dead and so no longer corporeal, but spiritually alive and active as intercessory presences—any bodily image of the saint must necessarily be somewhat unsuitable or touched by incongruity, since the saint is now "alive" in a different register and no longer inhabits a literal body. Like the bodies of their literary counterparts, the imagistic bodies of icons partook of an ambiguous corporeality: they were only pictures, but they might bubble over with the power of healing that was spiritual and material at once, as in the case of Saint Theodore of Sykeon discussed earlier.

I think Kitzinger was correct in discerning a stylistic shift in the art that portrayed saints. The material image is so crafted that it is a showing of transfiguration, a celebration of spiritual presence that avoids idolizing the flesh by endowing the saint with a subtracted but still recognizably human body. *Pace* Kitzinger, the icon is not an erasure of the human but a revelation of divine power in the human form that conveys it. In order to picture the animate presence of a figure who no longer has a body, that figure must be not *de*materialized, but *re*-materialized as a sign whose very dissimilarity advertises its own status as a contemplative, not a descriptive, object. The icon stages a play of difference *and* sameness with regard to its prototype. Kitzinger's view concerning the "actual presence of the saints" in their icons thus needs to be tempered with Charles Barber's view of the "icon as directed absence, functioning as a point of departure for contemplation."[68]

Similar and dissimilar at once, the saintly icon can be conceptualized as "theology in color" precisely insofar as it is a witness to central aspects of Christian belief, not only intercession—the power of God to affect human life by means of saintly mediation—but also transfiguration. Long before her mosaic portrait was placed in the apse of her church, Saint Agnes had been saluted by Prudentius as a "noble inhabitant of the celestial heights" who, despite her lofty abode, can "turn her face" to assuage human misery. Indeed, Prudentius felt sure that her "radiant glance" would cleanse him because she visits and touches her devotees.[69] Agnes's abode is double, both on earth and in heaven, and her powers of spiritual healing are materialized through the eye and the touch. Prudentius's text offers a literary picture of a transfigured human being, a revelation of the transformative effects of the Incarnation on the human self. Two centuries later, the icon of Saint Agnes shows, in mosaic tiles, the doubled quality of the transfigured self: rather than losing organic substance, she has (re)gained dimensionality, but of a sort that suggests that her (mere) humanity has been touched by transcendence.

Artistic Style and Iconic Doubleness

Agnes's icon as a portrayal of saintly paradox, disembodied and corporeal at once, can also be described in purely stylistic terms. There is something right about Kitzinger's observation about dematerialization as a characterization of Saint Agnes's "elongated body, diminutive head and chalk-white face."[70] However, she has life-blood too—in the form of decidedly rosy cheeks that function like a second pair of eyes that draw the viewer's gaze. Saint Agnes may be two-dimensional, but she is also animate, even emotionally animated with a flushed face.

Kitzinger is also right that she is linear and, clothed in purple like Popes Honorius and Symmachus who flank her, she is subsumed "colouristically" in "a unified pattern" that emphasizes "static" symmetry.[71] These three figures in the apse "rise like so many vertical pillars on a vast expanse of gold ground."[72] There is more to be said, however, about these "dematerializing" aspects of color.[73] While Kitzinger saw figures against plain gold expanses as floating in solitary splendor "in a luminous sphere which is not of this world," there is another aspect of the color gold, and indeed of color itself, that gives embodied substance to these ethereal figures.

In late antiquity and on into the Byzantine period, "colour was seen as a touchstone of truth in art."[74] As Maguire has pointed out, "the essence of Byzantine portraiture lay in the underdrawings of the images," but without color the images were considered to be incomplete.[75] As John of Damascus, using the simile of color to explain the relation between the Old and New Testaments, wrote, "As the Law [is] . . . a preliminary foreshadowing of the colored picture, so grace and truth are the colored picture."[76] Three centuries earlier, Cyril of Alexandria used the same simile: "The outlines [the Law] are the first marks made by the skill of those who paint on panels, and if the brightness of the colors is laid upon these, then indeed the beauty of the picture flashes forth."[77] In this long and consistent tradition, it was color that animated the artistic image and further, it was color that indicated the nature of the human being as image of God.

Color could be used to depict the human and divine status of the person-as-image because it was implicated in ethics. As Gregory of Nyssa explained, "As painters transfer the human forms to their pictures by means of certain colors, applying to their work of imitation the proper and corresponding tints, so that the archetypal beauty may be transferred exactly to this likeness, thus it would seem to me that our Maker also, with certain tints as it were, by putting on virtues, paints the image with various colors according to his own beauty."[78] Here Gregory links color with the virtues, which are the locus of human likeness to God. Humans are not, however, simply the passive recipients of the virtues in the divine palette: "Since it is possible, we must prepare the pure colors of the virtues, mixing them with each other according to some artistic formula for the imitation of beauty, so that we become as images of the image having achieved the beauty of the prototype through activity as a kind of imitation, as Paul did, who became an imitator of Christ through his life of virtue."[79] As this passage shows, color could indicate an active cultivation of the virtues in imitation of Christ. Gregory stood at the beginning of a conception of color that developed fully in Byzantine theory, where a theology *of* color underlay mosaic art as theology *in* color.[80]

Color, then, could "complete the mimesis of the model," as Gregory wrote, because it was a marker of human spiritual achievement.[81] Looking at Saint Agnes in her golden surround, the Byzantine viewer beheld not an abstraction punctuating a vast flat field of color, but a human embodiment of Christomimetic virtue. Color was ethically charged, and gold was the color that carried the greatest ethical significance. Gold represented celestial light and, looking at gold, ancient viewers saw the sparkle of heavenly goodness that enveloped the figure of the saint.[82] The golden expanse is luminous and otherworldly, as Kitzinger argued, but those qualities do not make it remote and alien since it provides the fundament for the showing of human goodness in the figure of the saint.

Actually, Agnes is not only enveloped by gold; her purple garment is emblazoned with a golden panel that is encrusted with jewels, as is her crown. This sets her apart from her companion figures, who are not so adorned, and interrupts, though it does not erase, what Kitzinger saw as a static alignment of rigid figures spaced symmetrically in the apse. Because of his emphasis on pattern, on "a new order of geometric simplicity," he saw no "tension . . . between dramatic action and static pattern."[83] But if one views this apse from the perspective of color, there *is* dramatic action: not only does the gold scintillate, the jewels on Agnes's body and in her crown flash with the virtuous struggles of the martyr. As we have seen in previous chapters, there was a polychromatic poetics at work in the ancient Christian imagination that connected jewels—especially the jewels in martyrs' crowns—with such virtues as wisdom, courage, endurance, chastity, and justice. The still symmetry of the apse's pattern harbors a condensed narrative of a martyr's drama. In this icon, Agnes as human martyr and Agnes as resident of the celestial heights are both present. Even stylistically, the icon draws on the double-ness that any showing of transfiguration needs.

An artistic image such as the icon of Saint Agnes cannot show the holy itself, but it can signify a "being toward" the spiritual realm that might indeed invite veneration and petition.[84] It can also signify a "being toward" the human realm since, when it is positioned in statuesque iso-lation in the center of an apse (to recall Kitzinger's description of Saint Agnes), the icon is the visual focal point in the space of the beholder, and in that space saint and viewer are constituted as an interactive pair. In the *vita* of Saint Symeon the Stylite the Younger, one venerator says of the saint, "If only I might look at his likeness, I shall be saved."[85] Agnes's is another such likeness, a visible image of invisible power, all the more beckoning for its incongruous dissimilarity.

Conclusion

In his work *Earth and Reveries of Will,* devoted to what he called the "imagination of matter," Gaston Bachelard wrote the following about images that "seek substance": "In a world of metal and stone, wood and rubber, images of terrestrial matter abound. They are stable and steady; visible to the eye; palpable to the hand. They arouse a muscular pleasure the moment we experience a desire to work them. It would seem, then, a simple task to illustrate the philosophy of the four elements through such images."[1] It would *seem* a simple task to elucidate material images but, as Bachelard went on to observe about "the substances of earthen matter," they are so familiar, "their forms so manifest, so evident, so real, that it is not readily apparent how dreams of their deepest essence are to be extracted."[2] Quoting Baudelaire, he concludes, "'The more concrete and solid matter seems, the more delicate and difficult the work of the imagination.'"[3]

The central difficulty in imagining matter, as Bachelard saw it, is that the apparent solid palpability of earthy objects seduces one into the realist trap of thinking that perception precedes imagination: "first we see things, and only then do we imagine them, combining in the imagination fragments of perceived reality with memories of actual experience."[4] Bachelard rejected this positivistic view: images (and the imagining process) do not passively reproduce "reality"; they actively create it.[5] Images, that is to say, do not function to confirm habituated modes of understanding; they are themselves constitutive of insight.[6] In addressing specifically the imagination of matter, Bachelard would have joined Daniel Tiffany (himself a reader of Bachelard's work) in arguing against the positivist equation of materialism and realism and for the intrinsic role of word-pictures in shaping Western knowledge of material substance.[7] Ian Hacking's position on the relation of image and matter, quoted in the Introduction, bears repeating here: "Without pictures, there can be no claim to reality."[8]

The inherently figurative character of late ancient Christianity's appropriation of "matter" as a locus of religious meaning is the perspective that articulates the unifying standpoint of this book. Engaging the "material turn"—the shift in late ancient sensibilities regarding the positive signifying potential of the material world—has led me to see the paramount importance of the corporeal imagination for Christian meaning-making in the late Roman and early Byzantine period. How Christians imagined matter—specifically, the matter of the human body as presented in relics, hagiography, and icons—as a primary locus of spiritual presence, power, and activity has been the focus of the foregoing discussions. The sanctifying potential of human physicality as locus and mediator of the transcendent in the material world was, I argue, the product of the poetics of matter developed by a variety of Christian authors in a variety of contexts, artistic as well as literary.

I have discussed this "magic by which objects become values"[9] using several different vocabularies drawn from contemporary literary and cultural theory: W. J. T. Mitchell's "pictorial turn," Michael Roberts's "aesthetics of discontinuity," Bill Brown's "thing theory," Daniel Tiffany's "poetics of material substance" and "ambiguous corporeality," Gaston Bachelard's understanding of imagination's creativity as a deformation of images, James Elkins's notion of "visceral seeing," and the New Historicism's "touch of the transcendent" and "touch of the real." In addition to these, there is one phrase that I have mentioned only in passing but that in fact encapsulates and underscores the import and impact of the various theories to which I have appealed to articulate my position, and I will conclude by elaborating briefly on it.

In Chapter 5, when discussing the visceral images of saints in hagiography, I noted that "the ocular and affective quality of these images is an appeal to the sensory imagination of the reader, and their visual and emotional intensity aid in naturalizating the fictive—because textual—world of which they are a part." Next I remarked about these images—and here is the operative phrase—that "they are *figuratively real*, that is, they are narrative pictorial strategies that seduce the reader into forgetting that these are images in texts."[10]

Perhaps no phrase better captures the sublime carnality of the early Christian imagination of matter than "figural realism." As articulated by Hayden White, figural realism is a kind of historical discourse that is "less a matching of an image or a model with some extrinsic reality than a making of a verbal image, a discursive 'thing' that interferes with our perception of its putative referent even while fixing our attention on and illuminating it."[11] From White's perspective (and my own), "figurative language can be said to refer to reality quite as faithfully and much more effectively than any putatively literalist idiom or mode of discourse might do."[12]

While White is writing in the main about the discourse of historians, I think his perspective on figural realism is applicable as well to historical discourse understood as texts from the past, whether by historians, theologians, or poets. Insofar as White argues that "events happen, whereas facts are constituted by linguistic description" such that "facts" are not "found," they are made, he would seem to agree with Tiffany's argument that "the foundation of material substance [White's "events"] is intelligible to us, and therefore appears to be real, only if we credit the imaginary pictures [White's "facts"] we have composed of it."[13] To use White's terms, this book has been about the "real event" of the material turn in late ancient Christianity and the "facts"—the imaginal stories that embodied that turn—that early Christians elaborated in order to make sense of the material world as a medium for the disclosure of the divine. In my view, the kinds of discourse examined in this book exemplify the full force of "figural realism," nowhere expressed so forthrightly as in the following set of comments: "To emplot real events as a story of a specific kind . . . is to trope those events. This is because stories are not lived; there is no such thing as a real story. Stories are told or written, not found. And as for the notion of a true story, this is virtually a contradiction in terms. All stories are fictions. Which means, of course, that they can be true only in a metaphorical sense and in the sense in which a figure of speech can be true. Is this true enough?"[14] The premise of this book is that the answer to White's question is: yes.

Abbreviations

ACW	Ancient Christian Writers
AJP	*American Journal of Philology*
CCL	*Corpus Christianorum, Series Latina*
CH	*Church History*
CQ	*Classical Quarterly*
CSEL	*Corpus Scriptorum Ecclesiasticorum Latinorum*
DOP	*Dumbarton Oaks Papers*
FOTC	Fathers of the Church
GCS	Die griechischen christlichen Schriftsteller der ersten drei Jahrhunderte
HTR	*Harvard Theological Review*
JAAR	*Journal of the American Academy of Religion*
JAC	*Jahrbuch für Antike und Christentum*
JECS	*Journal of Early Christian Studies*
JFSR	*Journal of Feminist Studies in Religion*
JHS	*Journal of Hellenic Studies*
JMEMS	*Journal of Medieval and Early Modern Studies*
JRS	*Journal of Roman Studies*
JTS, n.s.	*Journal of Theological Studies*, new series
LCC	Loeb Classical Library
NHC	Nag Hammadi Corpus
PG	*Patrologia Graeca*, ed. J. P. Migne
PGM	*Papyri Graecae Magicae*
PL	*Patrologia Latina*, ed. J. P. Migne
PLS	*Patrologia Latina Supplementa*, ed. J. P. Migne
SC	Sources Chrétiennes
TAPA	*Transactions of the American Philological Association*
VC	*Vigiliae Christianae*

Notes

Introduction

1. Brown, "Thing Theory," 9.
2. See Petroski, *The Pencil;* Cranz, *The Chair;* Jenkins, *Bananas;* Zuckerman, *The Potato.* I owe these references to Brown, "Thing Theory," 2, n. 4.
3. What follows is a representative list of studies whose bibliographies will yield further sources. On amulets, see Maguire, *The Icons of Their Bodies;* on *ampullae,* see the work of Vikan, especially *Byzantine Pilgrimage Art,* and Davis, *The Cult of St. Thecla;* on relics, Crook, *The Architectural Setting of the Cult of the Saints;* on statues, Bassett, *The Urban Image of Late Antique Constantinople;* on shrines and mosaics, Wharton, *Refiguring the Post Classical City,* and Mathews, *The Clash of Gods;* on pilgrimage, Wilken, *The Land Called Holy,* and Bitton-Ashkelony, *Encountering the Sacred.*
4. Merleau-Ponty, "Eye and Mind," 163.
5. Brown, "Thing Theory," 4.
6. Ibid.
7. Ibid., 5.
8. Ibid.
9. Ibid. (emphasis in original).
10. *Laudatio S. Theodori, PG* 46.737C–D.
11. *Laudatio S. Theodori, PG* 46.740A.
12. *Laudatio S. Theodori, PG* 46.740B: ὡς ὁλοκλήρῳ καὶ φαινομένῳ.
13. *Laudatio S. Theodori, PG* 46.740A.
14. *Laudatio S. Theodori, PG* 46.737D.
15. Gregory's encomium is in effect a martyrology since its central portion details the martyr's bravery in the face of torture. Relevant here is David Frankfurter's observation that the purpose of martyrologies "as narrative is not only to dramatize the brave saints' struggles against heathen powers, but even more to transform imaginatively a pious human being into sacred stuff for the populace." See "On Sacrifice and Residues: Processing the Potent Body," 518.
16. Harvey, *Scenting Salvation,* 122.
17. Ibid., 44.
18. Ibid.
19. Ibid., 122.
20. Ibid., 46, 58.
21. On the concept of Palestine as holy land, see Wilken, *The Land Called Holy,* and Bitton-Ashkelony, *Encountering the Sacred;* on the activities of Damasus (bishop of Rome, 366–84), see Trout, "Damasus and the Invention of Early Christian Rome," 298–315; on liturgy, see Harvey, *Scenting Salvation,* esp. 57–98, 134–47, 181–85.

22. Harvey, *Scenting Salvation*, 46.

23. Cyril of Jerusalem, *Cat. Hom.* 4.22, *The Works of Saint Cyril of Jerusalem*, 1: 130. On Cyril's view of the body, see Georgia Frank, " 'Taste and See,' " 626, on Cyril's use of scriptural passages in order to map "a new body capable of perceiving suprasensory realities. Such senses began at the body, but perceived what was beyond it." For Ephrem, *Hymns on Virginity* 35.12, trans. McVey, *Ephrem the Syrian*, 419.

24. Taylor, *Hiding*, 89. See also the following: Cameron, *Christianity and the Rhetoric of Empire*, 68: "The theme of the incarnation imposed the language of the body, and with it bodily symbolism, on Christian writing. All the central elements in orthodox Christianity—the Incarnation, the Resurrection, the Trinity, the Virgin Birth, and the Eucharist—focus on the body as symbolic of higher truth"; Frank, "Pilgrim's Gaze," 102: "According to fourth-century theologians, such as Cyril of Jerusalem, the sanctifying effect of God's incarnation extended to the physical world; in this broader understanding of incarnation, God was revealed not only in Jesus and humanity but also throughout creation"; Harvey, *Scenting Salvation*, 59: The trinitarian and Christological controversies of the fourth and fifth centuries developed "the teaching that at the incarnation the divine itself had entered into matter, sanctifying and renewing the whole of material existence."

25. For desert fathers with shining faces, see *Apophthegmata Patrum*, Pambo, 12; Sisoes, 14, Silvanus, 12; Arsenius, 27; for discussion, see Miller, "Desert Asceticism and 'The Body from Nowhere,' " 137–53. Good examples of mosaic portraits of saints against gold backgrounds are the images in this volume of Saint Victor in the Chapel of San Vittore in Ciel d'Oro at Sant'Ambrogio in Milan and of Saint Agnes in Sant'Agnese fuori le Mura in Rome. For a discussion of gold as a signifier of divinity, see Janes, *God and Gold in Late Antiquity*, 94–152.

26. For examples and discussion, see Miller, *Dreams in Late Antiquity*, 234–35, 238–39.

27. *Or.* 38.11 (*PG* 36.321–24). For the same cosmological positioning of the human, see Gregory of Nyssa, *De hom. opif.* 16.9 (*PG* 44.181B–C). He placed his sister Macrina similarly on the boundary (μεθόριος) between human life and bodiless nature; see *Vita sanctae Macrinae* 11.3435 (*PG* 46.972A).

28. Gregory of Nazianzus, *Or.* 38.11 (*PG* 36.324A); Gregory of Nyssa, *De hom. opif.* 14.2 (*PG* 44.176B); see also 8.5 (*PG* 44.145C). For discussion, see Behr, The Rational Animal," 226–30.

29. *HR*, pro.,6, trans. Price, *Theodoret of Cyrrhus*, 6.

30. Ibid.

31. *On the Lord's Prayer* 5 (*PG* 44.1185), trans. Graef, ACW 18: 78–79.

32. *Laudatio S. Theodori* (*PG* 46.740B).

33. Athenagoras, *A Plea Regarding Christians* 4, in LCC, vol. 1: *Early Christian Fathers*, trans. Richardson, 304.

34. Ibid., 15 (trans. Richardson, 312).

35. See n. 15, above.

36. Epiphanius, fragments from *Testament, Letter to the Emperor Theodosius,* and *Letter to John, bishop of Aelia*, in Mango, trans., *The Art of the Byzantine Empire*, 41–43; Augustine, *Serm.* 198.17, trans. Hill, *Sermons* 193–94. For Augustine's views, see Jensen, *Face to Face*, 34, 85, 109–115, discussing various sermons as well as passages from *The City of God*.

37. Jensen, *Face to Face*, 34.

38. Tiffany, *Toy Medium*, 2–3.

39. Ibid., 9.

40. Ibid.

41. Ibid., 3.

42. Ibid., 4, quoting Hacking, *Representing and Intervening* (no page number given).

43. Tiffany, *Toy Medium*, 267, following Hacking, *Representing and Intervening*, 137.

44. Tiffany, *Toy Medium*, 200 (emphasis in original).

45. Ibid., 195.

46. Onians, "Abstraction and Imagination in Late Antiquity," 4, 12, 23.

47. James and Webb, " 'To Understand Ultimate Things,' " 4.

48. Ibid., 6.

49. For the date of the dedication, see Van Dam, *Leadership and Community in Late Antique Gaul*, 169.

50. *Ep.* II.10.11–15, 20–21, trans. Onians, "Abstraction and Imagination," 7; text in *Sidonius: Poems and Letters*, vol. 1, ed. and trans. Anderson 464, 466: "distinctum vario nitore marmor/percurrit cameram solum fenestras,/ac sub versicoloribus figuris vernans herbida crusta sapphiratos/flectit per prasinum vitrum lapilos./ . . . et campum medium procul locatas/vestit saxea silva per columnas."

51. Onians, "Abstraction and Imagination," 11.

52. For references to the ancient Christian picture of paradise as a grassy, flowery meadow, see Delumeau, *History of Paradise*, 11–13, and Roberts, *The Jeweled Style*, 76.

53. Paul the Silentiary, *Descr. Ambonis* 224, trans. Mango, *Art of the Byzantine Empire*, 95; *Narratio de S. Sophia* 26, trans. Mango, *Art of the Byzantine Empire*, 101; both discussed by Onians, "Abstraction and Imagination in Late Antiquity," 8–9.

54. On the inner and outer man, see, e.g., Origen, *Hom. Gen.* 1.2, 1.13, 1.15, ed. and trans. Doutreleau, *Origène: Homélies sur la Genèse*, 29–31, 57–59, 67.

55. Dawson, *Christian Figural Reading and the Fashioning of Identity*, 56. Origen, *Cels.* 7.33, in *Origène: Contre Celse*, ed. and trans. Borret, 88, trans. Chadwick, *Origen: Contra Celsum*, 421. For a defense of the physical sense of smell in Origen's work, see Harvey, *Scenting Salvation*, 172–75.

56. Walker, *Holy City, Holy Places?* 81.

57. Frank, "Pilgrim's Gaze," 103.

58. Ibid., 104, quoting Cyril of Jerusalem, *Cat. Hom.* 13.22, trans. McCauley and Stephenson, *Works of Saint Cyril of Jerusalem*, 2: 19; for the association of sight and touch, Frank, "Pilgrim's Gaze," 104–9; "eyes as hands," 109.

59. Kelly, *Early Christian Doctrines*, 443–44, referring to John Chrysostom, *In Ioh. Hom.* 46.3 and *In Matt. Hom.* 82.4.

60. *Myst.* 9.50 (SC 25bis: 184; FOTC 44: 23).

61. *Sacr.* 4.4.20 (SC 25bis: 112; FOTC 304).

62. Frank, " 'Taste and See,' " 619.

63. Barber, "The Koimesis Church, Nicaea," 48.

64. One of the best discussions of Cyril's theology on this point is by Chadwick, "Eucharist and Christology in the Nestorian Controversy," 145–64.

65. See the discussion of McGuckin, *Saint Cyril of Alexandria and the Christological Controversy*, 174–93, esp. 187–88.

66. *De incarnatione Unigeniti*, in *Cyrille d'Alexandrie: Deux Dialogues Christologiques*, ed. and trans. De Durand, 279.

67. See Horn, *Asceticism and Christological Controversy*, 74–91.

68. John Rufus, *Life of Peter the Iberian*, ed. Raabe, *Petrus der Iberer*, 65; trans. Menze, "Priests, Laity and the Sacrament of the Eucharist," para. 1.

69. John Rufus, *Plerophoria*, in Nau, "Jean Rufus," 175; trans.. Gerstel, *Beholding the Sacred Mysteries*, 46. For similar images, see *Plerophoria* 10 (Nau, 24), 78 (Nau, 135), 86 (Nau, 140).

70. Perrone, "Dissenso Dottrinale e Propaganda Visionaria," 477.

71. *Serm.* 313A.3, in *Miscellanea Agostiniana*, ed. Morin, 1: 58; trans. Hill, *The Works of Saint Augustine, Part III—Sermons, 9* 92.

72. Bryson,, "Philostratus and the Imaginary Museum," 266.

73. See, e.g., *Imagines* 1.4, 1.11, 1.16, 2.10, 2.23, 2.28.

74. Bryson, "Philostratus and the Imaginary Museum," 266.

75. Vernant, "Dim Body, Dazzling Body," 20.

76. Turner, "Body in Western Society," 15–16.

77. Turner, "Body in Western Society," 16–17; on the naturalized body, see Knauft, "Bodily Images in Melanesia," 203.

78. Coakley, *Religion and the Body*, 2.

79. Butler, *Bodies That Matter*, ix.

80. Ibid.

81. MacDonald, *Transgressive Corporeality;* Johnson, *The Body in the Mind;* Leder, *The Absent Body;* Dalmolin, *Cutting the Body;* Cavarero, ed., *Stately Bodies;* Elkins, *Pictures of the Body;* and Grosz, *Volatile Bodies.*

82. Butler, *Bodies That Matter*, ix.

83. Comaroff, *Body of Power, Spirit of Resistance*, 6–7. For useful bibliographies of recent scholarly work on ancient Christian asceticism, holy bodies, and hagiography, see the articles in *JECS* 6 (1998), all written in acknowledgment of the work of Peter Brown on the holy man; see also articles collected in Montserrat, ed., *Changing Bodies, Changing Meanings;* for a thorough bibliography relating to the study of gender in early Christianity, see Castelli, "Heteroglossia, Hermeneutics, and History," 73–98, and more recently, Castelli and Boyarin, guest editors, *Sexuality in Late Antiquity*, special issue of *Journal of the History of Sexuality* (2001). On topics that are more theologically oriented, see, for example, Bynum, *The Resurrection of the Body in Western Christianity*, and Burrus, *"Begotten, Not Made."*

84. Roberts, *Jeweled Style*, esp. 47–53, 73–75.

Chapter 1. Bodies and Selves

1. The "power of pomp and glitter" in architecture, language, and costume is discussed by MacMullen, "Some Pictures in Ammianus Marcellinus," 435–55. See also the major study by MacCormack, *Art and Ceremony in Late Antiquity.*

2. MacMullen, "Some Pictures," 437 (theatricality); Matthews, *The Roman Empire of Ammianus*, 460 (expressionistic manner). See the discussion of late ancient mosaics by Roberts, *Jeweled Style*, where Roberts refers to "the liberation of the individual stone and its investment with light and color" (72) and to the "verbal dazzle" of poetry (75), in which individual words were used as though they possessed "a physical presence of their own, distinct from any considerations of sense or syntax" (58). Part of his point is that, with the loss of organic relationship in poetry and the arts, the eye of the spectator is focused on the part, and the relationships among such parts must be reconstituted or imagined by the spectator.

3. For discussion of Eunapius's *Vitae philosophorum et sophistarum* and the *Historia monachorum* in this light, see Miller, "Strategies of Representation in Collec-

tive Biography," 209–54; on visual imagination and Christian holiness, see, *inter alia*, Frank, *The Memory of the Eyes*, for discussion of such phenomena as "embracing with the eyes" (14) and "the readable body" (150).

4. Onians, "Abstraction and Imagination," 4, 12, 23.

5. Marinus, *Vita Procli* 23, ed. J. Boissanade, *Marini: Vita Procli* 19 (my translation).

6. See the discussion by Blumenthal, "Marinus' Life of Proclus," 477–81.

7. *Vita Procli* 3, ed. Boissanade, 3; trans. Guthrie, *The Life of Proclus*, 17–18.

8. *Vita Procli* 4, ed. Boissanade, 4; trans. Guthrie, *The Life of Proclus*, 19.

9. Plotinus, *Enn.* 1.1.1.1–3 (all translations of Plotinus's *Enneads* are by A. H. Armstrong in the Loeb edition).

10. See *Enn* 1.1.4 on "mixture" and "being interwoven." Note that *Enn.* 1.1 is #53 in Porphyry's chronological ordering of the *Enneads*, hence Plotinus's penultimate treatise.

11. *Enn.* 6.4.14.17. See discussion in Hadot, *Plotinus or the Simplicity of Vision*, trans. Michael Chase, 31–32 with reference to "the divisive alienation of [the] conscious self" (32).

12. *Enn.* 4.3.8.15–16.

13. *Meditations* 5.11 (trans. Staniforth, 83) (slightly emended).

14. Barton, "Being in the Eyes," 227.

15. For the images of serpent- and horse-man, see *Hom. in Ezek.* 3.8 (*GCS* 8, 355–57).

16. *Hom. in Luc.* 8.3 (ed. and trans. Crouzel, Fournier, and Périchon, 166–68).

17. Jay, "Freud: The Death of Autobiography," 104.

18. Ibid., 105.

19. *Enn.* 1.1.13.1–3 (italics added by Armstrong).

20. See, for example, *Enn.* 4.8.8.1–6; 4.8.1.1–11; and the many passages, like 6.5.12.13–29, in which Plotinus argues that the "All" is continuously present, even when we turn away from it.

21. See discussion by Dawson, *Christian Figural Reading and the Fashioning of Identity*, 79. For an example of Origen's understanding of the "inner man," composed of a union of spirit and soul, as "invisible, incorporeal, incorruptible, and immortal," see his *Hom. in Gen.* 1.13 (ed. and trans. Doutreleau, 56).

22. For a survey of ancient conceptions of the soul, see Corrigan, "Body and Soul in Ancient Religious Experience," 360–83; see also Schroeder, "Self in Ancient Religious Experience," 337–59, especially with regard to the Platonic tradition, in which soul is the location of human identity (350).

23. Schroeder, "Self in Ancient Religious Experience," 337.

24. Ibid., 348.

25. Goldhill, "Refracting Classical Vision," 18.

26. Gallagher and Greenblatt, *Practicing New Historicism*, 31. Gallagher and Greenblatt define "the touch of the real" as their commitment to particularity in historical explanation: "We wanted to recover in our literary criticism a confident conviction of reality, without giving up the power of literature to sidestep or evade the quotidian and without giving up a minimally sophisticated understanding that any text depends upon the absence of the bodies and voices that it represents. We wanted the touch of the real in the way that in an earlier period people wanted the touch of the transcendent" (31). While they don't specify who those earlier people were, their sense for what they are moving away from— "the touch of the transcendent"—is captured in such phrases as "a unitary

story, a supreme model of human perfection" (5) and "the path to a transhistorical truth" (7), and in this sentence, "the task of understanding then depends not on the extraction of an abstract set of principles, and still less on the application of a theoretical model, but rather on an encounter with the singular, the specific, and the individual" (6). Though I have adapted these phrases for my own purposes, the distinction that they make between the transhistorical and the particular will continue to inform my use of them.

27. Note that ancient authors such as Origen and Epiphanius tended to interweave Gen. 1 and 2, so that the "waters" of Gen. 1 become the more specific "rivers" of Gen. 2.

28. *Hom. in Gen.* 1.2 (ed. and trans. Doutreleau, 30). Note Origen's intertextual use of allusions to Jn. 7:38 and 4:14 (pertaining to the connection between Jesus and living water), suggesting a conflation of the spiritual water above the firmament, the rivers of Eden, and the rivers of living water.

29. *Hom. in Gen.* 1.3 (ed. and trans. Doutreleau, 34), for the first quotation; for seeds, 1.4 (Doutreleau, 36); stars, 1.7 (Doutreleau, 40); birds, 1.8 (Doutreleau, 44).

30. For Epiphanius's role in the Origenist controversy, see Clark, *The Origenist Controversy*, 86–104.

31. *Ancoratus* 58 (*PG* 43.113).

32. *Panarion* 64.4.3, in *GCS* 31², ed. Holl and Drummer, 410; see the discussion in Young, *From Nicaea to Chalcedon*, 141–42. To the point of the force of concrete seeing, the following statement is attributed to Epiphanius: "He also said, 'The acquisition of Christian books is necessary for those who can use them. For the mere sight of these books renders us less inclined to sin, and incites us to believe more firmly in righteousness'" (*Apophthegmata Patrum*, Epiphanius 8, trans. Ward, *The Sayings of the Desert Fathers*, 58).

33. *Ep. ad Johannem Episcopum*, *PG* 43.386.

34. Smith, *Map Is Not Territory*, 143.

35. Brown, *The Body and Society*, 381.

36. Gallagher and Greenblatt, *Practicing New Historicism*, 19.

37. Ibid., 15.

38. *Ezra Pound: A Critical Anthology*, ed. J. P. Sullivan, 41, 57.

39. See especially Barton, *Sorrows of the Ancient Romans*, 90–95; Barton, "Being in the Eyes," 216–35.

40. For a succinct ancient discussion of the aggressive eye as well as the self-bewitching eye, see Plutarch, *Quaestiones convivales* 5.7 (*Moralia* 680C–682B); for discussion of Narcissus and the self-consuming eye, see Barton, *Sorrows of the Ancient Romans*, 92; Elsner, "Naturalism and the Erotics of the Gaze," 248–61.

41. *Enn.* 1.6.8.4–16.

42. For the "eye" of Narcissus as self-consuming, see Barton, *Sorrows of the Ancient Romans*, 92; on self-splitting, see Elsner, "Naturalism and the Erotics of the Gaze," 255, discussing the presentation of Narcissus in Callistratus, *Descriptiones* 5.3: "The terrifying confrontation with the self's gaze as if it were other causes a psychic move whereby Narcissus looks at himself as another would look at him"—i.e., he objectivizes himself, much like Plotinus's self thrown into a world of objects.

43. *Enn.* 4.3.26.54.

44. *Enn.* 4.8.2.43–45.

45. *Enn.* 4.8.2.46–49.

46. *Enn.* 4.8.2.23–27.

47. *Enn.* 1.6.5.50–58 (on being mixed); 2.3.9.31–32 (on being double); 4.8.4.15–18 (on being isolated).

48. Clark, "Plotinus: Body and Soul," 280.

49. Clark, "Plotinus: Body and Soul," 284, quoting *Enn.* 3.7.11.14–17 and 3.7.11.21–22.

50. Halliwell, *The Aesthetics of Mimesis*, 322.

51. Preface to *Enn.* 6.7, p. 79. See the discussion of reality as a "structure of dependence" and as a continuous whole by O'Meara, "The Hierarchical Ordering of Reality in Plotinus," 66–81, citing especially such passages as *Enn.* 5.2.2.24–29 ("the whole is continuous with itself, but with one part differentiated from another, and the prior does not perish in the posterior," 76).

52. *Enn.* 6.4.14.18–22.

53. *Enn.* 6.4.14.22–26; Rappe, "Self-knowledge and Subjectivity in the *Enneads*," 266.

54. Ibid.

55. *Enn* 1.6.8.26–28.

56. *Enn.* 5.8.9.8–17.

57. Schroeder, "The Vigil of the One and Plotinian Iconoclasm," 67.

58. Earlier in *Enn.* 5.8, Plotinus describes the real beings of the noetic world as follows: "they see themselves in other things; for all things are transparent, and there is nothing dark or opaque; everything and all things are clear to the inmost part to everything; for light is transparent to light" (*Enn.* 5.8.4.4–7).

59. Schroeder, "The Vigil of the One," 68; Berchman, "Aesthetics as a Philosophic Ethos," 190.

60. See Rappe, "Self-Perception in Plotinus and the Later Neoplatonic Tradition," 433–51, on the problem of "being aware that one is aware": "To be aware that one is engaged in the act of knowing an object is to be distracted by a different object of awareness as well as to be excessively removed from the object with which one is engaged" (440). See also Rappe, "Metaphor in Plotinus' *Enneads* v 8.9," 155–72, esp. 161–63.

61. *Enn.* 5.3.17.37–39.

62. Hadot, *Plotinus*, 27.

63. *Enn.* 4.3.12.5 (trans. Hadot, *Plotinus*, 27). See the famous passage at *Enn.* 4.8.1.1–6: "Often I have woken up out of the body to my self and have entered into myself, going out from all other things; I have seen a beauty wonderfully great and felt assurance that then most of all I belonged to the better part; I have actually lived the best life and come to identity with the divine." See Hadot, "Neoplatonist Spirituality," 230–49: Plotinus "shows the soul trying to renounce its individuality, trying not to be 'someone,' in order to become the whole" (241).

64. Rappe, "Self-knowledge and Subjectivity," 266, 270.

65. *Enn.* 6.9.10.3 (body as hindrance); 6.9.9.52–53 (cutting away); 6.9.9.57–59 (self glorified).

66. *Dial. with Heraclitus* 13.3–6 (ed. and trans. Scherer, 82).

67. *De prin.* 3.4.1 (ed. and trans. Crouzel and Simonetti, 3:200).

68. See the discussion of Gal. 5.17 (on flesh warring against spirit) in *De prin.* 3.4.4; see also *Hom. in Gen.* 1.15 (ed. and trans. Doutreleau, 68) on the "insolence" of the "flesh" and its connection to "carnal vices." For a discussion of flesh as "the force that attracts the soul towards the body," see Crouzel, *Origen*, 89.

69. See *Comm. in Ioh.* 32.27.338 (trans. Trigg, *Origen*, 237) on the mind being

"divinized by those things that it contemplates"; on being subjected to "the passions of the mind," see *De prin.* 3.4.4; on the inner and outer man, see *Hom. in Gen.* 1.2, 1.13, 1.15, *Hom. in Luc.* 39.5 (of the two images in the human being, one is earthly, the other "made in the image and likeness of God"); *Comm. in Cant.*, prologue 2.4; *Hom. in Ezek.* 3.8 (*GCS* 8, 355–57); *Dial. with Heraclides* 16.

70. See *Comm. in Cant.* 1.4; *Contra Cels.* 1.48; *Dial. with Heraclides* 16–22. For discussion, see Dillon, "Aisthêsis Noêtê: A Doctrine of Spiritual Senses in Origen and in Plotinus," in his *Golden Chain*, 443–55.

71. Dawson, *Christian Figural Reading*, 56, 63.

72. *Comm. in Cant.*, prologue 2 (ed. Baehrens, *GCS, Origenes Werke*, vol. 8:72.11–24, trans. Lawson, ACW 26:36).

73. *Comm. in Cant.*, prologue 2 (ed. Baehrens, 72.25–26; trans. Lawson, 36).

74. *De prin.* 3.3.4 (ed. and trans. Crouzel and Simonetti, 198). For a discussion of Origen's use of animal imagery as a way of characterizing the soul's many dimensions, see Cox, "Origen on the Bestial Soul," 115–40.

75. These false *personae* are "the masks of the lion, the dragon, and the fox" referred to in *Hom. in Luc.* 8.3 (ed. and trans. Crouzel, Fournier, Périchon, 166–68). In *Hom. in Luc.* 8.2 (ed. and trans. Crouzel et al., 166), Origen explains that the human soul was "created as the image of an Image that already existed. . . . Each one of us shapes his soul into the image of Christ and makes either a larger or a smaller image of him. The image is either dingy and dirty, or it is clean and bright and corresponds to the form of the original" (trans. Lienhard, FOTC 94, 34). Sin dirties the soul, whereas virtue makes it bright.

76. Origen, *Dial. with Heraclides* 14 (ed. and trans. Scherer, 84).

77. *Comm. in Cant.*, prologue, 2 (ed. Baehrens, 8:66.2–17). See *Comm. in Ioh.* 1.8.44–45: Origen argues that it is necessary to "differentiate the sensible aspect of the gospel from its intelligible and spiritual aspect. And now our task is to change the sensible gospel into the spiritual, for what is interpretation of the sensible gospel unless it is transforming it into the spiritual?" (ed. and trans. Blanc, *Origène: Commentaire sur Saint Jean*, vol. 1, SC 120, 82; trans. Trigg, 113).

78. Dawson, *Christian Figural Reading*, 61.

79. *Comm. in Ioh.* 32.27.338 (trans. Trigg, 237). See Dawson, *Christian Figural Reading*, 54, for discussion of the link between allegorical reading and the spiritual transformation of the interpreter in Origen's thought.

80. Berchman, "Self-knowledge and Subjectivity in Origen," *Origeniana Octava* 1: 445.

81. *Hom. in Gen.* 2.6 (ed. and trans. Doutreleau, 108; trans. Heine, 86–87). Note should be made here of Origen's argument in *De prin.* 4.2.4, where another way of envisioning the relation between human beings and Scripture is outlined: as Mark Julian Edwards observes, "the division of the person into body, soul and spirit was the charter for his [Origen's] own ascription of a threefold meaning to the text" (*Origen Against Plato*, 89).

82. Dawson, *Christian Figural Reading*, 54.

83. *Philocalia* 15.19.15–16 (ed. Robinson, 85): ἀεὶ γὰρ ἐν ταῖς γραφαῖς ὁ λόγος σὰρξ ἐγένετο, ἵνα κατασκηνώσῃ ἐν ἡμῖν.

84. *Philocalia* 15.19.25–28 (ed. Robinson, 85). See the discussion by Jean Daniélou on Origen's equation of touching the flesh of the Word with allegorical interpretation in his *Hom. in Lev.* 4.8 (*Origène*, 182–83). See also Trigg, *Origen*, who summarizes Origen's view of human transformation in the first book of the *Commentary on John* as follows: "the person thus transformed [by participation in Christ] becomes, like John the evangelist, another Jesus, not differing from

Christ and knowing the Father as the Son does. . . . Origen states that such a person no longer encounters Christ as a rod of chastisement, or even as a flower, but as a fruit coming to mature perfection within him. Such human transformation derives from and extends the union of the divine and human in Christ" (103–4).

85. Dawson, *Christian Figural Reading*, 65. Addressing the importance of "flesh as the site of divine becoming" in Origen's incarnational theology, Virginia Burrus has argued that "flesh, including the flesh of textuality, is the place of transformation and striving where time and eternity, difference and identity, multiplicity and unity fleetingly coincide through the ever-creative power of God's love" (*Saving Shame*, 64, 72). Her argument that, for Origen, "Word is always becoming flesh and flesh is always the becoming of Word" would support the view that Origen was more positive than Plotinus regarding the orientation of the self vis-à-vis materiality precisely owing to his christology, a view with which I agree (65). She recognizes, however, the point that I have emphasized here: in her words, Origen's "narration of the Word's becoming flesh . . . remains haunted by a subtle ambivalence. . . . It is within materiality that divine transcendence is manifested. Yet materiality also marks a loss of unity within the divine" (65).

86. *The Body and Society*, 167.

87. *De prin.* 3.6.6 (ed. and trans. Crouzel et al., 246).

88. *The Resurrection of the Body in Western Christianity, 200–1336*, 68. See also Dawson, *Christian Figural Reading*, who discusses a fragment from Origen's *Commentary on Psalm* 1 in which Origen distinguished between the body's material substratum, always in flux, and a corporeal form (εἶδος) that endures and accounts for continuity of personal identity (78–79). He comments, following Bynum, that "despite Origen's insistence that the body is intrinsic to personal identity, his recourse to the category of 'form' to distinguish the body from mere materiality-without-identity still leaves hanging the pertinence of flesh or physicality to personal identity" (80).

89. See Berchman, "Self-knowledge and Subjectivity in Origen," 447, who refers to Origen's goal of achieving "a self that is beyond itself." His point, succinctly put, is that "complete self-knowledge requires a grasp of first principles, and this kind of knowledge is an uncovering of self-knowledge through a two-fold process of gradual detachment from the objects of everyday consciousness, and an immersion in the sources of consciousness itself."

90. *Enn.* 6.9.9.56.

91. For Plotinus, see *Enn.* 4.8.8.1–6 and for discussion, O'Meara, *Plotinus: An Introduction to the Enneads*, 102–3; Iamblichus, *In Tim.*, frag. 87.28–32, in *Iamblichi Chalcidensis: In Platonis dialogos commentariorum fragmenta*, ed. and trans. Dillon. See also Kenney, *The Mysticism of Saint Augustine*, 53, on the Neoplatonic "debate about the efficacy of philosophical contemplation, *theoria*. Was contemplation, achieved through the practice of the philosophic life, sufficient for the soul's reassociation with the eternal world of the forms and with the One? For Iamblichus it was not. He and his influential followers . . . regarded the Plotinian school's notion of a higher, undescended self as a mistaken innovation. For Iamblichus the soul did descend entirely into the material world." It should be noted that it was the school of Iamblichus that dominated Neoplatonism until the end of the Academy in the sixth century. See Wallis, *Neoplatonism*, 138–59.

92. See Shaw, "After Aporia," 3–41, esp. 18–19.

93. Dodds, *Proclus: The Elements of Theology*, xx: "the humbler cosmic status

assigned by Iamblichus and most of his successors to the human soul"; Athanassiadi, "Dreams, Theurgy and Freelance Divination," 120, n. 59, on Iamblichus's "more pessimistic view of humanity" when compared with Plotinus; see Shaw, "After Aporia," for a more nuanced view: "According to Iamblichus, all souls had to mediate [between immortal and mortal, as part of their role in cosmogenesis], and in the case of human souls their mediation included the experience of suffering, dividedness, and mortality. Since the soul's original nature was immortal and coordinate with the gods it meant that—as human—the soul was alienated not only from the divinity of the gods but from its own divinity as well. And this alienation was not an accident or a temporary condition that could be rectified when the soul corrected the 'error' of identifying with the body: *the experience of self-alienation constituted the soul's very essence as human*" (20–21, emphasis in original).

94. Shaw, *Theurgy and the Soul*, 35.

95. Priscianus, *De anima* 223.32, quoting Iamblichus (trans. Shaw, "After Aporia," 25). On the presence of the divine traces in the cosmos, see Iamblichus, *De mysteriis* 1.21 (ed. and trans. Des Places, *Jamblique: Les mystères d'Egypt*, 76–77).

96. Shaw, *Theurgy and the Soul*, 157; Sheppard, "Proclus' Attitude to Theurgy," 220; Berchman, "Rationality and Ritual in Neoplatonism," 239.

97. *De mysteriis* 5.23 (ed. Des Places, 178; trans. Shaw, *Theurgy and the Soul*, 165).

98. Iamblichus, *De mysteriis* 5.23 (ed. Des Places, 178; trans. Lewy, *Chaldean Oracles and Theurgy*, 496).

99. *De mysteriis* 4.2 (τὸ τῶν θεῶν σχῆμα περιτίθεσθαι) (ed. Des Places, 148).

100. "Theurgy: Rituals of Unification in the Neoplatonism of Iamblichus," 21. See also Rappe, *Reading Neoplatonism*: "the human soul, through its realization of unity with the divine, thereby sacralizes its own world and thus 'saves' the world of matter" (177), and Berchman, "Rationality and Ritual," 238: "the soul's purification and ascent not only begins but ends in the sensible realm."

101. *Elements of Theology*, prop. 144 (trans. Dodds, 127). See Sheppard, "Proclus' Attitude to Theurgy," 220: "In Proclus' metaphysical system everything in both the natural and the intelligible world belongs both to a particular level of being and to a particular 'chain' (σειρά or τάξις) by which it is inherently related to other members of the same 'chain' on other levels."

102. "Origen's Doctrine of the Trinity and Some Later Neoplatonic Theories," 22. See also *Elements of Theology*, props. 140, 142–143, 145. Proclus developed a very complex view of a multiple spiritual realm, anchored by first principles (the henads indentified with Greek gods) that activate the chains of *sympatheia* that permeate the cosmos. As Dodds explains, "the doctrine of the henads is an attempt to account for the existence of individuality by importing plurality into the first hypostasis, yet in such a manner as to leave intact the perfect unity of the One. They are the transcendent sources of individuality" (*Elements of Theology*, 259). See also Wallis, *Neoplatonism*, 147–48.

103. *Elements of Theology*, prop. 145 (trans. Dodds, 129).

104. Ibid., prop. 211 (trans. Dodds, 185); *Commentary on Plato's Parmenides* 948 (trans. Dillon, *Proclus' Commentary on Plato's Parmenides*, hereafter cited as *Comm. Parm.*).

105. *Comm. Parm.* 948; see *Elements of Theology*, prop. 190, on the soul's position between the indivisible and the divided realms as, in Dodds's words, "a frontier between two worlds," following the Neoplatonic understanding of the creation of the soul in the Timaeus (Dodds, *Elements of Theology*, 297).

106. *Comm. Parm.* 948.

107. See *Elements of Theology*, prop. 145 (trans. Dodds, 129): "all things are dependent from the gods, some being irradiated by one god, some by another, and the series extend downwards to the last orders of being"; see Wallis, *Neoplatonism*, 153, for discussion.

108. See n. 63 above for Hadot's view of Plotinus's renunciation of being "someone" in order to become the whole.

109. *De myst.* 3.30 (ed. Des Places, 143); see Athanassiadi, "Dreams, Theurgy, and Freelance Divination," 123, 128, for discussion.

110. Shaw, *Theurgy and the Soul*, 167, n. 9.

111. Proclus, *In Tim.* 3.155.18: once the *symbola* that participate in the god activate the statue, the statue "foretells the future" (προλέγειν τὸ μέλλον) (text in Dodds, *The Greeks and the Irrational*, 292). See also Pselles, quoting from Proclus's (now mostly lost) commentary on the *Chaldean Oracles*: "The practitioners of the telestic science fill the cavities of the statues with substances belonging to the potencies presiding over the statues: animals, plants, stones, herbs, seals, engravings, sometimes also sympathetic spices . . . and they vivify the images and move them with a secret power" (*Ep.* 187, trans. in Lewy, *Chaldean Oracles and Theurgy*, 496). On the animation of statues in Chaldean theurgy, see Johnston, *Hekate Soteira*, esp. ch. 6 ("Theurgy and Magic") and ch. 8 ("The Epiphany of Hekate").

112. *Catalogue des Manuscrits Alchimiques Grecs* IV.149.22 (bel stone); IV.149.12 (lotus); VI.148.14–18 (heliotrope); IV.150.3–4 (lion and cock) (ed. Joseph Bidez). For discussion, see Shaw, *Theurgy and the Soul*, 47–49; Sheppard, "Proclus' Attitude to Theurgy," 220.

113. *Comm. Parm.* 847.

114. *Comm. Parm.* 847.

115. *Commentary on Plato's Timaeus* 1.51.25–31 (trans. Festugière, *Proclus: Commentaire sur la Timée*, 1:85).

116. *Eclogae de Philosophia Chaldaica* 5.8–11, ed. Jahn, trans. Rappe, *Reading Neoplatonism*, 176.

117. See Rappe, *Reading Neoplatonism*, 176–78, for the importance of ritual.

118. Ibid., 178; see also p. 192: "theurgic rite involves the creation of a ritual cosmos, which is then sacralized through its capacity to draw down the power of the gods."

119. *Contra Cels.* 7.33 (trans. Chadwick, 421).

120. For discussion of the "angelic" bodies of desert ascetics in such texts as Palladius's *Historia Lausiaca*, Theodoret's *Historia religiosa*, the *Historia monachorum in Aegypto*, and others, see Miller, "Desert Asceticism and 'The Body from Nowhere.'"

121. "Asceticism: Pagan and Christian," 624.

122. Ibid., 625, summarizing his overall argument in *The Body and Society*, esp. ch. 11, "The Desert Fathers: Anthony to John Climacus."

123. Views of the body as integral to human identity were developed in the contexts of the Arian and Origenist controversies; for the former, see Brakke, *Athanasius and Asceticism*, 145–61, and Clark, *The Origenist Controversy*, esp. pp. 86–104 (on Epiphanius), 121–51 (on Jerome); on the resurrection of the body and the late fourth-century linking of bodily integrity with material continuity, see Bynum, *Resurrection of the Body*, 59–94.

124. On the new sense of the instability of the created order, as well as the intensifying of the difference between creator and created, see Lyman, *Christol-*

ogy and Cosmology, 141–46, esp. 146 on Athanasius: "Indeed, as τρέπτος rather than αὐτεξούσιος, human nature is alienated more profoundly from history or the world, as well as from eternal divine nature, than it is in Irenaeus or, ironically, even Origen. The body, if the locus of transformation, has become to an even greater extent the principal distraction."

125. See Brown, *The Body and Society*, 236: "Theologians of ascetic background, throughout the fourth and fifth centuries, would not have pursued with such ferocious intellectual energy the problems raised by the Incarnation of Christ, and the consequent joining of human and divine in one single human person, if this joining had not been sensed by them as a haunting emblem of the enigmatic joining of body and soul within themselves."

126. Burrus, *"Begotten, Not Made,"* 5.

127. Athanasius, *Contra Gentes* 2.20–21; 3.3–5, 16–17 (ed. and trans. Thomson, *Athanasius: Contra Gentes and De Incarnatione*). For discussion, see Brakke, *Athanasius and Asceticism*, 146–47; Lyman, *Christology and Cosmology*, 141–43.

128. Brakke, *Athanasius and Asceticism*, 149, 239.

129. Brown, "Arbiters of Ambiguity," 140.

130. It should be noted, however, that it was the specifically physical aspect of martyrs' endurance of suffering on behalf of their faith that was often highlighted as a sign of divinity working through them; descriptions of martyrdoms in the *Peristephanon* of Prudentius are good examples.

131. Hunter, "Vigilantius of Calagurris and Victricius of Rouen," 401–30; see also Brown, *The Cult of the Saints*, 66–67.

132. On localizing the holy, see Brown, *The Cult of the Saints*, 86–105.

133. Like an animated statue, the body of a holy man or a relic is a *vehicle* for divine power, not the divine itself; on the relation between spirit and matter in relics, see Chapter 3.

134. The quotation is from Hunter, "Vigilantius," 428.

135. Dated ca. C.E. 396, this sermon was given on the occasion of the arrival of Ambrose's gift of relics; for an account of Victricius's life, see the preface to the edition of *De laude sanctorum* (hereafter cited as *De laude*), 53–93; the text has been translated, with an introduction, by Clark, "Victricius of Rouen," 365–99.

136. *De laude* 10.1–5 (*CCL* 64: 84; trans. Clark, 391).

137. *De laude* 9.15–16 (*CCL* 64: 83; trans. Clark, 389).

138. Clark, "Victricius of Rouen," 371–72.

139. *De laude* 11.46–50 (*CCL* 64: 88) (healing and bond of eternity); 1.30 (*CCL* 64: 70) (heavenly brilliance) (trans. Clark, 395, 377). For many examples of these healings at martyrs' shrines, see MacMullen, *Christianity and Paganism in the Fourth to Eighth Centuries*, 120–34; as he notes, martyria served as hospitals (121).

140. *De laude* 9.30–31; 7.12 (*CCL* 64: 83–84, 79; trans. Clark, 386, 385).

141. *De laude* 7.39–42 (*CCL* 64: 80; trans. Clark, 386).

142. *De laude* 8.15–16 (*CCL* 64: 81; trans. Clark, 388).

143. Clark, "Victricius of Rouen," 367.

144. *De laude* 8.21–22 (*CCL* 64: 82; trans. Clark, 388).

145. *De laude* 8.25–40; 12.1–8 (*CCL* 64: 82, 88–89; trans. Clark, 388, 395–96).

146. *De laude* 11.27 (*CCL* 64: 87; trans. Clark, 394): "I touch fragments; I affirm that in these relics is perfect grace and perfect virtue." Victricius's sermon is studded with references to fire, light, brilliance, and radiance, reminiscent of the divine and illuminative fire in theurgy (see Shaw, *Theurgy and the Soul*, 150).

147. *De laude* 1.18 (*CCL* 64: 70; trans. Clark, 377).

148. *De laude* 12.25–33 (*CCL* 64: 89; trans. Clark, 396–97).

149. Ritual practices included processions such as the one described by Victricius in *De laude* 3.11–42 (*CCL* 64:73–74), candle-lit processions, sermons such as Victricius's own, prayers; martyria were often decorated with paintings and mosaics; for discussion of the aesthetic contexts of relics, see Chapter 3.

150. *De laude* 7.1 (*CCL* 64: 79; trans. Clark, 385).

151. There is little information about where the animation of statues took place, although temples seem a likely choice in light of Eunapius's account of the theurgist Maximus's animation of a statue of Hekate in Pergamom (*Vitae philosophorum et sophistarum*, 475). The ritual may also have taken place in private homes; see the discussion, with pictures, of private lararia containing statues with hollows, perhaps for containing theurgical herbs and other substances, by St. Clair, "Imperial Virtue," 156–57.

Chapter 2. Bodies in Fragments

1. See Introduction.
2. Calvino, *Six Memos for the Next Millennium*, 51.
3. Ibid., 35.
4. Ibid., 33.
5. Ibid., 35.
6. Roberts, *Jeweled Style*, 38.
7. Ibid., 39, 56–61, 75.
8. Ibid., 103; see also 56, 75, 84–85.
9. Ibid., 3.
10. Ibid., 58.
11. Ibid., 72.
12. In discussing late ancient mosaics, Roberts refers to the "liberation of the individual stone and its investment with light and color" (72); on the "verbal dazzle" of poetry, see *Jeweled Style*, 75.

13. Kitzinger, *Byzantine Art in the Making*, 18. On these stylistic developments, see Brandenburg, "Stilprobleme der frühchristlichen Sarkophagkunst Roms im 4. Jahrhundert," 439–71, and idem., "*Ars Humilis*," 71–84.

14. See Lavin, "The Hunting Mosaics of Antioch and Their Sources," 181–286, esp. 235–44, and Tromzo, *The Via Latina Catacomb*, esp. 65–70.

15. Kitzinger, *Byzantine Art in the Making*, 7–8. Brandenburg points to the "paratactic arrangement" of the figures in this frieze, as well as their schematic formation without regard to perspective or naturalistic presentation ("Stilprobleme der frühchristlichen Sarkophagkunst," 442–43).

16. Roberts, *Jeweled Style*, 84; these comments are about mosaics, but the same holds true for sarcophagi (see 94–100). See also Brandenburg, "Ars Humilis," 71–74, for discussion of similarities between the Arch of Constantine and sarcophagi of the early fourth century.

17. Kitzinger, *Byzantine Art in the Making*, 23.

18. Ibid., 23. On early Christian frieze sarcophagi of the Constantinian period, see Brandenburg, "Stilprobleme der frühchristlichen Sarkophagkunst," 454–60.

19. The quotations are from, respectively, Roberts, *Jeweled Style*, 94, and Kitzinger, *Byzantine Art in the Making*, 25.

20. Roberts, *Jeweled Style*, 95.

21. Brown, "Thing Theory," 5.

22. Onians, "Abstraction and Imagination in Late Antiquity," 19.

23. Roberts, *Jeweled Style*, 6. Brandenburg argues that early Christian art did not represent a new departure but was part of a wider cultural phenomenon in the development of artistic style ("Ars Humilis," 78–80).

24. See Delehaye, *Les Origines du Culte des Martyrs*, 60; the source of the report of Lucilla's practice is Optatus of Milevus, *Against the Donatists* 1.16, in *Optatus: Against the Donatists*, ed. and trans. Edwards, 15–16 (Latin text in *Optat de Milève: Traité contre les Donatistes*, vol. 1: 206–8); see Brown, *Cult of the Saints*, 34, for a discussion of Lucilla's practice in terms of a "privatization of the holy" and the rise of spiritual patronage in the fourth century.

25. Levitan, "Dancing at the End of the Rope," 249.

26. Ibid., 249, n. 15: *vincula* and *scrupea*.

27. Ausonius, *Epigrams* 8–13 (which lampoon the character of "Rufus the Rhetorician" by drawing parallels between the lifelike stillness of artistic representations of the man and his real-life stiffness), and *Epigrams* 107–112 (which are puns on the phrase "a good Briton," then an oxymoron); text in *Ausonius*, vol. 2 (trans. White).

28. *Ep. Symmachi ad Ausonium*, in *Ausonius*, vol. 1 (trans. White, 267); for discussion, see Nugent, "Ausonius' 'Late-Antique' Poetics and 'Post-Modern' Literary Theory," 33.

29. For a graphic defense of belief in "full presence" in the Eucharistic elements, see *Apophthegmata Patrum*, Alphabetical Collection, "Daniel 7" (trans. Ward, 53–54); on full presence in relics, see the comments of Victricius of Rouen, below.

30. See Brown, *Cult of the Saints*, 34.

31. See Paulinus of Nola, *Ep.* 31.6 (*CSEL* 29.274): "Indeed this cross of inanimate wood has living power, and ever since its discovery it has lent its wood to the countless, almost daily, prayers of men. Yet it suffers no diminution; though daily divided, it seems to remain whole to those who lift it, and always entire to those who venerate it" (trans. Walsh, *Letters of St. Paulinus of Nola*, ACW, vol. 36, 2:132–33). For discussion, see Hunt, *Holy Land Pilgrimage in the Late Roman Empire A.D. 312–460*, 129.

32. See Levitan, "Dancing at the End of the Rope," 245, for the few biographical details known about Optatian. For dating, see Barnes, "Publilius Optatianus Porfyrius," 173–86.

33. Malamud, *Prudentius and Classical Mythology*, 39–40.

34. For the estimation of the unreadability of Optatian's poems, see Malamud, *Prudentius and Classical Mythology*, 39; the quotation is from Levitan, "Dancing at the End of the Rope," 246.

35. On Optatian's compositional techniques, the best discussion is by Levitan, "Dancing at the End of the Rope," 249–62 and *passim*.

36. Levitan, "Dancing at the End of the Rope," 255.

37. Ibid., 257–58.

38. Ibid., 249 (first quotation); the second quotation is from Malamud, *Prudentius and Classical Mythology*, 40.

39. Malamud, *Prudentius and Classical Mythology*, 39.

40. Stewart, *Poetry and the Fate of the Senses*, 34. T. E. Hulme's comments about the Imagist movement in poetry in the early twentieth century are also relevant to ancient pattern poems: "This new verse appeals to the eye rather than to the ear. It has to mould images, a kind of spiritual clay, into definite shapes. The material . . . is image and not sound. It builds up a plastic image which it hands

over to the reader." "A Lecture on Modern Poetry," in *Further Speculations by T. E. Hulme*, ed. Sam Hynes, 75, quoted in Stewart, *Poetry*, 35.

41. Levitan, "Dancing at the End of the Rope," 263.

42. Victricius of Rouen, *De laude* 9 (*CCL* 64: 83–84). See also Theodoret of Cyrrhus, *Curatio affectionum graecarum* 8.11 (ed. Canivet, SC 57): "The body has been divided up, but the grace remains undivided, and the tiniest particle of a relic has a power equal to that which the martyr would have had if not divided."

43. See Wyschogrod, *Saints and Postmodernism*, 43: "The cultic veneration of saints attests the ongoing character of their moral influence. It is just this post-mortem effectiveness that enables them to become historical figures." This, I think, is the appropriate context in which to understand statements such as the following one by Augustine: speaking about the relics of St. Stephen, he remarks, "he would not be visiting us dead, if in death he were not alive. How so little a handful of dust can draw so great a multitude!" (*Serm.* 317.1.1, in Markus, *The End of Ancient Christianity*, 94).

44. Jerome, *C. Vigil.* 5 (*PL* 23.358); see *Ep.* 109.1 (*CSEL* 55: 352), where Jerome counters the charge of Vigilantius's view that the practices of the cult of relics were precisely idolatrous: "he calls those of us who acknowledge them [i.e., relics of martyrs] ashmen (*cinerarios*) and idolaters who venerate dead men's bones." On the insistence by partisans of the cult of relics that saints and relics were not themselves divine but rather intermediaries for the work of God and Christ, an affirmation "répétée à satiété" as Pierre Maraval remarked, see Maraval, *Lieux Saints et Pèlerinages d'Orient*, 158.

45. Levitan, "Dancing at the End of the Rope," 249.

46. Ibid., 249.

47. Wilken, *The Land Called Holy*, 116.

48. *De laude* 11.50 (*CCL* 64.88).

49. Ausonius, "Technopaegnion," pref. 2 (trans. White, 1: 289).

50. Ibid. (I have revised White's translation.) For a discussion of the *Mosella* in this regard, see Fontaine, "Unité et diversité du mélange des genres et des tons chez quelques écrivains latins de la fin du IV° siècle," 438–46; see especially the discussion of "cette volonté de ruptures répétées" characteristic of this poem (440).

51. Ausonius, "Technopaegnion," pref. 1 (trans. White, 1:287 [emphasis added]).

52. Barthes, *Camera Lucida*, trans. Howard, 45.

53. For discussions of late ancient ekphrasis, see Nugent, "Ausonius' 'Late Antique' Poetics," 30–35, and Roberts, *Jeweled Style*, 38–57.

54. Mitchell, *Picture Theory*, 167.

55. See Quintillian, *Inst. Or.* 9.2.40 (in Butler, trans., *Quintillian*, 3: 396) and *Rhet. ad Herennium* 4.55.68 (in Caplan, trans., *[Cicero]: Rhetorica ad Herennium*, 404); for an overall discussion, see Onians, "Abstraction and Imagination in Late Antiquity," 1–24.

56. Roberts, *Jeweled Style*, 44.

57. Ibid., 56.

58. Nugent, "Ausonius' 'Late-Antique' Poetics," 30–37. For discussions of the way in which this taste for exaggerated realism affected other genres in the fourth century—notably the *Res Gestae* of Ammianus Marcellinus—see Palmer, *Prudentius on the Martyrs*, 32–56, and Matthews, *The Roman Empire of Ammianus*, 460–61. The phrase "reality-effect" comes from an essay by Barthes, "The Reality Effect," 141–48.

59. Nugent, "Ausonius' 'Late-Antique' Poetics," 32. See also Fontaine, "Unité et diversité," 443: "Cette Moselle poétique nous est bien présente, mais dans l'ordre d'une réalité *spectaculaire*" (emphasis in original).

60. Nugent, "Ausonius' 'Late-Antique' Poetics," 34.

61. Mitchell, *Picture Theory*, 158.

62. Nugent, "Ausonius' 'Late-Antique' Poetics," 34, 32. See also Fontaine, "Unité et Diversité," 443–44.

63. Ibid., 31. On the conversion of reader into spectator, see the statement of Nicolaus of Myra, a *rhetor* of the fifth century C.E.: ἥ δὲ (sc. ἔκφρασις) πειρᾶται θεατὰς τοὺς ἀκούοντας ἐργάζεσθαι, in *Progymnasmata* 68.11–12 (*Rhetores Graeci* 11, ed. Felten), cited in Roberts, *Jeweled Style*, 38.

64. Nugent, "Ausonius' 'Late-Antique' Poetics," 32.

65. Saxer, *Morts, Martyrs, reliques en Afrique chrétienne aux premiers siècles*, 312–13.

66. On the activities of Damasus with regard to the cult of relics, see Pietri, *Roma Christiana*, 529–46, 607–724. Pietri credits Damasus with establishing "a holy topography" in Rome (529). For a more recent discussion of "Damasus's invention of early Christian Rome around the tombs of the saints," see Trout, "Damasus and the Invention of Early Christian Rome," 302. For a discussion on ways in which "the cult of martyrs turned the spatial world into a network of holy places," see Markus, *End of Ancient Christianity*, 142–50, quotation at 142.

67. Damasus, *Epigr.* 7; 59 (ed. Ferrua, *Epigrammata Damasiana*); Augustine, *Serm.* 274.1 (*PL* 38.1252) (on Vincent); *Serm.* 273.6 (*PL* 38.1250) (Agnes); for a discussion of Prudentius's complicated puns, see Malamud, *A Poetics of Transformation*, 152 (Agnes), 116 (Cyprian), and 81 (Hippolytus); see also Petruccione, "Prudentius' Use of Martyrological Topoi in *Peristephanon*," 40 ff. and 111, for many references to this kind of wordplay on the names of martyrs.

68. Gregory of Nyssa, *Laudatio S. Theodori* (*PG* 46.737).

69. Ibid. The convention of art "speaking," of sight transmuted into voice, had a long history. In early Byzantium, as Maguire has pointed out, "references to works of art which were so close to nature that they might be capable of speech are very common in ekphraseis" (*Rhetoric, Nature and Magic in Byzantine Art*, Ch. I: 129). For example, in his sixth-century ekphrasis on the church of St. Sergius at Gaza, Choricius wrote about an artistic depiction in the lateral apses of a flock of partridges: "He [the artist] would, perhaps, have rendered even their musical sounds, had not this hindered the hearing of divine things" (Choricius, *Laudatio Marciani* 1.33, in Mango, *The Art of the Byzantine Empire 312–1453*, 16, 62). Presumably to look at the picture of the partridges and hear them singing would require the kind of synaesthesia discussed earlier with regard to Ausonius's poetic image of Cupid's wings.

70. Asterius of Amaseia, *Ekphrasis on Saint Euphemia* 1 (ed. Halkin, *Euphémie de Chalcédoine: Légendes Byzantines*, Subsidia Hagiographica 41, 5).

71. Paulinus of Nola, *Ep.* 32.10 (*CSEL* 29.286): *vox patris caelo tonat.*

72. On *praesentia* and relics, see the discussion by Brown, *Cult of the Saints*, 86–105; see also Hunt, *Holy Land Pilgrimage*, 133.

73. Gregory of Nyssa, *Laudatio S. Theodori* (*PG* 46.740B).

74. *De laude* 12.32–35 (*CCL* 64: 89–90).

75. Ross, "Dynamic Writing and Martyrs' Bodies in Prudentius' *Peristephanon*," 326; Prudentius's writing is a good example of what Matthews has called "the peculiarly expressionistic manner of the fourth century" (*The Roman Empire of Ammianus*, 460). See also Malamud, *Prudentius and Classical Mythology*, 43–46, and Roberts, *Poetry and the Cult of the Martyrs*, chs. 3–5.

76. Levitan, "Dancing at the End of the Rope," 266.

77. *Peristephanon* (hereafter *Pe*) 9.50 (*rubetque ab ictu curta et umens pagina*), in *Prudence, IV: Le Livre des Couronnes, Dittochaeon, Épilogue*, ed. Lavarenne, 114, trans. and discussed by Ross, "Dynamic Writing," 331.

78. Ross, "Dynamic Writing," 353.

79. On the poetic structure shared by Prudentius's poems, see Roberts, *Poetry and the Cult of the Martyrs*, 10; Malamud, *A Poetics of Transformation*, 177–80 and passim.

80. Ross, "Dynamic Writing," 326.

81. Roberts, *Jeweled Style*, 85, 98 (these comments refer respectively to mosaics of processions of saints in S. Apollinare Nuovo in Ravenna and to the Probus sarcophagus, a column sarcophagus from the late fourth century [see p. 99, fig. 13 in Roberts]).

82. *HM*, pro. 10 and epilogue 2 (ed. Festugière, *Historia Monachorum in Aegypto*).

83. Theodoret, *HR*, pro. 8 (ed. and trans. Canivet and Leroy-Molinghen, *Théodoret de Cyr: Histoire des Moines de Syrie*, SC 234, 257). Here I have summarized a longer passage, following the translation by Price, 7.

84. For the use of the term πολιτεία, see Theodoret, *HR* pro. 3; *HM*, pro. 2. For a discussion of the notion of "angelic life" in these collections, see Miller, "Desert Asceticism and 'The Body From Nowhere,'" 137–53.

85. Ibid., esp. 137–43, for a discussion of the visual immediacy constructed by the *Historia monachorum* and similar collections.

86. *HM* 21.5–12.

87. On the whole issue of figuration and the presentation of lives as artistic images, see Cameron, *Christianity and the Rhetoric of Empire*, 150–52.

88. Theodoret, *HR*, pro. 2.27–28; 3.19–20.

89. Gregory of Nazianzus, *Or.* 43.77, 76 (emphasis added) (*PG* 36.600A, 597C).

90. *Ep.* 109.1 (*CSEL* 55.352). On the idolatrous dangers of "ekphrastic utopianism," which would be akin to "mere" mimesis, see Mitchell, *Picture Theory*, 156.

91. *Ep.* 109.1 (*CSEL* 55.352).

92. Evodius, *De miraculis Sancti Stephani* 2.6 (*PL* 41.847), trans. Brown, *Cult of the Saints* 88; Brown takes this anecdote to be an example of the yearning for proximity to saints run amok.

93. Virginia Burrus, private correspondence, October 10, 2007.

Chapter 3. Dazzling Bodies

1. Klinkenborg, review of *Outside Passage: A Memoir of an Alaskan Childhood*, by Julia Scully , 7.

2. The phrase in quotations is taken from Brown, *Cult of the Saints*, 69. On the burgeoning of the cult of relics in the mid-fourth century, see MacMullen, *Christianity and Paganism in the Fourth to Eighth Centuries*, 120–29.

3. For discussion of a visual rhetoric of sanctity in saints' shrines, see Hahn, "Seeing and Believing ," 1079–1106.

4. Fontaine, "Unité et diversité du mélange des genres," 443. Fontaine makes this remark with regard to the poetic art of Ausonius's poem "Mosella,"

and goes on to observe that "cette Moselle poétique nous est bien présente, mais dans l'ordre d'une réalité *spectaculaire*" (emphasis in original). I am arguing that similar aesthetic effects conditioned how relics were presented and perceived.

5. Paulinus of Nola, *Carm.* 27.400–405 (*CSEL* 30: 279–80), describing the relics in the churches at Nola: "For the ashes even of apostles have been set beneath that table of heaven, and consecrated amongst other holy offerings they emit a fragrance pleasing to Christ from their living dust [*spirantis pulveris*]" (trans. Walsh, *The Poems of St. Paulinus of Nola* , 285).

6. Brown, *Cult of the Saints*, 78.

7. Stevens, *Collected Letters*, 785 (letter to Renato Poggioli, 29 June 1953), commenting on the phrase "the amorist adjective aflame" in his poem "The Man With The Blue Guitar." I thank David L. Miller for this reference.

8. *Serm.* 273.9 (*PL* 38.1252): *non enim alterius generic carnem portaverunt, quam vos portatis,* trans. Hill, *The Works of Saint Augustine: Sermons III/8* , 21 (hereafter cited as *Sermons III/8*).

9. *Hom.* 19.5 (*In sanctos quadraginta martyres*) (*PG* 31.516A–B), trans. Maguire, *Art and Eloquence in Byzantium* , 40.

10. Brown, *Cult of the Saints*, 82.

11. Jerome, *Ep.* 109.1 (*CSEL* 55: 352); *C. Vigil.* 4 (*PL* 23.357); for a discussion of Vigiliantius's position on relics, see Hunter, "Vigilantius," 401–30.

12. *Serm.* 273.7 (*PL* 38.1251; *Sermons III/8*, 20); *De mor. eccl. cath.* 1.34.75 (*PL* 32.1342).

13. *Serm.* 313C (*PLS* 2.611): *Multi usquequaque habent magnum corpus librorum eius. Sed nos uberiores gratias domino agamus, quod habere meruimus sanctum corpus membrorum eius*; trans. Hill, *The Works of Saint Augustine: Sermons III.9* , 103 (hereafter cited as *Sermons III/9*).

14. Victricius of Rouen, *De laude* 10.1–5; 8.10–11 (*CCL* 64: 84, 81; trans. Clark, 391, 387). The first passage noted here, in which Victricius asks, "Why, then, do we call them relics?" is quoted in full and discussed in Chapter 1, p. 37.

15. *Serm.* 301A.7, in *Miscellanea Agostiniana*, vol. 1, ed. Morin, 87 (hereafter cited as *MA*) (*Sermons III/8*, 296): "Well, anyway, I love the martyrs, I go and watch the martyrs; when the Passions of the martyrs are read, I am a spectator, watching them."

16. *Serm.* 313A.2–3, (*MA*, 67–68; *Sermons III/9*, 90–93) for the lust of the eyes; on singing and dancing "inwardly," see *Serm.* 311.7, (*PL* 38.1416; *Sermons III/9*, 74); on imitation, *Serm.* 311.1, (*PL* 38.1414; *Sermons III/9*, 71), where Augustine—in the presence of Cyprian's relics—writes, "the right way to celebrate the festivals of the martyrs should be by imitating their virtues."

17. *Serm.* 313A.3 (*MA*, 68; *Sermons III/9*, 92: "arms of the mind"); *Serm.* 335D.1 (*PLS* 2.777; *Sermons III/9*, 229: "holy drunkenness"). For a fuller account of Augustine's notion of a theater of the mind, see Chapter 4, pp. 85–90.

18. Gregory of Nyssa, *Laudatio S. Theodori* (*PG* 46.737, 740). See the Introduction, pp. 2–3, and Chapter 2, pp. 55–56.

19. See *Serm.* 305A.4 (*MA*, 58; *Sermons III/8*, 326–27); 311.5–6 (*PL* 38.1416; *Sermons III/9*, 73), and 335D.1–2 (*PLS* 2.777–78; *Sermons III/9*, 229). For discussion and further examples of debauchery at celebrations of martyrs, see Bitton-Ashkelony, *Encountering the Sacred*, 37–39.

20. *Serm.* 311.5 (*PL* 38.1416; *Sermons III/9*, 73).

21. *Serm.* 301A.7 (*MA*, 87; *Sermons III/8*, 296).

22. *Serm.* 305A.4 (*MA*, 58; *Sermons III/8*, 327). For an extended discussion of Augustine's understanding of martyr-narratives as a form of a spiritual theater, see Chapter 4, "Bodies and Spectacles."

23. *Carm.* 27.542–595 (*CSEL* 30: 287–88).

24. For the description of the paintings as a multicolored spectacle, see *Carm.* 27.582–83 (*CSEL* 30: 288): *si forte adtonitas haec per spectacula mentes agrestum caperet fucata coloribus umbra.* For the quotation on hunger, line 588.

25. *Carm.* 27.580–81 (*CSEL* 30: 288).

26. *Carm.* 27.513–15 (*CSEL* 30: 284).

27. I have borrowed the phrase "wrap-around environment" from Mathews, *The Clash of Gods*, 155, who uses it to describe the Orthodox baptistery in Ravenna.

28. James and Webb, "'To Understand Ultimate Things,'" 4; see also Roberts, *Jeweled Style*, 38–39.

29. James and Webb, "'To Understand Ultimate Things,'" 6.

30. See Mango, *Art of the Byzantine Empire, 312–1453*, 4–14, 26–39, for a collection of examples.

31. James and Webb, "'To Understand Ultimate Things,'" 6; see also pp. 8–9.

32. Callistratus, *Ekphraseis* 5.2, text in *Philostratus, Imagines; Callistratus, Descriptions*, ed. and trans. Fairbanks ; trans. Elsner, "Naturalism and the Erotics of the Gaze," 250.

33. Elsner, "Naturalism and the Erotics of the Gaze," 251.

34. Ibid., 250–51.

35. *Ekphrasis on Saint Euphemia* 1 (ed. Halkin, 5).

36. *Ekphasis on Saint Euphemia* 2 (ed. Halkin, 6): ἱερὸν θέαμα.

37. Ibid., 1 ("animated"); 4 (drops of blood) (ed. Halkin, 5, 7).

38. Ibid., 3 (ed. Halkin, 6).

39. Ibid., 4 (ed. Halkin, 8): ὥρα δέ σοι καὶ αὐτὴν εἰ βούλει τελέσαι τὴν γραφήν, ἵνα κατίδῃς ἀκριβῶς εἰ μὴ πολὺ κατόπιν τῆς ἐξηγήσεως ἤλθομεν.

40. See James and Webb, "'To Understand Ultimate Things,'" for the suggestion that Asterius's "listeners are invited to create a picture in their own minds which they themselves may embellish" (10).

41. Bryson, "Philostratus and the Imaginary Museum," 273, referring to one of the dynamics of the ekphrases in the *Imagines* of Philostratus the Elder. See also Elsner, "Naturalism and the Erotics of the Gaze," 259, n. 37, who discusses the "*aporia* of *trompe l'oeil*" in the *Imagines* of the elder Philostratus, i.e., the phenomenon, much discussed in classical and later antiquity, in which a painting is so realistic that it deceives the viewer (not to mention bees, birds, and horses!) with its "realistic" or "naturalistic" appearance. A similar collaboration between words and pictures is characteristic of Prudentius's poetic descriptions.

42. Fontaine, *Naissance de la poésie dans l'occident chrétien*, 188.

43. Prudentius, *Pe.* 11.123–44 (ed. Lavarenne, *Prudence, IV*, 169). I have adapted the translations of Malamud, *A Poetics of Transformation*, 85, and Roberts, *Poetry and the Cult of the Martyrs*, 154. For a discussion of the complicated hagiographic tradition of this saint, see Lavarenne, *Prudence, IV*, 159–64.

44. See James and Webb, "'To Understand Ultimate Things,'" 3–9.

45. Malamud, *A Poetics of Transformation*, 86.

46. *The Cult Center of the Martyr Hippolytus on the Via Tiburtina*, 42.

47. Malamud, *A Poetics of Transformation*, 86.

48. *Pe.* 11.139–40 (ed. Lavarenne, *Prudence, IV,* 170; trans. Roberts, *Poetry and the Cult of the Martyrs,* 156); concerning this passage, Roberts offers the following insight: "The reconstitution of the saint's body is simultaneously, then, an act of devotion and cult, and the restoration of meaning to the obscure traces of martyrdom. Prudentius, in writing his poem, repeats this original devotional and interpretive act" (156–57).

49. *Pe.* 11.153–70 (ed. Lavarenne, *Prudence, IV,* 170–71; trans. Roberts, *Poetry and the Cult of the Martyrs,* 157–58).

50. *Pe.* 11.167–68 (ed. Lavarenne, *Prudence, IV,* 171): *Sic datur absentis per subterranea solis/cernere fulgorem luminibusque frui.*

51. *Pe.* 11.183–86 (ed. Lavarenne, *Prudence, IV,* 171; translation adapted from Malamud, *A Poetics of Transformation,* 111): *ipsa, illas animae exuvias quae continet intus/aeidcula argento fulgurat ex solido./praefixit tabulas dives manus aequore levi / candentes, recavum quale nitet speculum.*

52. On the collapsing of spatial and temporal distinctions in Prudentius's poetry, see Roberts, *Poetry and the Cult of the Martyrs,* 20, 72.

53. Malamud, *A Poetics of Transformation,* 112.

54. *Pe.* 11.193 (ed. Lavarenne, *Prudence, IV,* 171): *oscula perspicuo figunt impressa metallo.*

55. Fontaine, *Études sur la poésie latine tardive d'Ausone à Prudence,* 443, describing Ausonius's technique in his poem "Mosella," a technique of the art of ποικιλία equally applicable here.

56. Roberts, *Jeweled Style,* 46–47, 75.

57. Ibid., 47–54. As Roberts points out, "the images of flowers and jewels tended to become conflated as the adjectives *gemmeus, gemmans,* and *gemmatus* are increasingly used in the sense of *floridus*" (53).

58. Ibid., 55, 48. As Roberts observes, in late antiquity "the increasing tendency to conceive literary composition in visual, specifically color, terms can be traced in the metaphorical language used of rhetorical and poetic *ornatus*" (47).

59. Prudentius, *Pe.* 12.54 (ed. Lavarenne, *Prudence, IV,* 180): *sic prata vernis floribus renident;* see Roberts, *Jeweled Style,* 51, 75, for discussion of the flower metaphor.

60. Janes, *God and Gold in Late Antiquity,* 151.

61. *Oxford Classical Dictionary,* s.v. "*rosalia,*" 936–37.

62. Salzman, *On Roman Time,* 97–99.

63. Hoey, "Rosaliae Signorum," 22–27.

64. *Carm.* 14.110–16 (*CSEL* 30: 50).

65. *Carm.* 21.60–62 (*CSEL* 30: 160): *nam quasi fecundo sancti Felicis in agro/ emersere novi flores, duo germina Christi;* on the two new "plants of Christ" who blossom in the fertile field of Saint Felix (Turcius and Pinian), see Walsh, trans., *The Poems of St. Paulinus of Nola,* 386, nn. 7–8.

66. Paulinus, *Carm.* 27.206 (*CSEL* 30: 271): *hic quoque ades* (the context makes it clear that *ades* refers to Felix's presence in the company of those in heaven). On relics and presence, see Brown, *Cult of the Saints,* 86–105.

67. See Griffiths, *Apuleius of Madauros,* 160–61.

68. *Metamorphoses* 11.13 (trans. Lindsay, 242).

69. See the account of Arnobius, *Adv. Nationes* 5.7, in Meyer, ed., *The Ancient Mysteries,* 118.

70. *Metamorphoses* 10.728–35 (trans. Mandelbaum, 356).

71. *Org. Wld.,* 111.9–14 (=NHC II.5), in Robinson, ed., *The Nag Hammadi Library in English,* 169; see the discussion of Tardieu, *Trois Mythes Gnostiques* , 208–12.

72. Ausonius, *Cupido cuciatus*, lines 77, 90–93 (trans. White, 1: 212, 214).

73. *Pass. Perpetuae* 11.5; *Pass. Mar. et Iac.* 11.5, ed. and trans. Musurillo, *The Acts of the Christian Martyrs* , 119, 209.

74. *Cathemerinon* 12.125, ed. and trans. Lavarenne, *Prudence, I* .

75. For literary references, see Ross, "Dynamic Writing and Martyrs' Bodies," 338–40; Roberts, *Poetry and the Cult of the Martyrs*, 98–100; Palmer, *Prudentius on the Martyrs*, 167–75. In the early Christian imagination, the sexual element in the complex of blood, flowers, death and transformation appeared most frequently in connection with young women rather than with young men, as in the myths of Adonis, Attis, and Cupid. Traditional associations of virginity with roses and the association of flowers with young girls on the threshold of marriage appear to have combined here in a redirection of the virgin-martyr's sexuality toward a "chaste" fertility. For the association of virginity with roses, see Dulaey, *Le rêve dans la vie et la pensée de Saint Augustin*, 222–23; for flowers and marriageable girls, see Palmer, *Prudentius on the Martyrs*, 168.

76. Grabar, *Martyrium*, II, pl. LX.3: Anonymous martyr, fresco at Abou Girgeh.

77. Ross, "Dynamic Writing and Martyrs' Bodies," 340.

78. For many references, see Delumeau, *History of Paradise*, 11–14; Fontaine, *Études sur la poésie latine tardive d'Ausone à Prudence*, 490–95.

79. For Eulalia as a *flos tener*, see *Pe.* 3.109 (ed. Lavarenne, *Prudence, IV*, 58); for the quotation, see Ross, "Dynamic Writing and Martyrs' Bodies," 339.

80. *Pe.* 3.140, 201–2, 199–20, 205 (ed. Lavarenne, *Prudence, IV*, 58, 60–61; my translation); for his own verses as flowers, lines 208–10: *Ast ego, serta choro in medio/texta feram pede dactylico,/vilia, marcida, festa tamen* ("So I will bring into the midst of the celebration garlands of flowers woven from dactylic feet; they are paltry, wilted, but festal gifts nonetheless").

81. Paulinus, *Ep* 32.17.12–13 (*CSEL* 29.292).

82. *Laudatio S. Theodori* (*PG* 46.737).

83. *De laude* 12.28–37 (*CCL* 64: 89–90; trans. Clark, 396–97). On the connections that Victricius made among martyrs, relics, and spiritual jewels, see also Chapter 4, pp. 98–100.

84. The phrase is from Roberts, *Jeweled Style*, 75.

85. *Serm.* 319.6.6, quoted in Markus, *The End of Ancient Christianity*, 148.

86. *Civ. Dei* 22.8.10 (*PL* 41.766).

87. See Roberts, *Poetry of the Cult of the Martyrs*, 20, 72, for examples in art and architecture of such erasure of boundaries.

88. For many examples of healing as the major focus of the cult of relics, see MacMullen, *Christianity and Paganism in the Fourth to Eight Centuries*, 120–24.

89. The mosaic portrait of Saint Victor is from the Chapel of St. Victor at San Ambrogio, Milan.

90. Mackie, "Symbolism and Purpose in an Early Christian Martyr Chapel," 93.

91. Ibid., 95.

92. For a discussion of the early Christian "taste for brilliance," see Janes, *God and Gold*, 139–52; for the appreciation of color, see James, *Light and Colour in Byzantine Art*, 125–28.

93. Bachelard, *The Flame of a Candle*, 40, 43, 59.

94. Paulinus, *Carm.* 19.412–24 (*CSEL* 30.132–33): *at medio in spatio fixi laquearibus altis/pendebant per aëna cavi retinacula lychni,/qui specie arborea lentis quasi vitea virgis/bracchia iactantes summoque cacumine rami/vitreolos gestant tamquam sua poma*

*caliclos/et quasi vernantes accenso lumine florent/densaque multicomis imitantur sidera
flammis/distinguntque graves numerosa luce tenebras/et tenerum igniculis florentibus
aethera pingunt,/dumque tremunt liquidos crines crebrumque coruscant,/adsiduis facibus
sparsa caligine noctis/ambiguam faciem miscent lucem inter et umbras/et dubium trepidis
conspectibus aëra turbant.*

95. See n. 55.

96. Bachelard, *Air and Dreams*, 1 (emphasis in original).

97. Newman, *Locating the Romantic Subject* , 65, 1.

98. I owe this insight, as well as the comments by Stevens on incandescence, to an unpublished manuscript by David L. Miller, "The Amorist Adjective Aflame in the Works of Gaston Bachelard, Henry Corbin, and Wallace Stevens," originally presented at the Gaston Bachelard Conference, December 4, 1983, sponsored by the Dallas Institute of Humanities and Culture.

99. Bachelard, *The Psychoanalysis of Fire*, 41.

Chapter 4. Bodies and Spectacles

1. Tiffany, *Toy Medium*, 200.

2. For further discussion of the relevance of Tiffany's arguments for this book, see the Introduction.

3. This sentence draws on a discussion of the tradition of *ubi sunt qui ante nos fuerunt* (Where now are those who lived before us?) by Stewart, *Poetry and the Fate of the Senses*, 216: "The *ubi sunt* tradition addresses the farthest reaches of sensual apprehension, the point where such apprehension trails into unintelligibility and disappearance and so where memory turns to imagination." See also Frankfurter, "On Sacrifice and Residues," 518, who makes a similar point about Coptic martyrology: "This imagery [of martyrs' body parts as healing relics] makes clear that the martyrologies' purpose as narrative is not only to dramatize the brave saints' struggles against heathen powers, but even more to transform imaginatively a pious human being into sacred stuff for the populace."

4. John Chrysostom, *Homily Delivered After the Remains of the Martyrs* (*PG* 63.467), trans. Mayer and Allen, *John Chrysostom*, 86.

5. For dating and context, see Mayer and Allen, *John Chrysostom*, 85–86.

6. *A Homily on Martyrs* (*PG* 50.666), trans. Mayer and Allen, *John Chrysostom*, 97.

7. For a thorough discussion of Chrysostom's attack on the theater, see Leyerle, *Theatrical Shows and Ascetic Lives.*

8. *Homily Delivered After the Remains of the Martyrs* (*PG* 63.469), trans. Mayer and Allen, *John Chrysostom*, 88.

9. *A Homily on Martyrs* (*PG* 50.664), trans. Mayer and Allen, *John Chrysostom*, 96.

10. *Homily Delivered After the Remains of the Martyrs* (*PG* 63.469), trans. Mayer and Allen, *John Chrysostom*, 87.

11. *Discourse on the Blessed Babylas and Against the Greeks*, 65–66, in *Jean Chrysostome: Discours sur Babylas*, ed. and trans. Schatkin, SC 262, 174–76; Eng. trans. Schatkin, *St. John Chrysostom, Apologist*, 112–13.

12. *Baptismal Catecheses* 2.9, in *Jean Chrysostome*, ed. and trans. Wenger, SC 50,138. For discussion, see Frank, "'Taste and See,'" 635.

13. Carruthers, *The Craft of Thought*, 49.

14. For Chrysostom's distinction between the two kinds of eyes, see, e.g., *Baptismal Catecheses* 3.3.9–22, in *Jean Chrysostome: Trois catéchèses baptismales*, ed. and

trans. Piédagnel, SC 366, 220–22. As Frank, "'Taste and See,'" convincingly demonstrates, Chrysostom's goal was "not to reject bodily perceptions but to learn how to see more clearly and attentively through them" (636); further, "the mind's ability to generate the needed mental images was critical for the eyes of faith" (637).

15. *Serm.* 305A.4 (*MA*, 58; *Sermons III/8*, 326–27).

16. *Serm.* 311.5 (*PL* 38.1415; *Sermons III/9*, 73).

17. The phrase in quotation is from MacCormack, *The Shadows of Poetry*, 116. She quotes the following pertinent passage from Augustine's *De cura pro mortuis gerenda* 3.5: the body is not merely an "adornment or support applied to the soul from outside, but rather, it is part of the very nature of human beings" (116).

18. *Serm.* 311.5–6 (*PL* 38.1416; *Sermons III/9*, 73).

19. *Serm.* 311.7 (*PL* 38.1416, *Sermons III/9*, 74).

20. *Serm.* 277.10 (*PL* 38.1262; *Sermons III/8*, p. 38); see also Augustine, *De Genesi ad litteram* (hereafter cited as *De Gen. ad lit.*) 12.16.32: "Light, the finest element in bodies and hence more akin to soul than the others, is first of all diffused in a pure state through the eyes and shines forth in rays from the eyes to behold visible objects" (trans. Taylor, *St. Augustine: The Literal Meaning of Genesis*, 2: 199). On the theory of extramission, see Lindberg, *Theories of Vision from Al-Kindi to Kepler*; Nelson, "Introduction: Descartes' Cow and Other Domestications of the Visual," 1–21, esp. 4–5 on extramission and seeing as connective.

21. Jay, *Downcast Eyes*, 30.

22. On the malevolent power of the eye, see Barton, "Being in the Eyes," 216–35; *eadem, Sorrows of the Ancient Romans*, 90–95; Jay, *Downcast Eyes*, 28, referring to "vision's malevolent power" in the myths of Narcissus, Orpheus, and Medusa.

23. On the self-consuming eye, see Elsner, "Naturalism and the Erotics of the Gaze," 248–61; on self-bewitchment, see Plutarch, *Quaestiones convivales* 5.7 (*Moralia* 680C–682B). See also Chapter 1 for Plotinus's similar employment of the myth of Narcissus.

24. Nelson, "Descartes' Cow," 4.

25. *Serm.* 313A.3 (*MA*, 67; *Sermons III/9*, 92). In many of his sermons, as in this one, Augustine refers to the fact that the *passio* of the martyr was read on his or her feast day, and preceded his sermon.

26. See also *Serm.* 301A.7 (*MA*, 87; *Sermons III/8*, 295–96): "We have just now been spectators of the great contest of the seven brothers and their mother. What a contest, my brothers and sisters, if only our minds knew how to watch it! Compare with this holy spectacle the pleasures and delights of the theaters. There the eyes are defiled, here the heart is purified; here spectators are to be praised, if they become imitators; while there the spectator is base, and the imitator infamous."

27. *Serm.* 313A.3 (*MA*, 67–68; *Sermons III/9*, p. 92). On Augustine's view that Christians should imitate the martyrs, see Eno, *Saint Augustine and the Saints*, 59–64.

28. Ibid.

29. *Serm.* 301A.7 (*MA*, 87; *Sermons III/8*, 296): *Denique amo martyres, specto martyres: quando leguntur passiones martyrum, specto.*

30. *Serm.* 286.6 (*PL* 38.1300; *Sermons III/8*, 104); for other references to eyes of faith, inner eyes, and eyes of the heart, see *Serm.* 329.2; (*PL* 38.1455–1456; *Sermons III/9*, 183): "So look at them very carefully, dearly beloved; you can't do it with your eyes, but think about them with mind and heart"; *Serm.* 274; 277.1

(eyes of faith); *Serm.* 275.1 (inner eyes); *Serm.* 277A.1 (seeing in spirit); *Serm.* 280.2 (clear sight of faith).

31. *Serm.* 315.10 (*PL* 38.1431; *Sermons III/9*, 134): *Agnosce inimicam tuam: agnosce cum qua ignas in theatro pectoris tui. Angustum theatrum; sed Deus spectat.* Giselle de Nie has recently used Clifford Geertz's theory of ritual to explain the impact of the reading of saints' lives and miracle stories; her argument, which complements mine, is as follows: "Rituals, Geertz states, allow the worshipper to experience the precise coincidence of the everyday world with the belief world, and so they induce or even compel belief in the latter. One of the rituals Geertz mentions is the recitation of a myth. Such a myth would contain and present not only models *of* the reality postulated by religion, but also—and especially— models *for* what he calls 'producing' that reality in the perception of the worshipper. Saints' lives and miracles stories read in a liturgical context resemble such 'myths,' and an important means of what Geertz called 'producing, intensifying and rendering . . . inviolable by the discordant revelations of secular experience' the images and patterns—figures—of belief reality" ("Seeing and Believing in the Early Middle Ages," 70, emphasis in original).

32. Carruthers, *Craft of Thought*, 130. See also Chapter 3 for a discussion of the *ekphrasis*, a rhetorical practice related to *enargeia.*

33. Brilliant, " 'Let the Trumpets Roar!' " 224.

34. *De gen. ad lit.* 12.6.15; 12.7.16; 12.24.50 (*PL* 34.458, 459, 474; trans. Taylor, 2: 185–86, 213). The most succinct of these statements is at 12.6.15: *tria genera visionum occurrunt: unum per oculos, quibus ipsae litterae videntur; alterum per spiritum hominis quo proximus et absens cogitator; tertium per contuitum mentis, quo ipsa dilectio intellecta conspicitur.* Taylor translates "*spiritus*" as "spirit" but notes the special use of "*spiritus*" in this treatise to designate the imagination or the imaginative part of the soul (2: 301, n. 13). Thus where his translation uses "spirit," I have substituted "imagination," and for the adjectival form I have used "imaginal" rather than "imaginary" or "imaginative" in order to preserve the sense of mental image. See also Hill, trans., *The Works of Saint Augustine, Part I—Books*, vol. 13: *On Genesis*, 470, n. 9, on *De gen. ad lit.* 12.6.15: "Here 'spirit' is being used in its least spiritual meaning, for what are also called the inner senses, memory and imagination."

35. *De gen. ad lit.* 12.8.19 (*PL* 34.460; trans. Taylor, 2: 188). On signs, see Augustine, *De doctrina christiana* 2.1.1, where a sign is defined as "a thing which causes us to think of something beyond the impression the thing itself makes upon the senses" (trans. Robertson, *Saint Augustine: On Christian Doctrine*, 34). Discussions of Augustine's theory of signs are legion; among the best are Markus, "St. Augustine on Signs," 61–91; Dawson, "Sign Theory, Allegorical Reading, and the Motions of the Soul in *De doctrina Christiana*," 123–41.

36. *De gen. ad lit.* 12.24.51 (*PL* 34.475; trans. Taylor, 2: 213).

37. *De gen. ad lit.* 12.24.51 (*PL* 34.475; trans. Taylor, 2: 214).

38. *De trin.* 8.6.9 (*CCL* 50.281). For discussion, see O'Daly, *Augustine's Philosophy of Mind*, 106: "Imagination can be merely *reproductive* of the images in the memory, but Augustine can also talk of the *creative* exercise of the imagination" (emphasis in original). As O'Daly points out, *phantasia* and *phantasma* correspond respectively to the reproductive and creative representations of the imagination.

39. *De gen. ad lit.* 12.6.15 (*PL* 34.458).

40. See James and Webb, " 'To Understand Ultimate Things and Enter Secret Places,' " 1–17.

41. See O'Daly, *Augustine's Philosophy of Mind*, 109, on the connection between *phantasma* and intentional imagination (as opposed to flights of fancy); see also p. 110 for his discussion of Augustine, *Ep.* 7.4, where Augustine lists historical figures (as well as fictional figures and mythical places) as members of the class of *phantasmata*. Being historical figures, martyrs fit well in this class of images.

42. *De trin.* 8.4.7 (for the whole passage, see *CCL* 50.275.32–276.47); see the discussion by Carruthers, *Craft of Thought*, 121.

43. *De trin.* 8.4.7 (*CCL* 50.276.45–47; trans. Carruthers, *Craft of Thought*, 121).

44. *Serm.* 286.3 (*PL* 38.1298; *Sermons III/8*, 102).

45. *Serm.* 319.6 (*PL* 38.1441–1442; *Sermons III/9*, 153).

46. *Serm.* 275.3 (*PL* 38.1255; *Sermons III/8*, 28).

47. See *Serm.* 328.6 (*PL* 38.1454; *Sermons III/9*, p. 179) on the souls of martyrs being "already in bliss" with Christ.

48. As Eno, *Saint Augustine*, 53, has pointed out, "Augustine's view of the place of the saints in the general picture of things is a facet of his total picture of spiritual reality." In Augustine's *ordo caritatis*, martyrs occupy the top rung because they love God more than life, and they are exemplars of faith.

49. *Serm.* 277.1 (*PL* 38.1257–1258; *Sermons III/8*, 33).

50. *Naissance de la poésie dans l'occident Chrétien*, 188.

51. For discussion of Prudentius's use of ekphrasis, see Malamud, *Poetics of Transformation*, 86, 106, 110–13; Chapter 3, pp. 69–73.

52. Roberts, *Poetry and the Cult of the Martyrs*, 98, 137; see also 69–70, 189. On the motif of visiting martyria and there internalizing the martyrs' passion and sacrifice, see Ross, "Dynamic Writing and Martyrs' Bodies in Prudentius' *Peristephanon*," 325–55, esp. 344.

53. See Roberts, *Poetry and the Cult of the Martyrs*, 84, on the "dematerialization" of physical into spiritual landscape.

54. See *Serm.* 284.5; 297.3 on intercession; *Serm.* 313D.1; 313E.8; 316.5; 335H.2 on martyrs' prayers helping devotees.

55. In addition to material on imitation already cited, see also *Serm.* 284.6; 297.11. Augustine's caution on the topic of intercession is expressed most clearly in *De cura mortuis gerenda* 16.19–20, where he asks such questions as how martyrs know about earthly affairs and how they hear petitioners' prayers. See Eno, *Saint Augustine*, 68–70, for discussion.

56. See, e.g., *Pe.* 2.579–81; 4.189–91; 10.1134–40 (ed. Lavarenne, *Prudence, IV*, 49, 70, 158); on prayers taken immediately to heaven, see *Pe.* 1.16–20 (ed. Lavarenne, *Prudence, IV*, 23).

57. Malamud, *Poetics of Transformation*, 1. On Prudentius's expectation that his poems would be read aloud, see Ross, "Dynamic Writing," 327 and n. 9.

58. Lavarenne, *Prudence, IV*, 11. One of the most blatant uses of myth to enhance a saint's legend is in *Pe.* 11, where the death of the martyr Hippolytus is conflated with the death of the mythical figure of the same name. See Malamud, *Poetics of Transformation*, 79–113, for discussion.

59. For Prudentius's view of relics as both corporeal and spiritual, see, e.g., *Pe.* 5.517–20 (ed. Lavarenne, *Prudence, IV*, 90), where the relics of Saint Vincent are described as "set in the shrine and buried beneath the altar, [the bones] below are drenched and drink in the breath of heavenly bounty" (trans. Roberts, *Poetry and the Cult of the Martyrs*, 195); also *Pe.* 4.189–90 (ed. Lavarenne, *Prudence, IV*, 70), in which the martyr Encratis is said to "ask for mercy for our sins from her place at the foot of the eternal altar." In this passage, as Lavarenne

notes, Prudentius refers to the practice of placing relics beneath altars but is also alluding to the saint's heavenly home (*Prudence*, IV, 221, n. 3 to p. 70).

60. *Pe* 9.47–50 (ed. Lavarenne, *Prudence*, IV, 113–14) (trans. adapted from *The Poems of Prudentius*, trans. Eagan, FOTC 43, 185).

61. *Pe.* 9.99–100 (ed. Lavarenne, *Prudence*, IV, 115).

62. *Pe.* 9.50 (ed. Lavarenne, *Prudence*, IV, 114) : *rubetque ab ictu curta et umens pagina.*

63. Ross, "Dynamic Writing," 330; see further pp. 331–34 on the equation of words and wounds in the *Peristephanon.* In *Pe.* 3.136 (ed. Lavarenne, *Prudence*, IV, 58), for example, Eulalia exclaims about her wounds, "You write on me here, Lord" (*Scriberis ecce mihi, Domine*), and in *Pe.* 10.1119 (ed. Lavarenne, *Prudence*, IV, 158), Romanus is described as "a page inscribed by Christ" (*inscripta Christo pagina*).

64. *Pe.* 9.7–8 (ed. Lavarenne, *Prudence*, IV, 112). See Roberts, *Poetry and the Cult of the Martyrs*, 137, who notes that Cassian's wounds are also referred to as *acumina* in *Pe.* 9.51 (ed. Lavarenne, *Prudence*, IV, 114); thus "the language for bodily and spiritual suffering coincides exactly."

65. Ross, "Dynamic Writing," 334.

66. *Pe.* 9.101–105 (ed. Lavarenne, *Prudence*, IV, 115–16).

67. *Pe.* 10.928 (ed. Lavarenne, *Prudence*, IV, 151; trans. Egan, 230).

68. *Pe.* 10.2–15 (ed. Lavarenne, *Prudence*, IV, 120; trans. adapted from Egan, 190–91).

69. *Pe.* 10.21–22 (ed. Lavarenne, *Prudence*, IV, 120–21).

70. Roberts, *Poetry and the Cult of the Martyrs*, 13; see also Brown, *Cult of the Saints*, 81.

71. *Poetics of Transformation*, 43.

72. On the collapsing of spatial distinctions at martyr's tombs, see Chapter 3, p. 77, and Brown, *Cult of the Saints*, 3–5.

73. *Pe.* 3.31–65 (ed. Lavarenne, *Prudence*, IV, 55–56).

74. *Pe.* 3.46–50, 170 (ed. Lavarenne, *Prudence*, IV, 55–56, 59; trans. adapted from Egan, 130, 135).

75. *Pe.* 3.51–55 (ed. Lavarenne, *Prudence*, IV, 56).

76. *Poetry and the Cult of the Martyrs*, 103; quotation from *Pe.* 3.60 (ed. Lavarenne, *Prudence*, IV, 56). On Prudentius's use of biblical *exempla*, see Roberts, *Poetry and the Cult of the Martyrs*, 102–108.

77. *Pe.* 5.241–42, 248 (ed. Lavarenne, *Prudence*, IV, 82; trans. Roberts, *Poetry and the Cult of the Martyrs*, 84).

78. *Poetry and the Cult of the Martyrs*, 84.

79. *Pe.* 5.276 (ed. Lavarenne, *Prudence*, IV, 83).

80. *Pe.* 5.277–88 (ed. Lavarenne, *Prudence*, IV, 83).

81. On Paradise as a flowery garden, see Chapter 3, p. 75.

82. As Cameron has observed, the body is "the most characteristic of Christian metaphors"; as she goes on to argue, "the theme of the Incarnation of Christ imposed the language of the body, and with it bodily symbolism, on Christian writing" (*Christianity and the Rhetoric of Empire*, 68). In the case of Prudentius, it would seem that the Crucifixion was equally important as a source of bodily imagery.

83. *A Poetics of Transformation*, 175.

84. As Roberts notes, every poem in the *Peristephanon* "contains a formula of heavenly ascent" (*Poetry and the Cult of the Martyrs*, 70).

85. Frank, *Memory of the Eyes*, 68.

86. The phrase in quotations is from Frank, *Memory of the Eyes*, 4, 69, where it refers to readers of monastic travel literature such as the *Historia monachorum*. I think it applies equally well to a text such as the *Peristephanon*.

87. Chapter 1, pp. 37–39. In that brief discussion, I focused on Victricius's view of relics as condensed bits of an ideal self. Here I present his ideas in counterpoint to those of Prudentius and Augustine and offer a fuller presentation of his position on the phenomenon of relics, elaborating especially on the connection between relics, light, and gems. In order to minimize cross-referencing to other mentions of Victricius's sermon in this book, I have repeated some passages of *De laude sanctorum* for ease in reading.

88. The date of the sermon is ca. C.E. 397; for discussion of Victricius's career, especially his contacts with Ambrose and also with Paulinus of Nola, see Clark's introduction to her translation of the sermon, "Victricius of Rouen," 365–99, esp. 365–66, 372–75.

89. Hunter, "Vigilantius of Calagurris," esp. 425.

90. *De laude* 9.14–16 (*CCL* 64: 83; trans. Clark, 389).

91. On Victricius's radically incarnational theology, see Hunter, "Vigilantius of Calagurris," 428.

92. *De laude* 7.1, 15, 35 (*CCL* 64: 76–78; trans. Clark, 385–86).

93. *De laude* 8.10–11 (*CCL* 64: 81; trans. Clark, 387).

94. "Victricius of Rouen," 387, n. 118. See Hunter, "Vigilantius of Calagurris," 428: "Victricius apparently means that, since blood is present in the fragments of the relics, then, by virtue of the consubstantiality of matter, the entirety of the saint is present; and if the saint, who is united to the very substance of God is present, then so is the very power of God."

95. *De laude* 8.21–22 (*CCL* 64: 82; trans. Clark, p. 388).

96. On God being "diffused" (*diffunditur*) everywhere but not divided, see *De laude* 8.15; for the quotation, *De laude* 9.29–30 (*CCL* 64: 81, 83; trans. Clark, 388, 390).

97. *De laude* 9.30–34 (*CCL* 64: 83–84; trans. Clark, 390).

98. *De laude* 12.115 ("*primae resurrectionis exordia*") (*CCL* 64: 92; trans. Clark, 399).

99. *De laude* 10.32–40 (*CCL* 64: 86; trans. Clark, 393).

100. See Clark, "Victricius of Rouen," 391, n. 141: "Victricius will argue, in effect, that 'leftover' prompts the question 'leftover what'? Just as (for instance) 'it's a finger' is not a helpful definition unless the finger is related to the hand, and subsequently the human body, of which it is a part, so 'it's a relic' requires an account of the body of the saint." Hence Victricius's concern to establish the unity of substance between martyrs and God, which moves the status of relics to another level of coherence that has nothing to do with a literally "whole" body.

101. See *De laude* 11.26–29 (*CCL* 64: 87; trans. Clark, 394): "I point with my hand to what is sought; I touch fragments; I affirm that in these relics is perfect grace and perfect virtue." Here Victricius effects a shift in how meaning is discerned, moving from physical sense to faith.

102. *De laude* 10.1–5 (*CCL* 64: 84; trans. Clark, 391).

103. On the late ancient tendency to see more than was literally there, particularly in the arts, see Onians, "Abstraction and Imagination in Late Antiquity," 1–24, esp. p. 20: "The vitality of Christianity depended partly on its insistence that people should disregard the evidence of their eyes," developing a rich inner sight instead.

104. On this convention, see Roberts, *Jeweled Style*; Janes, *God and Gold*; James,

Light and Colour in Byzantine Art; James, "Color and Meaning in Byzantium," 223–33.

105. For a full discussion of relics and aesthetics, see Chapters 2–3.

106. On the early Christian taste for brilliance, see Janes, *God and Gold*, 139–52.

107. *De laude* 1.12–13 (*CCL* 64: 69; trans. Clark, 376).

108. *De laude* 10.38–39; 12.41–42 (brighter than the sun; *CCL* 64: 86, 90; trans. Clark, 393, 397); 1.29–30 (heavenly brilliance; *CCL* 64: 70; trans. Clark, 377); 9.1–3 (radiance; *CCL* 64: 82; trans. Clark, 389).

109. Janes, *God and Gold*, 74–79, 89–91, 144–52.

110. *De laude* 8.37–38 (*CCL* 64: 82; trans. Clark, 388).

111. *De laude* 8.31 (*CCL* 64: 82; trans. Clark, 388).

112. *De laude* 8.25–29 (*CCL* 64: 82; trans. Clark, 388).

113. *De laude* 9.20–22, 33–34 (*CCL* 64: 83, 84; trans. Clark, 390).

114. "Vigilantius of Calagurris," 429–30.

115. On the staging of the entry of relics into a city as an *adventus*, see Holum and Vikan, "The Trier Ivory, *Adventus* Ceremonial, and the Relics of St. Stephen," 113–33.

116. *De laude* 3.11–23 (CCL 64: 73; trans. Clark, 379).

117. *De laude* 3.33–36 (CCL 64: 74; trans. Clark, 380).

118. *De laude* 1.18 (*CCL* 64: 70; trans. Clark, 377).

119. *De laude* 12.26–33 (*CCL* 64: 89; trans. Clark, 396–97).

120. Elkins, *Pictures of the Body*, 223.

121. Ibid., 220. Elkins does not address the issue of relics, but I think his formulation of the problem of seeing visually intractable objects is relevant in this context.

122. Ibid.

123. Brown, *Cult of the Saints*, 82–83.

Chapter 5. Ambiguous Bodies

1. *De doctrina Christiana* 2.VI.7 (trans. Robertson, 37).

2. Ibid.

3. There has been much recent work on the increasing role of the senses in Christian epistemology and ritual from the fourth century onward. See, for example, Harvey, *Scenting Salvation;* Frank, *The Memory of the Eyes;* eadem, " 'Taste and See' "; Hahn, "Loca Sancta Souvenirs," 85–95.

4. See Rapp, " 'For Next to God, You Are My Salvation,' " 63–81, arguing that hagiography is not a genre.

5. I have borrowed the phrase "ambiguous corporeality" from Tiffany, *Toy Medium*, 8. Tiffany explores strategies of "depicting unobservable phenomena" in science and art (5). The relevance of his analytical perspective for a consideration of depictions of saints' bodies and relics can be seen from the following quotation: "Certain plausible correspondences between science and poetry can therefore be traced to shared forms of material and imaginative practice, but also to the basic inclination of materialism: to make the intangible tangible. Both science and poetry proceed, in part, by making pictures of what we cannot see (or what merely escapes our notice), by attributing corporeal qualities to inscrutable events" (5).

6. Elkins, *Pictures of the Body*, viii. Although Elkins's interest, as an art historian, is primarily in pictures of the body in art, his preface makes clear that his

theories regarding "the represented body," as he calls it (ix), can refer also to pictures or depictions of the body in texts.

7. Tiffany, *Toy Medium*, 2–3, 9.

8. Ibid., 9.

9. Translations are my own. For a discussion of Asterius's ekphrasis in another context, that of the creation of an aesthetics of relics, see Chapter 3, pp. 68–69.

10. Ibid., 1 (ed. Halkin, 5).

11. Ibid., 3 (ed. Halkin, 7), colors; 1 (ed. Halkin, 5), animated.

12. Ibid., 4 (ed. Halkin, 7).

13. *The Cult of St Thecla*, 170–71, n. 69.

14. *Ekphrasis on Saint Euphemia* 4 (ed. Halkin, 8).

15. On ancient seeing as connective, embodied, and performative, see Nelson, "Descartes' Cow," 1–21.

16. Elkins, *Pictures of the Body*, x.

17. Ibid.

18. *Ekphrasis on St. Euphemia* 4 (ed. Halkin, 8), where Euphemia rejoices that she is about to depart for the "bodiless and blessed life."

19. Cameron, "Language of Images," 15.

20. See Dagron, *Vie et Miracles de Sainte Thècle*, 152, on miracles as repetitive like an incantation. Texts hereafter abbreviated *Life* and *Mir.*

21. See *Life* 28.24–28; *Mir.*, pro. 11–18; *Mir.* 44.6–19 (ed. Dagron, 280, 284, 404); *Life of St. Symeon the Stylite the Younger*, pro. 9–10 (ed. and trans. Van Den Ven, *La Vie Ancienne de S. Syméon le Jeune*, 1:1).

22. Frank, "The Pilgrim's Gaze in the Age Before Icons," 107.

23. *Mir.* 22.7 (ed. Dagron, 348: piercing gaze); *Mir.* 26.37–40 (ed. Dagron, 358: no obstacles); *Mir.* 34.49 (ed. Dagron, 382: eye always open). On the role of seeing and visuality at pilgrimage sites such as that of Saint Thekla, see Hahn, "Seeing and Believing," 1086–87.

24. See *Mir.* 23–25 and 27 (ed. Dagron, 349–55, 391).

25. *Mir.* 24 (ed. Dagron, 351–53).

26. *Mir.* 17 (ed. Dagron, 334–36).

27. For text and translation, see *The Miracles of St. Artemios*, ed. and trans. Crisafulli and Nesbitt. On violence in miracle collections, see Maraval, *Lieux Saints*, 227, who remarks that in some of these stories "the odd vies with the absurd, even to the point of the scandalous."

28. On incubation as a late ancient and early Byzantine Christian practice, see Maraval, *Lieux Saints*, 224–29.

29. See *Mir.* 2, 5, 20, 32, 35, 37, 44 (ed. Crisafulli and Nesbitt, 78–81, 84–87, 122–25, 164–75, 184–89, 192–97, 218–23). It should be noted that while seeing and touching are constant, the touching is not always presented as painful.

30. See Crisafulli and Nesbitt, *Miracles of St. Artemios*, xv, discussing Artemios's "sense of humor" in several of the anecdotes.

31. For discussion, see Davis, "Crossed Texts, Crossed Sex," 1–36; Anson, "The Female Transvestite in Early Monasticism," 1–32; Patlagean, "L'histoire de la femme déguisée en moine et l'évolution de la sainteté feminine à Byzance," 597–623.

32. See *Apophthegmata patrum* N63, ed. Nau, "Histoire des Solitaires Égyptiens," 393; *Apophthegmata patrum*, Bessarion 4, *PG* 65.140–41; Moschus, *The Spiritual Meadow* 170 (trans. Wortley, 139). For discussion of the material in the *apophthegmata* literature, see Brakke, "The Lady Appears," 387–402.

33. *Life of St. Pelagia of Antioch* 15 (trans. Ward, *Harlots of the Desert*, 74); for discussion, see Miller, "Is There a Harlot in this Text?" 419–36.

34. *The Life and Conduct of the Blessed Mary Who Changed Her Name to Marinos*, trans. Constas, 11.

35. *Life of Eugenia* 15 (fol. 39b), in *Select Narratives of Holy Women*, trans. Smith Lewis, 21.

36. *Life of St. Symeon the Stylite the Younger* 138 (ed. Van Den Ven, 1:129; trans. 2:154).

37. For a discussion of the fictive nature of texts because they are linguistic, see White, *Figural Realism*, 5: "Language is never a set of empty forms waiting to be filled with a factual and conceptual content or attached to preexistent referents in the world but is itself in the world as one 'thing' among others and is already freighted with figurative, tropological, and generic contents before it is actualized in any given utterance."

38. Butler, *Bodies That Matter*, 187.

39. See Constas, "An Apology for the Cult of the Saints in Late Antiquity," 267–85, esp. 283.

40. For a representative, not exhaustive, list of studies, see n. 3 above.

41. For a theological discussion of this issue, see Williams, "Troubled Breasts," 63–78.

42. For discussion and examples, see Chapter 3, pp. 64–65.

43. For Vigilantius, see Jerome, *C. Vigil.* 4 (*PL* 23.357); Augustine, *Serm.* 273.7–8 (trans. Hill, *Sermons III/8*, 20–21).

44. Optatus of Milevis, *Against the Donatists* 1.16 (trans. Edwards, 16).

45. Basil of Caesarea, *In Ps. 115 hom.* (*PG* 30.112C); Cyril of Jerusalem, *Cat.* 18.16 (*PG* 33.1037A); these, and several more examples, are discussed by Maraval, *Lieux Saints*, 147–48.

46. Victricius's sermon is discussed in greater detail in Chapters 1 and 4.

47. *De laude* 10.1–5 (*CCL* 64: 84; trans. Clark, 391).

48. *De laude* 9.15–16 (*CCL* 64: 83; trans. Clark, 389). For an indication of how the term "idolatry" is being used here, see the Introduction.

49. Clark's observation ("Victricius of Rouen," 367), quoted in Chapter 1, bears repeating in this context: she writes that Victricius, having argued the point about the substantial union of God and relic, "preempts a shocked reaction: is he really saying that these relics are just what God is, the 'absolute and ineffable substance of godhead'? His answer, apparently, is yes." For discussion, see Hunter, "Vigilantius of Calagurris," 401–30, especially 428 on Victricius's "radically incarnational theology."

50. *De laude* 8.21–22 (*CCL* 64: 82; trans. Clark, 388).

51. See Williams, "Troubled Breasts," 75.

52. Athanasius, *Life of St. Antony*, 14.

53. Brakke, "'Outside the Places, Within the Truth,'" 459; see also 456–58. See also Brakke, *Athanasius and Asceticism*, 36–41, on Athanasius's view of holy places.

54. See Williams, "Troubled Breasts," 76.

55. Brown, "Arbiters of Ambiguity," 140. On the Christological debates and the subsequent "weakening of Christ's mediatorship," see Taft, "The Liturgy of the Great Church," 69.

56. Both quotations are from Eustratius of Constantinople, *On the State of Souls After Death* 2.340–41, trans. Constas, "An Apology for the Cult of Saints in Late Antiquity," 272–73.

57. *On the State of Souls After Death* 18.490–91 (trans. Constas, 276).

58. Constas, "An Apology for the Cult of Saints," 276, 275, 274 (emphasis in original).

59. Ibid., 283; see also 284: "it was the saints themselves who were the active bearers of their own transfigured images."

60. Tiffany, *Toy Medium*, 23.

61. Ibid. Tiffany understands "the romance of the ontology of pictures" as "the problem of the animate image as an allegory—a theatrical rendering of the enigma of corporeal substance. For the iconoclastic vision of eidetic 'life' (as well as the anxiety it arouses) invariably seizes on the uncertain *materiality* of images. Thus questions about the ontology of pictures can often be traced to certain paradoxical implications concerning their corporeality" (23, emphasis in original). See Déroche, "Pourquoi Écrivait-On des Recueils de Miracles?" 110–13, on Artemios and "real" presence.

62. For Thekla, see *Mir.*14.32–45; 12.96; 14.48; 2.9–10 (ed. Dagron, 326, 320, 329, 292); for Artemios, *Mir.* 39; 35 (see Crisafulli and Nesbitt, xiii–xiv, for a list of the miracles, indicating which ones involve disguises); for Symeon, *Life* 156; 118 (ed. Van Den Ven, 1: 137, 96; 2:161, 120); 213 (ed. Van Den Ven, 1: 181–82; 2:208).

63. One patristic author, Pseudo-Macarius, implied that saints as well as angels had subtle (λεπτά) bodies; see *Homilia* 4.9, in *Die fünfzig geistlichen Homilien des Makarios*, ed. Dörries, Klostermann, and Kroeger, 33–34; ET by Maloney, ed. and trans., *Pseudo-Macarius: The Fifty Spiritual Homilies and the Great Letter*, 54. As Peers has shown, some patristic theologians thought that angels were completely incorporeal, while "others stated that the angels are beings without body and without matter, but not *completely* so" (*Subtle Bodies*, 3, emphasis in original). Not surprisingly, the veneration and sometimes worship of angels in late ancient Christianity posed the problem of idolatry; see Peers, *Subtle Bodies*, 8–11.

64. For Artemios, see *Mir.* 16.28–31 (ed. Crisafulli and Nesbitt, 108); for Symeon, *Life* 116.17–22; 163.2–5; 231.39–41 (ed. Van Den Ven, 1: 95, 145, 206; 2:118–19, 169–70, 231).

65. For Artemios, see *Mir.* 34.26–28 (ed. Crisafulli and Nesbitt, 180); for Symeon, *Life* 118.9–11; 158.4–37 (ed. Van Den Ven, 1: 96, 140–41; 2:120–21, 164).

66. *Life* 231.39–41 (ed. Van Den Ven, 1: 206; 2:231).

67. For discussion of *eulogiae* and icons, see Vikan, "Icons and Icon Piety in Early Byzantium," 569–76, esp. 570–72 on Symeon; idem, *Byzantine Pilgrimage Art*, esp. 27–28 on Symeon; Hahn, "Loca Sancta Souvenirs," 85–96. The nature of "spiritual matter" as a phenomenon may well be more intelligible to those in antiquity than to those of us in modernity, especially in light of their cosmology. The revaluation of the human body and its potential for transformation in light of the incarnation of God may well have been indebted to late Roman philosophico-scientific discussions of a continuum, sometimes construed as material, between the human and the divine, especially in Stoicism. For the Latin tradition, see Colish, *The Stoic Tradition from Antiquity to the Early Middle Ages*, vol. 2: *Stoicism in Christian Latin Thought Through the Sixth Century*. For the Greek tradition, see, e.g., Daley's discussion of Gregory of Nyssa's "christology of transformation" and his appeal "to the natural science of his time for a likely metaphor" for Christ's progressive transformation or divinization (the metaphor being that of "the element of fire which always lies hidden within a piece of wood, only to be revealed when the wood is set ablaze"). This Stoic-sounding

metaphor, though not specified as such by Daley, is used by Gregory to explain not only Christ's transformation but also the mingling of ordinary human nature with the divine. See "'Heavenly Man' and 'Eternal Christ,'" 479, 481.

68. *Mir.* 46 (ed. Dagron, 408).

69. On Thekla and women, see Dagron, *Vie et Miracles*, 99–100; on Thekla and men of letters, see *Mir.* 38 and 41 (ed. Dagron, 392, 399); on the role of the hagiographer as devotee, see Krueger, *Writing and Holiness*, 63–93.

70. *Mir.* 31.7–14 (ed. Dagron, 372–74).

Chapter 6. Subtle Bodies

1. Harvey, *Scenting Salvation*, 58, 59.

2. For discussion, see the Introduction and Chapter 5, and Williams, "Troubled Breasts," 63–78.

3. Hahn, "Seeing and Believing," 1091–92.

4. Mondzain, *Image, Icon, Economy*, 81 (emphasis in original).

5. Cameron, "Language of Images," 4.

6. Basil of Caesarea, *Homilies on the Hexaemeron* 6.11, in *Basile de Césarée: Homélies sur l'Hexaéméron*, ed. and trans. Giet, SC 26 bis, 386: ἀμυδραῖς ἐμφάσεσι.

7. Brown, *Cult of the Saints*, 51.

8. Ibid. See also his "A Dark-Age Crisis," 15, discussing the phenomenon of the holy man as "translating the awesomely distant loving-kindness of God into the reassuring precision of a human face."

9. *Life of St. Symeon the Stylite the Younger* 118 (ed. Van den Ven, 1: 98).

10. Glück, *Proofs and Theories*, 73.

11. Sells, *Mystical Languages of Unsaying*, 2.

12. See Rapp, "'For Next to God, You Are My Salvation,'" 63–81, arguing that hagiography is not a genre.

13. Maximus of Turin, *Sermon* 56 "On Pentacost," trans. Ramsey, *The Sermons of Saint Maximus of Turin*, 234–37, quoted in Harvey, *Scenting Salvation*, 259–60, n. 20.

14. On the human body as a site for the expression and enactment of meaning in Christianity, the classic study remains that of Brown, *The Body and Society*; for a recent study of divine presence and the use of the human senses to detect it, see Harvey, *Scenting Salvation*, esp. 57–90.

15. The play between animation and immobility, especially as it pertains to icons, will be discussed in more detail in Chapter 7.

16. *Life of St. Theodore of Sykeon* 39, ed. Joannou, *Mnemeia Hagiologica*, 397–98; trans. Dawes and Baynes, *Three Byzantine Saint*, 115–16.

17. Brown, "Reification, Reanimation, and the American Uncanny," 199. Brown's discussion focuses on the confusion of person and thing in the "commodity fetishism" of modern capitalism, in which things that circulate in an economy appear to have social lives and biographies like persons; one example he gives is the "life story" (177) of a painting by Renoir. Most of his discussion focuses on objects in Spike Lee's film *Bamboozled* that are collectively called "Sambo art," including the infamous "Jolly Nigger banks" that worked like mechanically operated toys. Quoting Kenneth Goings (*Mammy and Uncle Mose: Black Collectibles and American Stereotyping*, 14), Brown makes the point that "such objects of material culture gave a tangible reality to the idea of racial inferiority" (186). Additionally, he observes that Lee's cinematography "effects an aura of animation—scenes in which the objects stare back, in which the objects stare

past (or all but stare through) the characters to establish contact with the cinematic spectator"—and finally ends by literally animating the objects of Sambo art such that they move by themselves (195). Although icons and mechanical toys are obviously very different culturally and artistically, they seem to me to share the function of giving life to ideas. I am most interested in Brown's vocabulary for describing a thing's habitation of an uneasy ground in which the subject-object binary is blurred; this idea of an animated object works well for analyzing ancient conceptualizations of icons. For a discussion of another of Brown's analysis of things and "thing theory," see the Introduction, pp. 1–2.

18. Ibid. On oscillation, see also Brilliant, *Portraiture*, 7: "The oscillation between art object and human subject, represented so personally, is what gives portraits their extraordinary grasp on our imagination."

19. Brown, "Reification," 197; the quotation on the uncanny that Brown gives is from Jentsch, "On the Psychology of the Uncanny," 12.

20. *Life of Theodore of Sykeon* 139 (ed. Joannou, 486; trans. Dawes and Baynes, 178).

21. Cormack, *Writing in Gold*, 39, 47.

22. Williams, "Troubled Breasts," 68, 73. See, for example, Athanasius's foundational hagiography, the *Life of Saint Antony*, in which Athanasius is careful (or anxious?) to specify that Antony's remarkable achievements were due not to his own agency but to Christ working through him. Athanasius seems to have been more wary of the localization of the holy—in geographical places as well as in the bodies of holy men—than later hagiographers. For discussion, see Brakke, "'Outside the Places, Within the Truth,'" 456–59.

23. The phrase in quotation is from Sells, *Mystical Languages*, 6.

24. The texts discussed here include *Historia monachorum in Aegypto* (*HM*); Theodoret of Cyrrhus, *Historia religiosa* (*HR*); and *Apophthegmata patrum* (*AP*). For discussion of the phenomenon of collective biography, see Miller, "Strategies of Representation in Collective Biography."

25. See Miller, "Desert Asceticism and 'The Body from Nowhere.'" Some of the material in this part of my discussion is drawn from this essay.

26. The literature on ancient Christian ascetic practice is voluminous. For a good discussion of the relation between bodily renunciation and spiritual well being, see Castelli, "Mortifying the Body, Curing the Soul," 134–53. On fasting, see Shaw, *The Burden of the Flesh*.

27. For Symeon, see Theodoret, *HR* 26.23 (ed. Canivet—Leroy-Molinghen, 2: 206); for Mary, see *Life of Mary of Egypt* 7 (trans. Ward, *Harlots of the Desert*); for Pelagia, see *Life of St. Pelagia of Antioch* 14 (trans. Ward, *Harlots of the Desert*). The two "harlot" hagiographies are not part of a collective biography, but they share a mindset with that literature in terms of their presentation of ascetic rigor in the desert.

28. Brown, *Body and Society*, 31.

29. *HM*, prologue 4 (ed. Festugière, 7; trans. Russell, 49).

30. *AP*, Pambo 12; Sisoes 14 (*PG* 65.372A; 395B; trans. Ward, 197, 214–15).

31. *HM* 2.1 (ed. Festugière, 35; trans. Russell, 63).

32. *AP*, Silvanus 12; Arsenius 27 (*PG* 65.411C; 80D; trans. Ward, 224, 13).

33. Harpham, *The Ascetic Imperative in Culture and Criticism*, 27.

34. On excess, surplus value, and the transforming of mere objects into meaningful "things," see Brown, "Thing Theory," 5.

35. For a list of the various charisms, see Russell, trans., *Lives of the Desert Fathers*, 175.

36. *HM* 10.20–21 (ed. Festugière, 89; trans. Russell, 85).

37. *HM* 2.9 (ed. Festugière, 36; trans. Russell, 64).

38. Harpham, *Ascetic Imperative*, 43.

39. *HM* 21.5 (ed. Festugière, 125; trans. Russell, 108).

40. *HM* 21.7 (ed. Festugière, 125; trans. Russell, 109).

41. *HM* 21.10–12 (ed. Festugière, 125–26; trans. Russell, 109).

42. Harpham, *Ascetic Imperative*, 43.

43. On constant progress, see Harpham, *Ascetic Imperative*, 43. For the concept of the ascetic as emergent, see Valantasis, "Constructions of Power in Asceticism," 801.

44. *AP*, Poemen 85 (trans. Ward, 179). A particularly striking anecdote in this regard is the deathbed scene of Abba Sisoes (*AP*, Sisoes 14 [*PG* 65.395B; trans. Ward, 215]): "The old men asked [Abba Sisoes], 'With whom are you speaking, Father?' He said, 'Look, the angels are coming to fetch me, and I am begging them to let me do a little penance.' The old man said to him, 'You have no need to do penance, Father.' But the old man [Sisoes] said to them, 'Truly, I do not think I have even made a beginning yet.' "

45. In its original form, this chapter was a presentation delivered at Drew University's Transdisciplinary Theological Colloquium 6: Apophatic Bodies. The respondent to the paper, Professor Karmen MacKendrick, suggestively noted the fact that these ascetic bodies "hover between material and light, damage and healing." Together with the hagiographical authors' emphasis on progress and action, this suggests "that we might read their bodies not as entities but as processes or as events, as constant transitions always-coming, and going, rather than arrivals already-come. The body is fleeting without quite disappearing, incomplete but not simply disintegrated, in transformation but not wholly transformed." I thank Prof. MacKendrick for her insightful comments.

46. Gregory of Nyssa, *VM* 22.27–31 (ed. Maraval, 214).

47. Krueger, *Writing Holiness*, 122, quoting *VM* 22.

48. Krueger, *Writing Holiness*, 120; see *VM* 20 (ed. Maraval, 206–8).

49. Ibid., 121.

50. Ibid., 130; see *VM* 24 (ed. Maraval, 218–24).

51. Ibid., 131.

52. *VM* 32.8–12 (ed. Maraval, 246). Gregory's narrative of his dream is at *VM* 15.15–19 (ed. Maraval, 192).

53. Burrus, "Macrina's Tattoo," 111.

54. *VM* 31 (ed. Maraval, 242–46).

55. *VM* 31.13–14 (ed. Maraval, 242). See Burrus, "Macrina's Tattoo," for a brilliantly evocative discussion of Macrina's scar as a "fleshly tattoo" that "lays claim to an irreducible materiality that is also the trace of divinity" (109). Another elegant discussion of the scar is by Frank, "Macrina's Scar," 511–30.

56. See, e.g., *VM* 11 (ed. Maraval, 174–80).

57. *VM* 39.3, 18 (ed. Maraval, 264, 266).

58. See Chapter 5, pp. 111–12.

59. See Williams, "Troubled Breasts," 76.

60. Brown, "Arbiters of Ambiguity," 140.

61. See Dagron, *Vie et Miracles de Sainte Thècle*, 152, on miracles as repetitive, like an incantation.

62. For a discussion of the rise in popularity of the cult of the martyrs and saints in light of the felt remoteness of the "high gods," see MacMullen, *Christianity and Paganism in the Fourth to Eighth Centuries*, 119–39.

63. This phrase is from Tiffany, *Toy Medium*, 23.

64. This is a revision of Kitzinger's argument that mediation of the divine by a human body requires dematerialization and abstraction. By arguing that saints and their images in art are "receptacles for divine substance," he comes close to erasing the saint's humanness. See Kitzinger, "The Cult of Images in the Age Before Iconoclasm," 150 (for the quotation in regard to divine substance). Full development of the idea of dematerialization is in Kitzinger, "Byzantine Art in the Period Between Justinian and Iconoclasm," 157–232. For an expanded treatment of Kitzinger's observations about dematerialization, see Chapter 9.

65. For discussion of saints as epiphanies of saintly transfiguration, see Constas, "An Apology for the Cult of the Saints in Late Antiquity," 283–84.

66. The phrase in quotation is from Sells, *Mystical Languages of Unsaying*, 8.

67. *Life of St. Symeon the Stylite the Younger* 231 (ed. Van den Ven, 1: 205–6); for Barber's discussion of this miracle, see his *Figure and Likeness*, 23.

68. See n. 45 above; I owe this insight about the saint's body as process or event to Professor Karmen MacKendrick.

69. Sells, *Mystical Languages of Unsaying*, 7.

70. See p. 118 above.

71. The idea of the ambiguous corporeality of the saints is addressed in Chapter 5.

72. *Miracles of St. Thekla* 38 (ed. Dagron, 391–95).

73. *Miracles of St. Thekla* 46 (ed. Dagron, 408).

74. I owe this observation to Johnson, *The Life and Miracles of Thekla*, 123.

75. See Sells, *Mystical Languages of Unsaying*, 8, on referential openness, which I am appropriating for my own purposes here. For Thekla and flying, see Dagron, *Miracles of Saint Thekla*, 96–97, for discussion and examples.

Chapter 7. Animated Bodies and Icons

1. For Brown's "thing theory," see the Introduction and Chapter 3.

2. *Miracula SS. Cosmae et Damiani* 15, in *Kosmas und Damian: Texte und Einleitung*, ed. Deubner, 137–38; trans. Mango, *The Art of the Byzantine Empire 312–1453*, 139 (slightly adapted).

3. See Liddell, Scott, and Jones, *A Greek-English Lexicon*, s.v. ἐπιφοιτάω, and Lampe, *A Patristic Greek Lexicon*, s.v. ἐπιφοίτησις. Note that the verb ἐπιφοιτάω is used to describe the presence of Saint Thekla as well; see Chapter 6.

4. I have borrowed the phrase "picture theory" from Mitchell, *Picture Theory*, a book that examines the relation between pictures and theory from different angles. Mitchell discusses "pictures 'in' theory" and "theory itself as a form of picturing," as well as "pictures 'as' theory," as second-order reflections on the practices of pictorial representation; in the latter case, he analyzes "what pictures tell us when they theorize (or depict) themselves" (9). My own interest in this chapter is in the concept of pictures *as* theory.

5. I am not, of course, attributing these anecdotes about icons to the explicit intentionality of the texts' authors. Instead, I am reading the intentionality of the texts' rhetoric for its implicit message. For a discussion of authorial and textual intentionality, see Foucault, "What Is an Author?" 141–60, and Barthes, "The Death of the Author," 142–48.

6. See Drake, *Constantine and the Bishops*, 181–85.

7. Bassett, *The Urban Image of Late Antique Constantinople*, 203.

8. Smith, "The Public Image of Licinius I," 185–87.

9. Ibid., 194.

10. Francis, "Living Icons," 577.

11. Price, "From Noble Funerals to Divine Cult," 97–98.

12. Smith, *Hellenistic Royal Portraits*, 33.

13. Philostorgius, *Hist. eccles.* 2.17 (*GCS* 21 3, 28, no. 17), as cited by Price, "Gods and Emperors," 92.

14. St. Clair, "Imperial Virtue," 159.

15. Maraval, *Lieux Saints et Pèlerinages d'Orient*, 145, discussing Philostorgius, *Hist. eccl.* 7.3, on the inhabitants of Panias in northern Palestine protesting that they did not "adore" (προσκυνοῦμεν) the statue of Christ in their town. For Christian attitudes toward pagan statues of the gods, see James, "'Pray Not to Fall into Temptation and Be on Your Guard,'" 12–20, and Mango, "Antique Statuary and the Byzantine Beholder," 55–75.

16. Lane Fox, *Pagans and Christians*, 133, referring to Aristophanes, *Wasps* 819; *Peace* 661ff.; *Knights* 1169; *Birds* 518.

17. Ibid., 133; for further examples, see MacMullen, *Pagan and Christian in the Fourth to Eighth Centuries*, 49–52.

18. Lane Fox, *Pagans and Christians*, 133, referring to the account of Suetonius, *Aug.* 16.

19. Libanius, *Or.* XIX.48, trans. Norman, *Libanius. Selected Works*, 2: 299. On the relation between statues and divine power in the third and fourth centuries, see Francis, "Living Icons," 584–87.

20. Christian theologians of the fourth century used the idea that the emperor and his portrait shared an identity to express the relation of the Father and the Son in the Trinity. See, for example, Basil of Caesarea, *De spirito sancto* 18.45, and Athanasius, *Third Oration Against the Arians* 5 (*PG* 26.329C–332B These two texts are quoted and discussed in Chapter 8.

21. Julian, *Hymn to the Mother of the Gods* 161A, trans. Francis, "Living Icons," 585; text in Cave Wright, *The Works of the Emperor Julian*, 1:448: οὔτε ὡς ἀνθρώπινον τοῦτον, ἀλλὰ ὄντως θεῖον, οὔτε ἄψυχον γῆν, ἀλλὰ ἔμπνουν τι χρῆμα καὶ δαιμόνιον. As Francis remarks, "Of course, Julian is no mere idol worshipper. He makes clear that images of the gods are no more the gods themselves than images of the emperor are the emperor. But neither are they mere stones or wood. They are something in between that is constructed not by the artist but by the image and especially by the viewer" (585). The position of many Christians vis-à-vis icons of the saints echoed this stance. On "the stone that was the Goddess" and ancient Roman views of the sacrality of matter, see Ando, *The Matter of the Gods*, 21–27.

22. See Lane Fox, *Pagans and Christians*, especially the section entitled "Seeing the Gods," 106–67.

23. Pausanias, *Description of Greece* 7.22.2 (marketplace Hermes); Rufinus, *HE* 11.23 (statue of Serapis), discussed in Trombley, *Hellenic Religion and Christianization, c. 370–529*, 1: 132.

24. *Monumenta Asiae Minoris Antiqua* 8.446, trans. Lane Fox, *Pagans and Christians*, 134.

25. *CIL* 9.3375 a. 156, trans. MacMullen, *Christianity and Paganism*, 52; the phrase in quotation marks is from Virgil, *Aen.* 9.157f.

26. Gross, *The Dream of the Moving Statue*, 142–43, commenting on dedicatory inscriptions in *The Greek Anthology*.

27. See Vikan, "Art, Medicine, and Magic in Early Byzantium," 69, for discussion; for other examples of Christian-inscribed votives, see Vikan, "Icons and Icon Piety," 569–71.

28. For a detailed discussion of these spells, see Ciraolo, "The Warmth and Breath of Life," 240–54.

29. *PGM* IV.1830–1870, trans. Betz, *The Greek Magical Papyri in Translation*, 71.

30. *PGM* XII.30–34 (trans. Betz, 154).

31. *PGM* IV.1855–1860 (trans. Betz, 71); *PGM* XII.83–84 (trans. Betz, 156).

32. Shaw, *Theurgy and the Soul*, 157; Sheppard, "Proclus' Attitude to Theurgy," 220; Berchman, "Rationality and Ritual in Neoplatonism," 229–68.

33. The quotation is from Iamblichus, Proclus's predecessor who laid the groundwork for theurgical thinking; see his *De mysteriis* 5.23 (ed. and trans. Des Places, 178).

34. Proclus, *in Ti.* 3.155.18 (text in Dodds, *The Greeks and the Irrational*, 292).

35. This aspect of Proclus's thought is more fully discussed in Chapter 1, pp. 33–35.

36. Proclus, *in Ti.* 1,51,25–31 (trans. Festugière, *Proclus: Commentaire sur la Timée*, 1: 85).

37. Proclus, *Eclogae de Philosophia Chaldaica* 5.8–11 (ed. Jahn; trans. Rappe, *Reading Neoplatonism*, 176).

38. On the whole topic of what he calls "signs stained by reality" (48) that are "images that *do* something" (50), see Bettini, *The Portrait of the Lover*.

39. Eunapius, *VS* 472, trans. Wright, *Philostratus and Eunapius: The Lives of the Sophists*, 421.

40. Ibid., 489 (trans. Wright, 497). See also *VS* 492: a crowd listening to Prohaeresius speak "marveled at his physical beauty and great stature, while they gazed up at him . . . as though to behold some statue" (trans. Wright, 507).

41. Brown, "A Dark-Age Crisis," 13, n. 2.

42. Gregory of Nazianzus, *Or.* 43.52.2 (*Eulogy on Basil of Caesarea*), *PG* 36.561D–564A.

43. Basil of Caesarea, *Ep.* 2, ed. and trans. Deferrari, *Saint Basil*, 1:17.

44. Monastic standing is reported in the major collective hagiographies: the *Historia monachorum*, Palladius's *Lausiac History*, and Theodoret's *Historia religiosa*. For examples and discussion of monastic "immovability," see Williams, *The Immoveable Race*, 86–96.

45. *Historia monachorum* 13.3 (standing) and 13.11 (withdrawal from sensible things) (trans. Russell, 93–94).

46. See James, "'Pray Not to Fall into Temptation and Be on Your Guard,'" 18: "The image of the antique statue survived into Christian Byzantium: the stylite saint on his pillar, with its elaborate capital, . . . is an image of a living Christian statue replacng an ancient pagan power." See also Eastmond, "Body vs. Column," 98: "The visual similarity between the great monumental columns, each surmounted by a statue of the emperor, and that of St Symeon standing atop his own column in the Syrian desert is undeniable, but the comparison can be taken much further. The two types of column also shared similarities in the way they functioned. In the same way that the statue of an emperor on a pedestal or column acted as an object worthy of veneration, so too did people come to pray to Symeon. . . . Whereas on the imperial column the statue stood in for the prototype, at Qalat Siman, Symeon became the image."

47. *Life of Theodore of Sykeon* 115, text in Festugière, ed., *Vie de Théodore de Sykéon*, vol. 1: *Texte grec*, Subsidia hagiographica 48, 91; trans. Dawes and Baynes, 164.

48. Theodoret, *HR*, pro. 2, lines 27–28 (ed. Canivet and Leroy-Molinghen, 1: 128; trans. Price, 4).

49. Palladius, *Lausiac History* 18.14–17, summarized by Williams, *Immoveable Race*, 87 (text in Butler, ed., *The Lausiac History of Palladius*, 1: 52–53).

50. On the relation between immobility, stability, and the transcendent realm, see Williams, *Immoveable Race*, esp. 8–34.

51. Palladius, *Lausiac History* 18.17 (ed. Butler, 1: 54, ll. 14–22; trans. Williams, *Immovable Race*, 88).

52. Palladius, *Lausiac History* 18.18, l. 2 (ed. Butler, 1: 54).

53. Although debate about idolatry did not assume full-blown proportions in Christianity until the iconoclastic controversy of the eighth and ninth centuries, problems regarding idolatry arose already in the fourth century in connection with both the veneration of relics and with artistic representations of Christ. See Introduction.

54. For a discussion of opposition to sculpture in the round in early Byzantium (sixth century), see Hjort, " 'Except on Doors,' " 615–25.

55. See, for example, the comment by Barasch, *Icon*, 1–2: "Even the most enthusiastic champion of pictures acknowledges, by the very fact that he or she has to defend the image's validity, that the object of his or her veneration is problematic."

56. Barber, *Figure and Likeness*, 13.

57. Kitzinger, "Cult of Images," 94–100; Cameron, "The Language of Images," 4.

58. Peers, *Subtle Bodies*, 142.

59. *Life of Saint Symeon the Stylite the Younger* 118 (ed. Van den Ven, 1: 98). Kitzinger, "Cult of Images," takes this passage to envisage a "perpetual bond between the incarnation and man-made images" (144). I thank Prof. Eugene Rogers for alerting me to the biblical uses of the verb ἐπισκιάζω, especially in the New Testament, where it is used to describe both the Holy Spirit's overshadowing of Mary at the annunciation (Lk. 1:35) and the cloud that overshadows the disciples with Jesus at the transfiguration (Mt. 17:5 = Mk. 9:7 = Lk. 9:34). Its use to describe Saint Symeon's icon places the icon in powerful company in terms of spiritual presence.

60. Leontius of Neapolis, *Contra Iudaeos orationes* 5, ed. and trans. Déroche, "L'*Apologie contre les Juifs de Léontios de Néapolis*," 66–78, quotation at p. 67, lines 47–52. For discussion, see Baynes, "The Icons Before Iconoclasm," 100, and Barber, *Figure and Likeness*, 17–20.

61. Barber, *Figure and Likeness*, 57, 56. The bibliography on iconoclasm is of course immense; in what follows I rely on Barber's lucid presentation.

62. See Kahzdan and Maguire, "Byzantine Hagiographical Texts as Sources on Art," 10.

63. Barber, *Figure and Likeness*, 56.

64. Ibid.

65. Ibid., 36.

66. Ibid., 34.

67. Ibid., 76, discussing the implications of John of Damascus, *On the Divine Images* 3.18–23. A helpful discussion of John's ideas about icons, especially in terms of how they signify, is in Barasch, *Icon*, 188–253.

68. John of Damascus, *On the Divine Images* 1.16, ed. Kotter, *Die Schriften des Johannes von Damaskos*, vol. 3: *Contra imaginum calumniators orationes tres*, 90, lines 31–32.

69. As Vikan has noted about healing saints such as Cosmas and Damian, epiphanies were "critical for the saint's miraculous intervention." Further, their

patients "needed mystically to experience a vision of the saint in order for an appropriate diagnosis to be made and treatment applied. . . . Significantly, the figure seen in the epiphany seems usually to have matched in features and costume the saint as he was portrayed in art" ("Icons and Icon Piety," 573).

70. *Life of Saint Theodore of Sykeon* 39 (ed. Joannou, 397–98; trans. Dawes and Baynes, 115–16).

71. Brown, "Reification, Animation, and the American Uncanny," 199.

72. Ibid., 197.

73. Brown, "Thing Theory," 186.

74. *Eulogiae* made of clay and stamped with Saint Symeon's image were given to pilgrims at his column. They were often inscribed not only with the saint's likeness atop his pillar but also with words of blessing. See Vikan, "Icons and Icon Piety," 572. For a discussion of *eulogiae* as secondary relics, see Maraval, *Lieux Saints*, 237–41.

75. *Life of Saint Simeon the Stylite the Younger* 231 (ed. Van den Ven, 1: 205–6).

Chapter 8. Saintly Bodies as Image-Flesh

1. Mitchell, *Picture Theory*, 16.

2. Mitchell, *What Do Pictures Want?*, 348 (italics in original).

3. On "image-rich culture," see Barber, *Figure and Likeness*, 13; see also Cameron, "Language of Images," 4; Kitzinger, "Cult of Images," 95–100.

4. Icons did not originate in the sixth and seventh centuries. Rather, this was the period of their flourishing; hence they were newly central, and increasingly problematic. See Cameron, "Byzantium and the Past in the Seventh Century," 252. For discussion of the origins of icons, see Mathews, *Clash of Gods*, 177–90. For a discussion of the iconophiles' understanding of the origin and legitimation of icons in Christian tradition and history, see Giakalis, *Images of the Divine*, 22–50.

5. In a similar vein, Cameron ("Language of Images," 31) has noted briefly that "Of the surviving pre-Iconoclastic images, a high proportion depict the Virgin and Child, a fact which is indicative of her Christological importance, and which, in itself, illustrates the way in which visual art was being used to make doctrinal points."

6. John Moschus, *Spiritual Meadow* (*Pratum Spirituale*) 81, *PG* 87.3: 2940.A–B, trans. Mango, *The Art of the Byzantine Empire*, 135 (slightly emended).

7. Cameron, "Language of Images," 29 (quoting Lossky, *The Mystical Theology of the Eastern Church*, 189).

8. Kitzinger, "Cult of Images," 101, 104; see also Barber, *Figure and Likeness*, 34.

9. Basil of Caesarea, *On the Holy Spirit* 18 (*PG* 32: 149C; trans. Francis, "Living Icons," 587–88, n. 33). For discussion, see Barber, *Figure and Likeness*, 61–81.

10. Brown, "A Dark-Age Crisis," 11.

11. Barber, *Figure and Likeness*, 34–35; see also Francis, "Living Icons," 584–88.

12. Athanasius, *Third Oration Against the Arians* 5, trans. Francis, "Living Icons," 587.

13. See Barber, *Figure and Likeness*, 20–23, for a discussion of the relation of relics and icons.

14. Mondzain, *Image, Icon, Economy*, 39.

15. Leontius of Neapolis, *Contra Iudaeos orationes* 5 (ed. Déroche, 67, lines 43–

46). Leontius's text is extant as excerpts in the florilegia appended to the iconophile John of Damascus's *On the Divine Images* and is dated by Déroche
between c.e. 610 and 630 (46). For the debate on the authenticity of attribution
to Leontios, see Barber, *Figure and Likeness*, 146, n. 12.

16. *Contra Iudaeos orationes* 5 (ed. Déroche, 67, lines 50–52).

17. Déroche, "L'*Apologie contre les Juifs* de Léontios de Néapolis," 89.

18. Leontios, *Contra Iudaeos orationes* 5 (ed. Déroche, 67, lines 39–42; see also
p. 70, lines 179–81).

19. Barber, *Figure and Likeness*, 18; see also Déroche, "L'*Apologie contre les Juifs*
de Léontios de Néapolis," 92–93.

20. Leontius, *Contra Iudaeos orationes* 5 (ed. Déroche, 68, lines 83–86).

21. Leontius, *Contra Iudaeos orationes* 5 (ed. Déroche, 69, lines 144–45).

22. Lk. 1:35 (Annunciation); Matt. 17.5 = Mk. 9:7 = Lk. 9:34 (Transfiguration).

23. Barber, *Figure and Likeness*, 19.

24. *Life of Saint Symeon the Stylite the Younger* 118 (ed. Van den Ven, 1:96).

25. *Life of Saint Symeon the Stylite the Younger* 118 (ed. Van Den Ven, 1:97, italics
added).

26. *Life of Saint Symeon the Stylite the Younger* 118 (ed. Van Den Ven, 1:98).

27. Ibid.

28. See Mk. 5:26, where the woman suffering from hemorrhages says, "If I
but touch his clothes, I will be made well." On Symeon's Christomimeticism,
Vikan has pointed out the express parallels between Symeon's posture and
behavior on the column with those of Christ on the cross. He also discusses textual and artistic connections among Symeon, doves, Christ's baptism, and the
statement, discussed above, about Symeon's being overshadowed by the Holy
Spirit. See "Art, Medicine, and Magic in Early Byzantium," 69; *Byzantine Pilgrimage Art*, 35–37.

29. Discussed by Vikan, "Art, Medicine, and Magic in Early Byzantium," 69.

30. *Life of Saint Daniel the Stylite* 59, in *Three Byzantine Saints*, trans. Dawes and
Baynes, 42.

31. Gross, *Dream of the Moving Statue*, 234, n. 2, discussing the view of Barkan,
The Gods Made Flesh.

32. Vikan, "Icons and Icon Piety," 573.

33. *Miracles of Saint Artemios* 16 (ed. Crisafulli and Nesbitt, 106–9).

34. Vikan, "Icons and Icon Piety," 573.

35. Ibid.

36. *Miracles of Saint Artemios* 6 (ed. Crisafulli and Nesbitt, 89).

37. See Crisafulli and Nesbitt, 238, first note to Miracle 6, where they defend
their reading of ὀφθαλμοφανῶς as designating a waking state as opposed to a
dreaming one.

38. *Miracles of Saint Artemios* 6, (ed. Crisafulli and Nesbitt, 89).

39. Ibid.

40. I have borrowed this phrasing from a peculiarly apt comment by Richard
Dorment in his review of *Plane Image: A Brice Marden Retrospective*, *New York Review
of Books*, December 21, 2006, p. 8. When describing a recent painting by Marden
of the Muses, Dorment observes, "For an instant the goddesses are luminously
present, but more as immanence than as solid forms, semitransparent shapes
flickering against the light. . . . But the moment you sense their presence, the
Muses disappear, receding back into the 'landscape' to become swirls and eddies
of paint on a flat plane, mere material." This comment captures nicely, I think,

the oscillation between animate presence and inanimate art-object that hagiographical anecdotes depict.

41. John of Damascus, *On the Divine Images* 2.14 (ed. Kotter, 105; trans. Louth, *St. John of Damascus*, 70–71).

42. Barber, *Figure and Likeness*, 57.

43. The quotation is from Mondzain, *Image, Icon, Economy*, 81.

44. Barber, *Figure and Likeness*, 57–58, quoting (on the issue of carnality) a letter from Patriarch Germanios to Thomas of Claudiopolis that is a defense against the charge of turning to more carnal things, i.e., to idolatry.

45. John of Damascus, *On the Divine Images* 1.7 (first quotation) and 1.4 (ed. Kotter, 80, 78; trans. Louth, 23, 22).

46. Ibid., 1.8 (ed. Kotter, 82; trans. Louth, 24).

47. Louth, *St. John Damascene*, 218.

48. Ibid., 216.

49. See *On the Divine Images* 1.24 (on pagan idols); for the quotation, see 1.33 (ed. Kotter, 145; trans. Louth, 41). For a discussion of John's differentiated conception of image (*On the Divine Images* 3.18–23), see Barber, *Figure and Likeness*, 76; Barasch, *Icon*, 192–98.

50. *On the Divine Images* 3.34 (ed. Kotter, 139; trans. Louth, 108).

51. Barber, *Figure and Likeness*, 76.

52. *On the Divine Images* 1.36 (ed. Kotter, 147; trans. Louth, 42).

53. *On the Divine Images* 1.25 (ed. Kotter, 125; trans. Louth, 95). See the enlightening discussion in Barasch, *Icon*, 206–11, which concludes: "John faced the problem of whether a material image can actually portray an idea or a spiritual being, in its purest form, without the aid of 'conventional' concepts or psychological explanations. On this level John does not give a clear answer; the mystery of how an image carries an intimation of the invisible remains in full force" (211).

54. *On the Divine Images* 1.16 (Kotter, 90; trans. Louth, 30).

55. This line is a summary of part of the story in Mango, *The Art of the Byzantine Empire*, 138–39.

56. *Miracles of Saints Cosmas and Damian* 13 (ed. Deubner, 132–33; trans. Mango, *The Art of the Byzantine Empire*, 139).

57. *Life of Saint Theodore of Sykeon* 39 (ed. Joannou, 397–98; trans. Dawes and Baynes, 115–16).

58. In *Life of Saint Theodore of Sykeon* 8, the twelve-year-old Theodore is stricken with bubonic plague. He is taken to a shrine of St. John the Baptist and placed underneath an icon of Christ, from which drops of dew fall on the child and cure him (ed. Joannou, 367–68; trans. Dawes and Baynes, 91–92). In section 108, Theodore, who is suffering from an eye ailment, enters a church of the Virgin Mary in Sozopolis, where he gazes at the "icon of myrrh": "By divine working [ἐνεργείᾳ δὲ θείᾳ], the myrrh gathered into a bubble and then rained down plentifully upon his eyes and anointed his whole face," presumably easing his ocular affliction (ed. Joannou, 457–58; trans. Dawes and Baynes, 159–60).

59. Cormack, *Writing in Gold*, 46.

60. *Life of Saint Symeon the Stylite the Younger* 231 (ed. Van den Ven, 1: 204–8).

61. Vikan, "Icons and Icon Piety," 572.

62. Vikan, *Byzantine Pilgrimage Art*, 13.

63. *Life of Saint Symeon the Stylite the Younger* 148, 235, 230.

64. Vikan, *Byzantine Pilgrimage Art*, 36, calls this "a chain of sanctifying contact."

65. I owe the insight about constant arrival to Professor Karmen MacKendrick.

66. *Life of Saint Symeon the Stylite the Younger* 118 (ed. Van den Ven, 98). For a discussion of Symeon's Christomimeticism, see Vikan, *Byzantine Pilgrimage Art*, 36–37.

67. See Cameron, "Language of Images," 41: "they [images] raised fundamental issues about matter and about what they could actually be held to represent, in a period concerned about charges of idolatry and still dominated by basic Christological issues."

Chapter 9. Incongruous Bodies

1. Cameron, "The Language of Images," 5.
2. Ibid.
3. See Chapter 4, n. 3.
4. For a discussion of Brown's theory, see the Introduction, pp. 1–2.
5. Mitchell, *What Do Pictures Want?*, 93.
6. Ibid., 105.
7. *Life of Saint Theodore of Sykeon*, 8 (dew), 13 (memory), 108 (myrrh) (ed. Joannou, 367–68, 457–58; Dawes and Baynes, 91–92, 95–96, 159–60).
8. See Chapter 6, pp. 119–20, and Chapter 8, p. 160.
9. Cormack, *Writing in Gold*, 46.
10. See Chapter 7, p. 142. The phrase in quotation is from Barber, *Figure and Likeness*, 13; on the increase of icon veneration, see Kitzinger, "Cult of Images," 94–100.
11. Brown, "A Dark-Age Crisis," 13.
12. On icons, memory, and tangibility, see Barber, *Figure and Likeness*, 23–24, especially p. 23: "an icon was a means of extending the relic's touch through a tangible reiteration," and p. 36 on the "translation" of tangibility "into the domain of sight." Hans Belting makes a similar point about the emergence of images "that behaved in exactly the same way as relics": "the image, both in its physical reality and as a testimony to authenticity, inherited the functions otherwise characteristic of the relics. It became a carrier of the highly actual presence of a saint" (*Likeness and Presence*, 59). See also Cameron, "Language of Images," 15, on recall and presence.
13. Belting, *Likeness and Presence*, 99; see also Cormack, *Painting the Soul*, 63, on the icon as "the present witness of a past moment captured in art."
14. Brown, "A Dark-Age Crisis," 20; see also Kitzinger, "Cult of Images," 37; Jensen, *Face to Face*, 172.
15. Belting, *Likeness and Presence*, 46 (Belting's referent here is icons of Christ, but his point works with regard to images of saints as well).
16. Hahn, "Seeing and Believing," 1105.
17. Barber, *Figure and Likeness*, 36. Contrasting the difficulty of making an icon of Christ as compared with making an icon of the Virgin Mary, Cormack comments: "Mary, despite her special role in history, was an ordinary woman; thus, her portraits offered an authentic record of a sanctified human being. In the case of Christ, the problem of portraiture is far more complex. It is one thing to describe in words in the Gospels the charismatic appearance of the Son of God, but another thing entirely for the artist to provide an acceptable visual version of the verbal concept. The problem was not exactly unique to Christian artists; the artists of imperial Rome had faced a similar problem. For the Romans

too it was one thing to describe the appearance of the emperor Augustus in words—whether eulogistic or not, as in some cases—but it was another to portray the leader to his public in the form of a permanent visual record. But Roman artists and image-makers were set one further challenge. When Augustus died, they had to answer a more difficult question: How do you convey through art the external appearance of a man who has become a god (*Divus Augustus*)? This is a dilemma which mirrors the challenge to the Christian church in the imagery of Jesus" (*Painting the Soul*, 93–94). While I agree with the point about icons of Christ, I disagree about the ease of showing the heavenly *persona* of Mary—and the *personae* of the saints—in art. As I will argue, depicting human sanctity also required artistic finesse.

18. Cormack, *Painting the Soul*, 81.

19. Jensen, *Face to Face*, 185; see also 172.

20. Brown, "A Dark-Age Crisis," 15, quoting *Life of Saint Symeon the Stylite the Younger* 118.

21. Ibid.

22. Hahn, "Seeing and Believing," 1104.

23. Ibid., 1079; Cormack, *Painting the Soul*, 88.

24. Hahn, "Seeing and Believing," 1079.

25. Kitzinger, *Byzantine Art in the Making*, 105.

26. Kitzinger, *Byzantine Art in the Making*, 103. Kitzinger developed his arguments about this shift in two articles: "Cult of Images" and "Byzantine Art in the Period Between Justinian and Iconoclasm," 157–232; repr. from *Berichte zum XI. Internationalen Byzantinisten-Kongress, München 1958*, IV/1, 1–50; page references are to the reprinted edition.

27. Kitzinger, "Byzantine Art in the Period Between Justinian and Iconoclasm," 173.

28. Ibid., 172.

29. Ibid., 196 (sharp upswing); *Byzantine Art in the Making*, 105 (statuesque isolation).

30. Kitzinger, "Byzantine Art in the Period Between Justinian and Iconoclasm," 176.

31. Kitzinger, "Cult of Images," 101, 116.

32. Ibid., 137.

33. Kitzinger, "Byzantine Art in the Period Between Justinian and Iconoclasm," 202.

34. Ibid., 202 (first quotation); Kitzinger, "Cult of Images," 139 (second quotation).

35. Kitzinger, *Byzantine Art in the Making*, 106; see also "Cult of Images," 150.

36. Kitzinger, "Cult of Images," 150.

37. Ibid.

38. Kitzinger, *Byzantine Art in the Making*, 104 (gaunt and remote); "Byzantine Art in the Period Between Justinian and Iconoclasm," 173 (ghost), 178 (anaemic).

39. Kitzinger, *Byzantine Art in the Making*, 106–7.

40. Brown, "A Dark-Age Crisis," 14–15.

41. Symeon the Stylite the Younger, *On icons*, frag., *PG* 86bis.3220, also quoted by John of Damascus, *On the Divine Images* 3.126 (ed. Kotter, 194–95; trans. Louth, 151–52). The passage is discussed by Kitzinger, "Cult of Images," 147.

42. See Chapter 8.

43. Kitzinger, "Cult of Images," 141, 144.

44. Leontius of Neapolis, *Contra Iudaeos orationes* 5 (ed. and trans. Déroche, 69).

45. Kitzinger, "Cult of Images," 141.

46. Constas, "An Apology for the Cult of the Saints in Late Antiquity," 283.

47. Kitzinger, "Cult of Images," 150.

48. Kitzinger, *Byzantine Art in the Making*, 107.

49. *Life of Saint Theodore of Sykeon* 39 (ed. Joannou, 397; trans. Dawes and Baynes, 115).

50. Maguire, *The Icons of Their Bodies*, 16.

51. Ibid.

52. Saint Agnes was burned to death according to one of the poetic epigrams of Pope Damasus (*PL* 13.402–3); Ambrose, *On Virgins* 1.2.9 (*PL* 16.189; trans. Clark, *Women in the Early Church*, 109) and Prudentius, *Pe.* 14.88–89 (ed. and trans. Lavarenne, *Prudence, IV,* 198), report an alternative tradition that Agnes was beheaded.

53. Kitzinger, *Byzantine Art in the Making*, 106.

54. The quotation is from Cameron, "Language of Images," 29–30 (emphasis added). For Kitzinger's denial of paradox, see "Byzantine Art in the Period Between Justinian and Iconoclasm," 201–2.

55. Halliwell, *The Aesthetics of Mimesis*, 335, referring to John of Damascus.

56. For discussion, see Rorem, *Pseudo-Dionysius*, 53–57; Louth, " 'Truly Visible Things Are Manifest Images of Invisible Things,' " 15–24.

57. *The Celestial Hierarchy* 2.3 (*PG* 3:141B), trans. Luibheid, *Pseudo-Dionysius: The Complete Works*, 150.

58. *The Celestial Hierarchy* 2.3 (*PG* 3:141B-C; trans. Luibheid, 150).

59. *The Celestial Hierarchy* 2.4 (*PG* 3:144B-C; trans. Luibheid, 151–52).

60. *The Celestial Hierarchy* 2.3 (*PG* 3:141B; trans. Luibheid, 151).

61. *The Celestial Hierarchy* 2.3 (*PG* 3:141A; trans. Luibheid, 150), 2.4 (*PG* 3:144C; trans. Luibheid, 152).

62. *Divine Names* 9.7 (*PG* 3:916A; trans. Luibheid, 118).

63. Peers, *Subtle Bodies*, 90; Cameron, "Language of Images," 25; see also Louth, " 'Truly Visible Things,' " 15–16, 23–24.

64. Louth, " 'Truly Visible Things,' " 23, quoting Pseudo-Dionysius, *Ep.* 10.1.

65. *Ep.* 10.1 (*PG* 3. 1117), trans. by Luibheid, 289, as "The visible is truly the plain image of the invisible."

66. See the comment of Louth, " 'Truly Visible Things,' " 19: "Though [Dionysius] does not use the word, he sees the whole cosmos, both visible and invisible, as a theophany: a manifestation of God, in which God is calling the whole order of things 'after him' back into union with him."

67. On John of Damascus's theory of icons, see Chapter 8.

68. Kitzinger, "Cult of Images," 148; Barber, *Figure and Likeness*, 121.

69. Prudentius, *Pe.* 14.124–33 (ed. and trans. Lavarenne, *Prudence, IV,* 200).

70. Kitzinger, *Byzantine Art in the Making*, 104.

71. Ibid., 103; "Byzantine Art in the Period Between Justinian and Iconoclasm," 173.

72. Kitzinger, *Byzantine Art in the Making*, 103.

73. Ibid., 62, discussing the mosaic portrait of Saint Victor, also against a plain gold background, in the center of the dome of the chapel of San Vittore in Ciel d'Oro in Milan. For another view of Saint Victor, see Chapter 3.

74. James, *Light and Colour in Byzantine Art*, 129.

75. Maguire, *The Icons of Their Bodies*, 48.

76. John of Damascus, *On the Divine Images* 3.51 (ed. Kotter, 155; trans. Maguire, *The Icons of Their Bodies*, 48).

77. Cyril of Alexandria, *Ep.* 41 (*PG* 77.217C; trans. Maguire, *The Icons of Their Bodies*, 48).

78. Gregory of Nyssa, *Hom. opif.* 5 (*PG* 4.137A).

79. Gregory of Nyssa, *On perfection* (*PG* 46.272A), trans. Callahan, *Saint Gregory of Nyssa: Ascetical Works*, 110–11.

80. See James, *Light and Colour in Byzantine Art*, 127, 129.

81. Gregory of Nyssa, *In Cantica Canticorum* 1 (*PG* 44.776A; trans. James, *Light and Colour in Byzantine Art*, 128).

82. See Janes, *God and Gold in Late Antiquity*, esp. 74–79, 89–91, 144–52, and the discussion in Chapter 4.

83. Kitzinger, "Byzantine Art in the Period Between Justinian and Iconoclasm," 173.

84. Barber, *Figure and Likeness*, 121.

85. *Life of Saint Symeon the Stylite the Younger* 118 (ed. Van den Ven, 1: 98).

Conclusion

1. Bachelard, *Earth and Reveries of Will*, 1.

2. Ibid., 2.

3. Ibid., 2, quoting Baudelaire, *Curiosités esthétiques*, 317.

4. Bachelard, *Earth and Reveries of Will*, 2.

5. Ibid., 3; see also Bachelard, *Air and Dreams*, 1, discussed at the end of Chapter 3.

6. See Black, "More About Metaphor," 431–57, who makes a similar point about the dynamic creativity of metaphor.

7. Tiffany, *Toy Medium*, 2–3.

8. Hacking, *Representing and Intervening*, 137.

9. Brown, "Thing Theory," 5.

10. Chapter 5, p. 109.

11. White, *Figural Realism*, 6, elaborating on E. H. Gombrich's studies of Western pictorial realism.

12. Ibid.,vii.

13. Ibid., 18; Tiffany, *Toy Medium*, 3.

14. White, *Figural Realism*, 9.

Bibliography

Primary Sources

Ambrose. *On the Mysteries* and *On the Sacraments*. Ed. and trans. Bernard Botte. *Ambroise de Milan: Des Sacrements; Des Mystères; Explication du symbole*. SC 25 bis. Trans. R. J. Deferrari. *Saint Ambrose: Theological and Dogmatic Works*. FOTC 44. Washington, D.C.: Catholic University of America Press, 1963.

―――. *On Virgins*. PL 16.197–243. Trans. Elizabeth A. Clark. *Women in the Early Church*. Message of the Fathers of the Church 13. Collegeville, Minn.: Liturgical Press, 1983.

Apophthegmata patrum: Alphabetical Collection. PG 65.71–440. Trans. Benedicta Ward. *The Sayings of the Desert Fathers: The Alphabetical Collection*. Kalamazoo, Mich.: Cistercian Press, 1987. See also François Nau. "Histoire des Solitaires Égyptiens." *Revue de l'Orient chrétien* 12 (1907): 393–413.

Apuleius. *Metamorphoses*. Trans. Jack Lindsay. *Apuleius: The Golden Ass*. Bloomington: Indiana University Press, 1960.

Arnobius. *Adversus nationes*. In *The Ancient Mysteries: A Sourcebook*. Ed. Marvin W. Meyer. San Francisco: Harper & Row, 1987.

Asterius of Amaseia. *Ekphrasis on Saint Euphemia*. Ed. François Halkin. *Euphémie de Chalcédoine: Légendes Byzantines*. Subsidia Hagiographica 41. Brussels: Société des Bollandistes, 1965.

Athanasius. *Contra Gentes*. Ed. and trans. R. W. Thomson. *Athanasius: Contra Gentes and De Incarnatione*. Oxford: Clarendon Press, 1971.

―――. *Third Oration Against the Arians*. PG 26.321B–468A.

Athenagoras. *A Plea Regarding Christians*. In *The Library of Christian Classics*, vol. 1: *Early Christian Fathers*, trans. Cyril C. Richardson, 300–340. Philadelphia: Westminster Press, 1953.

Augustine. *De civitate Dei*. PL 41.13–804.

―――. *De doctrina christiana*. Trans. D. W. Robertson. *Saint Augustine: On Christian Doctrine*. Upper Saddle River, N.J.: Prentice Hall, 1958.

―――. *De Genesi ad litteram*. PL 34.245–466. Trans. John Hammond Taylor, S.J. *St. Augustine: The Literal Meaning of Genesis*, 2 vols. ACW 41–42. New York: Newman Press, 1982. I have also consulted Edmund Hill, O.P., trans., *The Works of Saint Augustine, Part I—Books*, vol. 13: *On Genesis*. Hyde Park, N.Y.: New City Press, 2002.

―――. *De moribus ecclesiae catholicae et de moribus manichaeorum*. PL 32.1300–1377.

―――. *De trinitate*. Ed. W. J. Mountain. CCL 50–50A (1968).

―――. *Sermones*. Texts in PL 38, 39 and in G. Morin, ed., *Miscellanea Agostiniana*, vol. 1. Rome: Tipografia Poliglotta Vaticana, 1930. Trans. Edmund Hill, O.P. *The Works of Saint Augustine, Part III—Sermons*, vols. 8–9. Hyde Park, N.Y.: New City Press, 1994.

Ausonius. *Epigrams*. 2 vols. Trans. Hugh G. Evelyn White. LCL. Cambridge, Mass.: Harvard University Press, 1921; repr. ed. 1985.

Basil of Caesarea. *De spirito sancto*. Ed. and trans. Benoît Pruche. SC 17. Paris: Les Éditions du Cerf, 1947.

———. *Epistulae*. Ed. and trans. Roy J. Deferrari. *Saint Basil: The Letters*. 4 vols. London: William Heinemann, 1926.

———. *Homiliae*. PG 30–31.

———. *Homilies on the Hexaemeron*. Ed. and trans. Stanislas Giet. *Basile de Césarée: Homélies sur l'Hexaéméron*. SC 26 bis. Paris: Les Éditions du Cerf, 1968.

Callistratus. *Ekphraseis*. In *Philostratus, Imagines; Callistratus, Descriptions*. Ed. and trans. Arthur Fairbanks. LCL. London: W. Heinemann, 1931.

Catalogue des Manuscrits Alchimiques Grecs. Ed. Joseph Bidez. Brussels: Maurice Lamertin, 1928.

Choricius. *Laudatio Marciani*. Trans. Cyril Mango, *The Art of the Byzantine Empire, 312–1453: Sources and Documents*. Medieval Academy Reprints for Teaching 16. Toronto: University of Toronto Press and the Medieval Academy of America, 1986.

[Cicero]. *Rhetorica ad Herennium*. Trans. Harry Caplan. LCL. Cambridge, Mass.: Harvard University Press, 1954.

Corpus Inscriptionum Latinarum. Berlin: G. Reimerum, 1862–.

Cyril of Alexandria. *De incarnatione Unigeniti*. Ed. and trans. G. M. De Durand. *Cyrille d'Alexandrie: Deux Dialogues Christologiques*. SC 97. Paris: Les Éditions du Cerf, 1964.

———. *Epistulae*. PG 77.10A-390C.

Cyril of Jerusalem. *Catechetical Homilies*. PG 33.369A–1128A. Trans. Leo P. McCauley and Anthony Stephenson. *The Works of Saint Cyril of Jerusalem*, vol. 1. FOTC 61. Washington, D.C.: Catholic University of America Press, 1969.

Damasus. *Epigrammata*. Ed. Antonio Ferrua. *Epigrammata Damasiana*. Rome: Pontificio istituto di archeologia cristiana, 1942.

Ephrem the Syrian. *Hymns*. Trans. Kathleen McVey. Mahwah, N.J.: Paulist Press, 1989.

Epiphanius of Salamis. *Ancoratus*. PG 43.12A–236D.

———. *Epistula ad Johannem Episcopum* (*Letter to John, bishop of Aelia*). PG 43.380C–391A. Trans. Cyril A. Mango. *The Art of the Byzantine Empire 312–1453: Sources and Documents*, 42–43. Medieval Academy Reprints for Teaching 16. Toronto: University of Toronto Press and the Medieval Academy of America, 1986.

———. *Letter to the Emperor Theodosius*. In Georgije Ostrogorsky, ed. *Studien zur Geschichte des byzantinische Bilderstreites*, fragment 31, pp. 74–75. Breslau: Marcus, 1929.

———. *Panarion*. GCS 31², ed. Karl Holl and J. Drummer. Leipzig: J. Hinrichs, 1980.

———. *Testament*. In Georgije Ostrogorsky, ed. *Studien zur Geschichte des byzantinische Bilderstreites*, fragment 2, p. 67. Trans. Cyril A. Mango. *The Art of the Byzantine Empire 312–1453: Sources and Documents*, 41. Medieval Academy Reprints for Teaching 16. Toronto: University of Toronto Press and the Medieval Academy of America, 1986.

Eunapius. *Vitae philosophorum et sophistarum*. Ed. J. Boissonade. Paris: Didot, 1849. Trans. Wilmer Cave Wright. *Philostratus and Eunapius: The Lives of the Sophists*. LCL. Cambridge, Mass.: Harvard University Press, 1968.

Evodius. *De miraculis Sancti Stephani*. PL 41.833–854.

Gregory of Nazianzus. *Orationes. PG* 35–36.

Gregory of Nyssa. *De hominis opificium. PG* 44.123–256.

————. *In Cantica Canticorum. PG* 44.756A–1120A.

————. *Laudatio S. Theodori. PG* 46.736–748.

————. *On the Lord's Prayer. PG* 44.1120B–1193A. Trans. Hilda Graef. *Gregory of Nyssa: The Lord's Prayer, The Beatitudes.* ACW 18. Mahwah, N.J.: Paulist Press, 1954.

————. *On perfection. PG* 46.252A–285D. Trans. Virginia Callahan. *Saint Gregory of Nyssa: Ascetical Works.* FOTC 58. Washington, D.C.: Catholic University Press of America, 1967.

————. *Vita sanctae Macrinae. PG* 46.960–1000. Ed. and trans. Pierre Maraval. *Grégoire de Nysse: Vie de Sainte Macrine.* SC 178. Paris: Les Éditions du Cerf, 1971.

Historia Monachorum in Aegypto. Ed. A.-J. Festugière. Brussels: Société des Bollandistes, 1961. Trans. Norman Russell. *The Lives of the Desert Fathers.* Cistercian Studies 34. Kalamazoo, Mich.: Cistercian Publications, 1980.

Iamblichus. *De mysteriis.* Ed. and trans. Eduard des Places. *Jamblique: Les mystères d'Egypte.* Paris: Les Belles Lettres, 1966. Trans. also by H. Lewy. *Chaldean Oracles and Theurgy.* Cairo: L'Institut Français d'Archéologie Orientale, 1956.

————. *In Timaeum commentarium,* in *Iamblichi Chalcidensis: In Platonis dialogos commentariorum fragmenta.* Ed. and trans. John Dillon. Leiden: E. J. Brill, 1973.

Jerome. *Contra Vigilantium. PL* 23.353–368.

————. *Epistulae.* Ed. I. Hilberg. *CSEL* 54–56 (1910, 1912).

John Chrysostom. *Baptismal Catecheses.* Ed. and trans. Auguste Piédagnel. *Jean Chrysostome: Trois catéchèses baptismales.* SC 366. Paris: Les Éditions du Cerf, 1990.

————. *Baptismal Catecheses.* Ed. and trans. Antoine Wenger. *Jean Chrysostome: Huit catéchèses baptismales inédites.* SC 50. Paris: Les Éditions du Cerf, 1957.

————. *Discourse on the Blessed Babylas and Against the Greeks.* Ed. and trans. Margaret A. Schatkin. *Jean Chrysostome: Discours sur Babylas.* SC 362. Paris: Les Éditions du Cerf, 1990; Eng. trans. Margaret A. Schatkin. *St. John Chrysostom, Apologist.* FOTC 73. Washington, D.C.: Catholic University Press of America, 1985.

————. *A Homily on Martyrs. PG* 50.661–666. Trans. Wendy Mayer and Pauline Allen. *John Chrysostom.* London: Routledge, 2000.

————. *Homily Delivered After the Remains of the Martyrs. PG* 63.467–72. Trans. Wendy Mayer and Pauline Allen. *John Chrysostom.* London: Routledge, 2000.

John of Damascus. *On the Divine Images.* Ed. P. Bonifatius Kotter, O.S.B. *Die Schriften des Johannes von Damaskos,* vol. 3: *Contra imaginum calumniators orationes tres.* Berlin: Walter de Gruyter, 1975. Trans. Andrew Louth. *St. John of Damascus: Three Treatises on the Divine Images.* Crestwood, N.Y.: St. Vladimir's Seminary Press, 2003.

John Moschus. *Pratum Spirituale. PG* 87.3: 2852A–3112B. Trans. John Wortley. *John Moschus: The Spiritual Meadow.* Kalamazoo, Mich.: Cistercian Publications, 1992.

John Rufus. *Life of Peter the Iberian.* Ed. R. Raabe. *Petrus der Iberer. Ein Charakterbild zur Kirchen und Sittengeschichte des fünften Jahrhunderts.* Leipzig: J. C. Hinrichs, 1895. Trans. Volker Menze. "Priests, Laity and the Sacrament of the Eucharist in Sixth-Century Syria." *Hugoye: Journal of Syriac Studies* 7 (2004), para. 1. http://syrcom.cua.edu/Hugoye/Vol7No2/HV7N2Menze.html.

————. *Plerophoria.* Text in François Nau, "Jean Rufus, Évéque de Maïouma: Plérophories." *Patrologia Orientalis* 8 (1911): 175. Trans. Sharon E. J. Gerstel. *Beholding the Sacred Mysteries: Programs of the Byzantine Sanctuary.* Seattle: College Art Association with University of Washington Press, 1999.

Julian. *Hymn to the Mother of the Gods.* Ed. and trans. Wilmer Cave Wright. *The Works of the Emperor Julian.* 3 vols. LCL. London: William Heinemann, 1913.

Leontius of Neapolis. *Contra Iudaeos orationes.* Ed. and trans. Vincent Déroche. "L'*Apologie contre les Juifs de Léontios de Néapolis.*" *Travaux et mémoires* 12 (1994): 66–78.

Libanius. *Orations.* Trans. A. F. Norman. *Libanius. Selected Works.* 3 vols. LCL. Cambridge, Mass.: Harvard University Press, 1977.

The Life and Conduct of the Blessed Mary Who Changed her Name to Marinos. Trans. Nicholas Constas. In *Holy Women of Byzantium: Ten Saints' Lives in English Translation.* Ed. Alice-Mary Talbot. Washington, D.C.: Dumbarton Oaks, 1996.

Life of Eugenia. Trans. Agnes Smith Lewis. *Select Narratives of Holy Women.* Studia Sinaitica 10. London: C. J. Clay and Sons, 1900.

Life of Mary of Egypt. Trans. Benedicta Ward. *Harlots of the Desert.* Kalamazoo, Mich.: Cistercian Publications, 1987.

Life and Miracles of Saint Thekla. Ed. and trans. Gilbert Dagron. *Vie et Miracles de Sainte Thècle: Texte Grec, Traduction et Commentaire.* Brussels: Société des Bollandistes, 1978.

Life of St. Pelagia of Antioch. Trans. Benedicta Ward. *Harlots of the Desert.* Kalamazoo, Mich.: Cistercian Publications, 1987.

Life of St. Symeon the Stylite the Younger. Ed. and trans. Paul Van den Ven. *La Vie Ancienne de S. Syméon le Jeune.* 2 vols. Brussels: Société des Bollandistes, 1962, 1970.

Life of St. Theodore of Sykeon. Ed. Theophilos Joannou. *Mnemeia Hagiologica.* Leipzig: Zentralantiquiariat der Deutschen Demonkratischen Repubik, 1884, repr. ed. 1973; Greek text also in A.-J. Festugière, ed. *Vie de Théodore de Sykéon,* vol. 1: *Texte grec.* Subsidia hagiographica 48. Brussels: Société des Bollandistes, 1970. Trans. Elizabeth Dawes and Norman H. Baynes. *Three Byzantine Saints: Contemporary Biographies of St. Daniel the Stylite, St. Theodore of Sykeon, and St. John the Almsgiver.* Oxford: Blackwell, 1948.

Marcus Aurelius. *Meditations.* Trans. Maxwell Staniforth. London: Penguin Books, 1964.

Marinus. *Vita Procli.* Ed. J. Boissanade, *Marini: Vita Procli.* Amsterdam: Adolf M. Hakkert, 1966. Trans. Kenneth Guthrie. *The Life of Proclus or Concerning Happiness.* Grand Rapids, Mich.: Phanes Press, 1986.

Maximus of Turin. *Sermons.* Trans. Boniface Ramsey. *The Sermons of Saint Maximus of Turin.* ACW 50. New York: Newman Press, 1989.

Michael Pselles. *Epistula* 187. Trans. in H. Lewy, *Chaldean Oracles and Theurgy.* Cairo: L'Institut Français d'Archéologie Orientale, 1956.

Miracles of St. Artemios. Ed. and trans. Virgil S. Crisafulli and John W. Nesbitt. Leiden: E. J. Brill, 1997.

Miracula SS. Cosmae et Damiani. Ed. Ludwig Deubner. *Kosmas und Damian: Texte und Einleitung.* Leipzig: B. G. Teubner, 1907; trans. Cyril Mango, *The Art of the Byzantine Empire 312–1453.* Medieval Academy Reprints for Teaching 16. Toronto: University of Toronto Press and the Medieval Academy of America, 1986.

Monumenta Asiae Minoris Antiqua. Ed. William Moir Calder, Ernst Herzfeld, and Samuel Guyer. London: Longmans, Green, 1928–.

Narratio de Sancta Sophia. Trans. Cyril A. Mango. *The Art of the Byzantine Empire*

312–1453: Sources and Documents, 96–102. Medieval Academy Reprints for Teaching 16. Toronto: University of Toronto Press and the Medieval Academy of America, 1986.

Nicolaus of Myra. *Progymnasmata.* In *Rhetores Graeci* 11. Ed. Joseph Felten. Leipzig: B. G. Teubner, 1913.

On the Origin of the World (= NHC II.5). In *The Nag Hammadi Library in English.* Ed. James M. Robinson. New York: Harper and Row, 1977.

Optatus of Milevus. *Against the Donatists.* Ed. and trans. Mark Edwards. Translated Texts for Historians 27. Liverpool: Liverpool University Press, 1997. Latin text in *Optat de Milève: Traité contre les Donatistes*, vol. 1. Ed. and trans. Mireille Labrousse. Paris: Les Éditions du Cerf, 1995.

Origen. *Commentarium in Canticum Canticorum.* Ed. W. A. Baehrens. GCS, *Origenes Werke*, vol. 8. Leipzig: J. Hinrichs, 1925. Trans. R. P. Lawson. *Origen: The Song of Songs, Commentary and Homilies.* ACW 26. New York: Newman Press, 1956.

———. *Commentarium in Iohannem.* Ed. and trans. Cécile Blanc. *Origène: Commentaire sur Saint Jean*, vol. 1. SC 120. Paris: Les Éditions du Cerf, 1996. Selections also trans. by Joseph W. Trigg. *Origen.* London: Routledge, 1998.

———. *Contra Celsum.* Ed. and trans. Marcel Borret, S.J. *Origène: Contre Celse.* SC 150. Paris: Les Éditions du Cerf, 1969. Trans. Henry Chadwick. *Origen: Contra Celsum.* Cambridge: Cambridge University Press, 1965.

———. *De principiis.* Ed. and trans. Henri Crouzel and Manlio Simonetti. Vol. 3 (books 3 and 4). SC 268. Paris: Les Éditions du Cerf, 1980.

———. *Dialogue with Heraclitus.* Ed. and trans. Jean Scherer. SC 67. Paris: Les Éditions du Cerf, 1960.

———. *Homiliae in Ezekielem.* GCS, *Origenes Werke*, vol. 8. Ed. W. Baehrens. Leipzig: J. Hinrichs, 1925.

———. *Homiliae in Genesim.* Ed. and trans. Louis Doutreleau. *Origène: Homélies sur la Genèse.* SC 7 bis. Paris: Les Éditions du Cerf, 1976. Trans. Ronald E. Heine. *Origen: Homilies on Genesis and Exodus.* FOTC 71. Washington, D.C.: Catholic University of America Press, 1982.

———. *Homiliae in Lucam.* Ed. and trans. Henri Crouzel, François Fournier, and Pierre Périchon. SC 87. Paris: Les Éditions du Cerf, 1962. Trans. Joseph T. Lienhard. *Origen: Homilies on Luke.* FOTC 94. Washington, D.C.: Catholic University of America Press, 1996.

———. *Philocalia.* Ed. J. Armitage Robinson. *The Philocalia of Origen: The Text Revised with a Critical Introduction and Indices.* Cambridge: Cambridge University Press, 1893.

Ovid. *Metamorphoses.* Trans. Allen Mandelbaum. *The Metamorphoses of Ovid.* San Diego: Harcourt Brace, 1993.

Palladius. *Lausiac History.* Ed. Cuthbert Butler. *The Lausiac History of Palladius* repr. ed. 2 vols. Hildesheim: Georg Olms Verlagsbuchhandlung, 1967.

Papyri Magicae Graecae. Trans. Hans Dieter Betz. Chicago: University of Chicago Press, 1986.

Passio Marciani et Iacobi. In *The Acts of the Christian Martyrs.* Ed. and trans. Herbert Musurillo. Oxford: Clarendon Press, 1972.

Passio Perpetuae et Felicitatis. In *The Acts of the Christian Martyrs.* Ed. and trans. Herbert Musurillo. Oxford: Clarendon Press, 1972.

Paul the Silentiary. *Descriptio ambonis.* Trans. Cyril A. Mango. *The Art of the Byzantine Empire 312–1453: Sources and Documents*, 91–96. Medieval Academy Reprints for Teaching 16. Toronto: University of Toronto Press and the Medieval Academy of America, 1986.

Paulinus of Nola. *Carmina.* Ed. W. Hartel. *CSEL* 30 (1904). Trans. P. G. Walsh. *The Poems of Paulinus of Nola.* New York: Newman Press, 1975.

———. *Epistulae.* Ed. W. Hartel. *CSEL* 29 (1894). Trans. P. G. Walsh. *Letters of St. Paulinus of Nola.* ACW 36. New York: Newman Press, 1967.

Pausanias. *Description of Greece.* Trans. W. H. S. Jones. 5 vols. LCL. Cambridge, Mass.: Harvard University Press, 1960–64.

Philostorgius. *Historia ecclesiastica.* Ed. Joseph Bidez and Friedhelm Winkelmann. GCS 21. Berlin: Akademie-Verlag, 1981.

Philostratus. *Imagines.* Ed. and trans. Arthur Fairbanks. *Philostratus, Imagines; Callistratus, Descriptions.* LCL. London: W. Heinemann, 1931.

Plotinus. *Enneads.* 7 vols. Trans. A. H. Armstrong. LCL. Cambridge, Mass.: Harvard University Press, 1966–88.

Plutarch. *Quaestiones convivales.* In *Plutarch's Moralia,* vol. 8. Trans. Paul A. Clement and Herbert B. Hoffleit. LCL. Cambridge, Mass.: Harvard University Press, 1969.

Priscianus. *De anima.* Trans. Gregory Shaw, "After Aporia: Theurgy in Later Platonism." *Journal of Neoplatonic Studies* 5 (1996): 25.

Proclus. *Commentary on the Chaldean Oracles,* fragment. In *Eclogae de Philosophia Chaldaica.* Ed. H. Jahn. Halle: Preffer, 1891. Trans. in Sara Rappe, *Reading Neoplatonism: Non-discursive Thinking in the Texts of Plotinus, Proclus, and Damascius.* Cambridge: Cambridge University Press, 2000.

———. *Commentary on Plato's Parmenides.* Trans. John Dillon. *Proclus' Commentary on Plato's Parmenides.* Princeton, N.J.: Princeton University Press, 1987.

———. *Commentary on Plato's Timaeus.* Trans. A. J. Festugière. *Proclus: Commentaire sur la Timée.* 5 vols. Paris: J. Vrin, 1966–68.

———. *Elements of Theology.* Trans. E. R. Dodds, *Proclus: The Elements of Theology.* Oxford: Clarendon Press, 1963.

Prudentius. *Cathemerinon.* Ed. and trans. M. Lavarenne. *Prudence, I: Cathemerinon liber.* Paris: Société d'Édition "Les Belles Lettres," 1955.

———. *Peristephanon.* Ed. and trans. M. Lavarenne. *Prudence, IV: Le Livre des Couronnes, Dittochaeon, Épilogue.* Paris: Société d'Édition "Les Belles Lettres," 1963. Also consulted: *The Poems of Prudentius.* Trans. M. Clement Eagan, C.C.V.I. FOTC 43. Washington, D.C.: Catholic University Press of America, 1962.

Pseudo-Dionysius the Areopagite. *The Celestial Hierarchy.* PG 3:121A–340B. Trans. Colm Luibheid. *Pseudo-Dionysius: The Complete Works.* New York: Paulist Press, 1987.

———. *Divine Names.* PG 3:585B–984A. Trans. Colm Luibheid. *Pseudo-Dionysius: The Complete Works.* New York: Paulist Press, 1987.

———. *Epistulae.* PG 3.1065A–1120A. Trans. Colm Luibheid, *Pseudo-Dionysius: The Complete Works.* New York: Paulist Press, 1987.

Pseudo-Macarius. *Homiliae.* Ed. H. Dörries, E. Klostermann, and M. Kroeger. *Die fünfzig geistlichen Homilien des Makarios.* Patristiche Texte und Studien 6. Berlin: De Gruyter, 1964; trans. by George A. Maloney, S.J. *Pseudo-Macarius: The Fifty Spiritual Homilies and the Great Letter.* New York: Paulist Press, 1992.

Quintillian. *Institutio oratoria.* 4 vols. Trans. H. E. Butler. LCL. London: William Heinemann, 1921.

Rufinus of Aquileia. *Historia Ecclesiastica.* In *Opera,* ed. Manlio Simonetti. *CCL* 20. Turnholt: Brepols, 1961.

Sidonius Apollinaris. *Epistulae.* Ed. and trans. W. B. Anderson. *Sidonius: Poems and Letters.* 2 vols. LCL. Cambridge, Mass.: Harvard University Press, 1936.

Symeon the Stylite the Younger. *On icons,* frag. *PG* 86bis.3220.

Theodoret of Cyrrhus. *Curatio affectionum graecarum.* Ed. and trans. Pierre Canivet. SC 57. Paris: Les Éditions du Cerf, 1958.

Theodoret of Cyrrhus. *Historia Religiosa.* Ed. and trans. Pierre Canivet and Alice Leroy-Molinghen. *Théodoret de Cyr: Histoire des Moines de Syrie.* 2 vols. SC 234, 257. Paris: Les Éditions du Cerf, 1977, 1979. Trans. R. M. Price. *Theodoret of Cyrrhus: A History of the Monks of Syria.* Cistercian Studies 88. Kalamazoo, Mich.: Cistercian Publications, 1985.

Victricius of Rouen. *De laude sanctorum.* Ed. R. Demeulenaere. *CCL* 64 (1985): 53–93. Trans. Gillian Clark. "Victricius of Rouen: Praising the Saints." *JECS* 7 (1999): 365–99.

Secondary Sources

Ando, Clifford. *The Matter of the Gods: Religion and the Roman Empire.* The Transformation of the Classical Heritage 44. Berkeley: University of California Press, 2008.

Anson, John. "The Female Transvestite in Early Monasticism: The Origin and Development of a Motif." *Viator* 5 (1974): 1–32.

Athanassiadi, Polymnia. "Dreams, Theurgy and Freelance Divination: The Testimony of Iamblichus." *JRS* 83 (1993): 115–30.

Bachelard, Gaston. *Air and Dreams.* Trans. Edith R. Farrell and C. Frederick Farrell. Dallas: Dallas Institute, 1988.

———. *Earth and Reveries of Will: An Essay on the Imagination of Matter.* Trans. Kenneth Haltman. Dallas: Dallas Institute, 2002.

———. *The Flame of a Candle.* Trans. Joni Caldwell. Dallas: Dallas Institute, 1988.

———. *The Psychoanalysis of Fire.* Trans. Alan C. M. Ross. Boston: Beacon Press, 1964.

Barasch, Moshe. *Icon: Studies in the History of an Idea.* New York: New York University Press, 1992.

Barber, Charles. *Figure and Likeness: On the Limits of Representation in Byzantine Iconoclasm.* Princeton, N.J.: Princeton University Press, 2002.

———. "The Koimesis Church, Nicaea: The Limits of Representation on the Eve of Iconoclasm." *Jahrbuch der österreichischen Byzantinistik* 41 (1991): 43–60.

Barnes, T. D. "Publilius Optatianus Porfyrius." *AJP* 96 (1975): 173–86.

Barthes, Roland. *Camera Lucida: Reflections on Photography.* Trans. Richard Howard. New York: Hill and Wang, 1981.

———. "The Reality Effect." In *The Rustle of Language,* trans. Richard Howard, 141–48. New York: Hill and Wang, 1986.

———. "The Death of the Author." In his *Image, Music, Text,* trans. Stephen Heath, 142–48. New York: Hill and Wang, 1977.

Barton, Carlin. "Being in the Eyes: Shame and Sight in Ancient Rome." In *The Roman Gaze: Vision, Power, and the Body,* ed. David Fredrick, 216–35. Baltimore: Johns Hopkins University Press, 2002.

———. *The Sorrows of the Ancient Romans: The Gladiator and the Monster.* Princeton, N.J.: Princeton University Press, 1993.

Bassett, Sarah. *The Urban Image of Late Antique Constantinople.* Cambridge: Cambridge University Press, 2004.

Baynes, Norman H. "The Icons Before Iconoclasm." *HTR* 44 (1951): 93–106.

Behr, John. "The Rational Animal: A Rereading of Gregory of Nyssa's *De hominis opificio.*" *JECS* 7 (1999): 219–47.

Belting, Hans. *Likeness and Presence: A History of the Image Before the Era of Art.* Trans. Edmund Jephcott. Chicago: University of Chicago Press, 1994.

Berchman, Robert M. "Aesthetics as a Philosophic Ethos: Plotinus and Foucault." In *Neoplatonism and Contemporary Thought, Part Two,* ed. R. Baine Harris, 181–215. Studies in Neoplatonism 11. Albany: State University of New York Press, 2002.

———. "Rationality and Ritual in Neoplatonism." In *Neoplatonism and Indian Philosophy,* ed. Paulos Mar Gregorios, 229–68. Studies in Neoplatonism: Ancient and Modern 9. New York: State University of New York Press, 2002.

———. "Self-knowledge and Subjectivity in Origen." In *Origeniana Octava: Origene e la Tradizione Alessandrina,* vol. 1, ed. Lorenzo Perrone, 437–50. Leuven: Leuven University Press and Peeters, 2003.

Bertonière, Gabriel. *The Cult Center of the Martyr Hippolytus on the Via Tiburtina.* BAR International Series 260. Oxford: Oxford University Press, 1985.

Bettini, Maurizio. *The Portrait of the Lover.* Trans. Laura Gibbs. Berkeley: University of California Press, 1999.

Bitton-Ashkelony, Brouria. *Encountering the Sacred: The Debate on Christian Pilgrimage in Late Antiquity.* The Transformation of the Classical Heritage 38. Berkeley: University of California Press, 2005.

Black, Max. "More About Metaphor." *Dialectica* 31 (1977): 431–57.

Blumenthal, Henry. "Marinus' Life of Proclus: Neoplatonist Biography." *Byzantion* 54 (1984): 469–94.

Brakke, David. *Athanasius and Asceticism.* Baltimore: Johns Hopkins University Press, 1998.

———. "The Lady Appears: Materializations of 'Woman' in Early Monastic Literature." *JMEMS* 33 (2003): 387–402.

———. "'Outside the Places, Within the Truth': Athanasius of Alexandria and the Localization of the Holy." In *Pilgrimage and Holy Space in Late Antique Egypt,* ed. David Frankfurter, 445–81. Leiden: E. J. Brill, 1998.

Brandenburg, Hugo. "*Ars Humilis*: Zur Frage eines christlichen Stils in der Kunst des 4. Jahrhunderts nach Christus." *Jahrbuch für Antike und Christentum* 24 (1981): 71–84.

———. "Stilprobleme der frühchristlichen Sarkophagkunst Roms im 4. Jahrhundert: Volkskunst, Klassizismus, spätantiker Stil." *Mitteilungen des Deutschen Archaeologischen Instituts,* Römische Abteilung, vol. 86 (1979): 439–71.

Brilliant, Richard. *Portraiture.* Cambridge, Mass.: Harvard University Press, 1991.

———. "'Let the Trumpets Roar!': The Roman Triumph." In *The Art of Ancient Spectacle,* Studies in the History of Art 56, ed. Bettina Bergmann and Christine Kondoleon, 221–29. Washington, D.C.: National Gallery of Art, 1999.

Brown, Bill. "Reification, Reanimation, and the American Uncanny." *Critical Inquiry* 32 (2006): 175–207.

———. "Thing Theory." *Critical Inquiry* 28 (2001): 1–21.

Brown, Peter. "Arbiters of Ambiguity: A Role of the Late Antique Holy Man." *Cassiodorus* 2 (1996): 123–42.

———. "Asceticism: Pagan and Christian." In *CAH* 13, ed. Averil Cameron and Peter Garnsey, 601–31. Cambridge: Cambridge University Press, 1998.

———. *The Body and Society: Men, Women, and Sexual Renunciation in Early Christianity.* New York: Columbia University Press, 1988.

———. *The Cult of the Saints: Its Rise and Function in Latin Christianity.* Chicago: University of Chicago Press, 1981.

———. "A Dark-Age Crisis: Aspects of the Iconoclastic Controversy." *The English Historical Review* 88 (1973): 1–34.

Bryson, Norman. "Philostratus and the Imaginary Museum." In *Art and Text in Ancient Greek Culture*, ed. Simon Goldhill and Robin Osborne, 255–83. Cambridge: Cambridge University Press, 1994.

Burrus, Virginia. *"Begotten, Not Made": Conceiving Manhood in Late Antiquity*. Stanford, Calif.: Stanford University Press, 2000.

———. "Macrina's Tattoo." In *The Cultural Turn in Late Ancient Studies: Gender, Asceticism, and Historiography*, 103–16. Ed. Dale B. Martin and Patricia Cox Miller. Durham, N.C.: Duke University Press, 2005.

———. *Saving Shame: Martyrs, Saints, and Other Abject Subjects*. Divinations: Rereading Late Ancient Religion. Philadelphia: University of Pennsylvania Press, 2008.

Butler, Judith. *Bodies That Matter: On the Discursive Limits of "Sex."* New York: Routledge, 1993.

Bynum, Caroline Walker. *The Resurrection of the Body in Western Christianity, 200–1336*. New York: Columbia University Press, 1995.

Calvino, Italo. *Six Memos for the Next Millennium*. Cambridge, Mass.: Harvard University Press, 1988.

Cameron, Averil. "Byzantium and the Past in the Seventh Century: The Search for Redefinition." In *The Seventh Century: Change and Continuity. Proceedings of a joint French and British Colloquium held at the Warburg Institute 8–9 July 1988*, ed. J. Fontaine and J. N. Hillgarth, 250–76. London: Warburg Institute, 1992.

———. *Christianity and the Rhetoric of Empire: The Development of Christian Discourse*. Sather Classical Lectures 55. Berkeley: University of California Press, 1991.

———. "The Language of Images: The Rise of Icons and Christian Representation." In *The Church and the Arts*, ed. Diana Wood, 1–42. Studies in Church History 28. Oxford: Blackwell Publishers, 1992.

Carruthers, Mary. *The Craft of Thought: Meditation, Rhetoric, and the Making of Images, 400–1200*. Cambridge Studies in Medieval Literature 34. Cambridge: Cambridge University Press, 1998.

Castelli, Elizabeth A. "Heteroglossia, Hermeneutics, and History: A Review Essay of Recent Feminist Studies of Early Christianity." *JFSR* 10 (1994): 73–98.

———. "Mortifying the Body, Curing the Soul: Beyond Ascetic Dualism in *The Life of Saint Syncletica*." *differences* 4.2 (1992): 134–53.

Castelli, Elizabeth A., and Daniel Boyarin, eds. *Sexuality in Late Antiquity*, special issue of *Journal of the History of Sexuality* 10 (2001).

Cavarero, Adriana, ed. *Stately Bodies: Literature, Philosophy, and the Question of Gender (The Body, in Theory)*. Trans. Robert de Lucca and Deanna Shemek. Ann Arbor: University of Michigan Press, 2002.

Chadwick, Henry. "Eucharist and Christology in the Nestorian Controversy," *JTS*, n.s., 2 (1951): 145–64.

Ciraolo, Leda J. "The Warmth and Breath of Life: Animating Physical Object πάρεδροι in the Greek Magical Papyri." In *Society of Biblical Literature 1992 Seminar Papers*, ed. Eugene H. Lovering, Jr., 240–54. Atlanta: Society of Biblical Literature, 1992.

Clark, Elizabeth A. *The Origenist Controversy: The Cultural Construction of an Early Christian Debate*. Princeton, N.J.: Princeton University Press, 1992.

Clark, Stephen R. L. "Plotinus: Body and Soul." In *The Cambridge Companion to Plotinus*, ed. Lloyd P. Gerson, 275–91. Cambridge: Cambridge University Press, 1996.

Coakley, Sarah. "Introduction: Religion and the Body." In *Religion and the Body*, ed. Sarah Coakley, 1–12. Cambridge Studies in Religious Traditions 8. Cambridge: Cambridge University Press, 1997.

Colish, Marcia L. *The Stoic Tradition from Antiquity to the Early Middle Ages,* vol. 2: *Stoicism in Christian Latin Thought Through the Sixth Century.* Leiden: E. J. Brill, 1985.

Comaroff, Jean. *Body of Power, Spirit of Resistance: The Culture and History of a South African People.* Chicago: University of Chicago Press, 1985.

Constas, Nicholas. "An Apology for the Cult of the Saints in Late Antiquity: Eustratius Presbyter of Constantinople, On the State of Souls after Death (CPG 7522)." *JECS* 10 (2002): 267–85.

Cormack, Robin. *Painting the Soul: Icons, Death Masks, and Shrouds.* London: Reaktion Books, 1997.

———. *Writing in Gold: Byzantine Society and its Icons.* New York: Oxford University Press, 1985.

Corrigan, Kevin. "Body and Soul in Ancient Religious Experience." In *Classical Mediterranean Spirituality,* ed. A. H. Armstrong, 360–83. New York: Crossroad, 1986.

Cox, Patricia. "Origen on the Bestial Soul: A Poetics of Nature." *VC* 36 (1982): 115–40.

Cranz, Galen. *The Chair: Rethinking Culture, Body, and Design.* New York: W. W. Norton, 2000.

Crook, John. *The Architectural Setting of the Cult of the Saints in the Early Christian West c. 300–1200.* Oxford: Clarendon Press, 2000.

Crouzel, Henri. *Origen: The Life and Thought of the First Great Theologian.* Trans. A. S. Worrall. San Francisco: Harper and Row, 1989.

Daley, Brian. "'Heavenly Man' and 'Eternal Christ': Apollinarius and Gregory of Nyssa on the Personal Identity of the Savior." *JECS* 10 (2002): 469–88.

Dalmolin, Eliane Françoise. *Cutting the Body: Representing Woman in Baudelaire's Poetry, Truffaut's Cinema, and Freud's Psychoanalysis.* Ann Arbor: University of Michigan Press, 2000.

Daniélou, Jean. *Origène.* Paris: La Table Ronde, 1948.

Davis, Stephen J. "Crossed Texts, Crossed Sex: Intertextuality and Gender in Early Christian Legends of Holy Women Disguised as Men." *JECS* 10 (2002): 1–36.

———. *The Cult of St. Thecla: A Tradition of Women's Piety in Late Antiquity.* Oxford: Oxford University Press, 2001.

Dawson, David. "Sign Theory, Allegorical Reading, and the Motions of the Soul in *De doctrina Christiana.*" In *De doctrina Christiana: A Classic of Western Culture,* ed. Duane W. H. Arnold and Pamela Bright, 123–41. Notre Dame: University of Notre Dame Press, 1995.

Dawson, John David. *Christian Figural Reading and the Fashioning of Identity.* Berkeley: University of California Press, 2002.

Delehaye, Hippolyte. *Les Origines du Culte des Martyrs.* Subsidia Hagiographica 20. Brussels: Société des Bollandistes, 1933.

Delumeau, Jean. *History of Paradise: The Garden of Eden in Myth and Tradition.* Trans. Matthew O'Connell. New York: Continuum, 1995.

De Nie, Giselle. "Seeing and Believing in the Early Middle Ages: A Preliminary Investigation." In *The Pictured Word,* ed. Martin Heusser et al., 67–76. Word and Image Interactions 2. Amsterdam: Rodopi, 1998.

Déroche, Vincent, ed. and trans. "L'*Apologie contre les Juifs de Léontios de Néapolis.*" *Travaux et mémoires* 12 (1994): 66–78.

———. "Pourquoi Écrivait-On des Recueils de Miracles? L'Exemple des Miracles de Saint Artémios." In *Les Saints et Leur Sanctuaire à Byzance,* ed. Catherine

Jolivet-Lévy, Michel Kaplan, and Jean-Pierre Sodini, 95–116. Byzantina Sorbonensia 11. Paris: Publications de la Sorbonne, 1993.

Dillon, John. "Aisthêsis Noêtê: A Doctrine of Spiritual Senses in Origen and in Plotinus." In his *The Golden Chain: Studies in the Development of Platonism and Christianity*, 443–55. London: Variorum, 1990.

———. "Origen's Doctrine of the Trinity and Some Later Neoplatonic Theories." In *Neoplatonism and Christian Thought*, ed. Dominic J. O'Meara, 19–56. Albany: State University of New York Press, 1981.

Dodds, E. R. "Introduction." *Proclus: The Elements of Theology*, ix–xlvi. Oxford: Clarendon Press, 1963.

———. *The Greeks and the Irrational*. Berkeley: University of California Press, 1966.

Dorment, Richard. Review of *Plane Image: A Brice Marden Retrospective*. *New York Review of Books*, December 21, 2006, 8–10.

Drake, H. A. *Constantine and the Bishops: The Politics of Intolerance*. Baltimore: Johns Hopkins University Press, 2000.

Dulaey, Martine. *Le rêve dans la vie et la pensée de Saint Augustin*. Paris: Études Augustinienes, 1973.

Eastmond, Antony. "Body vs. Column: The Cults of St Symeon Stylites." In Liz James, ed., *Desire and Denial in Byzantium*, 87–100. Aldershot: Ashgate, 1999.

Edwards, Mark Julian. *Origen Against Plato*. Aldershot: Ashgate, 2002.

Elkins, James. *Pictures of the Body: Pain and Metamorphosis*. Stanford, Calif.: Stanford University Press, 1999.

Elsner, John. "Naturalism and the Erotics of the Gaze: Intimations of Narcissus." In *Sexuality in Ancient Art: Near East, Egypt, Greece, and Italy*, ed. Natalie Boymel Kampen, 248–61. Cambridge: Cambridge University Press, 1996.

Eno, Robert Bryan, S.S. *Saint Augustine and the Saints*. The Saint Augustine Lecture 1985. Villanova, Pa.: Villanova University Press, 1989.

Fontaine, Jacques. *Études sur la poésie latine tardive d'Ausone à Prudence*. Paris: Belles Lettres, 1980.

———. *Naissance de la poésie dans l'occident chrétien: Esquisse d'une histoire de la poésie latine chrétienne du IIIe au VIe siècle*. Paris: Études augustiniennes, 1981.

———. "Unité et diversité du mélange des genres et des tons chez quelques écrivains latins de la fin du IV siècle: Ausone, Ambroise, Ammien." In *Christianisme et Formes Littéraires de L'Antiquité Tardive en Occident*, ed. Manfred Fuhrmann, 425–82. Entretiens sur L'Antiquité Classique 23. Vandoeuvres: Fondation Hardt, 1976.

Foucault, Michel. "What is an Author?" In *Textual Strategies: Perspectives in Post-Structuralist Criticism*, ed. Josué Harari, 141–60. Ithaca, N.Y.: Cornell University Press, 1979.

Francis, James A. "Living Icons: Tracing a Motif in Verbal and Visual Representation from the Second to Fourth Centuries C.E." *AJP* 124 (2003): 575–600.

Frank, Georgia. "Macrina's Scar: Homeric Allusion and Heroic Identity in Gregory of Nyssa's *Life of Macrina*." *JECS* 8 (2000): 511–30.

———. *The Memory of the Eyes: Pilgrims to Living Saints in Late Antiquity*. The Transformation of the Classical Heritage 30. Berkeley: University of California Press, 2000.

———. "The Pilgrim's Gaze in the Age Before Icons." In Robert S. Nelson, ed., *Visuality Before and Beyond the Renaissance*, 98–115. Cambridge: Cambridge University Press, 2000.

———. "'Taste and See': The Eucharist and the Eyes of Faith in the Fourth Century." *CH* 70 (2001): 619–43.

Frankfurter, David. "On Sacrifice and Residues: Processing the Potent Body." In *Religion im kulturellen Diskurs/Religion in Cultural Discourse*, ed. Brigitte Luchesi and Kocku von Stuckrad, 511–33. Berlin: Walter de Gruyter, 2004.

Gallagher, Catherine, and Stephen Greenblatt. *Practicing New Historicism.* Chicago: University of Chicago Press, 2001.

Gerson, Lloyd. *The Cambridge Companion to Plotinus.* Cambridge: Cambridge University Press, 1996.

Giakalis, Ambrosios. *Images of the Divine: The Theology of Icons at the Seventh Ecumenical Council.* Studies in the History of Christian Thought 54. Leiden: E. J. Brill, 1994.

Glück, Louise. *Proofs and Theories: Essays on Poetry.* Hopewell, N.J.: Ecco Press, 1994.

Goldhill, Simon. "Refracting Classical Vision: Changing Cultures of Viewing." In *Vision in Context: Historical and Contemporary Perspectives on Sight*, ed. Teresa Brennan and Martin Jay, 15–28. New York: Routledge, 1996.

Grabar, André. *Martyrium.* 2 vols. Paris: Collège de France, 1946.

Griffiths, J. Gwyn. *Apuleius of Madauros: The Isis Book (Metamorphoses, Book XI).* Leiden: E. J. Brill, 1975.

Gross, Kenneth. *The Dream of the Moving Statue.* Ithaca, N.Y.: Cornell University Press, 1992.

Grosz, Elizabeth. *Volatile Bodies: Toward a Corporeal Feminism.* Bloomington: Indiana University Press, 1994.

Hacking, Ian. *Representing and Intervening.* Cambridge: Cambridge University Press, 1983.

Hadot, Pierre. "Neoplatonist Spirituality." In *Classical Mediterranean Spirituality*, ed. A. H. Armstrong, 230–49. New York: Crossroad, 1986.

———. *Plotinus or the Simplicity of Vision.* Trans. Michael Chase. Chicago: University of Chicago Press, 1993.

Hahn, Cynthia. "Loca Sancta Souvenirs: Sealing the Pilgrim's Experience." In *The Blessings of Pilgrimage*, ed. Robert Ousterhout, 85–95. Urbana: University of Illinois Press, 1990.

———. "Seeing and Believing: The Construction of Sanctity in Early-Medieval Saints' Shrines." *Speculum* 72 (1997): 1079–1106.

Halliwell, Stephen. *The Aesthetics of Mimesis: Ancient Texts and Modern Problems.* Princeton, N.J.: Princeton University Press, 2002.

Hammond, N. G. L., and H. H. Scullard, ed. *Oxford Classical Dictionary*, 2nd ed. Oxford: Clarendon Press, 1970.

Harpham, Geoffrey Galt. *The Ascetic Imperative in Culture and Criticism.* Chicago: University of Chicago Press, 1987.

Harvey, Susan Ashbrook. *Scenting Salvation: Ancient Christianity and the Olfactory Imagination.* The Transformation of the Classical Heritage 42. Berkeley: University of California Press, 2006.

Hjort, Øystein. "'Except on Doors': Reflections on a Curious Passage in the Letter from Hypatios of Ephesus to Julian of Atramyttion." In *Byzantine East, Latin West: Art-Historical Studies in Honor of Kurt Weitzmann*, ed. Christopher Moss and Katherine Kiefer, 615–25. Princeton, N.J.: Department of Art and Archaeology, Princeton University, 1995.

Hoey, A. S. "Rosaliae Signorum," *HTR* 30 (1937): 15–35.

Holum, Kenneth, and Gary Vikan. "The Trier Ivory, *Adventus* Ceremonial, and the Relics of St. Stephen." *DOP* 33 (1979): 113–33.

Horn, Cornelia B. *Asceticism and Christological Controvery in Fifth-Century Palestine: The Career of Peter the Iberian.* Oxford: Oxford University Press, 2006.

Hulme, T. E. "A Lecture on Modern Poetry." In *Further Speculations by T. E. Hulme*, ed. Sam Hynes, 67–76. Minneapolis: University of Minnesota Press, 1955.

Hunt, E. D. *Holy Land Pilgrimage in the Late Roman Empire A.D. 312–460.* Oxford: Clarendon Press, 1982.

Hunter, David G. "Vigilantius of Calagurris and Victricius of Rouen: Ascetics, Relics, and Clerics in Late Roman Gaul." *JECS* 7 (1999): 401–30.

James, Liz. "Color and Meaning in Byzantium." *JECS* 11 (2003): 223–33.

———. *Light and Colour in Byzantine Art.* Oxford: Clarendon Press, 1996.

———. " 'Pray Not to Fall into Temptation and Be on Your Guard': Antique Statues in Byzantine Constantinople." *Gesta* 35 (1996): 12–20.

James, Liz, and Ruth Webb. " 'To Understand Ultimate Things and Enter Secret Places': Ekphrasis and Art in Byzantium." *Art History* 14 (1991): 1–17.

Janes, Dominic. *God and Gold in Late Antiquity.* Cambridge: Cambridge University Press, 1998.

Jay, Gregory. "Freud: The Death of Autobiography." *Genre* 19 (1986): 103–28.

Jay, Martin. *Downcast Eyes: The Denigration of Vision in Twentieth-Century French Thought.* Berkeley: University of California Press, 1993.

Jenkins, Virginia Scott. *Bananas: An American History.* Washington, D.C.: Smithsonian, 2000.

Jensen, Robin Margaret. *Face to Face: Portraits of the Divine in Early Christianity.* Minneapolis: Fortress Press, 2005.

Jentsch, Ernst. "On the Psychology of the Uncanny (1906)." Trans. Roy Sellars. *Angelaki* 2, no. 1 (1995): 7–16.

Johnson, Mark. *The Body in the Mind: The Bodily Basis of Meaning, Imagination, and Reason.* Chicago: University of Chicago Press, repr. ed., 1990.

Johnston, Sarah Iles. *Hekate Soteira: A Study of Hekate's Role in the Chaldean Oracles and Related Literature.* Atlanta: Scholars Press, 1990.

Johnson, Scott Fitzgerald. *The Life and Miracles of Thekla: A Literary Study.* Cambridge, Mass.: Center for Hellenic Studies, 2006.

Kahzdan, Alexander, and Henry Maguire. "Byzantine Hagiographical Texts as Sources on Art." *DOP* 45 (1991): 1–22.

Kelly, J. N. D. *Early Christian Doctrines,* 2nd ed. New York: Harper and Row, 1960.

Kenney, John Peter. *The Mysticism of Saint Augustine: Rereading the Confessions.* New York, Routledge: 2005.

Kitzinger, Ernst. *Byzantine Art in the Making: Main Lines of Stylistic Development in Mediterranean Art 3rd–7th Century.* Cambridge, Mass.: Harvard University Press, 1977.

———. "Byzantine Art in the Period Between Justinian and Iconoclasm." In his *The Art of Byzantium and the Medieval West: Selected Studies,* 157–232. Ed. W. Eugene Kleinbauer. Bloomington: Indiana University Press, 1976; repr. from *Berichte zum XI. Internationalen Byzantinisten-Kongress, München 1958* (Munich, 1958), IV/1, 1–50.

———. "The Cult of Images in the Age Before Iconoclasm." *DOP* 8 (1954): 83–150.

Klinkenborg, Verlyn. Review of Julia Scully, *Outside Passage: A Memoir of an Alaskan Childhood* (New York: Random House, 1998). *New York Times Book Review,* May 10, 1998: 7.

Knauft, Bruce. "Bodily Images in Melanesia: Cultural Substances and Natural Metaphors." In *Fragments for a History of the Human Body,* Part 3 (*Zone* 5), ed. Michel Feher, 198–279. New York: Urzone, 1989.

Krueger, Derek. *Writing and Holiness: The Practice of Authorship in the Early Christian East.* Divinations: Rereading Late Ancient Religion. Philadelphia: University of Pennsylvania Press, 2004.

Lampe, G. W. H. *A Patristic Greek Lexicon.* Oxford: Clarendon Press, 1962.

Lane Fox, Robin. *Pagans and Christians.* New York: Alfred A. Knopf, 1987.

Lavin, Irving. "The Hunting Mosaics of Antioch and Their Sources. A Study of Compositional Principles in the Development of Early Mediaeval Style." *DOP* 17 (1963): 181–286.

Leder, Drew. *The Absent Body.* Chicago: University of Chicago Press, 1990.

Levitan, W. "Dancing at the End of the Rope: Optatian Porfyry and the Field of Roman Verse." *Transactions of the American Philological Association* 115 (1985): 245–69.

Lewy, H. *Chaldean Oracles and Theurgy.* Cairo: L'Institut Français d'Archéologie Orientale, 1956.

Leyerle, Blake. *Theatrical Shows and Ascetic Lives: John Chrysostom's Attack on Spiritual Marriage.* Berkeley: University of California Press, 2001.

Liddell, H. G., R. Scott, and H. S. Jones. *A Greek-English Lexicon.* Oxford: Clarendon Press, 1968.

Lindberg, David C. *Theories of Vision from Al-Kindi to Kepler.* Chicago: University of Chicago Press, 1976.

Louth, Andrew. *St. John Damascene: Tradition and Originality in Byzantine Theology.* Oxford: Oxford University Press, 2002.

———. " 'Truly Visible Things Are Manifest Images of Invisible Things': Dionysios the Areopagite on Knowing the Invisible." In *Seeing the Invisible in Late Antiquity and the Early Middle Ages,* ed. Giselle de Nie, Karl F. Morrison, and Marco Mostert, 15–24. Utrecht Studies in Medieval Literacy 14. Turnhout: Brepols, 2005.

Lyman, J. Rebecca. *Christology and Cosmology: Models of Divine Activity in Origen, Eusebius, and Athanasius.* Cambridge: Clarendon Press, 1993.

MacCormack, Sabine. *Art and Ceremony in Late Antiquity.* The Transformation of the Classical Heritage 1. Berkeley: University of California Press, 1981.

———. *The Shadows of Poetry: Vergil in the Mind of Augustine.* The Transformation of the Classical Heritage 26. Berkeley: University of California Press, 1998.

MacDonald, Diane L. Prosser. *Transgressive Corporeality: The Body, Poststructuralism, and the Theological Imagination.* Albany: State University of New York Press, 1995.

Mackie, Gillian. "Symbolism and Purpose in an Early Christian Martyr Chapel: The Case of San Vittore in Ciel d'Oro, Milan." *Gesta* 34, 2 (1995): 91–101.

MacMullen, Ramsay. *Christianity and Paganism in the Fourth to Eighth Centuries.* New Haven, Conn.: Yale University Press, 1997.

———. "Some Pictures in Ammianus Marcellinus." *Art Bulletin* 46 (1964): 435–55.

Maguire, Henry. *Art and Eloquence in Byzantium.* Princeton, N.J.: Princeton University Press, 1981.

———. *The Icons of Their Bodies: Saints and Their Images in Byzantium.* Princeton, N.J.: Princeton University Press, 1996.

———. *Rhetoric, Nature and Magic in Byzantine Art.* Variorum Collected Studies Series. Aldershot: Ashgate, 1998.

Malamud, Martha A. *Prudentius and Classical Mythology.* Ithaca, N.Y.: Cornell University Press, 1989.

Mango, Cyril. "Antique Statuary and the Byzantine Beholder." *DOP* 17 (1963): 55–75.

——. *The Art of the Byzantine Empire 312–1453: Sources and Documents.* Medieval Academy Reprints for Teaching 16. Toronto: University of Toronto and the Medieval Academy of America, 1986.

Maraval, Pierre. *Lieux Saints et Pèlerinages d'Orient: Histoire et géographie des origins à la conquête arabe.* Paris: Les Éditions du Cerf, 1985.

Markus, Robert A. *The End of Ancient Christianity.* Cambridge: Cambridge University Press, 1990.

——. "St. Augustine on Signs." In his *Augustine: A Collection of Critical Essays,* 61–91. Garden City, N.Y.: Anchor Books, 1972.

Mathews, Thomas. *The Clash of Gods: A Reinterpretation of Early Christian Art,* rev. ed. Princeton, N.J.: Princeton University Press, 1999.

Matthews, John. *The Roman Empire of Ammianus.* Baltimore: Johns Hopkins University Press, 1989.

Mayer, Wendy, and Pauline Allen. *John Chrysostom.* London: Routledge, 2000.

McGuckin, John. *Saint Cyril of Alexandria and the Christological Controversy.* Crestwood, N.Y.: St. Vladimir's Seminary Press, 2004.

Merleau-Ponty, Maurice. "Eye and Mind." Trans. Carleton Dallery. In *The Primacy of Perception and Other Essays on Phenomenological Psychology, the Philosophy of Art, History, and Politics,* ed. James M. Edie, 159–90. Evanston, Ill.: Northwestern University Press, 1964.

Miller, David L. "The Amorist Adjective Aflame in the Works of Gaston Bachelard, Henry Corbin, and Wallace Stevens." Unpublished manuscript presented at the Gaston Bachelard Conference, December 4, 1983, sponsored by the Dallas Institute of Humanities and Culture.

Miller, Patricia Cox. "Desert Asceticism and 'The Body from Nowhere.'" *JECS* 2 (1994): 137–53.

——. *Dreams in Late Antiquity: Studies in the Imagination of a Culture.* Princeton, N.J.: Princeton University Press, 1994.

——. "Is There a Harlot in This Text?: Hagiography and the Grotesque." *JMEMS* 33 (2003): 419–36.

——. "Strategies of Representation in Collective Biography: Constructing the Subject as Holy." In *Greek Biography and Panegyric in Late Antiquity,* ed. Tomas Hägg and Philip Rousseau, 209–54. The Transformation of the Classical Heritage 31. Berkeley: University of California Press, 2000.

Mitchell, W.J.T. *Picture Theory: Essays on Verbal and Visual Representation.* Chicago: University of Chicago Press, 1994.

——. *What Do Pictures Want? The Lives and Loves of Images.* Chicago: University of Chicago Press, 2005.

Mondzain, Marie-José. *Image, Icon, Economy: The Byzantine Origins of the Contemporary Imaginary.* Trans. Rico Franses. Stanford, Calif.: Stanford University Press, 2005.

Montserrat, Dominic, ed. *Changing Bodies, Changing Meanings: Studies on the Human Body in Antiquity.* London: Routledge, 1998.

Nau, François. "Histoire des Solitaires Égyptiens." *Revue de l'Orient chrétien* 12 (1907): 393–413.

Nelson, Robert S. "Introduction: Descartes' Cow and Other Domestications of the Visual." In Robert S. Nelson, ed., *Visuality Before and Beyond the Renaissance: Seeing as Others Saw,* 1–21. Cambridge: Cambridge University Press, 2000.

Newman, Gail M. *Locating the Romantic Subject.* Detroit: Wayne State University Press, 1997.

Nugent, S. Georgia. "Ausonius' 'Late-Antique' Poetics and 'Post-Modern' Literary Theory." *Ramus* 19 (1990): 26–50.

O'Daly, Gerard. *Augustine's Philosophy of Mind*. Berkeley: University of California Press, 1987.

O'Meara, Dominic J. "The Hierarchical Ordering of Reality in Plotinus." In *The Cambridge Companion to Plotinus*, ed. Lloyd Gerson, 66–81. Cambridge: Cambridge University Press, 1996.

———. *Plotinus: An Introduction to the Enneads*. Oxford: Clarendon Press, 1995.

Onians, John. "Abstraction and Imagination in Late Antiquity." *Art History* 3 (1980): 1–24.

Palmer, Anne-Marie. *Prudentius on the Martyrs*. Oxford: Clarendon Press, 1989.

Patlagean, Evelyne. "L'histoire de la femme déguisée en moine et l'évolution de la sainteté feminine à Byzance." *Studi Medievali* 17 (1976): 597–623.

Peers, Glenn. *Subtle Bodies: Representing Angels in Byzantium*. The Transformation of the Classical Heritage 32. Berkeley: University of California Press, 2001.

Perrone, Lorenzo. "Dissenso Dottrinale e Propaganda Visionaria: Le *Pleroforie* di Giovanni di Maiuma." *Augustinianum* 29 (1989): 451–95.

Petroski, Henry. *The Pencil: A History of Design and Circumstance*. New York: Knopf, 1989.

Petruccione, John Francis. "Prudentius' Use of Martyrological Topoi in *Peristephanon*." Ph.D. dissertation, University of Michigan, 1985.

Pietri, Charles. *Roma Christiana: Recherces sur l'Église de Rome, son organisation, sa politique, son l'idéologie de Miltiade à Sixte III (311–440)*. Rome: École Française de Rome, 1976.

Price, Simon. "From Noble Funerals to Divine Cult: The Consecration of Roman Emperors." In *Rituals of Royalty: Power and Ceremonial in Traditional Societies*, ed. David Cannadine and Simon Price, 56–105. Cambridge: Cambridge University Press, 1987.

———. "Gods and Emperors: The Greek Language of the Roman Imperial Cult." *JHS* 104 (1984): 79–95.

Rapp, Claudia. " 'For Next to God, You Are My Salvation': Reflections on the Rise of the Holy Man in Late Antiquity." In *The Cult of the Saints in Late Antiquity and the Middle Ages: Essays on the Contribution of Peter Brown*, ed. James Howard-Johnston and Paul Antony Hayward, 63–81. Oxford: Oxford University Press, 1999.

Rappe, Sara. "Metaphor in Plotinus' *Enneads* v 8.9." *Ancient Philosophy* 15 (1995): 155–72.

———. *Reading Neoplatonism: Non-discursive Thinking in the Texts of Plotinus, Proclus, and Damascius*. Cambridge: Cambridge University Press, 2000.

———. "Self-knowledge and Subjectivity in the *Enneads*." In *The Cambridge Companion to Plotinus*, ed. Lloyd Gerson, 250–74. Cambridge: Cambridge University Press, 1996.

———. "Self-Perception in Plotinus and the Later Neoplatonic Tradition." *American Catholic Philosophical Quarterly* 71 (1997): 433–51.

Roberts, Michael. *Poetry and the Cult of the Martyrs: The Liber Peristephanon of Prudentius*. Ann Arbor: University of Michigan Press, 1993.

———. *The Jeweled Style: Poetry and Poetics in Late Antiquity*. Ithaca, N.Y.: Cornell University Press, 1989.

Rorem, Paul. *Pseudo-Dionysius: A Commentary on the Texts and an Introduction to Their Influence*. New York: Oxford University Press, 1993.

Ross, Jill. "Dynamic Writing and Martyrs' Bodies in Prudentius' *Peristephanon*." *JECS* 3 (1995): 325–55.

Salzman, Michele Renée. *On Roman Time: The Codex-Calendar of 354 and the*

Rhythms of Urban Life in Late Antiquity. The Transformation of the Classical Heritage 17. Berkeley: University of California Press, 1990.

Saxer, Victor. *Morts, Martyrs, Reliques en Afrique Chrétienne aux Premiers Siècles.* Paris: Éditions Beauchesne, 1980.

Schroeder, Frederic M. "The Vigil of the One and Plotinian Iconoclasm." In *Neoplatonism and Western Aesthetics*, ed. Aphrodite Alexandrakis, assoc. ed. Nicholas J. Moutafakis, 61–74. Studies in Neoplatonism 12. Albany: State University of New York Press, 2002.

———. "The Self in Ancient Religious Experience." In *Classical Mediterranean Spirituality*, ed. A. H. Armstrong, 337–59. New York: Crossroad, 1986.

Sells, Michael. *Mystical Languages of Unsaying.* Chicago: University of Chicago Press, 1994.

Shaw, Gregory. "After Aporia: Theurgy in Later Platonism." *Journal of Neoplatonic Studies* 5 (1996): 3–41.

———. *Theurgy and the Soul: The Neoplatonism of Iamblichus.* University Park: Pennsylvania State University Press, 1995.

———. "Theurgy: Rituals of Unification in the Neoplatonism of Iamblichus." *Traditio* 41 (1985): 1–28.

Shaw, Teresa M. *The Burden of the Flesh: Fasting and Sexuality in Early Christianity.* Minneapolis: Fortress Press, 1998.

Sheppard, Anne. "Proclus' Attitude to Theurgy." *CQ* 32 (1982): 212–24.

Smith, Jonathan Z. *Map Is Not Territory: Studies in the History of Religions.* Chicago: University of Chicago Press, 1993.

Smith, R. R. R. *Hellenistic Royal Portraits.* Oxford: Oxford University Press, 1988.

———. "The Public Image of Licinius I: Portrait Sculpture and Imperial Ideology in the Early Fourth Century." *JRS* 87 (1997): 170–202.

St. Clair, Archer. "Imperial Virtue: Questions of Form and Function in the Case of Four Late Antique Statuettes." *DOP* 50 (1996): 147–62.

Stevens, Wallace. *Collected Letters.* Ed. Holly Stevens. New York: Alfred A. Knopf, 1966.

———. *Opus Posthumous.* Ed. Samuel French Morse. New York: Alfred A. Knopf, 1977.

Stewart, Susan. *Poetry and the Fate of the Senses.* Chicago: University of Chicago Press, 2002.

Sullivan, J. P. *Ezra Pound: A Critical Anthology.* Baltimore: Harmondsworth, 1970.

Taft, Robert. "The Liturgy of the Great Church: An Initial Synthesis of Structure and Interpretation on the Eve of Iconoclasm." *DOP* 34 (1980–1981): 45–75.

Tardieu, Michel. *Trois Mythes Gnostiques: Adam, Éros et les animaux d'Égypte dans un écrit de Nag Hammadi (II.5).* Paris: Études Augustiniennes, 1974.

Taylor, Mark C. *Hiding.* Chicago: University of Chicago Press, 1997.

Tiffany, Daniel. *Toy Medium: Materialism and Modern Lyric.* Berkeley: University of California Press, 2000.

Trombley, Frank. *Hellenic Religion and Christianization, c. 370–529.* 2 vols. Leiden: E. J. Brill, 1995.

Tromzo, William. *The Via Latina Catacomb: Imitation and Discontinuity in Fourth-Century Roman Painting.* University Park: Pennsylvania State University Press, 1986.

Trout, Dennis E. "Damasus and the Invention of Early Christian Rome." In *The Cultural Turn in Late Ancient Studies: Gender, Asceticism, and Historiography*, ed. Dale B. Martin and Patricia Cox Miller, 298–315. Durham, N.C.: Duke University Press, 2005.

Turner, Bryan. "The Body in Western Society: Social Theory and Its Perspectives." In *Religion and the Body*, ed. Sarah Coakley, 15–41. Cambridge: Cambridge University Press, 1997.

Valantasis, Richard. "Constructions of Power in Asceticism." *JAAR* 63 (1995): 775–821.

Van Dam, Raymond. *Leadership and Community in Late Antique Gaul.* Berkeley: University of California Press, 1985.

Vernant, Jean Pierre. "Dim Body, Dazzling Body." In *Fragments for a History of the Human Body*, Part One (*Zone* 3), ed. Michel Feher, 18–47. New York: Urzone, 1989.

Vikan, Gary. "Art, Medicine, and Magic in Early Byzantium." *DOP* 38 (1984): 65–86.

———. *Byzantine Pilgrimage Art.* Washington, D.C.: Dumbarton Oaks, 1982.

———. "Icons and Icon Piety in Early Byzantium." In *Byzantine East, Latin West: Art-Historical Studies in Honor of Kurt Weitzman*, ed. Christopher Moss and Katherine Kiefer, 569–76. Princeton, N.J.: Department of Art and Archaeology, Princeton University.

Walker, P. W. L. *Holy City, Holy Places? Christian Attitudes to Jerusalem and the Holy Land in the Fourth Century.* Oxford: Clarendon Press, 1990.

Wallis, R. T. *Neoplatonism*, 2nd ed. London: Gerald Duckworth, 1995.

Wharton, Annabel. *Refiguring the Post Classical City: Dura Europa, Jerash, Jerusalem, and Ravenna.* Cambridge: Cambridge University Press, 1995.

White, Hayden. *Figural Realism: Studies in the Mimesis Effect.* Baltimore: Johns Hopkins University Press, 1999.

Wilken, Robert. *The Land Called Holy: Palestine in Christian History and Thought.* New Haven, Conn.: Yale University Press, 1992.

Williams, Michael Allen. *The Immoveable Race: A Gnostic Designation and the Theme of Stability in Late Antiquity.* Leiden: E. J. Brill, 1985.

Williams, Rowan. "Troubled Breasts: The Holy Body in Hagiography." In *Portraits of Spiritual Authority: Religious Power in Early Christianity, Byzantium and the Christian Orient*, ed. Jan Willem Drijvers and John W. Watt, 63–78. Leiden: E. J. Brill, 1999.

Wyschogrod, Edith. *Saints and Postmodernism: Revisioning Moral Philosophy.* Chicago: University of Chicago Press, 1990.

Young, Frances. *From Nicaea to Chalcedon: A Guide to the Literature and Its Background.* Philadelphia: Fortress Press, 1983.

Zuckerman, Larry. *The Potato: How the Humble Spud Rescued the Western World.* San Francisco: North Point Press, 1999.

Index

Page references in italics indicate illustrations.

Acknowledgments

Were it not for invitations to deliver papers at six special conferences, this book might not exist. Those special occasions proved to be formative for the course of research and writing that this book represents, and I am delighted to remember them here. It began with my presidential address to the North American Patristics Society in May 1997, in which I offered my first thoughts about aesthetics and bodies in late ancient Christianity. My heartfelt thanks go to the members of NAPS, not only for that special occasion but also for the many years of stimulating scholarly exchange. The train of thought regarding the odd materiality of holy bodies began when, with trepidation, I contemplated delivering the Inaugural Address to the Fourteenth International Patristics Conference at the University of Oxford in August 2003. I am grateful to the conference's directors, then headed by Frances Young, for honoring me with their invitation. Shortly after the Oxford conference, David Brakke, Michael L. Satlow, and Steven Weitzman convened a remarkable symposium on the self in ancient religions, and I thank them for providing me the occasion to articulate how the late ancient self was newly oriented toward materiality. For the genial gathering that they provided the evening before the symposium, I extend thanks to David Brakke and Bert Harrill for their hospitality.

Also in 2003, the University of Utrecht, under the auspices of the Utrecht Centre for Medieval Studies, sponsored a colloquium entitled "Verbal and Pictorial Imaging: Representing and Accessing Experience of the Invisible: 400–1000." I had never contemplated the connection between mental spectacles and relics until pondering what I might contribute to this colloquium. Many thanks to the organizers, Giselle de Nie, Karl F. Morrison, Herbert Kessler, and Marco Mostert, for this rich experience. Finally, two conferences held in 2006 pushed me to extend my thoughts about holy bodies to icons as well as to imagine those bodies in different theoretical terms. My compliments to Virginia Burrus, Catherine Keller, and Christopher Boesel of Drew University's Theological School for coming up with the most tantalizingly provocative colloquium title I have ever encountered ("Apophatic Bodies: Infinity, Ethics, and Incarnation"). It was a joy to participate in this, the sixth of

Drew's Transdisciplinary Theological Colloquia, and I offer special thanks to Karmen MacKendrick of Le Moyne College, whose insightful response to my paper helped me hone my thoughts about subtle bodies. Last, and in some ways best, of all, I acknowledge with gratitude my colleagues in our regional association, LARCNY (Late Ancient Religion in Central New York). They asked me to be the keynote speaker at our first conference, "Bodies and Boundaries in Late Antiquity," and then surprised me at the last minute by telling me that the conference was in my honor. It was an unforgettable experience. My best regards go to Kim Haines-Eitzen, whose arrangements at Cornell University made the conference possible, and to Georgia Frank, Jennifer Glancy, Anne Meredith, Gay Byron, and Suzanne Abrams. My LARCNY colleagues are one of the best features of academic life in upstate New York. Thanks also to friends who traveled to Cornell to give papers at the conference: David Brakke, Virginia Burrus, Elizabeth Clark, David Frankfurter, and Derek Krueger.

A fellowship from the John Simon Guggenheim Memorial Foundation in 2006–7 supported the writing of this book, and I am deeply grateful for the time to think that a year's leave provides. The Arts and Sciences Subvention Fund of Syracuse University, along with the Department of Religion, provided funds to cover the expenses of art-permissions and indexing. Special thanks go to Gerald Greenberg, Associate Dean of the College of Arts and Sciences, and Tazim Kassam, Chair of the Department of Religion, for their generous support. The staff at the University of Pennsylvania Press, especially Jerome Singerman, have been unfailingly gracious, and the editors of the Divinations series, Daniel Boyarin, Virginia Burrus, and Derek Krueger, have been collegially encouraging throughout. Virginia read the entire manuscript with an imaginatively critical eye, which was a great help at a crucial moment. At the end of all these thank-yous, words are not really adequate to express my appreciation to my husband, David L. Miller, for the extraordinary gift of his intelligent reading of my pages, day by day, as they emerged from the printer; my love to him.

Portions of this book appeared in earlier forms in other publications. Chapter 1 is a longer version of "Shifting Selves in Late Antiquity," in *Religion and the Self in Antiquity*, ed. David Brakke, Michael L. Satlow, and Steven Weitzman (Bloomington: Indiana University Press, 2005), 15–39. Chapter 2 first appeared as "'Differential Networks': Relics and Other Fragments in Late Antiquity," *Journal of Early Christian Studies* 6 (1998): 113–38. Chapter 3 was first published as "'The Little Blue Flower is Red': Relics and the Poetizing of the Body," *Journal of Early Christian Studies* 8 (2000): 213–36. Chapter 4, "Relics, Rhetoric, and Mental Spectacles," first appeared in *Seeing the Invisible in Late Antiquity and the Early Middle Ages*, Utrecht Studies in Medieval Literacy 14, ed. Giselle de Nie,

Karl F. Morrison, and Marco Mostert (Turnhout: Brepols Publishers, 2005), 25–52. Chapter 5 is a later version of "Visceral Seeing: The Holy Body in Late Ancient Christianity," *Journal of Early Christian Studies* 12 (2004): 391–412. A version of Chapter 7 will appear in *Journal of Early Christian Studies* 17 (June 2009).